Natsume's
BOOK of FRIENDS

Shojo Beat

Natsume's BOOK of FRIENDS

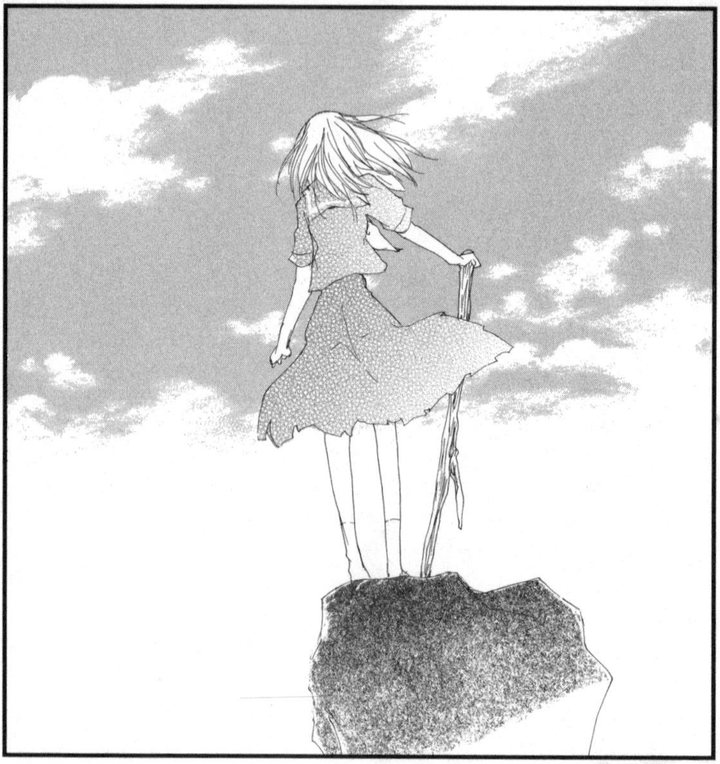

STORY and ART by
Yuki Midorikawa

VOLUME 18

Natsume's
BOOK of FRIENDS
VOLUME 18 CONTENTS

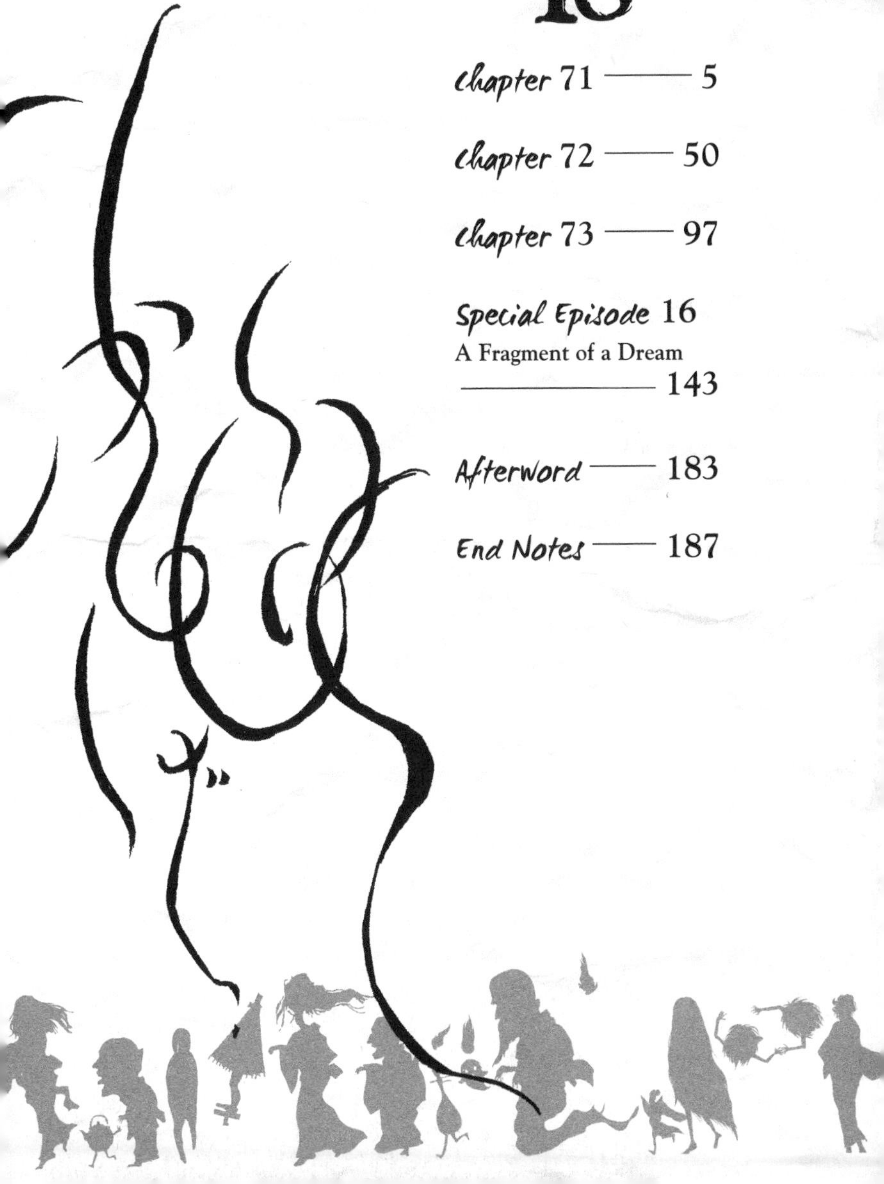

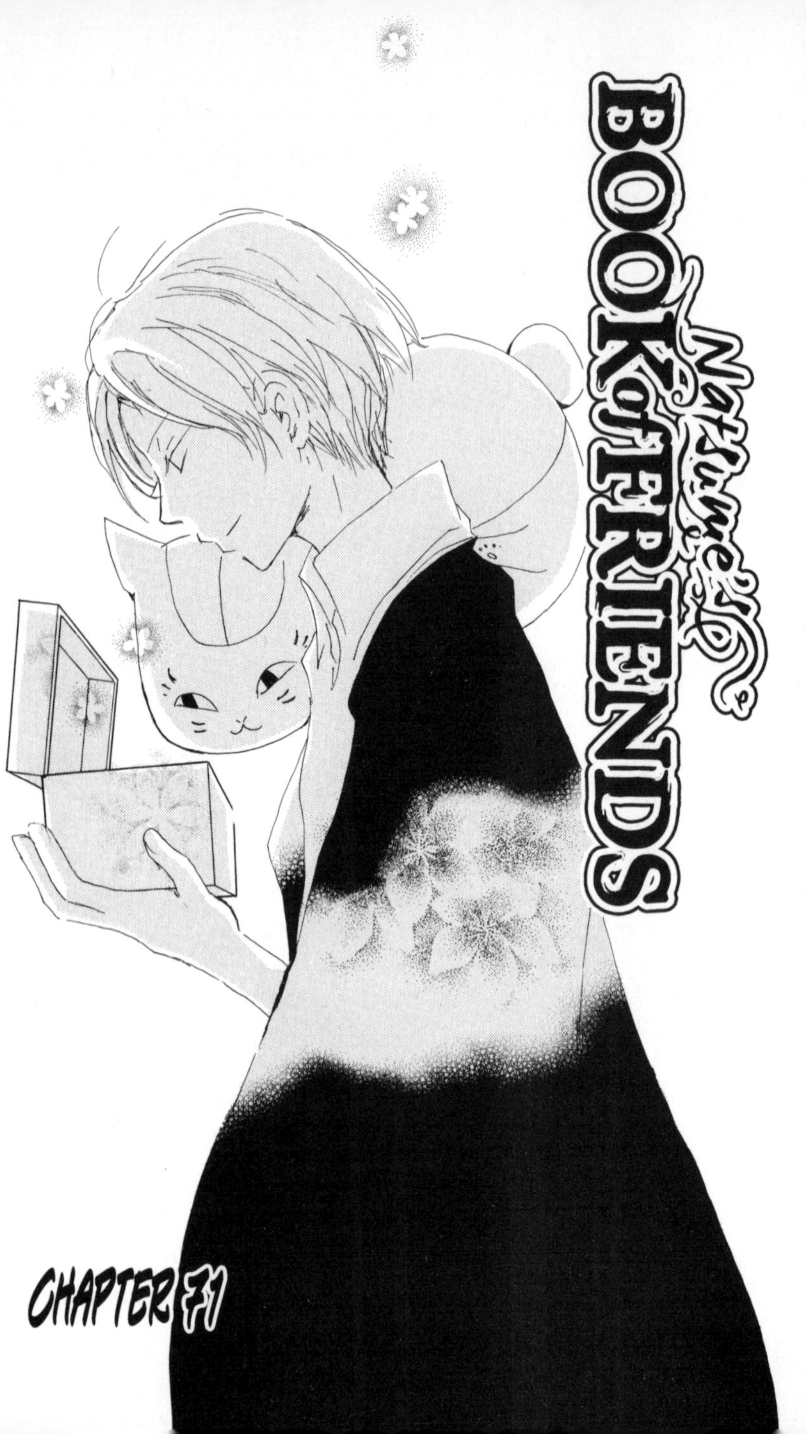
Natsume's
BOOK of FRIENDS
CHAPTER 71

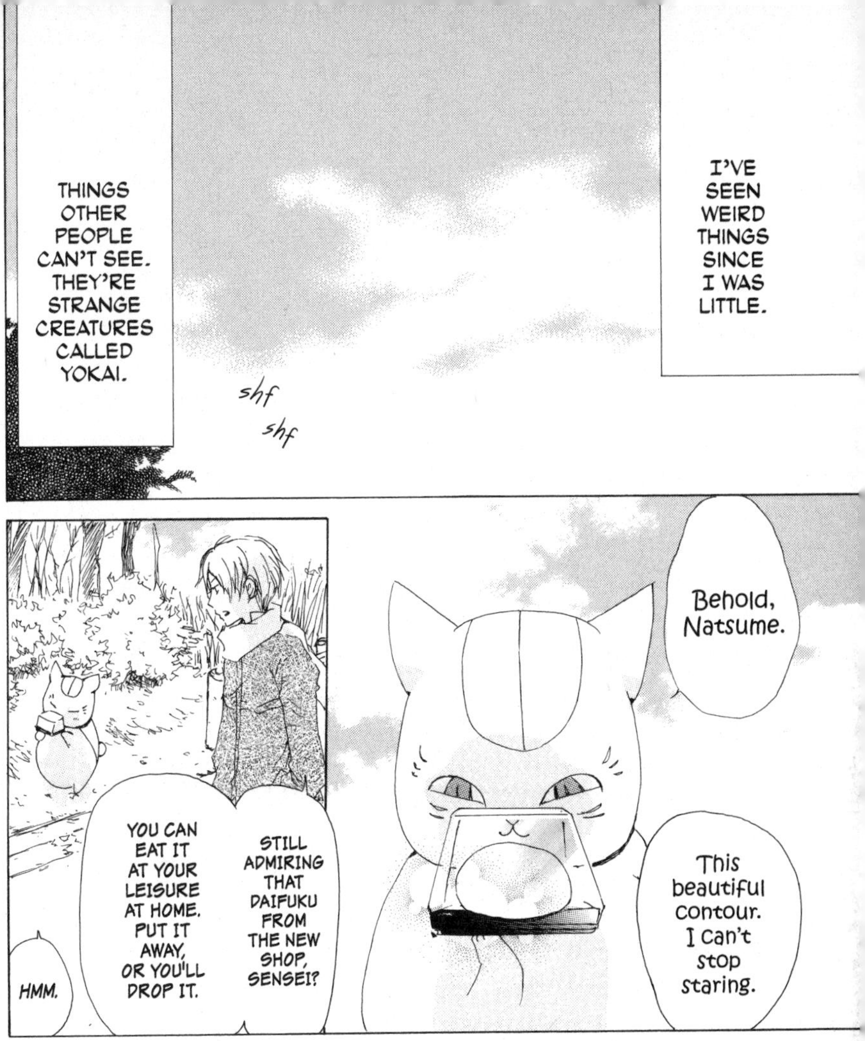
I'VE SEEN WEIRD THINGS SINCE I WAS LITTLE.
THINGS OTHER PEOPLE CAN'T SEE. THEY'RE STRANGE CREATURES CALLED YOKAI.
shf
shf
Behold, Natsume.
This beautiful contour. I can't stop staring.
STILL ADMIRING THAT DAIFUKU FROM THE NEW SHOP, SENSEI?
YOU CAN EAT IT AT YOUR LEISURE AT HOME. PUT IT AWAY, OR YOU'LL DROP IT.
HMM.
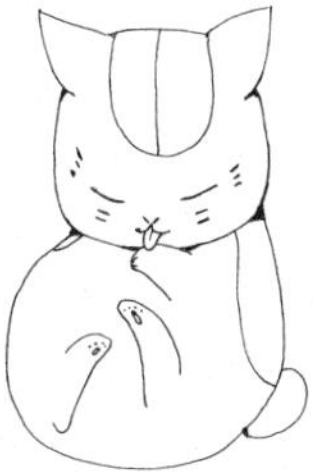

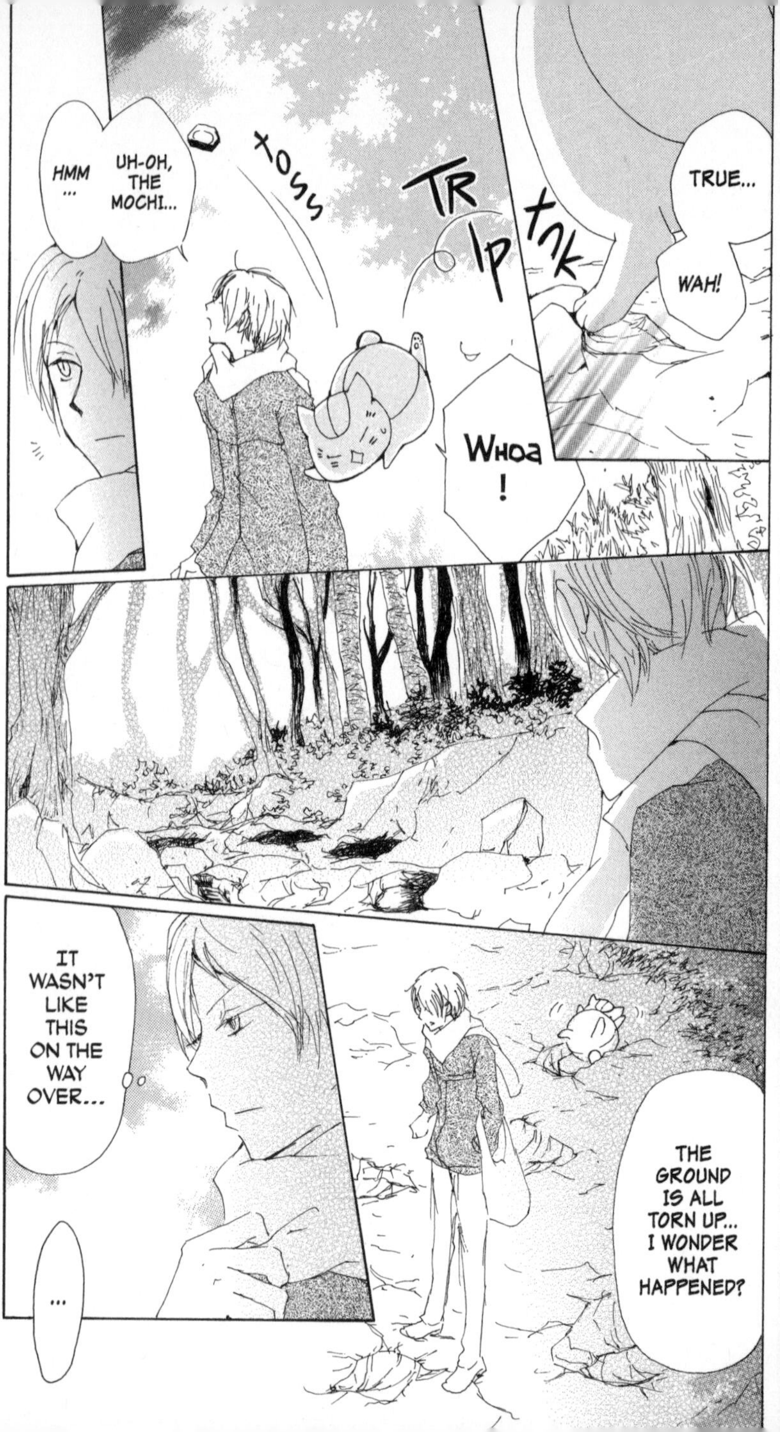
TRUE...
WAH!
toss
TRIP
Whoa!
HMM ... UH-OH, THE MOCHI...
THE GROUND IS ALL TORN UP... I WONDER WHAT HAPPENED?
IT WASN'T LIKE THIS ON THE WAY OVER...
...

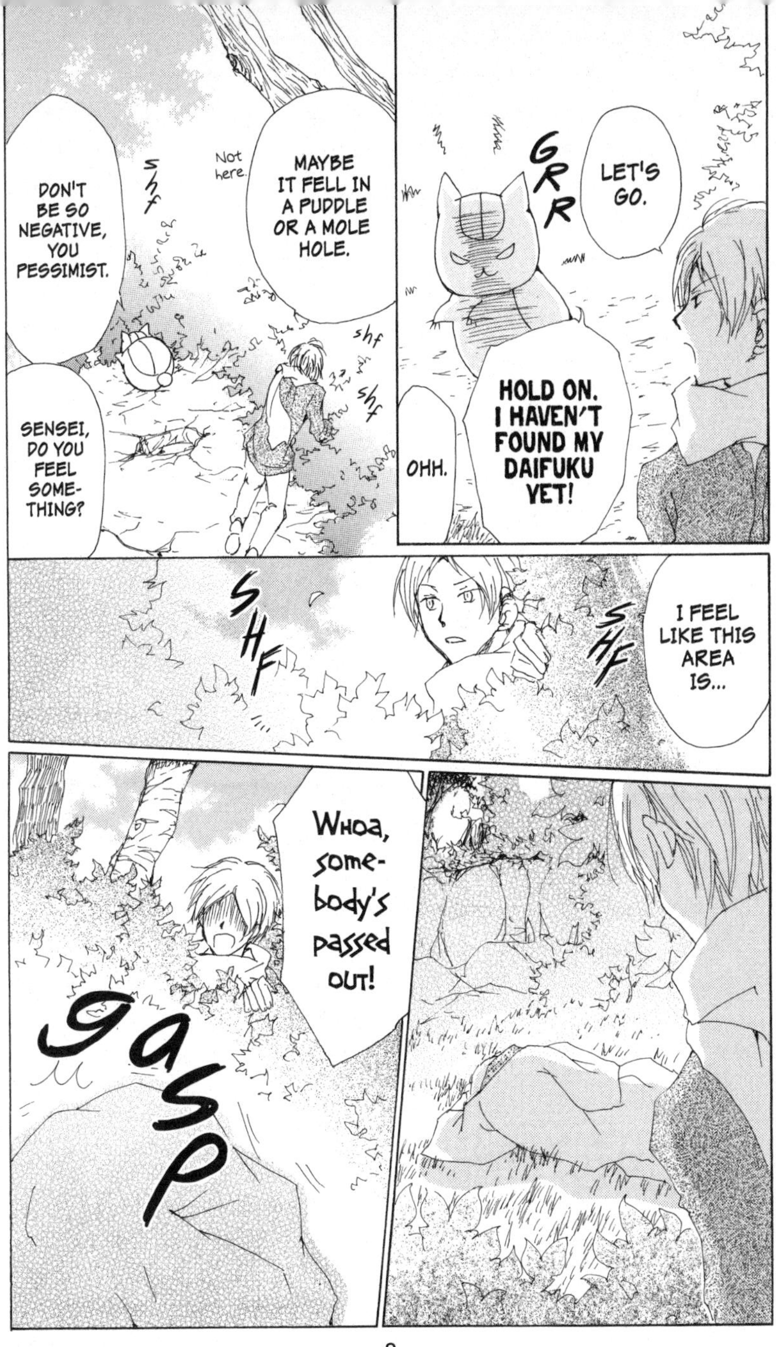
LET'S GO.
GRR
HOLD ON. I HAVEN'T FOUND MY DAIFUKU YET!
OHH.
MAYBE IT FELL IN A PUDDLE OR A MOLE HOLE.
Not here.
shf
DON'T BE SO NEGATIVE, YOU PESSIMIST.
shf
shf
SENSEI, DO YOU FEEL SOME-THING?
I FEEL LIKE THIS AREA IS...
SHF
SHF
Whoa, some-body's passed out!
gasp

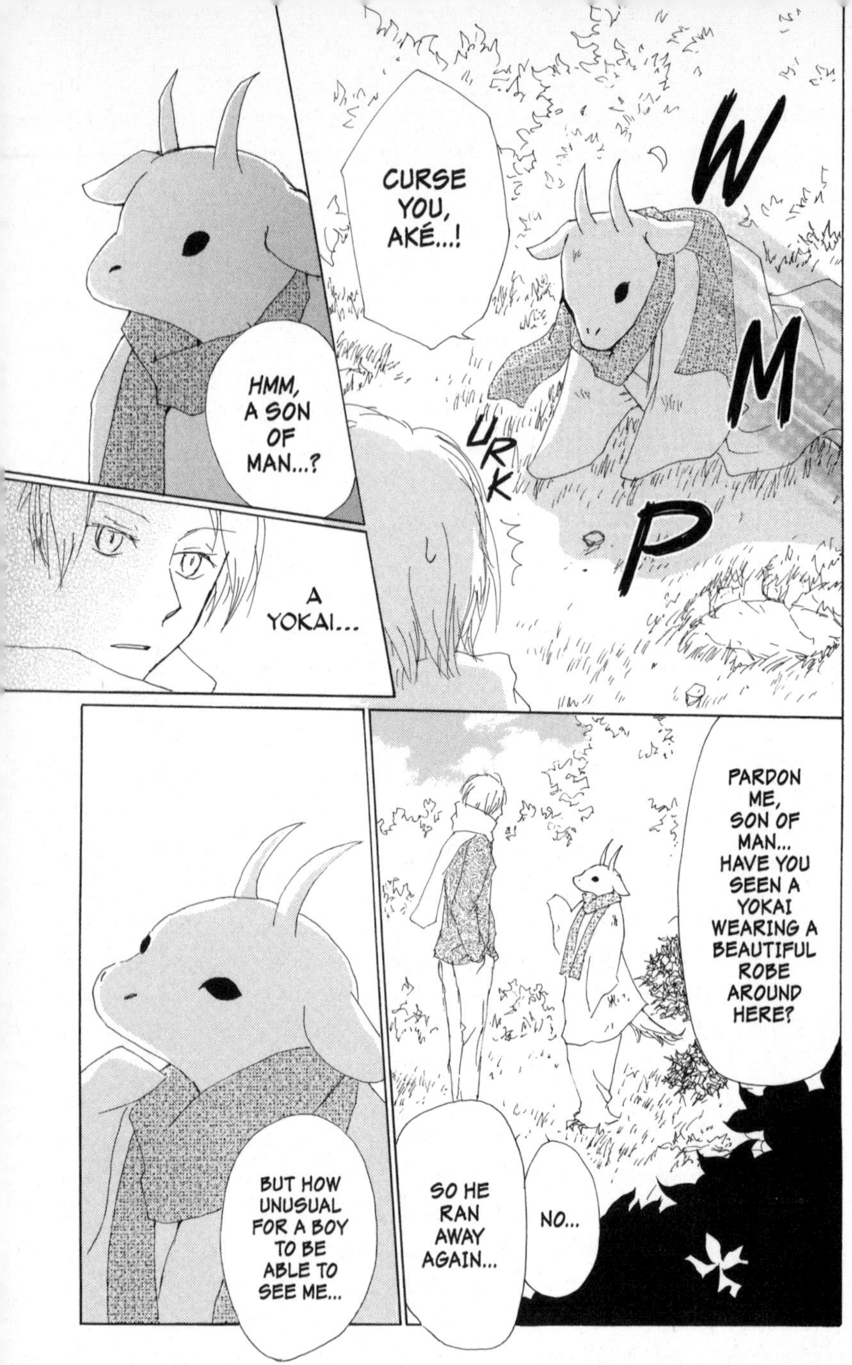
WMMP
CURSE YOU, AKÉ...!
URK
HMM, A SON OF MAN...?
A YOKAI...
PARDON ME, SON OF MAN... HAVE YOU SEEN A YOKAI WEARING A BEAUTIFUL ROBE AROUND HERE?
NO...
SO HE RAN AWAY AGAIN...
BUT HOW UNUSUAL FOR A BOY TO BE ABLE TO SEE ME...

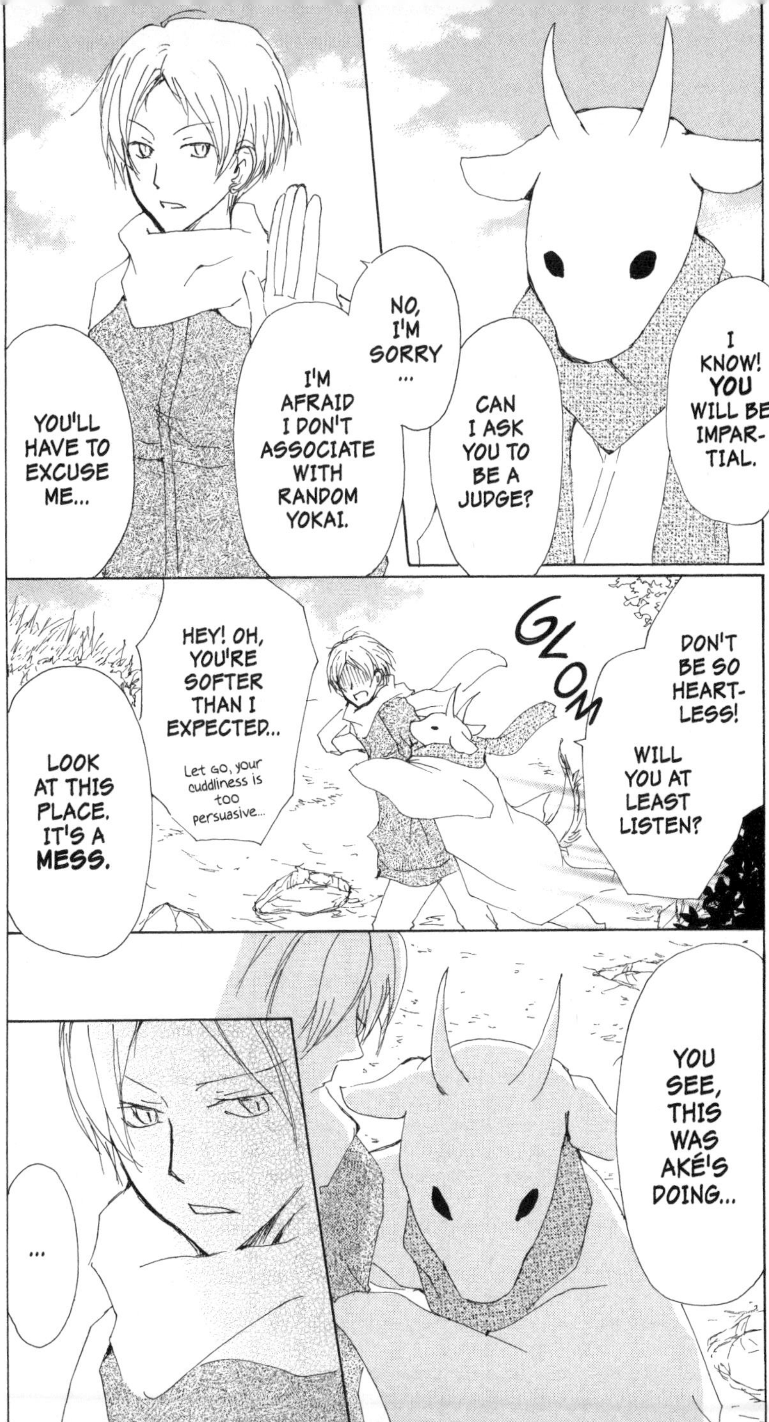
I KNOW! YOU WILL BE IMPARTIAL.
CAN I ASK YOU TO BE A JUDGE?
NO, I'M SORRY...
I'M AFRAID I DON'T ASSOCIATE WITH RANDOM YOKAI.
YOU'LL HAVE TO EXCUSE ME...
DON'T BE SO HEARTLESS!
GLOM
WILL YOU AT LEAST LISTEN?
HEY! OH, YOU'RE SOFTER THAN I EXPECTED...
Let go, your cuddliness is too persuasive...
LOOK AT THIS PLACE. IT'S A MESS.
YOU SEE, THIS WAS AKÉ'S DOING...
...

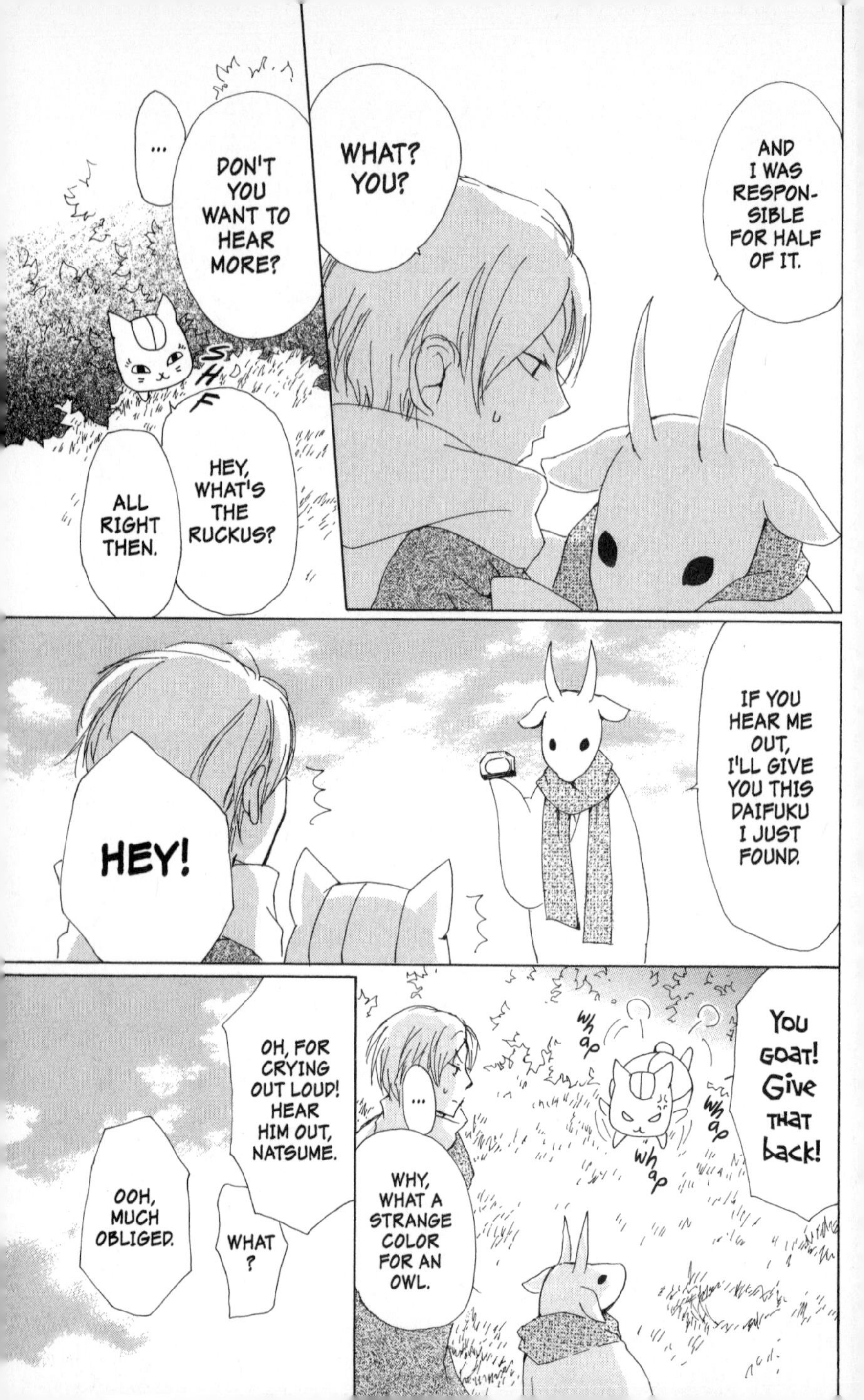
AND I WAS RESPONSIBLE FOR HALF OF IT.
WHAT? YOU?
DON'T YOU WANT TO HEAR MORE?
...
SHF
HEY, WHAT'S THE RUCKUS?
ALL RIGHT THEN.
IF YOU HEAR ME OUT, I'LL GIVE YOU THIS DAIFUKU I JUST FOUND.
HEY!
You goat! Give that back!
whap
whap
whap
...
WHY, WHAT A STRANGE COLOR FOR AN OWL.
OH, FOR CRYING OUT LOUD! HEAR HIM OUT, NATSUME.
WHAT?
OOH, MUCH OBLIGED.

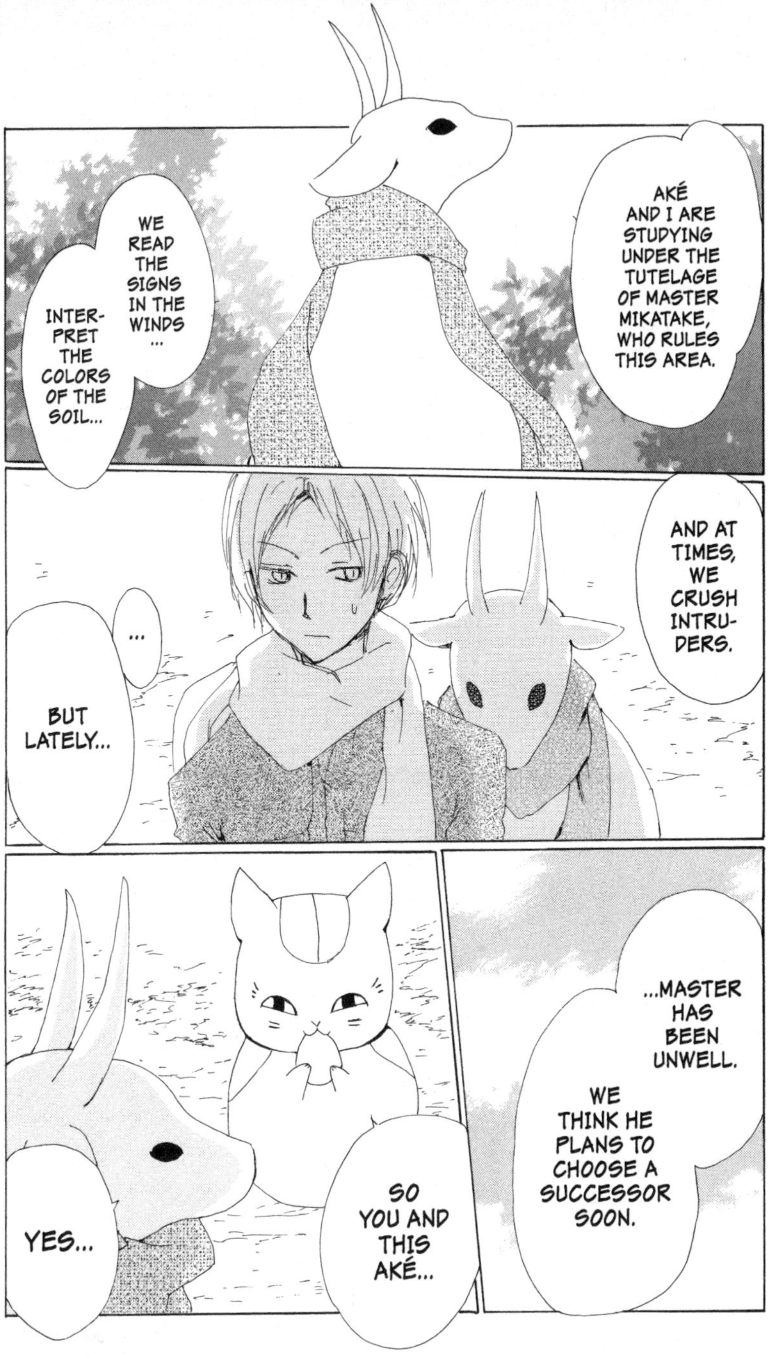
AKÉ AND I ARE STUDYING UNDER THE TUTELAGE OF MASTER MIKATAKE, WHO RULES THIS AREA.
WE READ THE SIGNS IN THE WINDS...
INTERPRET THE COLORS OF THE SOIL...
AND AT TIMES, WE CRUSH INTRUDERS.
...
BUT LATELY...
...MASTER HAS BEEN UNWELL.
WE THINK HE PLANS TO CHOOSE A SUCCESSOR SOON.
SO YOU AND THIS AKÉ...
YES...

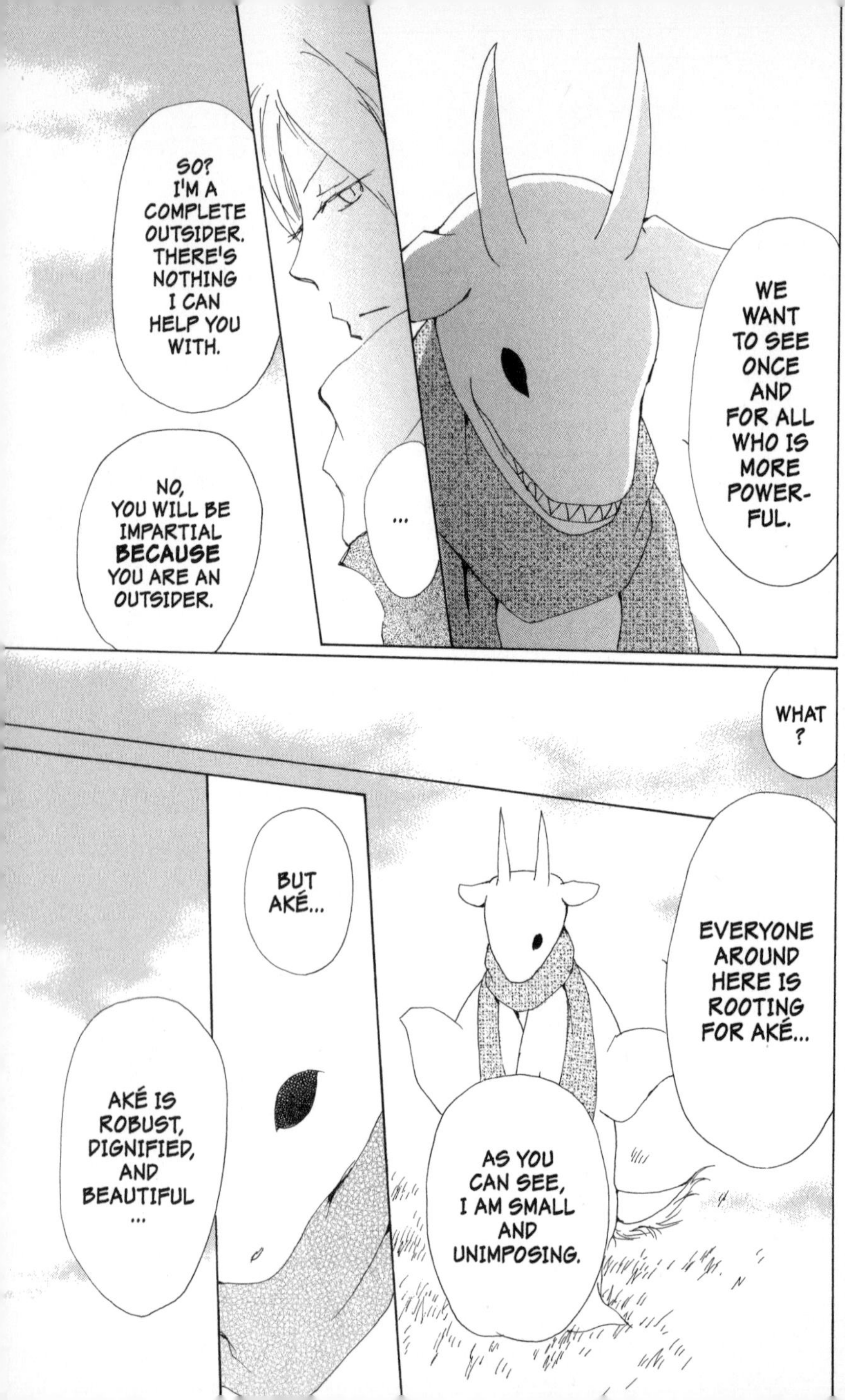
WE WANT TO SEE ONCE AND FOR ALL WHO IS MORE POWERFUL.
SO? I'M A COMPLETE OUTSIDER. THERE'S NOTHING I CAN HELP YOU WITH.
...
NO, YOU WILL BE IMPARTIAL **BECAUSE** YOU ARE AN OUTSIDER.
WHAT?
EVERYONE AROUND HERE IS ROOTING FOR AKÉ...
AS YOU CAN SEE, I AM SMALL AND UNIMPOSING.
BUT AKÉ...
AKÉ IS ROBUST, DIGNIFIED, AND BEAUTIFUL...

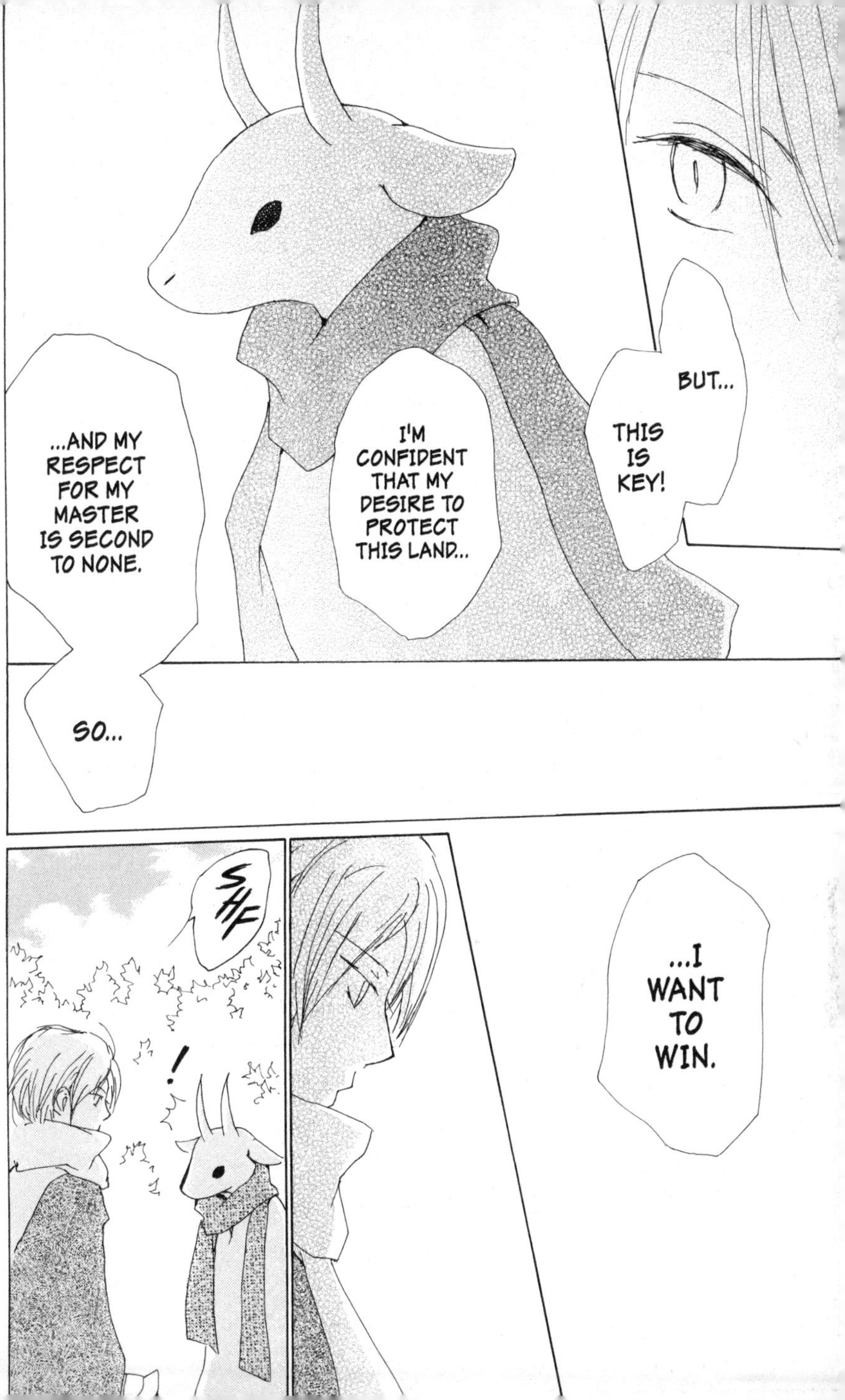
BUT...
THIS IS KEY!
I'M CONFIDENT THAT MY DESIRE TO PROTECT THIS LAND...
...AND MY RESPECT FOR MY MASTER IS SECOND TO NONE.
SO...
...I WANT TO WIN.
SHF
!

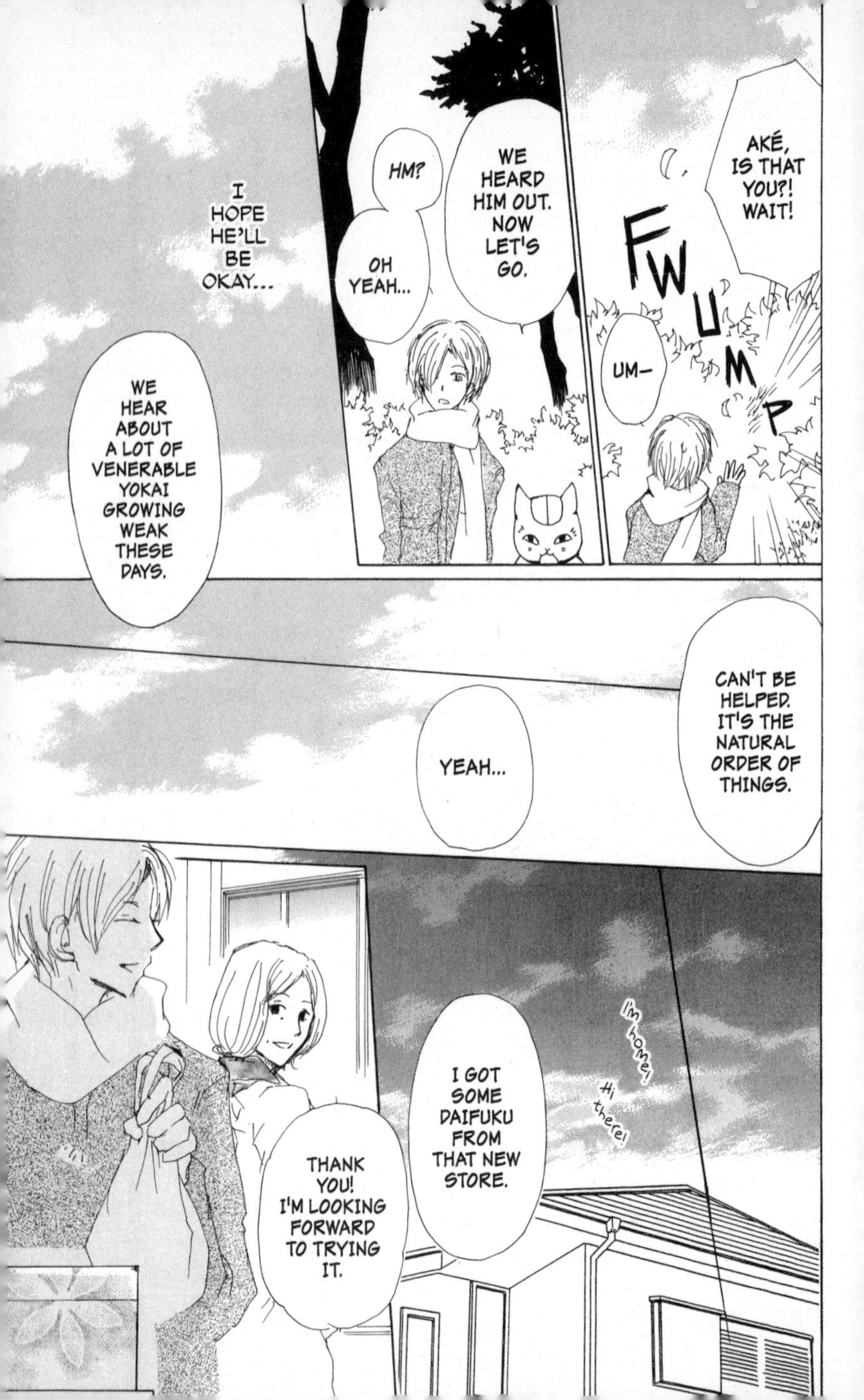
AKÉ, IS THAT YOU?! WAIT!
FWUMP
UM–
WE HEARD HIM OUT. NOW LET'S GO.
HM?
OH YEAH...
I HOPE HE'LL BE OKAY...
WE HEAR ABOUT A LOT OF VENERABLE YOKAI GROWING WEAK THESE DAYS.
CAN'T BE HELPED. IT'S THE NATURAL ORDER OF THINGS.
YEAH...
I'm home!
Hi there!
I GOT SOME DAIFUKU FROM THAT NEW STORE.
THANK YOU! I'M LOOKING FORWARD TO TRYING IT.

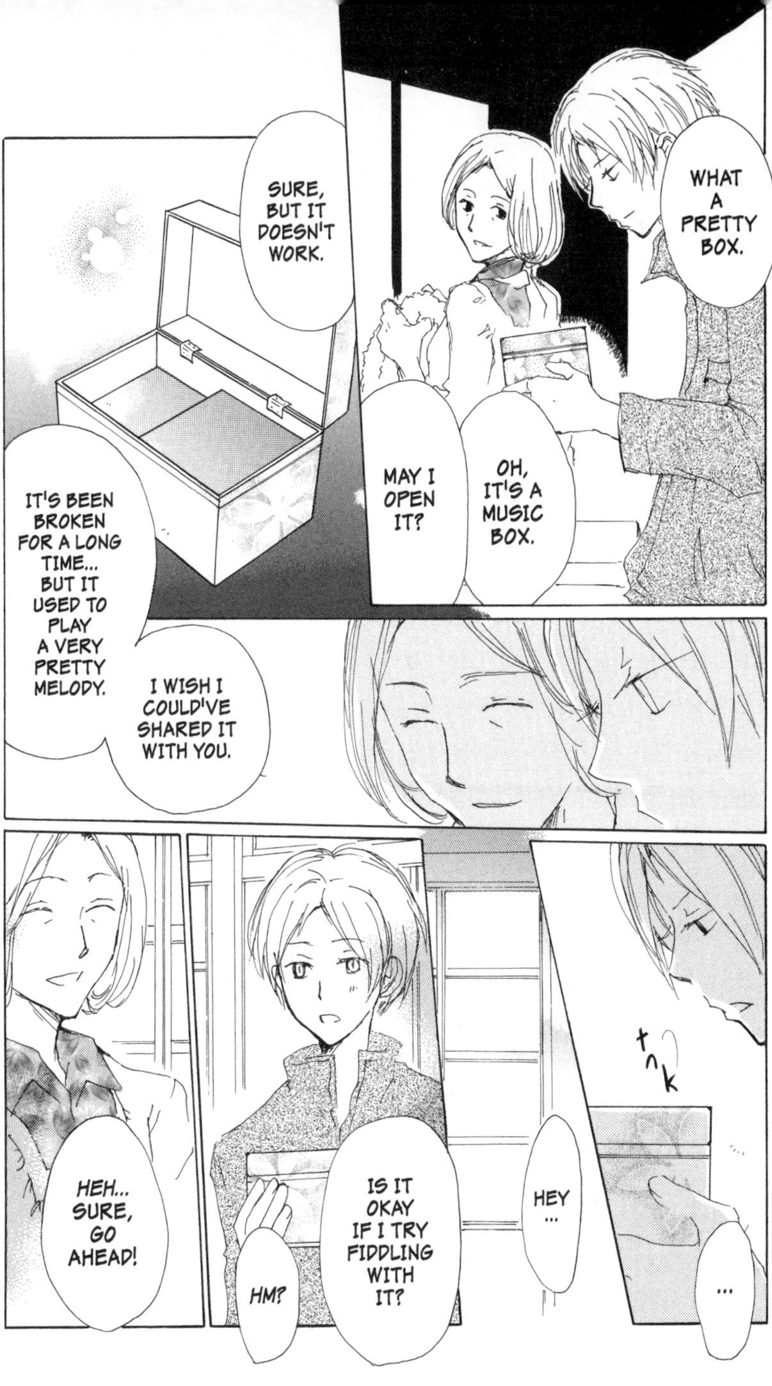
WHAT A PRETTY BOX.
OH, IT'S A MUSIC BOX.
MAY I OPEN IT?
SURE, BUT IT DOESN'T WORK.
IT'S BEEN BROKEN FOR A LONG TIME... BUT IT USED TO PLAY A VERY PRETTY MELODY.
I WISH I COULD'VE SHARED IT WITH YOU.
tnk
...
HEY ...
IS IT OKAY IF I TRY FIDDLING WITH IT?
HM?
HEH... SURE, GO AHEAD!

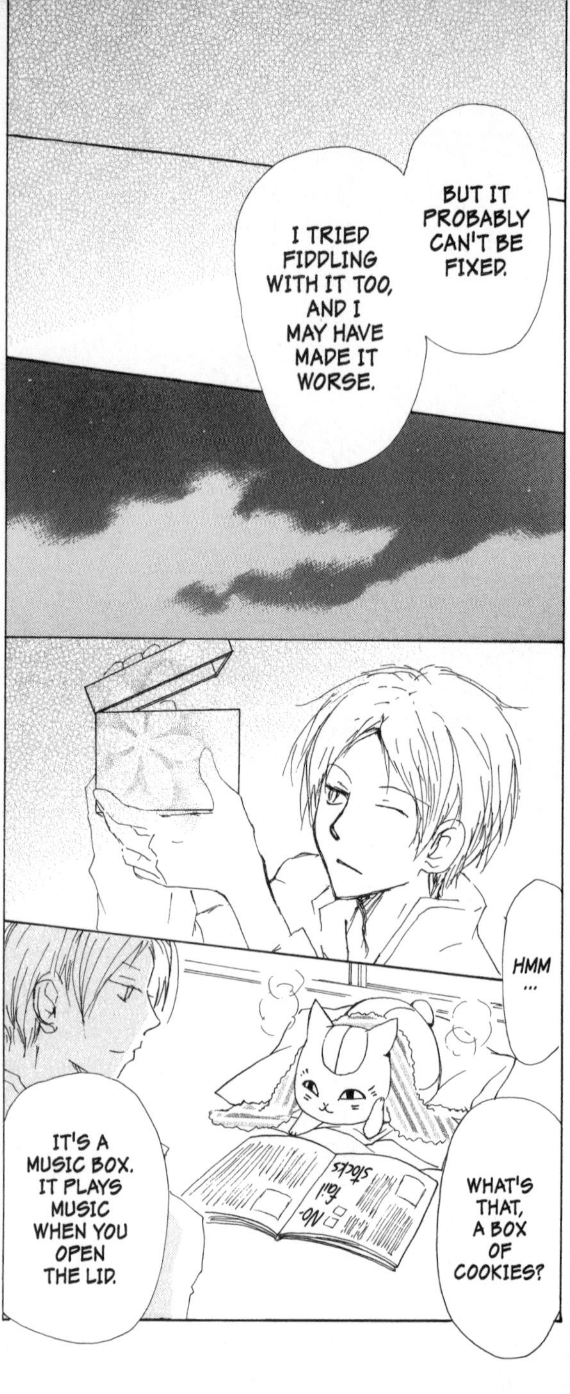
BUT IT PROBABLY CAN'T BE FIXED.
I TRIED FIDDLING WITH IT TOO, AND I MAY HAVE MADE IT WORSE.
HMM ...
WHAT'S THAT, A BOX OF COOKIES?
IT'S A MUSIC BOX. IT PLAYS MUSIC WHEN YOU OPEN THE LID.

01

Hello, Midorikawa here. Natsume's Book of Friends has reached the 18th volume.

I look forward to the letters and messages from my readers. I'd like to keep working hard to make compelling stories for you, so you'll keep coming back for more. Please keep up with your support.

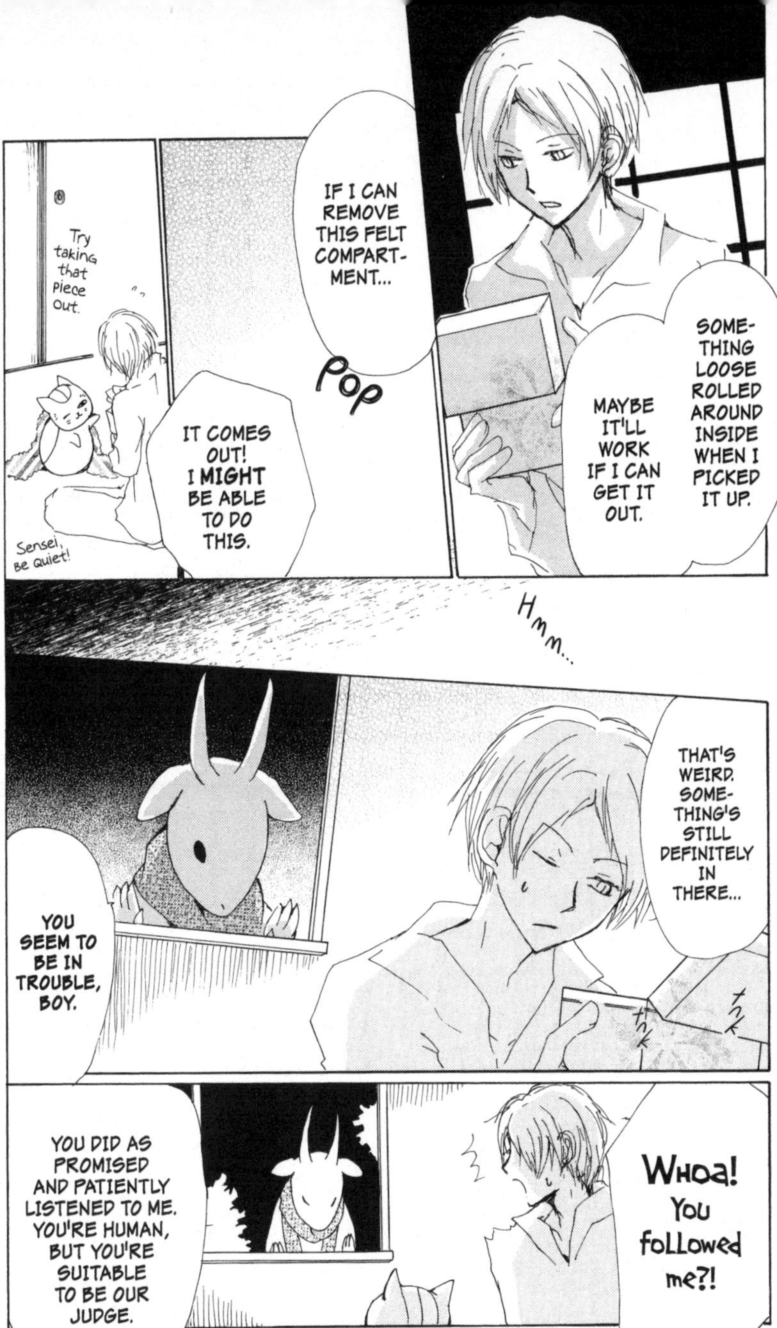
SOMETHING LOOSE ROLLED AROUND INSIDE WHEN I PICKED IT UP.
MAYBE IT'LL WORK IF I CAN GET IT OUT.
IF I CAN REMOVE THIS FELT COMPARTMENT...
POP
IT COMES OUT! I MIGHT BE ABLE TO DO THIS.
Try taking that piece out.
Sensei, Be Quiet!
Hmm...
THAT'S WEIRD. SOMETHING'S STILL DEFINITELY IN THERE...
YOU SEEM TO BE IN TROUBLE, BOY.
Whoa! You followed me?!
YOU DID AS PROMISED AND PATIENTLY LISTENED TO ME. YOU'RE HUMAN, BUT YOU'RE SUITABLE TO BE OUR JUDGE.

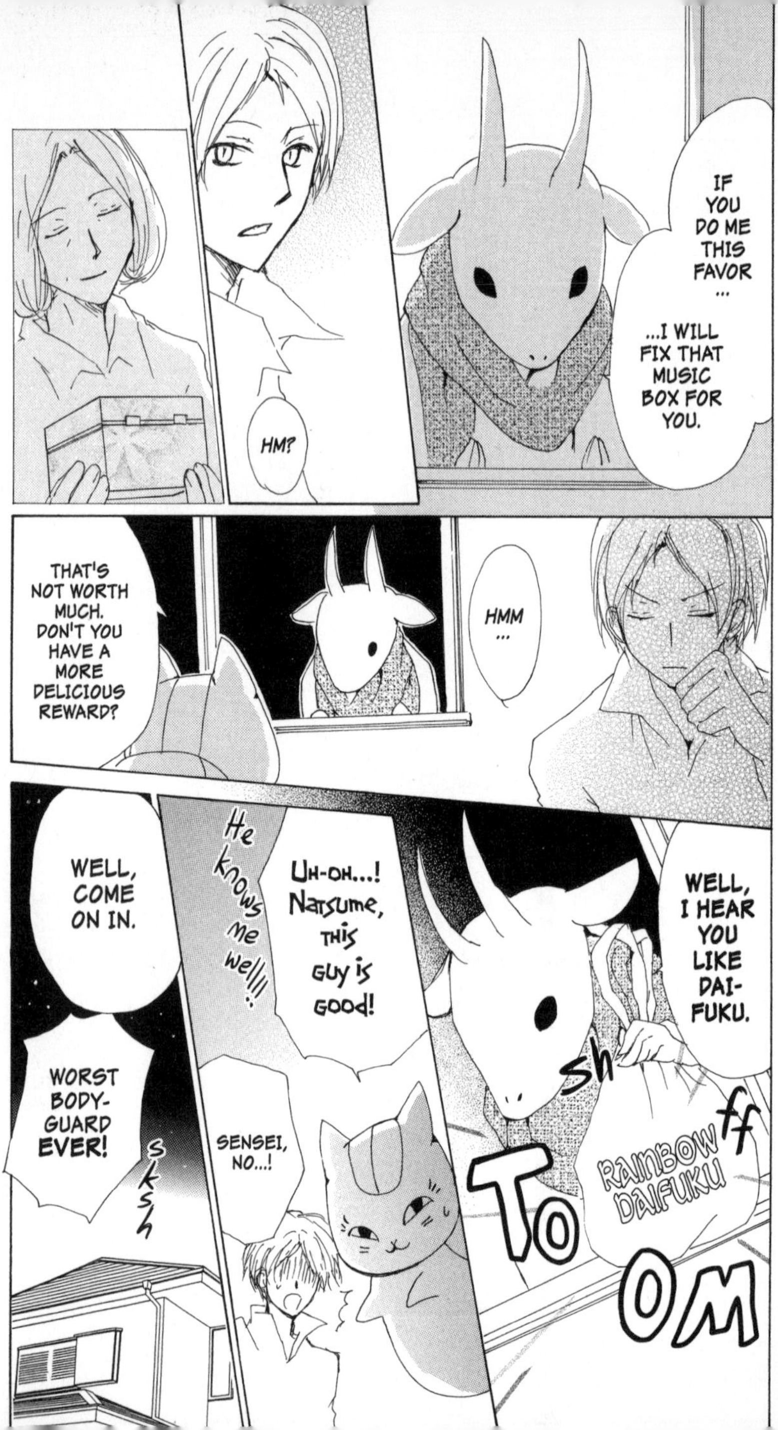
IF YOU DO ME THIS FAVOR...
...I WILL FIX THAT MUSIC BOX FOR YOU.
HM?
HMM...
THAT'S NOT WORTH MUCH. DON'T YOU HAVE A MORE DELICIOUS REWARD?
WELL, I HEAR YOU LIKE DAI-FUKU.
shff
RAINBOW DAIFUKU
TOOM
UH-OH...! Natsume, this guy is good!
He knows me well!!
SENSEI, NO...!
WELL, COME ON IN.
WORST BODY-GUARD EVER!
sksh

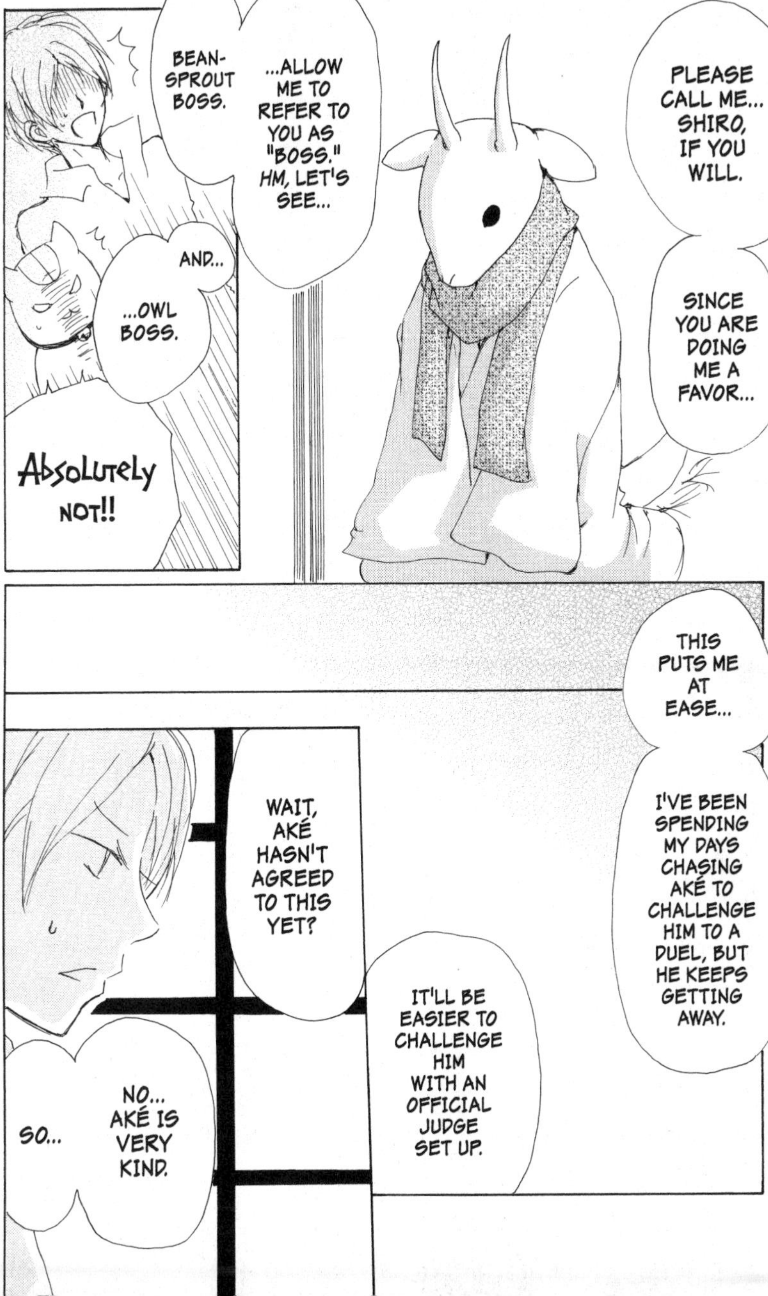
PLEASE CALL ME... SHIRO, IF YOU WILL.
SINCE YOU ARE DOING ME A FAVOR...
...ALLOW ME TO REFER TO YOU AS "BOSS." HM, LET'S SEE...
BEAN-SPROUT BOSS.
AND...
...OWL BOSS.
Absolutely NOT!!
THIS PUTS ME AT EASE...
I'VE BEEN SPENDING MY DAYS CHASING AKÉ TO CHALLENGE HIM TO A DUEL, BUT HE KEEPS GETTING AWAY.
IT'LL BE EASIER TO CHALLENGE HIM WITH AN OFFICIAL JUDGE SET UP.
WAIT, AKÉ HASN'T AGREED TO THIS YET?
NO... AKÉ IS VERY KIND.
SO...

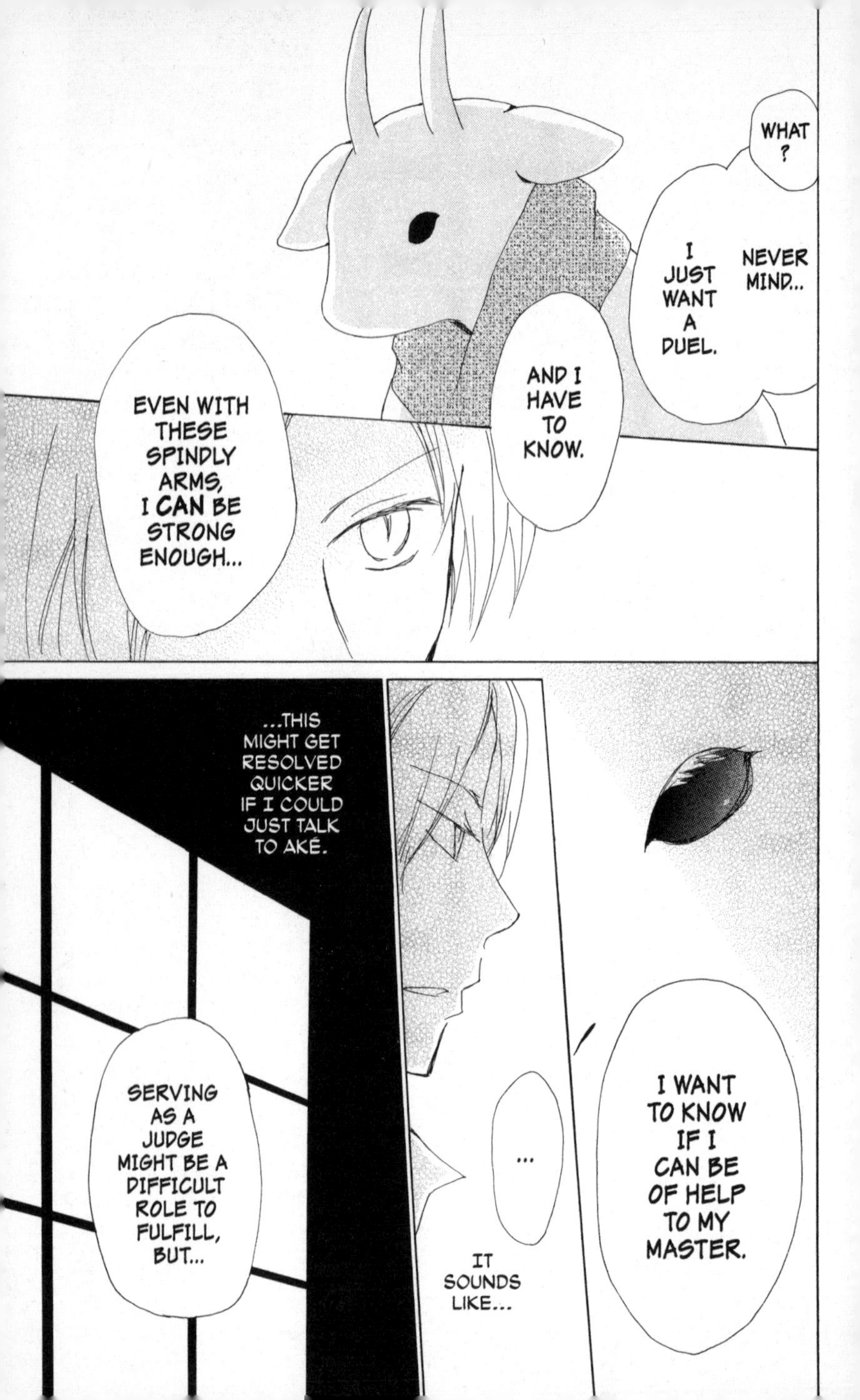
WHAT?
NEVER MIND...
I JUST WANT A DUEL.
AND I HAVE TO KNOW.
EVEN WITH THESE SPINDLY ARMS, I CAN BE STRONG ENOUGH...
I WANT TO KNOW IF I CAN BE OF HELP TO MY MASTER.
...
IT SOUNDS LIKE...
...THIS MIGHT GET RESOLVED QUICKER IF I COULD JUST TALK TO AKÉ.
SERVING AS A JUDGE MIGHT BE A DIFFICULT ROLE TO FULFILL, BUT...

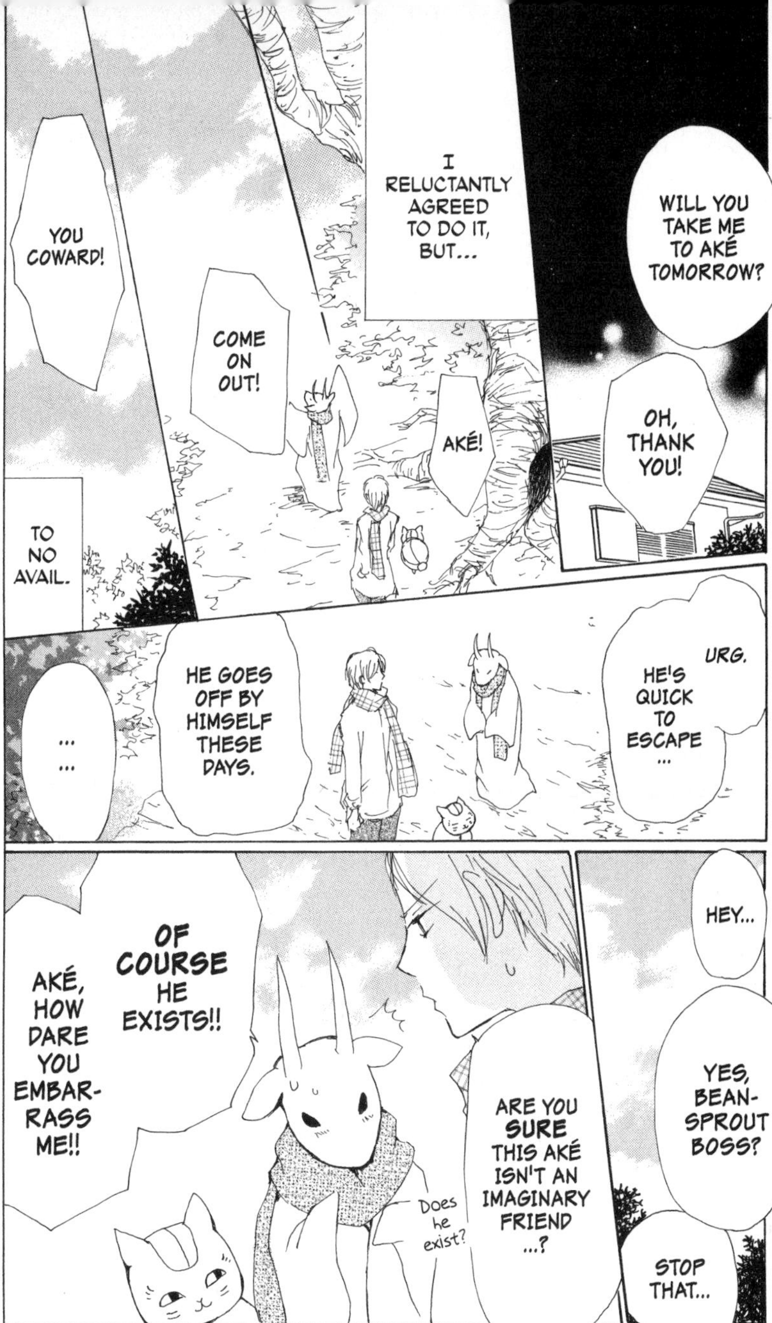

WILL YOU TAKE ME TO AKÉ TOMORROW?
OH, THANK YOU!
I RELUCTANTLY AGREED TO DO IT, BUT...
AKÉ!
COME ON OUT!
YOU COWARD!
TO NO AVAIL.
URG.
HE'S QUICK TO ESCAPE...
HE GOES OFF BY HIMSELF THESE DAYS.
... ...
HEY...
YES, BEAN-SPROUT BOSS?
STOP THAT...
ARE YOU SURE THIS AKÉ ISN'T AN IMAGINARY FRIEND...?
Does he exist?
OF COURSE HE EXISTS!!
AKÉ, HOW DARE YOU EMBARRASS ME!!

02

❃ Gallery in Osaka and Fukuoka

They graciously held a gallery show for me in Osaka and Fukuoka. They make such beautiful and fun event spaces every time, and so many people work so hard to make it happen, I feel unworthy. I get so emotional. Thank you so much to everyone who came.

About the art... I love to draw, but since I draw strange things, I'm grateful that people pick it up at all. That's really what keeps me going, so sometimes I feel embarrassed or self-conscious, but all my art is precious to me. I'm so happy that people were able to come in contact with it. Thanks to everyone who turned out. The guestbook that people wrote in will be treasured forever.

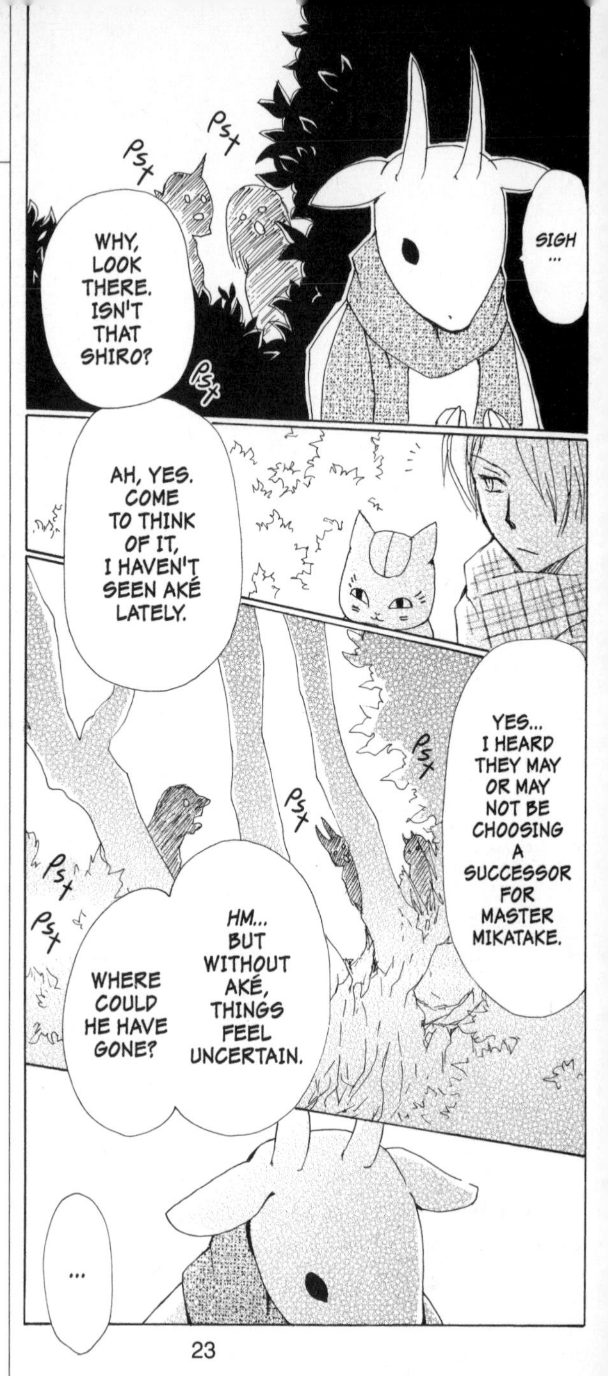
SIGH...
Pst
Pst
WHY, LOOK THERE. ISN'T THAT SHIRO?
Pst
AH, YES. COME TO THINK OF IT, I HAVEN'T SEEN AKÉ LATELY.
YES... I HEARD THEY MAY OR MAY NOT BE CHOOSING A SUCCESSOR FOR MASTER MIKATAKE.
Pst
Pst
Pst
Pst
HM... BUT WITHOUT AKÉ, THINGS FEEL UNCERTAIN.
WHERE COULD HE HAVE GONE?
...

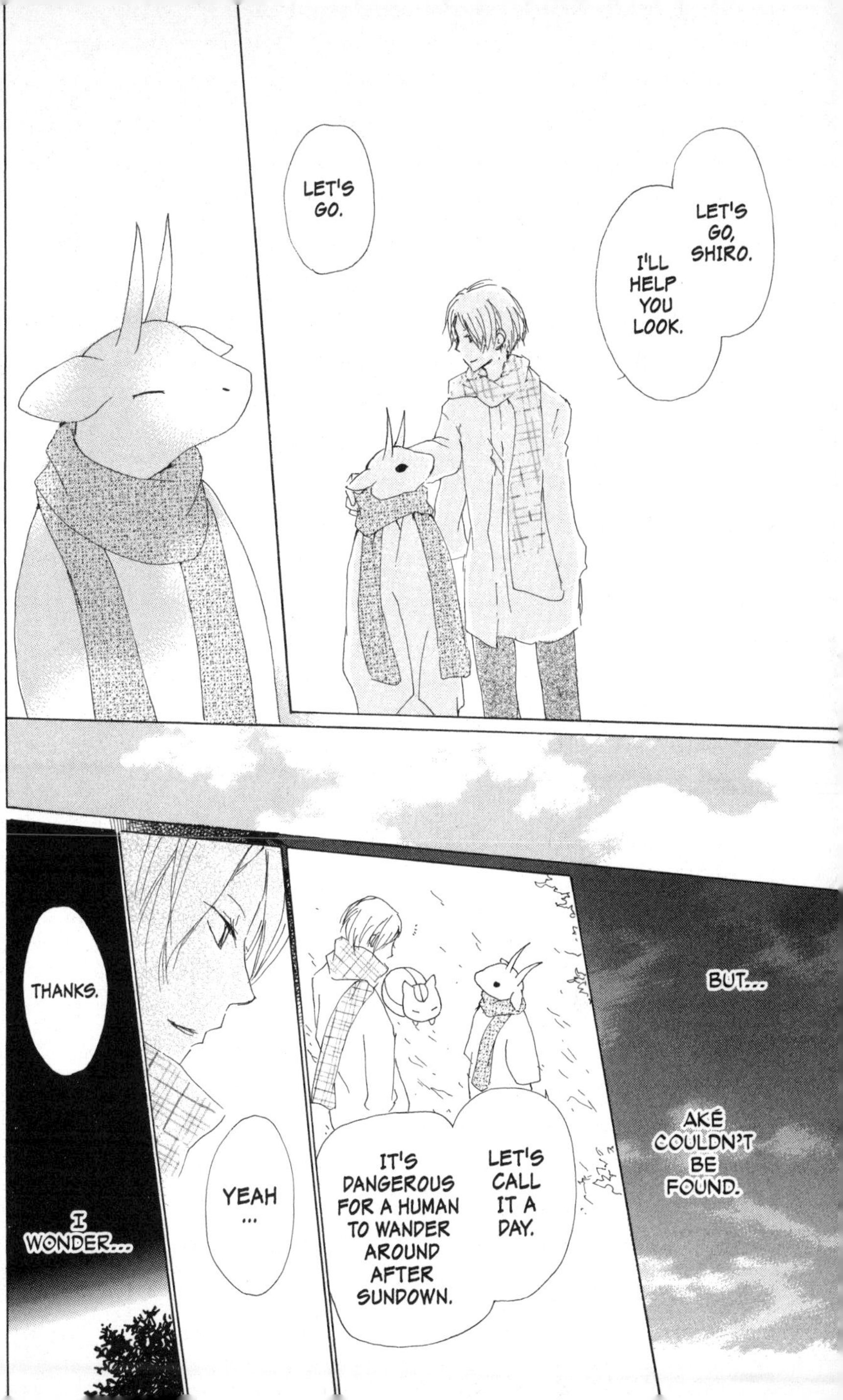
LET'S GO, SHIRO.
I'LL HELP YOU LOOK.
LET'S GO.
BUT...
AKÉ COULDN'T BE FOUND.
LET'S CALL IT A DAY.
IT'S DANGEROUS FOR A HUMAN TO WANDER AROUND AFTER SUNDOWN.
YEAH...
THANKS.
I WONDER...

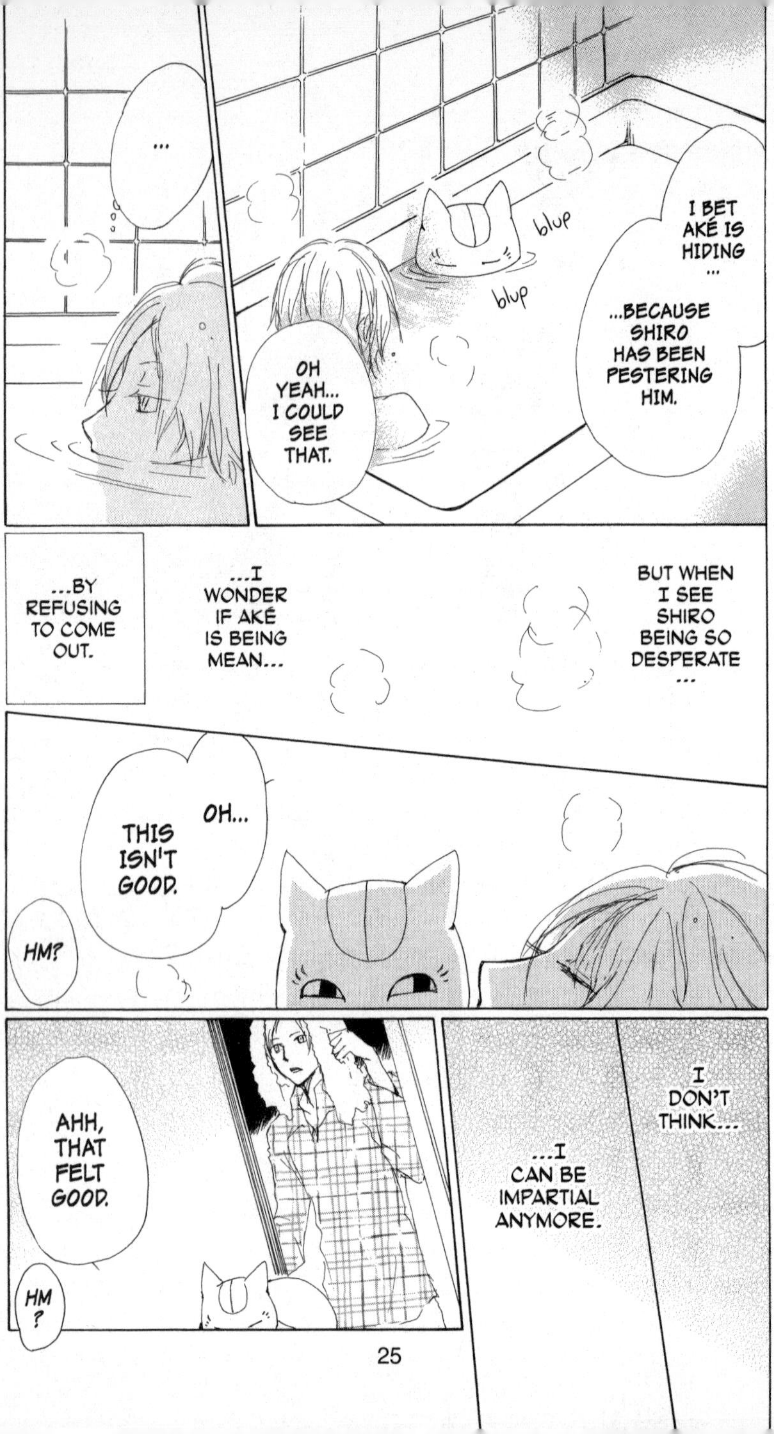

I BET AKÉ IS HIDING ...
...BECAUSE SHIRO HAS BEEN PESTERING HIM.
blup
blup
OH YEAH... I COULD SEE THAT.
...
BUT WHEN I SEE SHIRO BEING SO DESPERATE ...
...I WONDER IF AKÉ IS BEING MEAN...
...BY REFUSING TO COME OUT.
OH... THIS ISN'T GOOD.
HM?
I DON'T THINK...
...I CAN BE IMPARTIAL ANYMORE.
AHH, THAT FELT GOOD.
HM ?

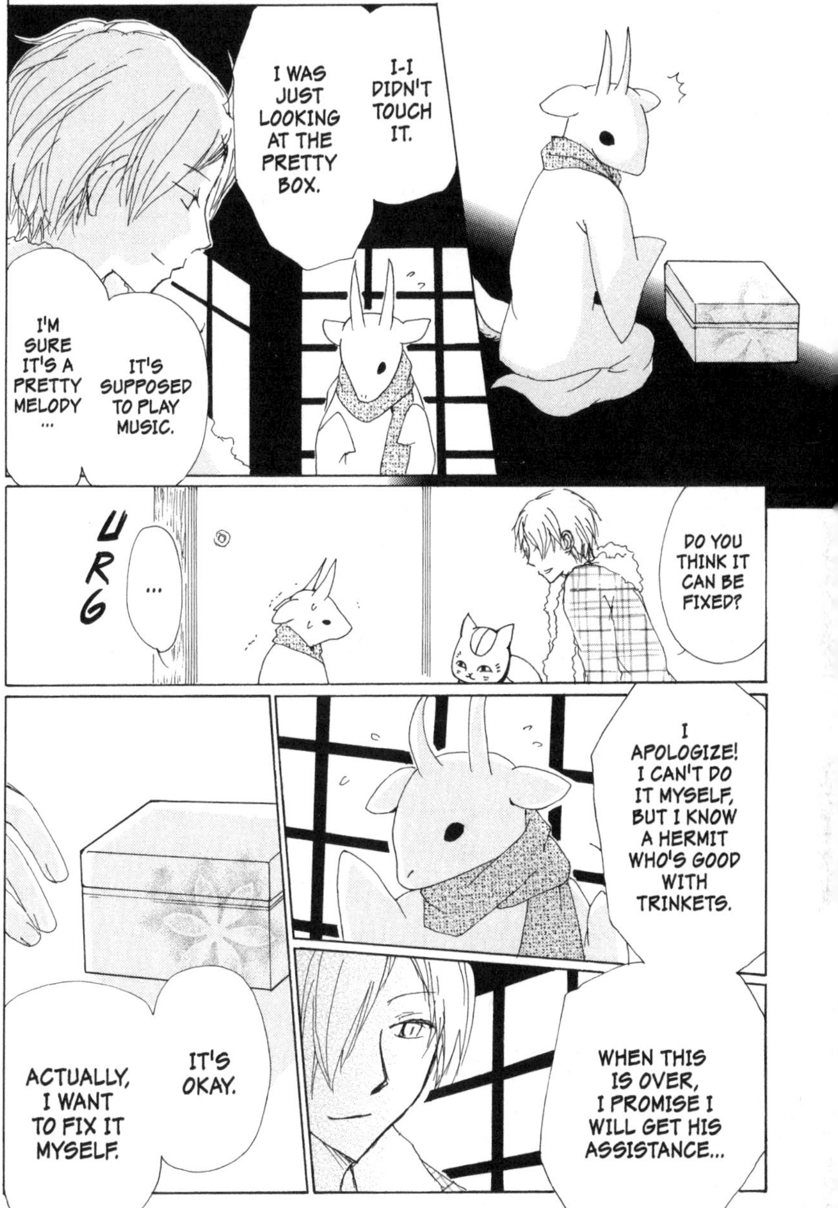
I-I DIDN'T TOUCH IT.
I WAS JUST LOOKING AT THE PRETTY BOX.
IT'S SUPPOSED TO PLAY MUSIC.
I'M SURE IT'S A PRETTY MELODY ...
DO YOU THINK IT CAN BE FIXED?
...
URG
I APOLOGIZE! I CAN'T DO IT MYSELF, BUT I KNOW A HERMIT WHO'S GOOD WITH TRINKETS.
WHEN THIS IS OVER, I PROMISE I WILL GET HIS ASSISTANCE...
IT'S OKAY.
ACTUALLY, I WANT TO FIX IT MYSELF.

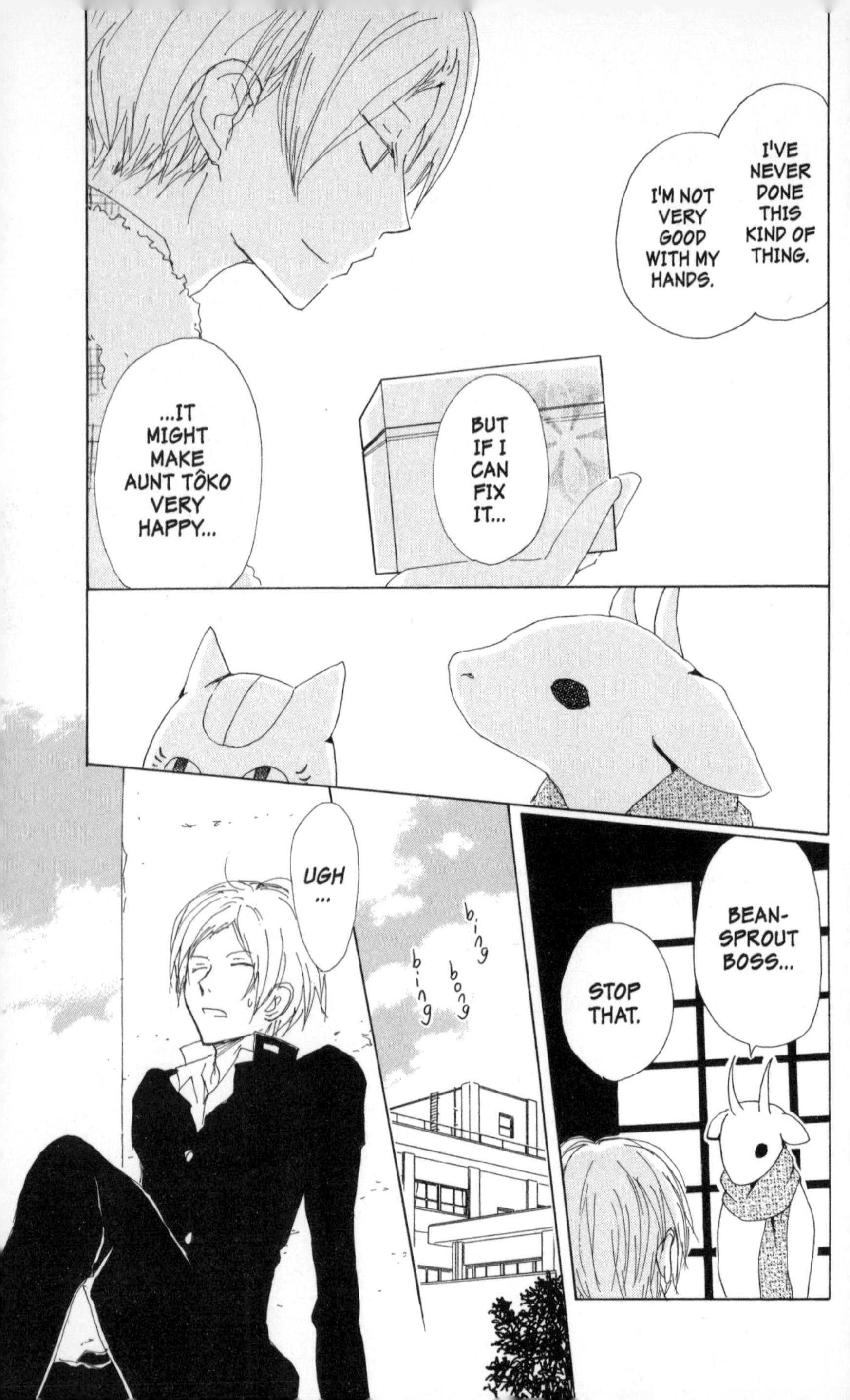
I'VE NEVER DONE THIS KIND OF THING.
I'M NOT VERY GOOD WITH MY HANDS.
BUT IF I CAN FIX IT...
...IT MIGHT MAKE AUNT TÔKO VERY HAPPY...
BEAN-SPROUT BOSS...
STOP THAT.
UGH...
bing
bong
bing

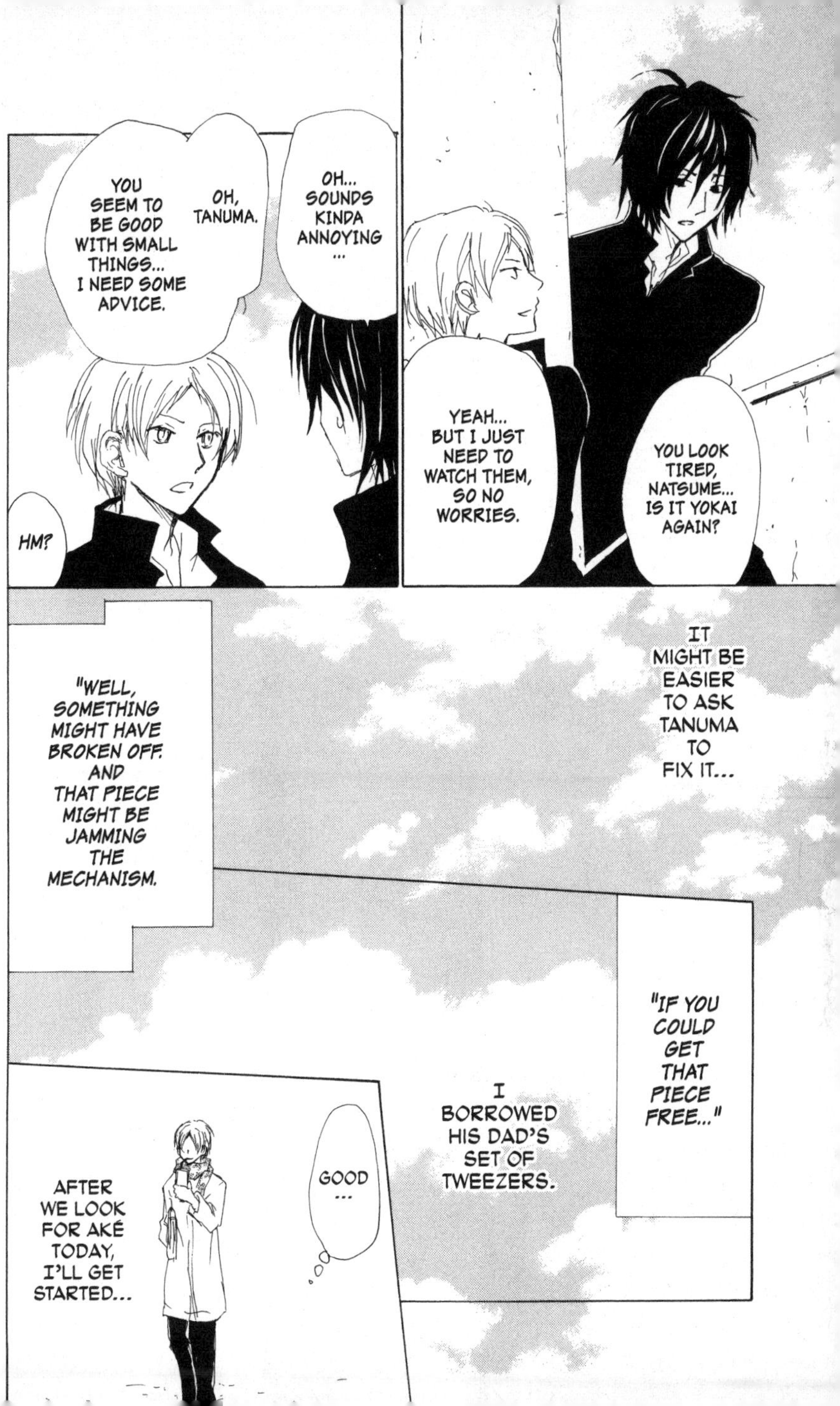
YOU LOOK TIRED, NATSUME... IS IT YOKAI AGAIN?
YEAH... BUT I JUST NEED TO WATCH THEM, SO NO WORRIES.
OH... SOUNDS KINDA ANNOYING...
OH, TANUMA.
YOU SEEM TO BE GOOD WITH SMALL THINGS... I NEED SOME ADVICE.
HM?
IT MIGHT BE EASIER TO ASK TANUMA TO FIX IT...
"WELL, SOMETHING MIGHT HAVE BROKEN OFF. AND THAT PIECE MIGHT BE JAMMING THE MECHANISM.
"IF YOU COULD GET THAT PIECE FREE..."
I BORROWED HIS DAD'S SET OF TWEEZERS.
GOOD...
AFTER WE LOOK FOR AKÉ TODAY, I'LL GET STARTED...

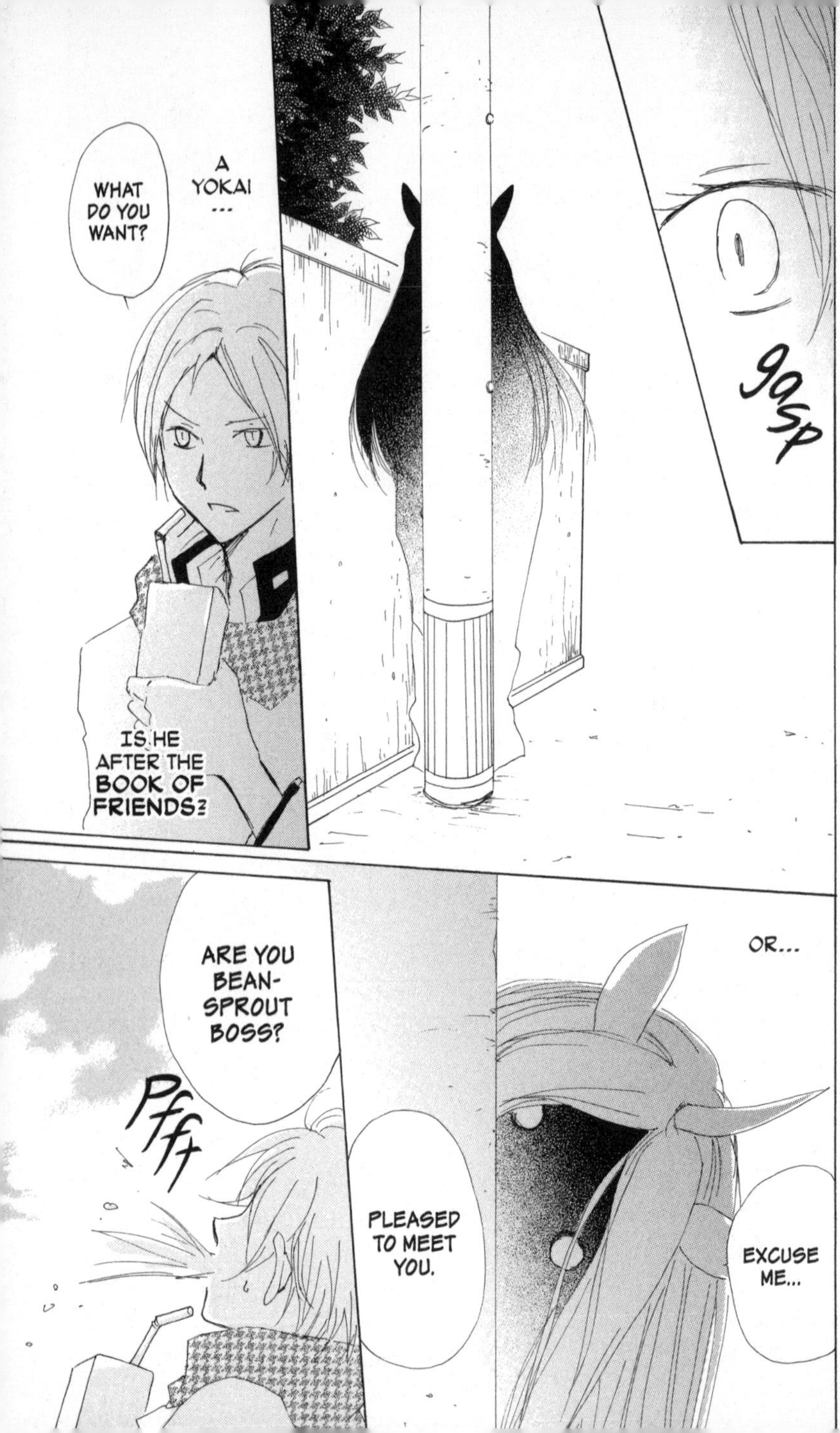
gasp
A YOKAI...
WHAT DO YOU WANT?
IS HE AFTER THE BOOK OF FRIENDS?
OR...
EXCUSE ME...
PLEASED TO MEET YOU.
ARE YOU BEAN-SPROUT BOSS?
Pffft

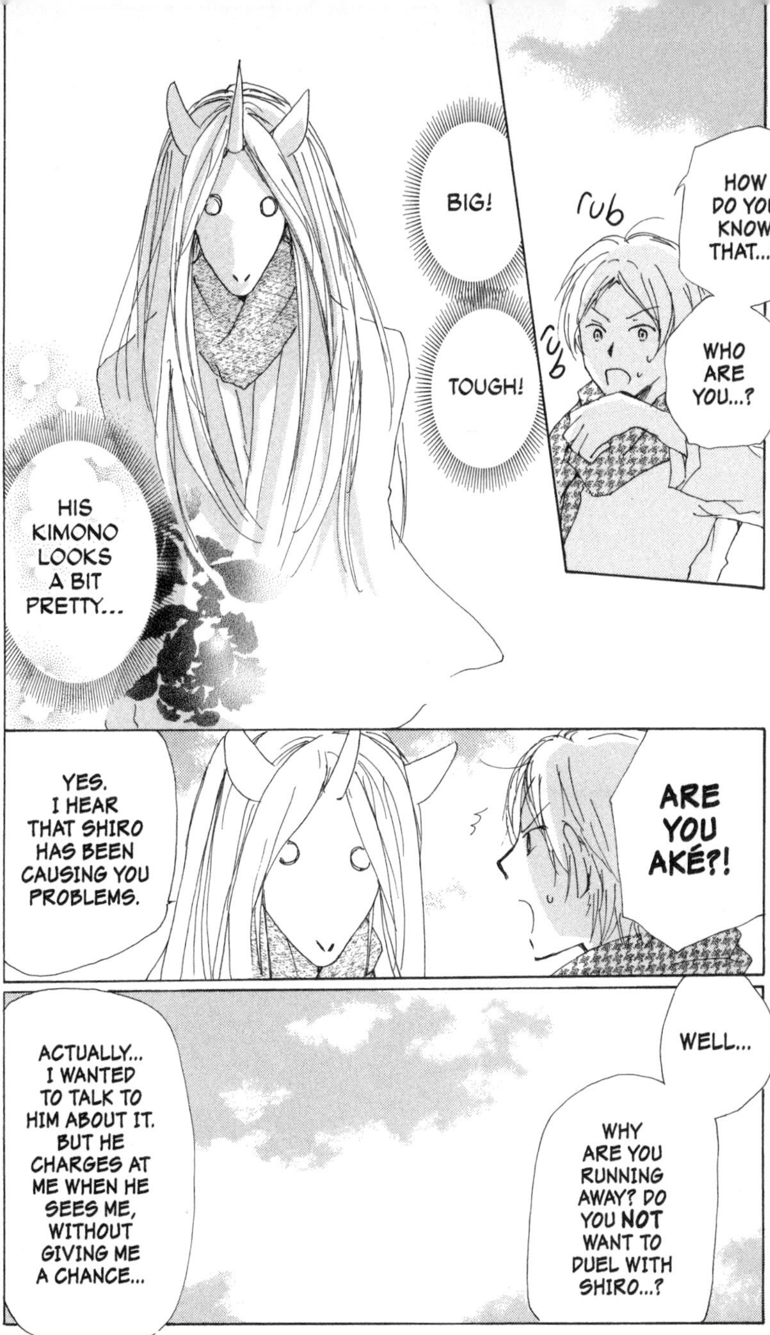
HOW DO YOU KNOW THAT...?
rub
rub
WHO ARE YOU...?
BIG!
TOUGH!
HIS KIMONO LOOKS A BIT PRETTY...
ARE YOU AKÉ?!
YES. I HEAR THAT SHIRO HAS BEEN CAUSING YOU PROBLEMS.
WELL...
WHY ARE YOU RUNNING AWAY? DO YOU **NOT** WANT TO DUEL WITH SHIRO...?
ACTUALLY... I WANTED TO TALK TO HIM ABOUT IT. BUT HE CHARGES AT ME WHEN HE SEES ME, WITHOUT GIVING ME A CHANCE...

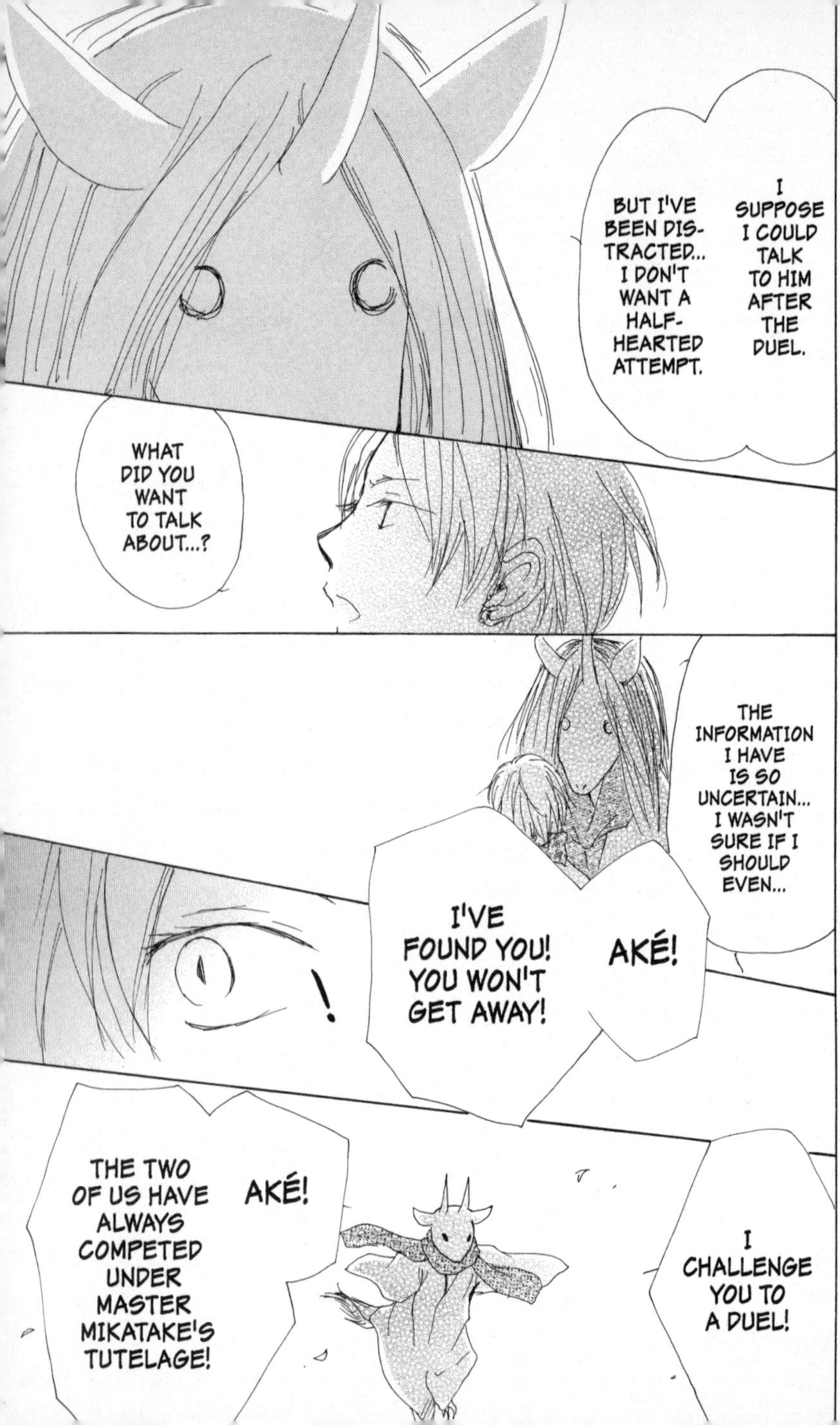
I SUPPOSE I COULD TALK TO HIM AFTER THE DUEL.
BUT I'VE BEEN DIS-TRACTED... I DON'T WANT A HALF-HEARTED ATTEMPT.
WHAT DID YOU WANT TO TALK ABOUT...?
THE INFORMATION I HAVE IS SO UNCERTAIN... I WASN'T SURE IF I SHOULD EVEN...
AKÉ!
I'VE FOUND YOU! YOU WON'T GET AWAY!
!
I CHALLENGE YOU TO A DUEL!
AKÉ!
THE TWO OF US HAVE ALWAYS COMPETED UNDER MASTER MIKATAKE'S TUTELAGE!

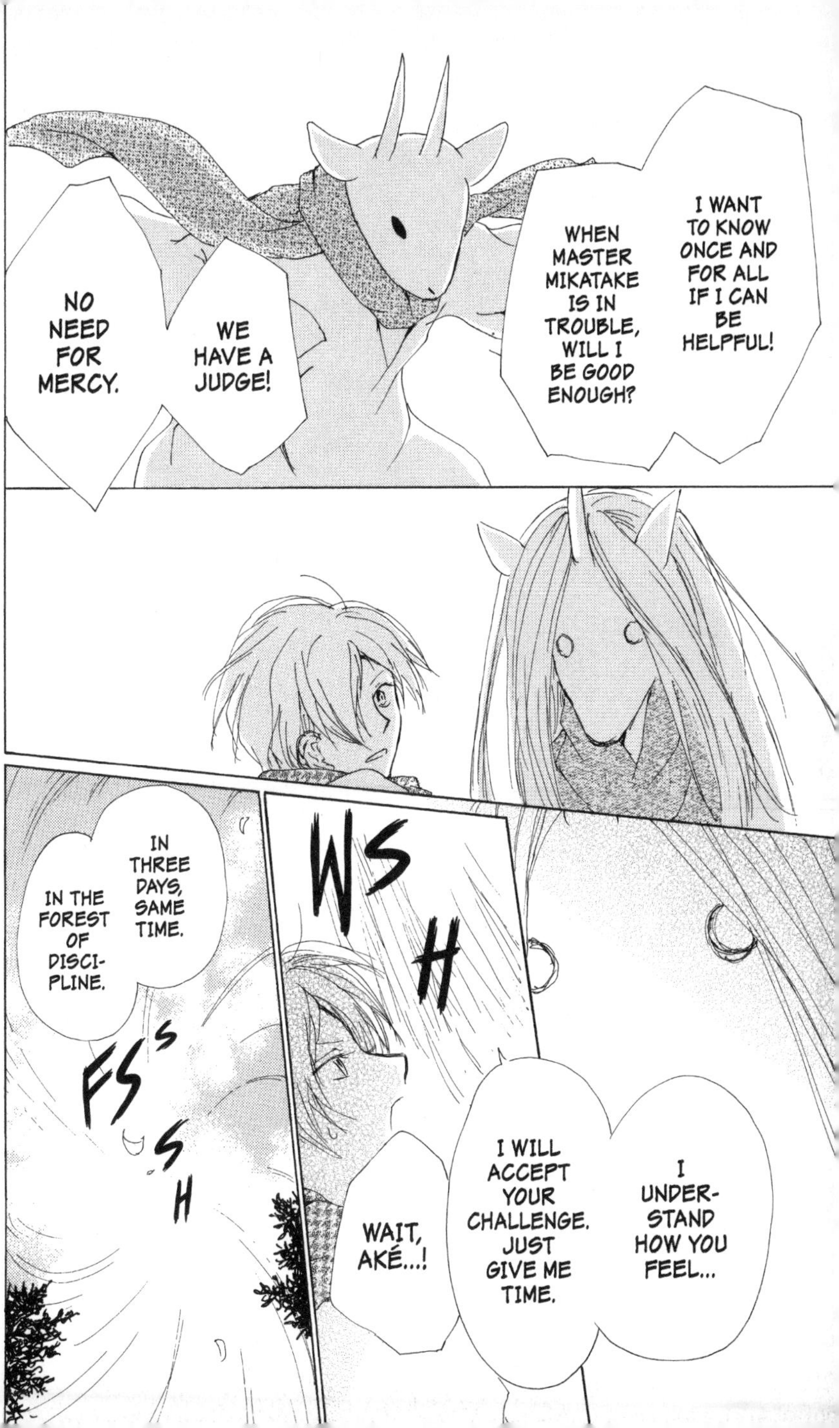
I WANT TO KNOW ONCE AND FOR ALL IF I CAN BE HELPFUL!
WHEN MASTER MIKATAKE IS IN TROUBLE, WILL I BE GOOD ENOUGH?
WE HAVE A JUDGE!
NO NEED FOR MERCY.
WSH
I UNDER-STAND HOW YOU FEEL...
I WILL ACCEPT YOUR CHALLENGE. JUST GIVE ME TIME.
WAIT, AKÉ...!
IN THREE DAYS, SAME TIME.
IN THE FOREST OF DISCI-PLINE.
FSSSH

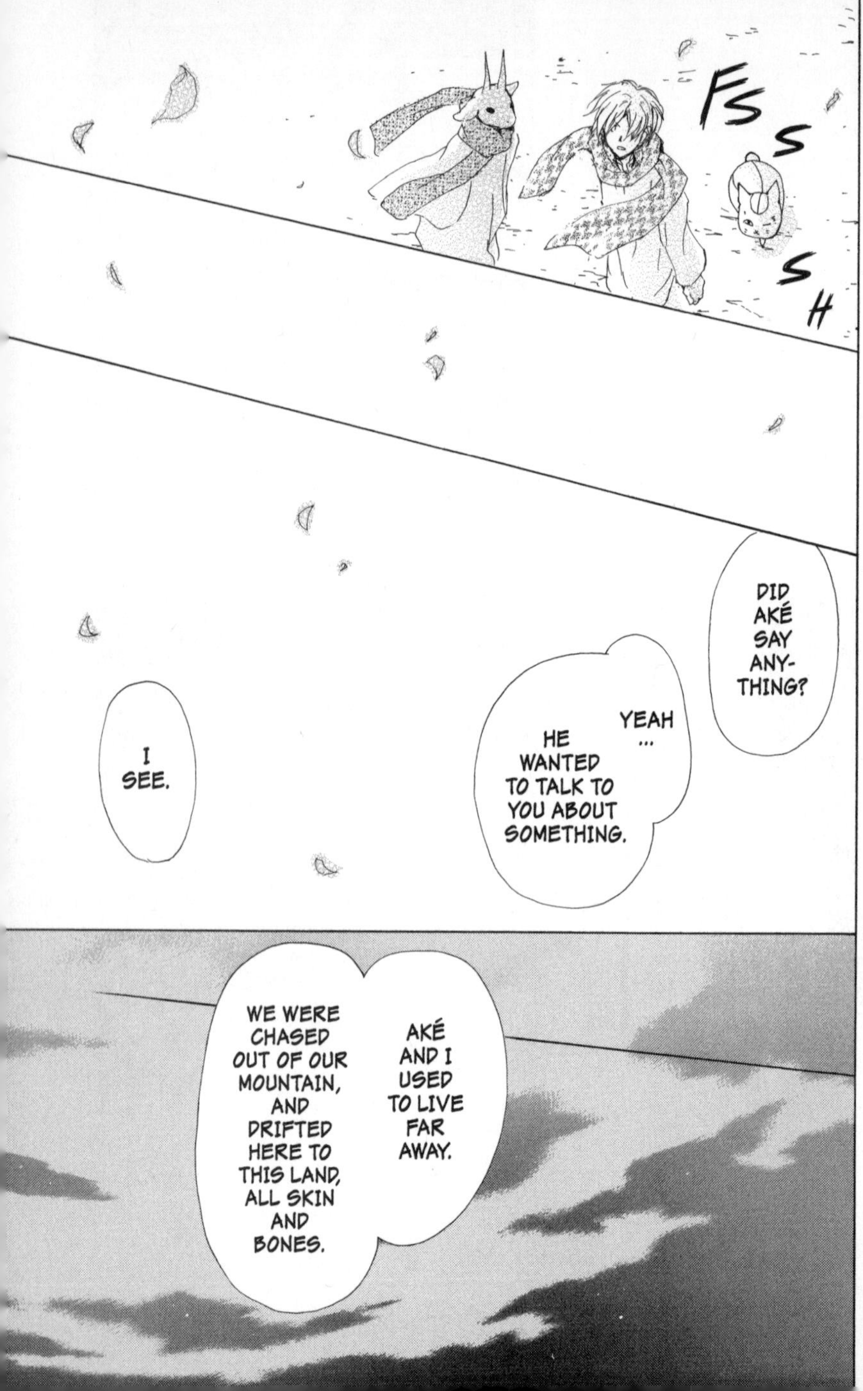
FSSSH
DID AKÉ SAY ANYTHING?
YEAH ...
HE WANTED TO TALK TO YOU ABOUT SOMETHING.
I SEE.
AKÉ AND I USED TO LIVE FAR AWAY.
WE WERE CHASED OUT OF OUR MOUNTAIN, AND DRIFTED HERE TO THIS LAND, ALL SKIN AND BONES.

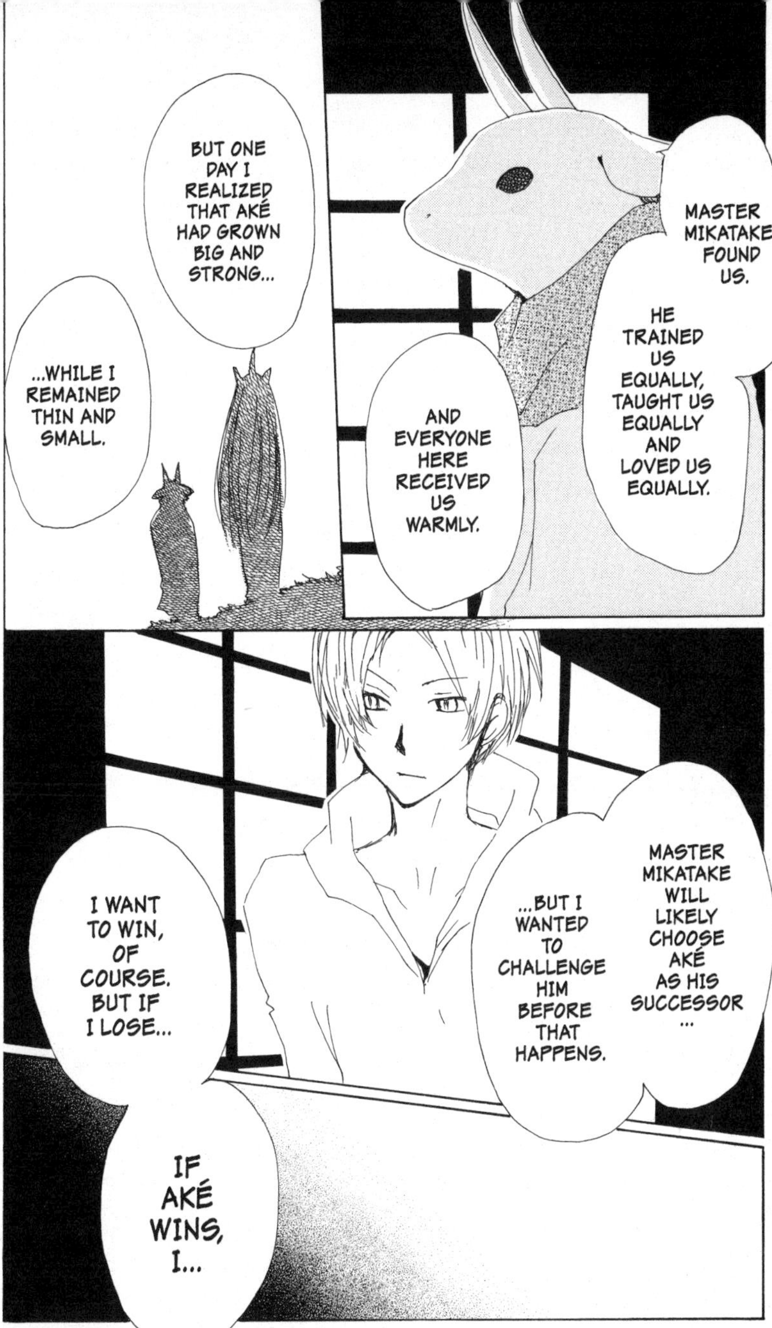
MASTER MIKATAKE FOUND US.
HE TRAINED US EQUALLY, TAUGHT US EQUALLY AND LOVED US EQUALLY.
AND EVERYONE HERE RECEIVED US WARMLY.
BUT ONE DAY I REALIZED THAT AKÉ HAD GROWN BIG AND STRONG...
...WHILE I REMAINED THIN AND SMALL.
MASTER MIKATAKE WILL LIKELY CHOOSE AKÉ AS HIS SUCCESSOR...
...BUT I WANTED TO CHALLENGE HIM BEFORE THAT HAPPENS.
I WANT TO WIN, OF COURSE. BUT IF I LOSE...
IF AKÉ WINS, I...

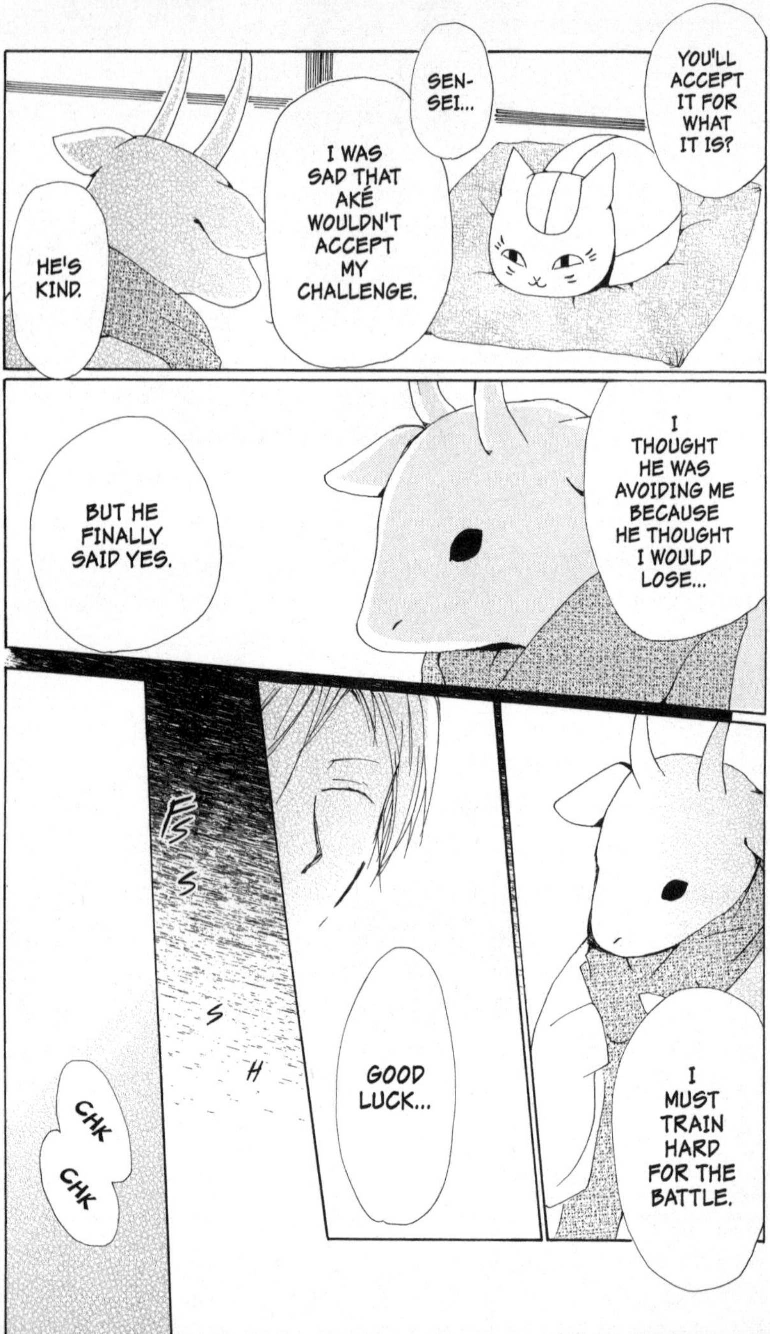
YOU'LL ACCEPT IT FOR WHAT IT IS?
SEN-SEI...
I WAS SAD THAT AKÉ WOULDN'T ACCEPT MY CHALLENGE.
HE'S KIND.
I THOUGHT HE WAS AVOIDING ME BECAUSE HE THOUGHT I WOULD LOSE...
BUT HE FINALLY SAID YES.
I MUST TRAIN HARD FOR THE BATTLE.
GOOD LUCK...
FSSSH
CHK CHK

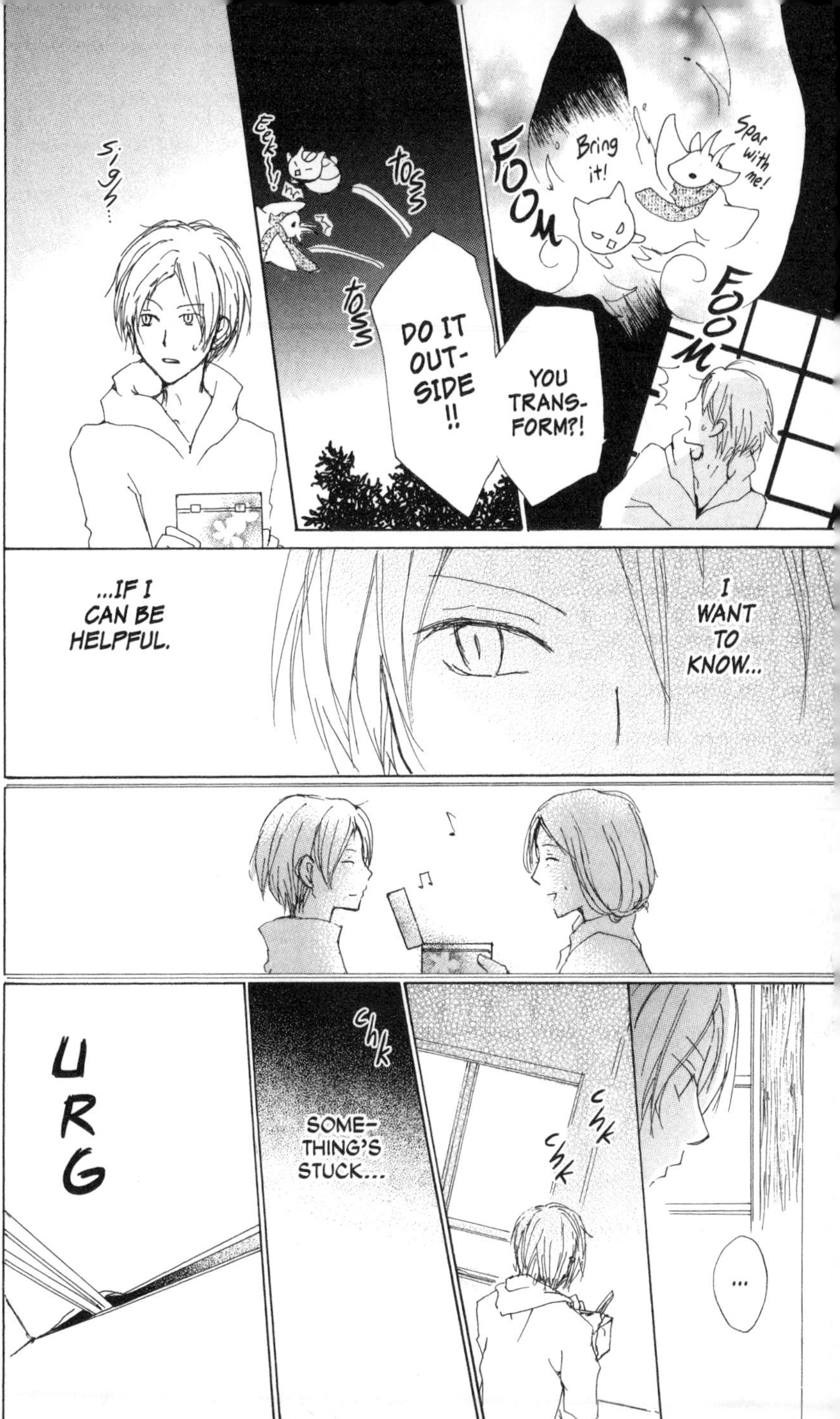

FOOM
Spar with me!
Bring it!
FOOM
YOU TRANSFORM?!
DO IT OUTSIDE!!
toss
toss
Eek~!
sigh...
I WANT TO KNOW...
...IF I CAN BE HELPFUL.
...
chk
chk
chk
SOME-THING'S STUCK...
URG

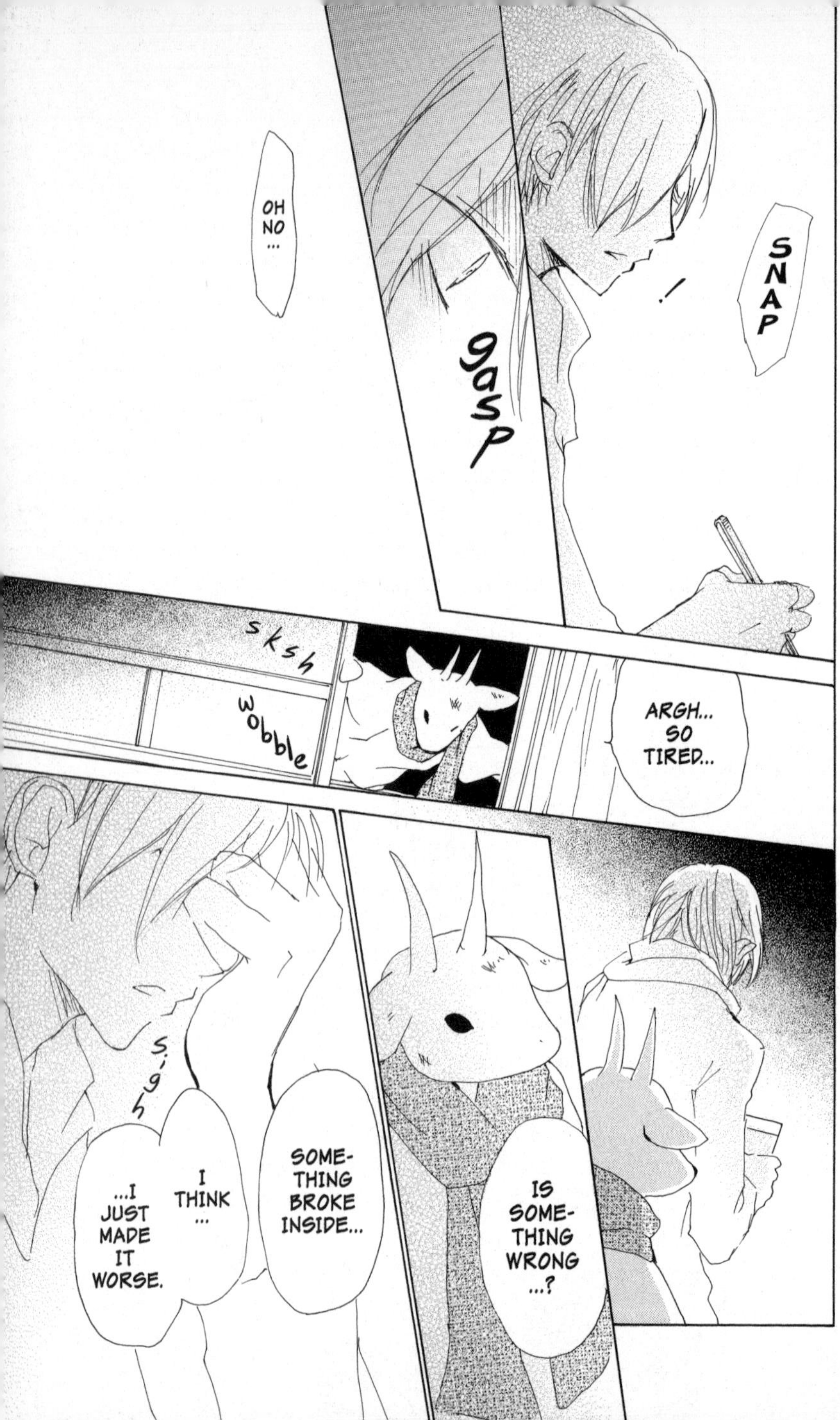
SNAP
!
gasp
OH NO ...
ARGH... SO TIRED...
sksh
wobble
IS SOME-THING WRONG ...?
SOME-THING BROKE INSIDE...
sigh
I THINK ...
...I JUST MADE IT WORSE.

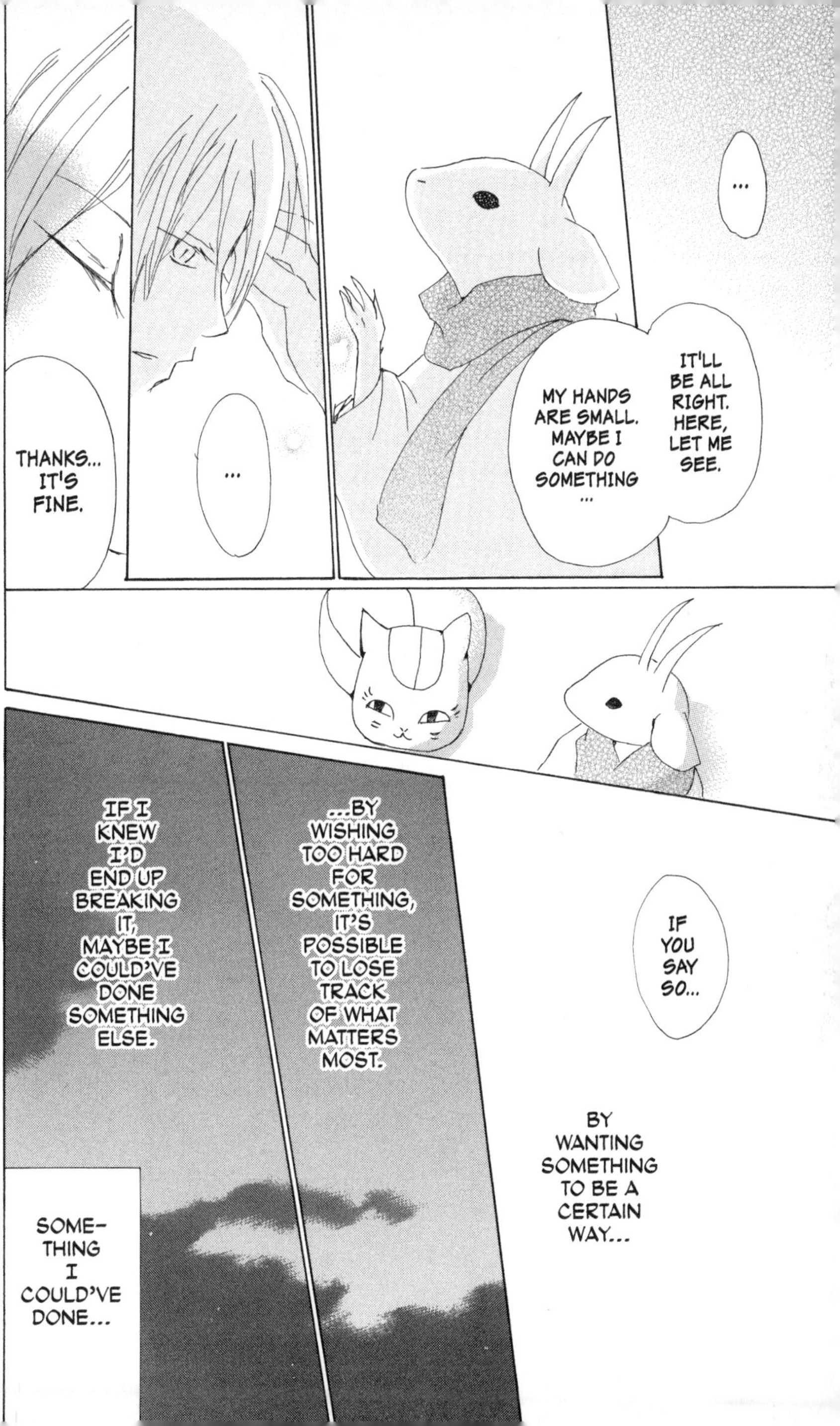
...
IT'LL BE ALL RIGHT. HERE, LET ME SEE.
MY HANDS ARE SMALL. MAYBE I CAN DO SOMETHING...
...
THANKS... IT'S FINE.
IF YOU SAY SO...
BY WANTING SOMETHING TO BE A CERTAIN WAY...
...BY WISHING TOO HARD FOR SOMETHING, IT'S POSSIBLE TO LOSE TRACK OF WHAT MATTERS MOST.
IF I KNEW I'D END UP BREAKING IT, MAYBE I COULD'VE DONE SOMETHING ELSE.
SOME-THING I COULD'VE DONE...

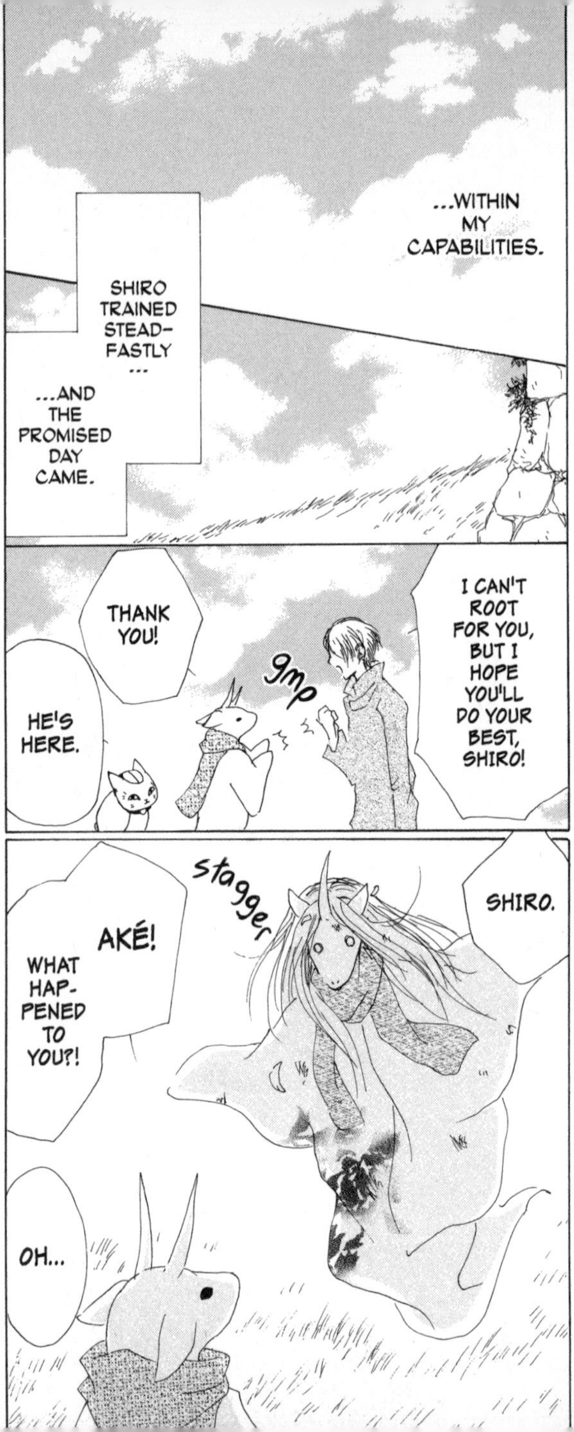

...WITHIN MY CAPABILITIES.
SHIRO TRAINED STEAD-FASTLY ...
...AND THE PROMISED DAY CAME.
I CAN'T ROOT FOR YOU, BUT I HOPE YOU'LL DO YOUR BEST, SHIRO!
gmp
THANK YOU!
HE'S HERE.
SHIRO.
stagger
AKÉ!
WHAT HAP-PENED TO YOU?!
OH...

03

❋ Natsume's Book of Friends Anime OVA

I got some help from the people who created the anime Natsume's Book of Friends, the people behind the other beautiful, unique and warm Natsume's Book of Friends. They made a wonderful OVA titled "One Snowy Day." There's a cute story where Nyanko Sensei goes on an errand for the first time, and a story where Natsume meets a mysterious yokai on a quiet snowy day. Also included is a "Sound Theater Gathering Chapter," the script and live music so delicately done. It's a memorable piece by the anime voice actors. I love it.

I highly recommend it to all anime Natsume fans, and anyone who hasn't seen the anime yet but is curious.

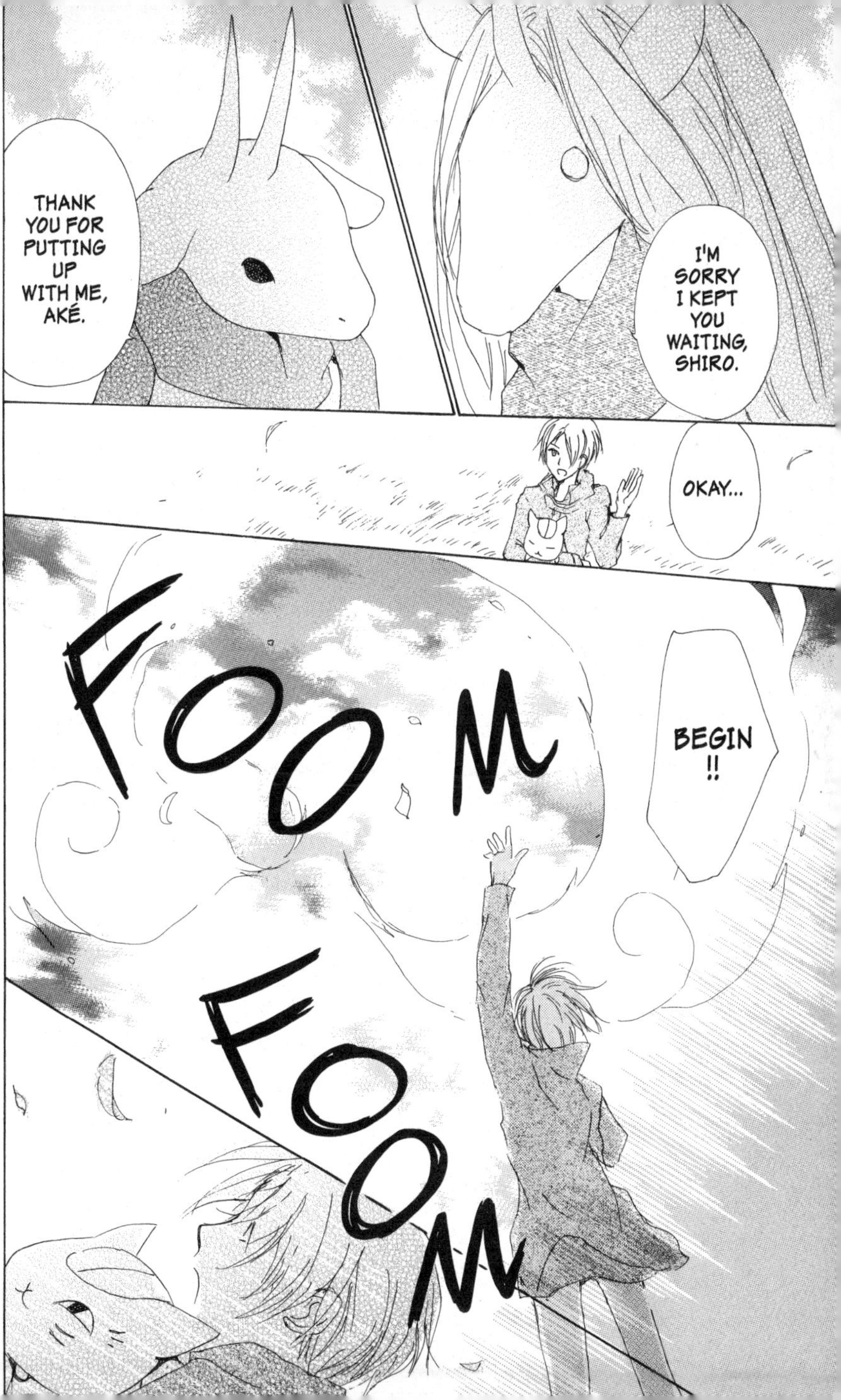
I'M SORRY I KEPT YOU WAITING, SHIRO.
THANK YOU FOR PUTTING UP WITH ME, AKÉ.
OKAY...
BEGIN!!
FOOM
FOOM

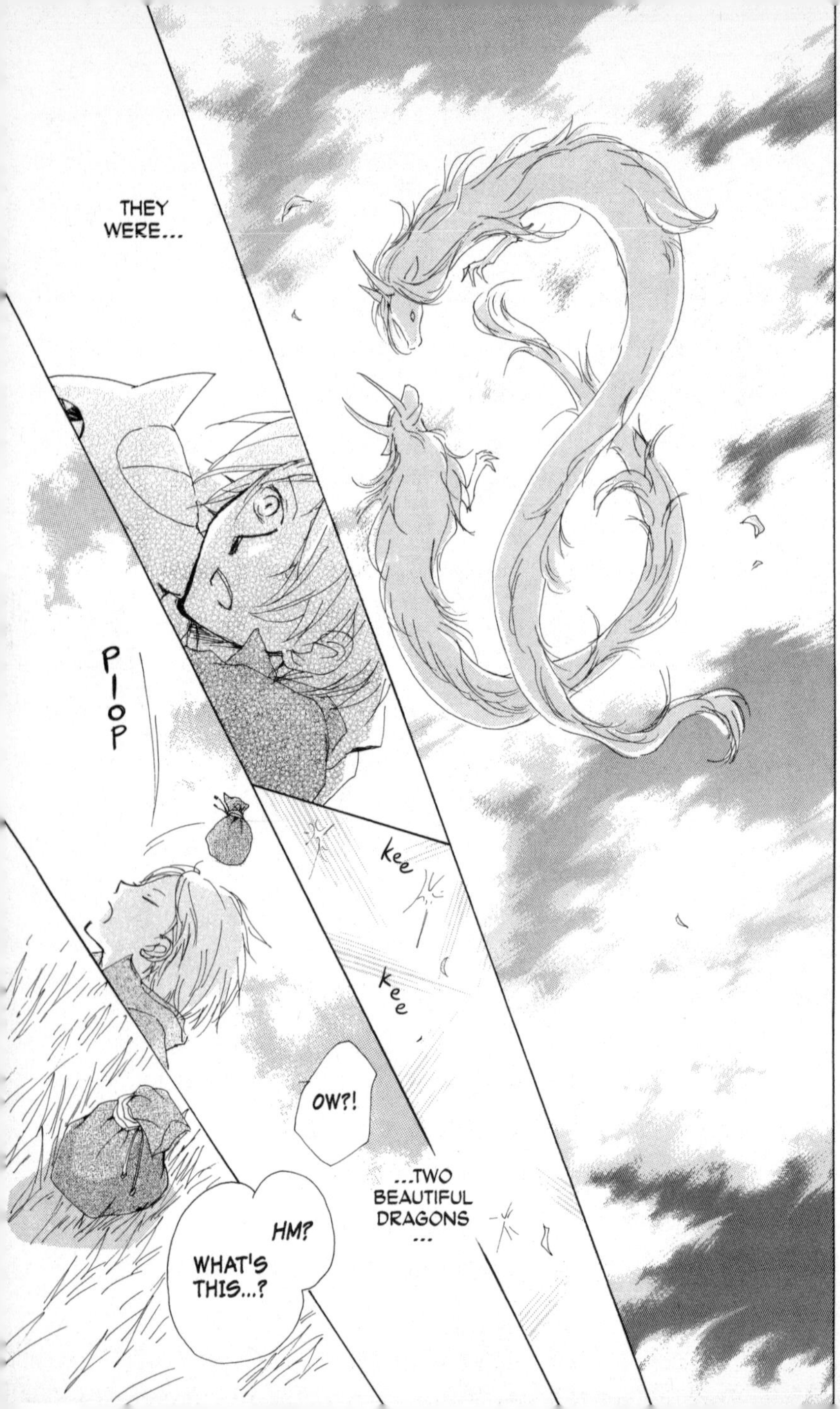
THEY WERE...
...TWO BEAUTIFUL DRAGONS ...
kee kee
PLOP
OW?!
HM? WHAT'S THIS...?

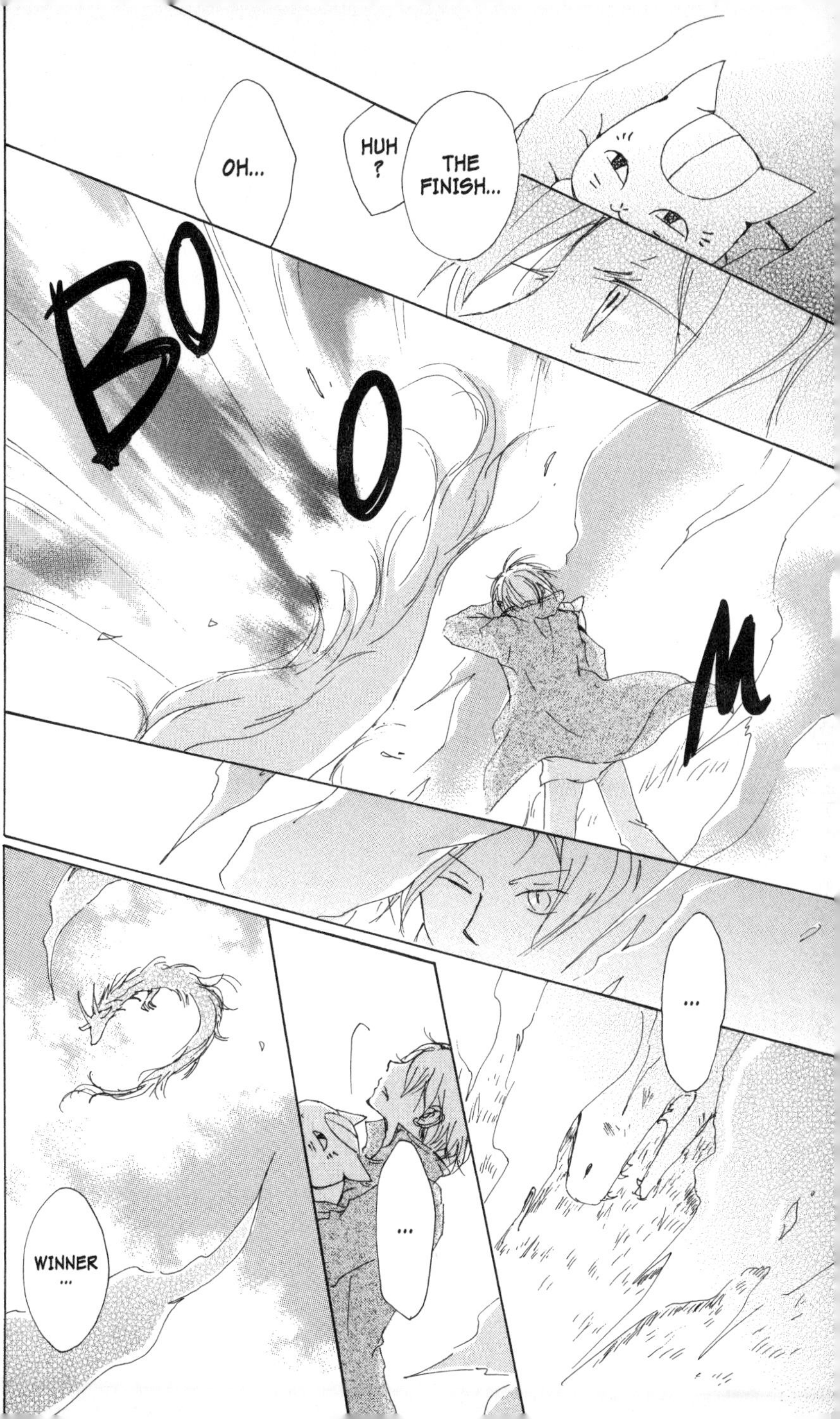
THE FINISH...
HUH ?
OH...
BOOM
...
...
WINNER ...

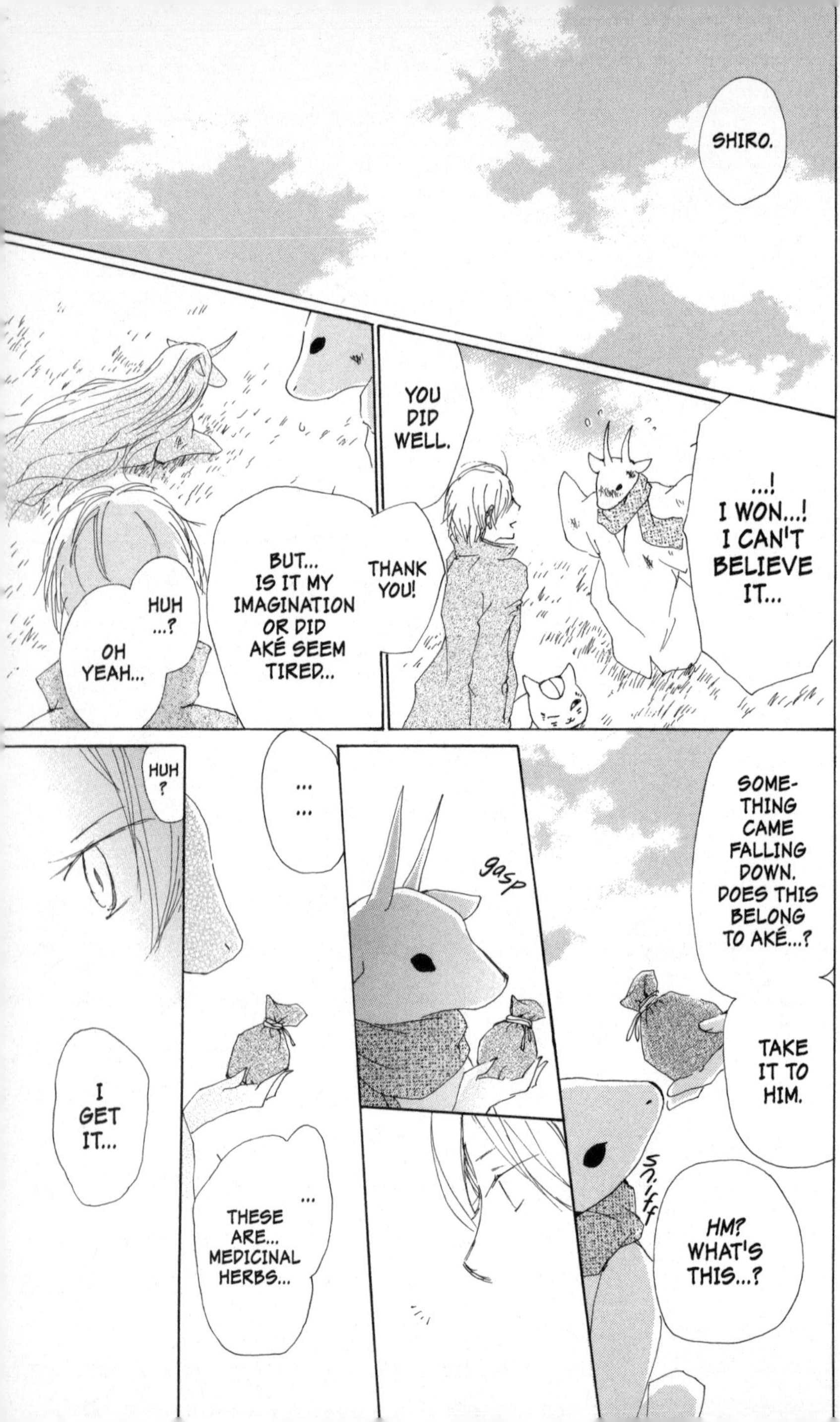
SHIRO.
...! I WON...! I CAN'T BELIEVE IT...
YOU DID WELL.
THANK YOU!
BUT... IS IT MY IMAGINATION OR DID AKÉ SEEM TIRED...
HUH ...? OH YEAH...
SOME-THING CAME FALLING DOWN. DOES THIS BELONG TO AKÉ...?
TAKE IT TO HIM.
HM? WHAT'S THIS...?
sniff
gasp
... ...
HUH ?
I GET IT...
... THESE ARE... MEDICINAL HERBS...

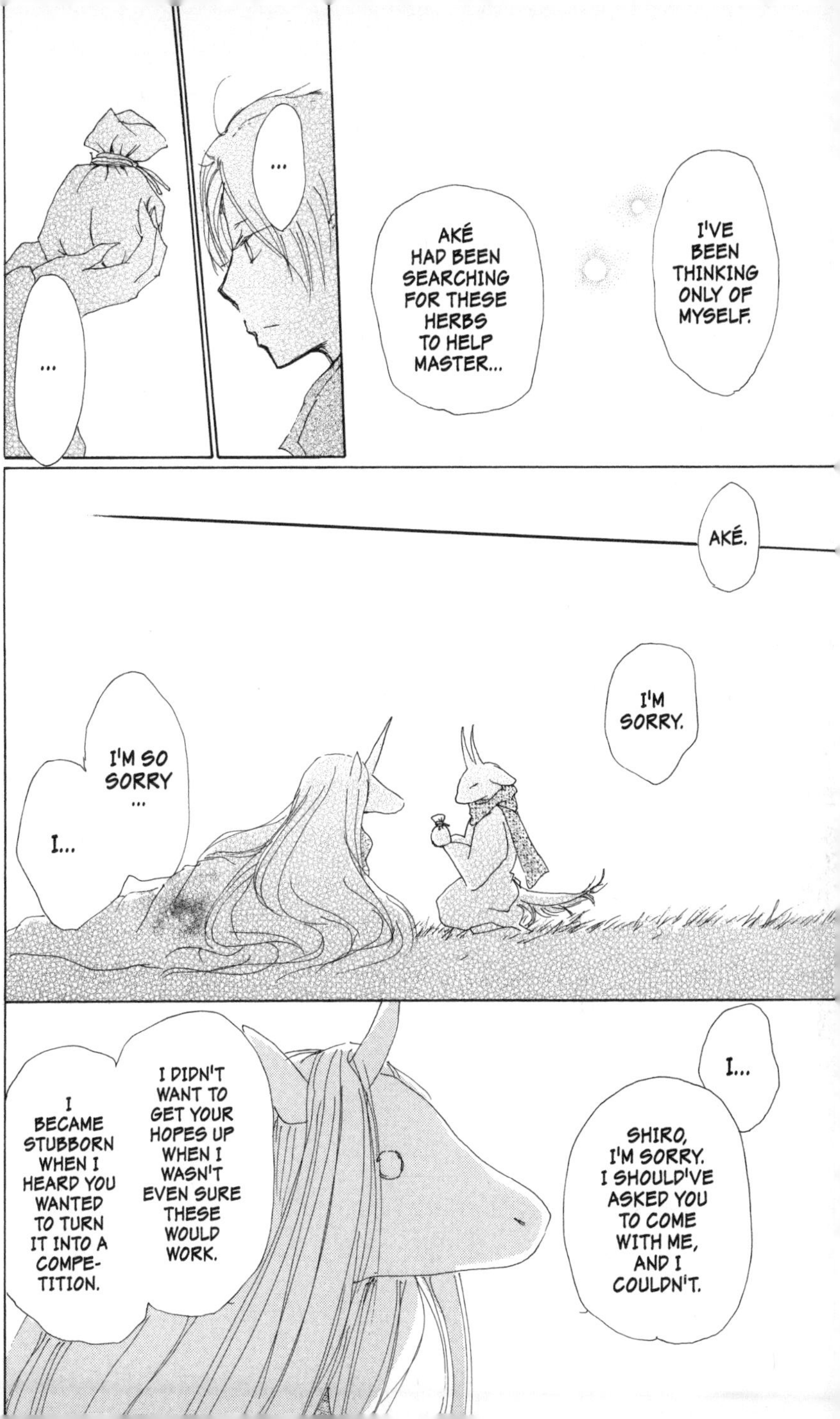
I'VE BEEN THINKING ONLY OF MYSELF.
AKÉ HAD BEEN SEARCHING FOR THESE HERBS TO HELP MASTER...
...
...
AKÉ.
I'M SORRY.
I'M SO SORRY ...
I...
I...
SHIRO, I'M SORRY. I SHOULD'VE ASKED YOU TO COME WITH ME, AND I COULDN'T.
I DIDN'T WANT TO GET YOUR HOPES UP WHEN I WASN'T EVEN SURE THESE WOULD WORK.
I BECAME STUBBORN WHEN I HEARD YOU WANTED TO TURN IT INTO A COMPE-TITION.

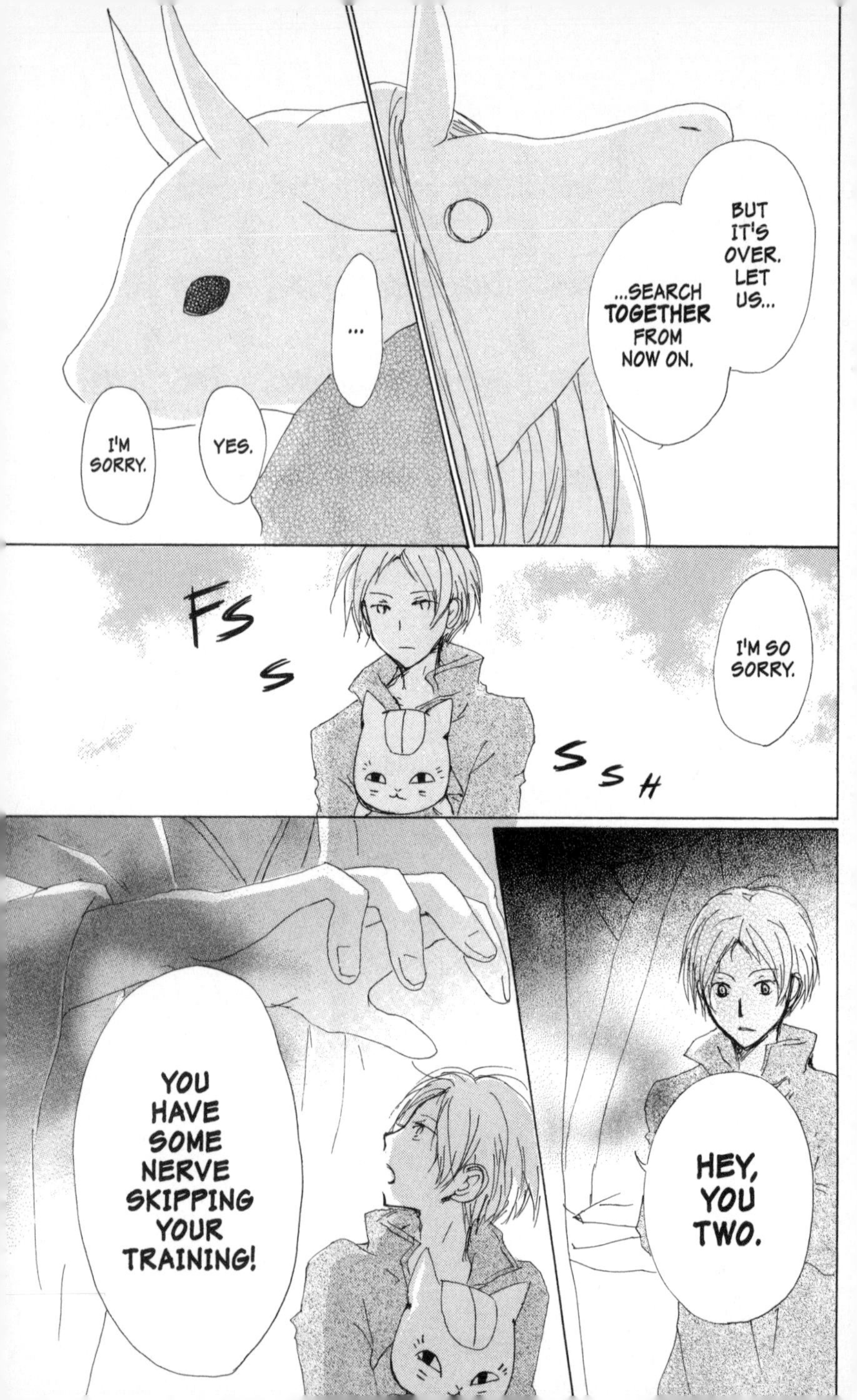
BUT IT'S OVER. LET US...
...SEARCH TOGETHER FROM NOW ON.
...
YES.
I'M SORRY.
I'M SO SORRY.
FSS
SSH
HEY, YOU TWO.
YOU HAVE SOME NERVE SKIPPING YOUR TRAINING!

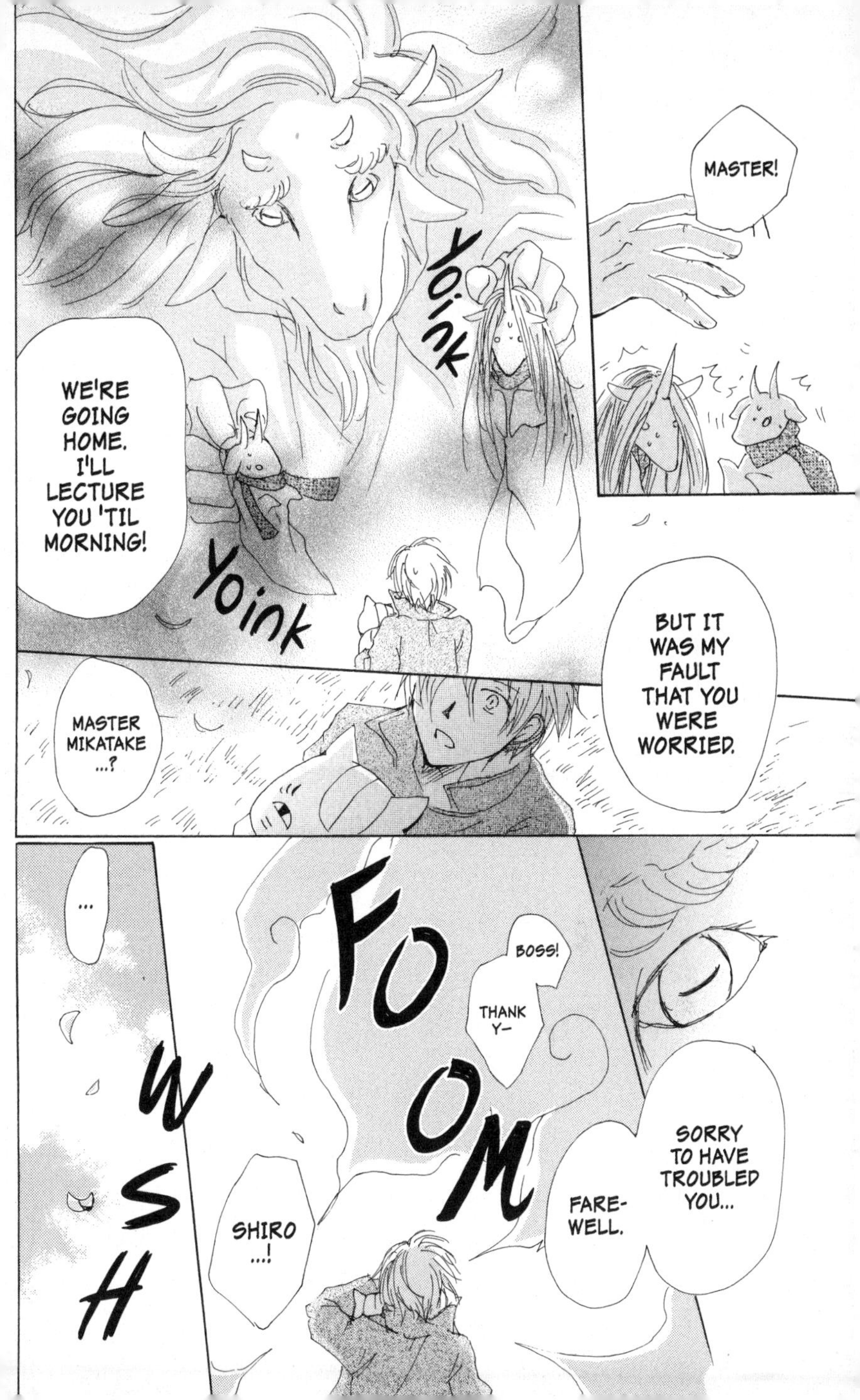
MASTER!
WE'RE GOING HOME. I'LL LECTURE YOU 'TIL MORNING!
Yoink
Yoink
BUT IT WAS MY FAULT THAT YOU WERE WORRIED.
MASTER MIKATAKE ...?
SORRY TO HAVE TROUBLED YOU...
FARE-WELL.
BOSS!
THANK Y—
FOOM
SHIRO ...!
...
WSH

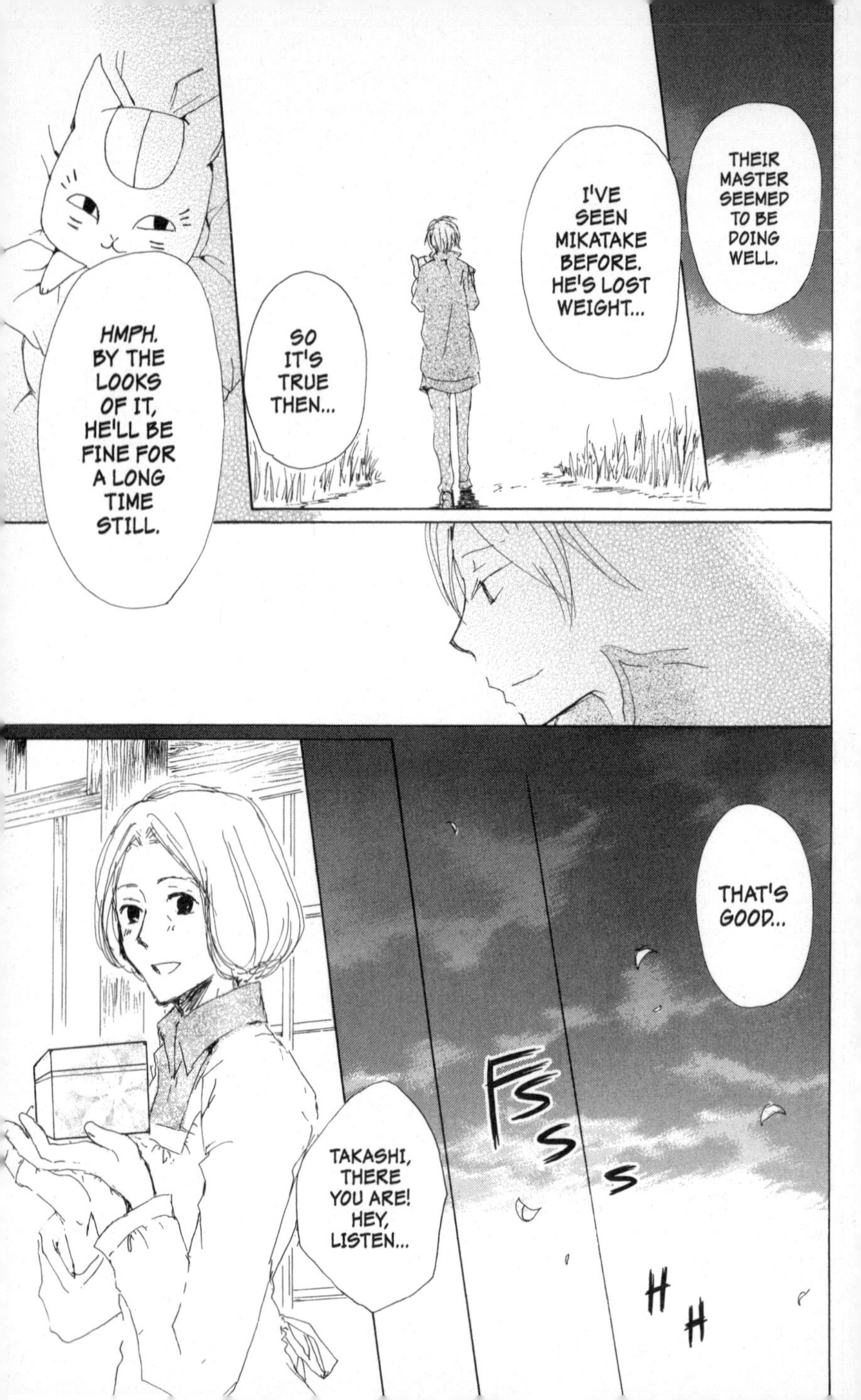
THEIR MASTER SEEMED TO BE DOING WELL.
I'VE SEEN MIKATAKE BEFORE. HE'S LOST WEIGHT...
SO IT'S TRUE THEN...
HMPH. BY THE LOOKS OF IT, HE'LL BE FINE FOR A LONG TIME STILL.
THAT'S GOOD...
FSSS
HH
TAKASHI, THERE YOU ARE! HEY, LISTEN...

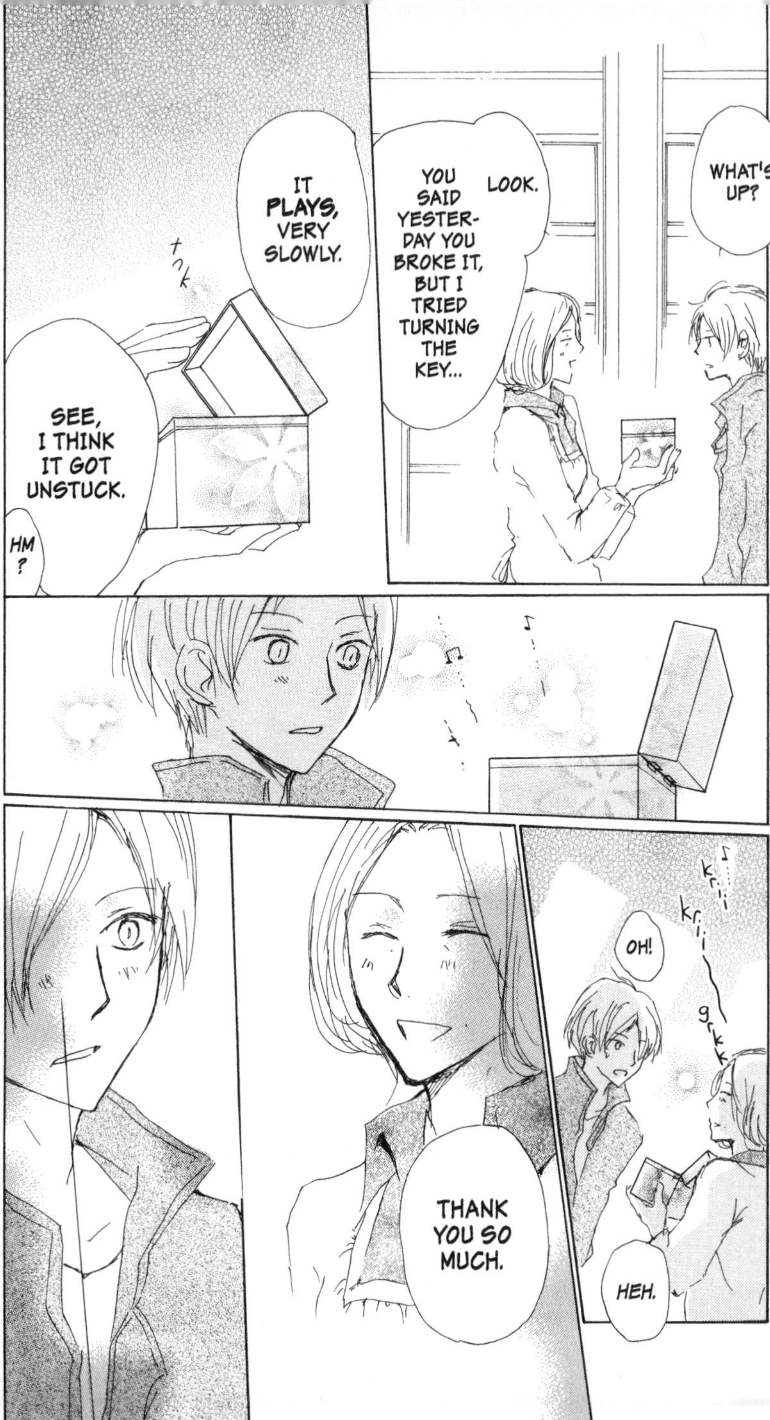

WHAT'S UP?
LOOK.
YOU SAID YESTER-DAY YOU BROKE IT, BUT I TRIED TURNING THE KEY...
IT **PLAYS**, VERY SLOWLY.
SEE, I THINK IT GOT UNSTUCK.
HM?
kri
kri
grkk
OH!
HEH.
THANK YOU SO MUCH.

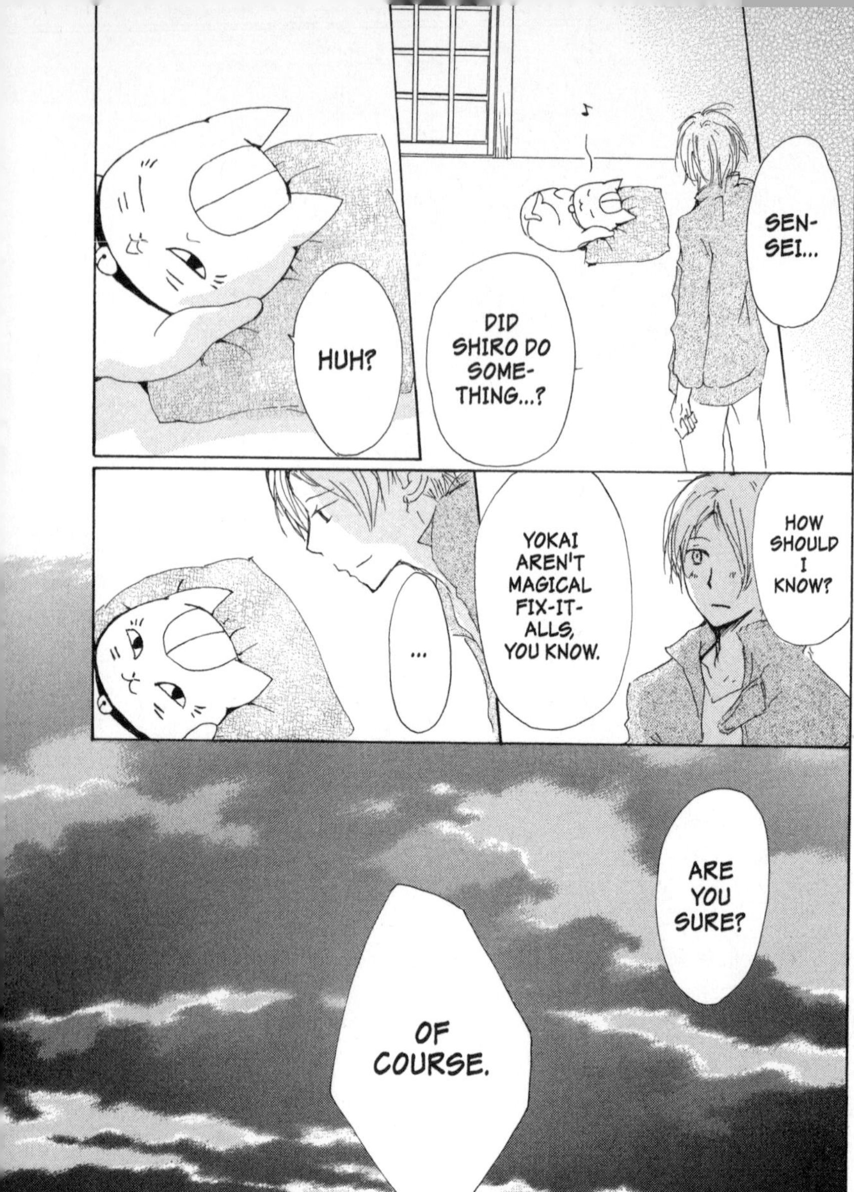
SEN-SEI...
DID SHIRO DO SOMETHING...?
HUH?
HOW SHOULD I KNOW?
YOKAI AREN'T MAGICAL FIX-IT-ALLS, YOU KNOW.
...
ARE YOU SURE?
OF COURSE.

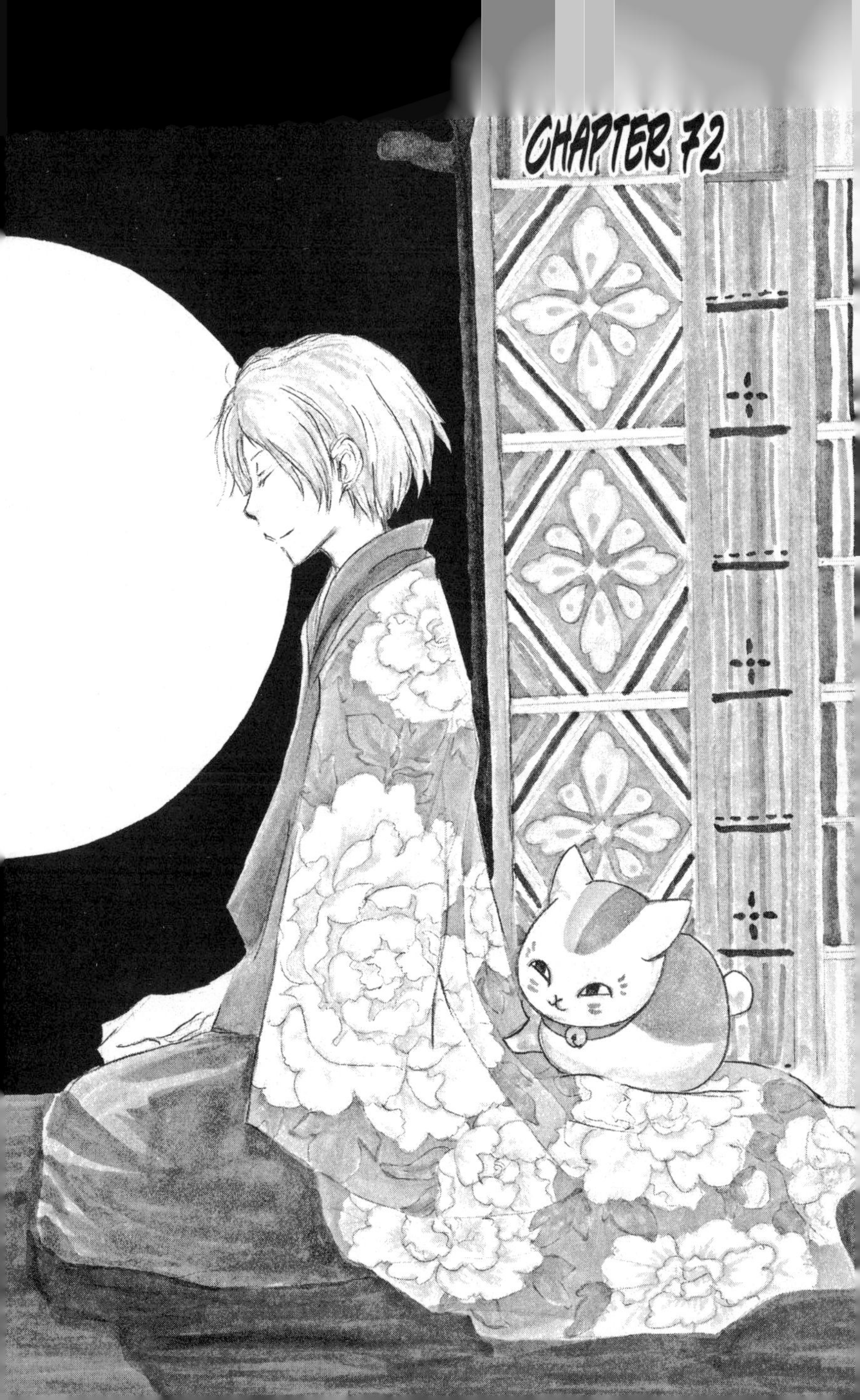
CHAPTER 72

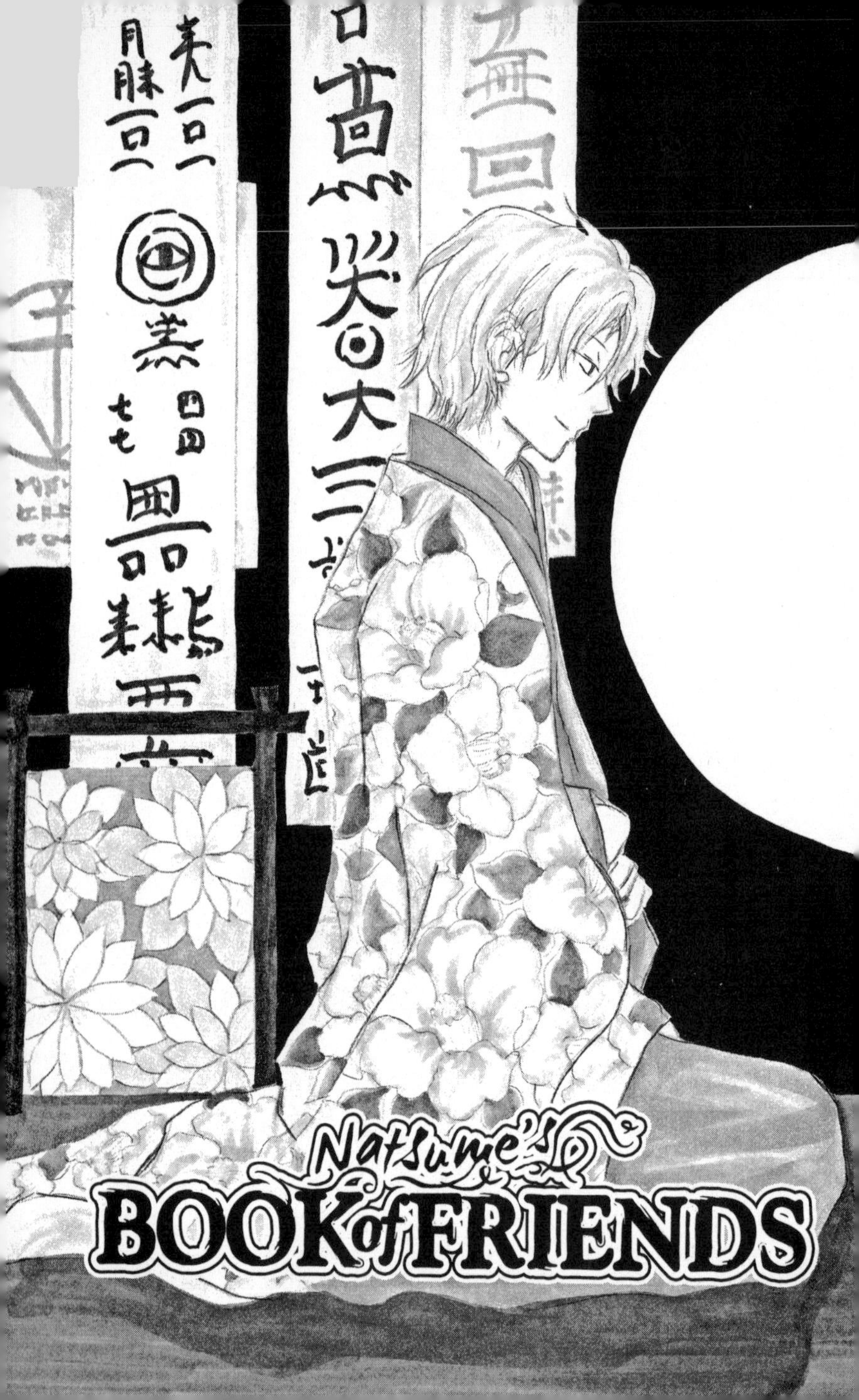
Natsume's
BOOK of FRIENDS

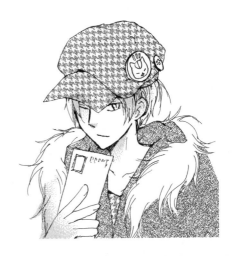

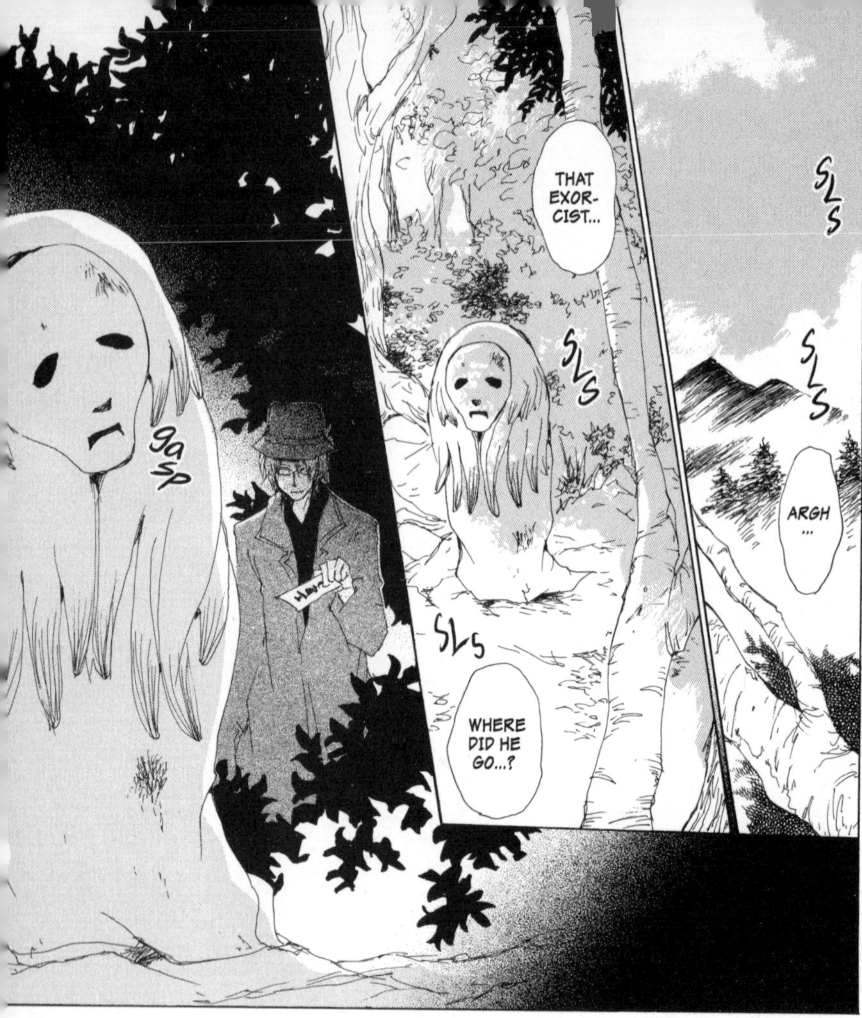
SLS
SLS
ARGH...
THAT EXORCIST...
SLS
SLS
WHERE DID HE GO...?
gasp

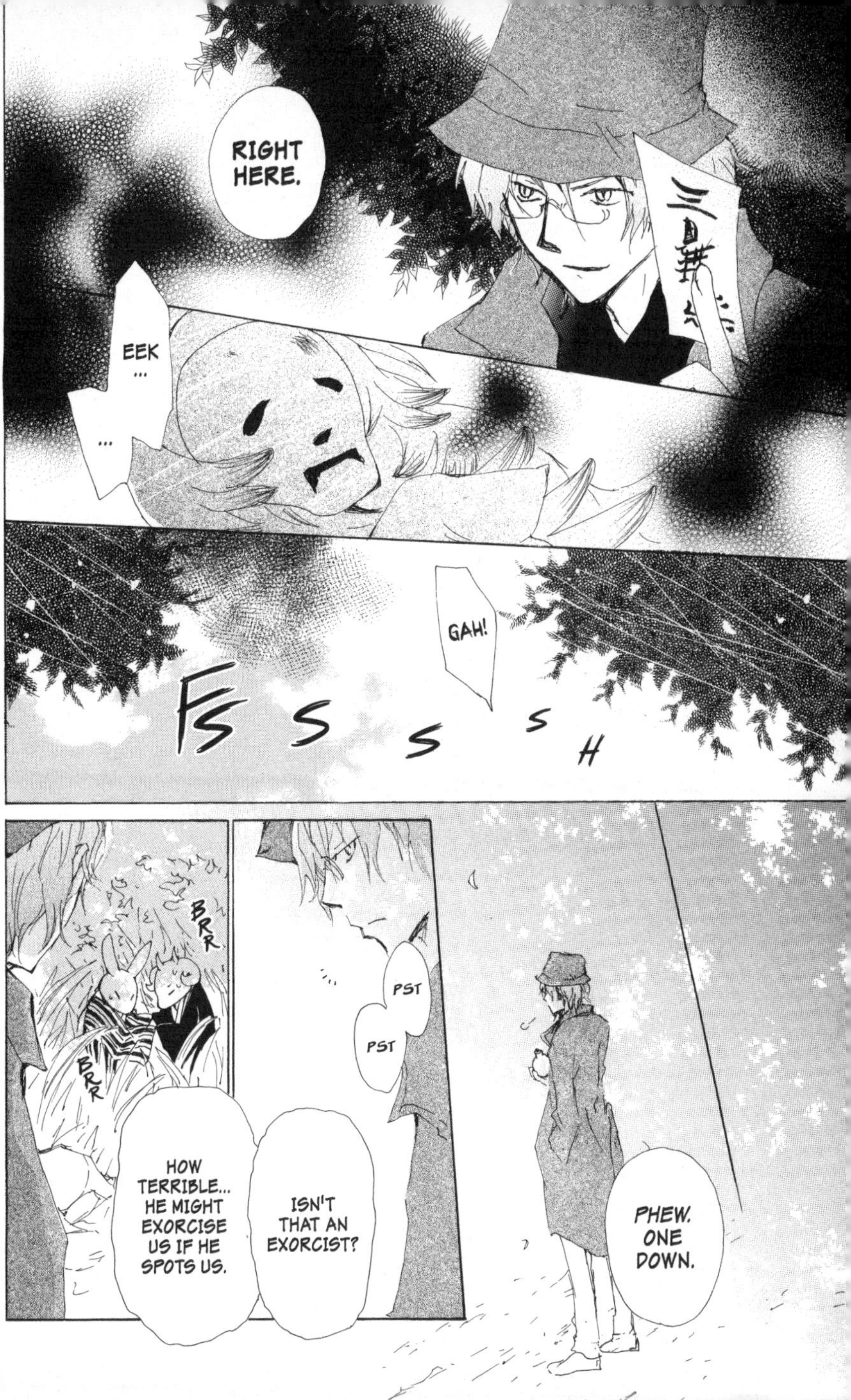
RIGHT HERE.
EEK ... ...
GAH!
FSSSSH
PHEW. ONE DOWN.
...
PST
PST
ISN'T THAT AN EXORCIST?
BRR
BRR
HOW TERRIBLE... HE MIGHT EXORCISE US IF HE SPOTS US.

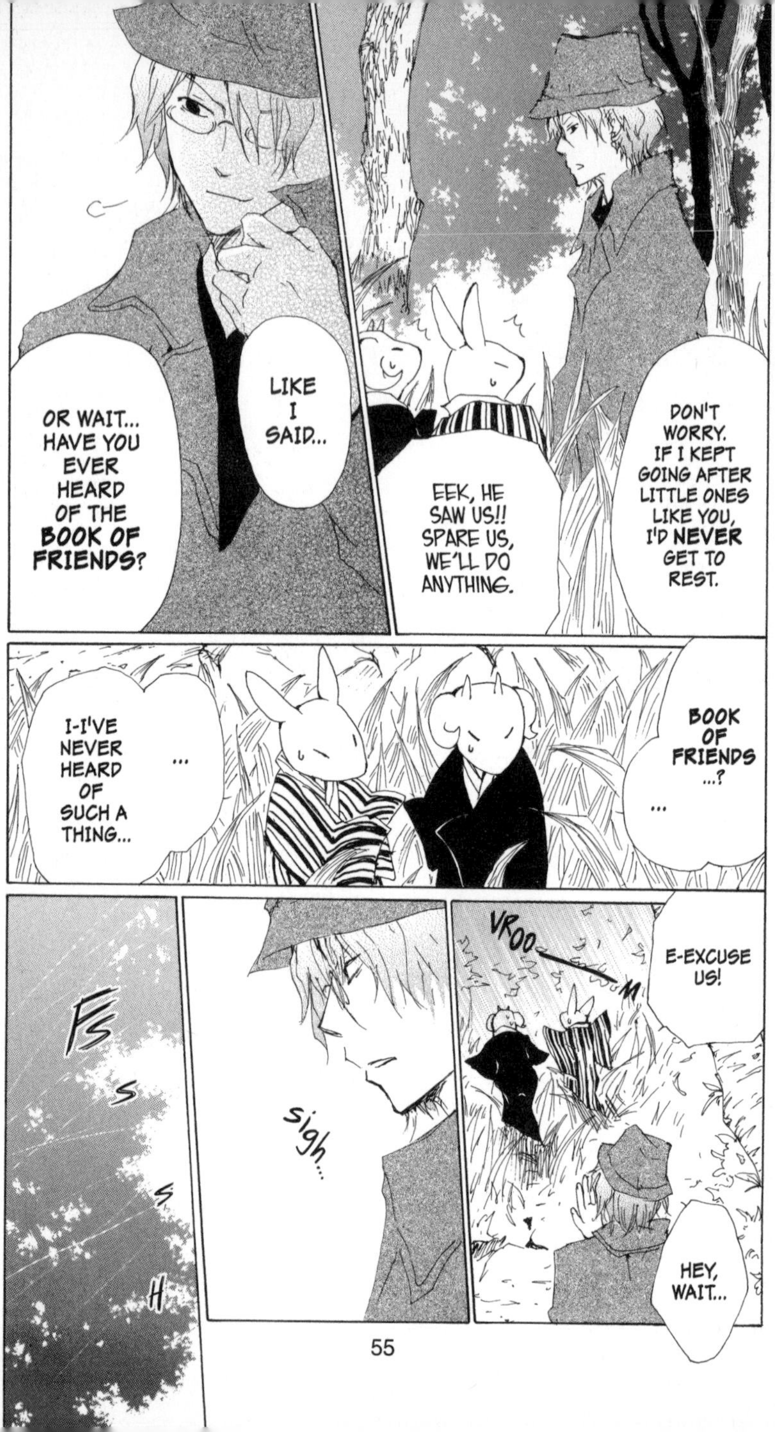
DON'T WORRY. IF I KEPT GOING AFTER LITTLE ONES LIKE YOU, I'D NEVER GET TO REST.
EEK, HE SAW US!! SPARE US, WE'LL DO ANYTHING.
LIKE I SAID...
OR WAIT... HAVE YOU EVER HEARD OF THE BOOK OF FRIENDS?
BOOK OF FRIENDS ...?
...
...
I-I'VE NEVER HEARD OF SUCH A THING...
E-EXCUSE US!
VROOOOM
HEY, WAIT...
sigh...
FSSSH

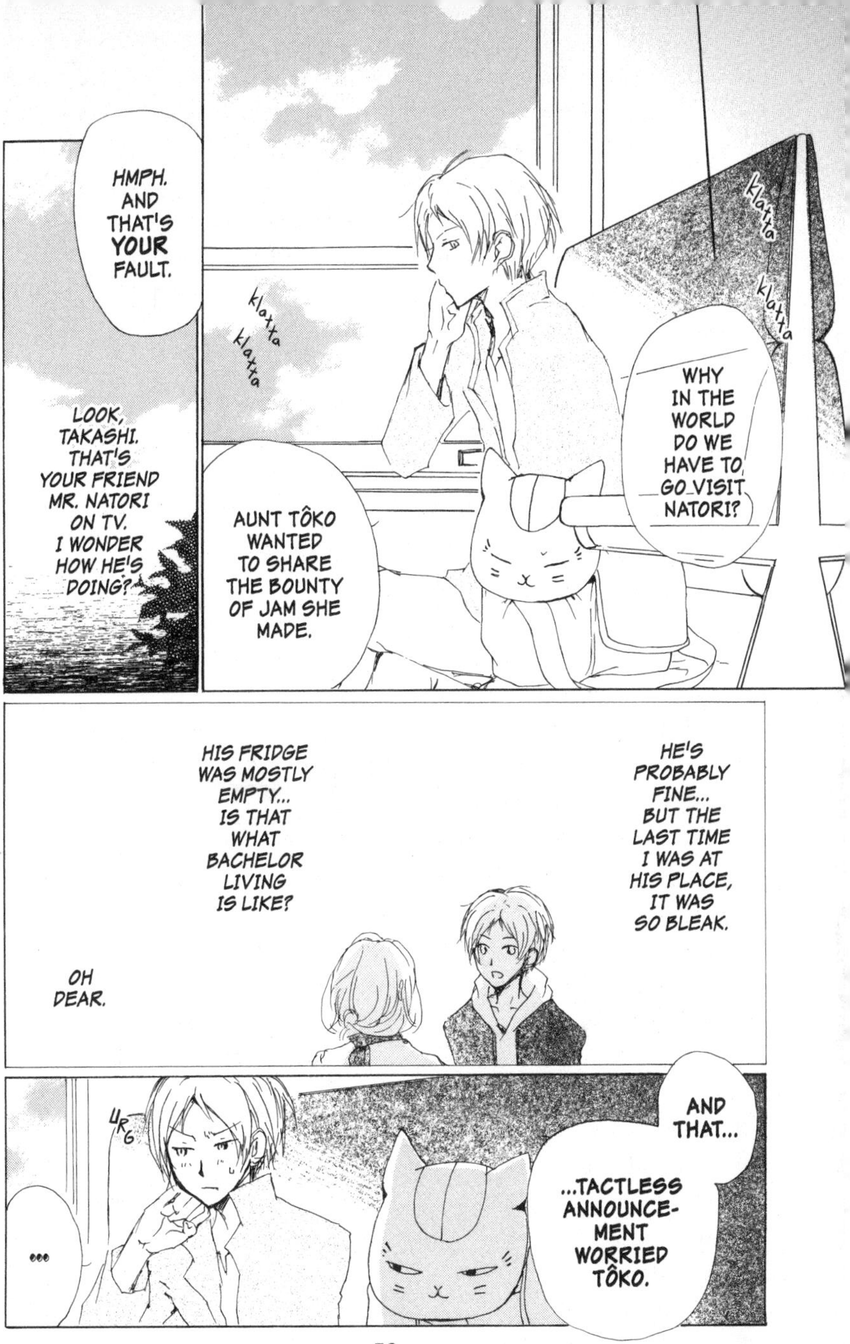
klatta
klatta
WHY IN THE WORLD DO WE HAVE TO GO VISIT NATORI?
AUNT TÔKO WANTED TO SHARE THE BOUNTY OF JAM SHE MADE.
klatta
klatta
HMPH. AND THAT'S **YOUR** FAULT.
LOOK, TAKASHI. THAT'S YOUR FRIEND MR. NATORI ON TV. I WONDER HOW HE'S DOING?
HE'S PROBABLY FINE... BUT THE LAST TIME I WAS AT HIS PLACE, IT WAS SO BLEAK.
HIS FRIDGE WAS MOSTLY EMPTY... IS THAT WHAT BACHELOR LIVING IS LIKE?
OH DEAR.
AND THAT...
...TACTLESS ANNOUNCEMENT WORRIED TÔKO.
URG
...

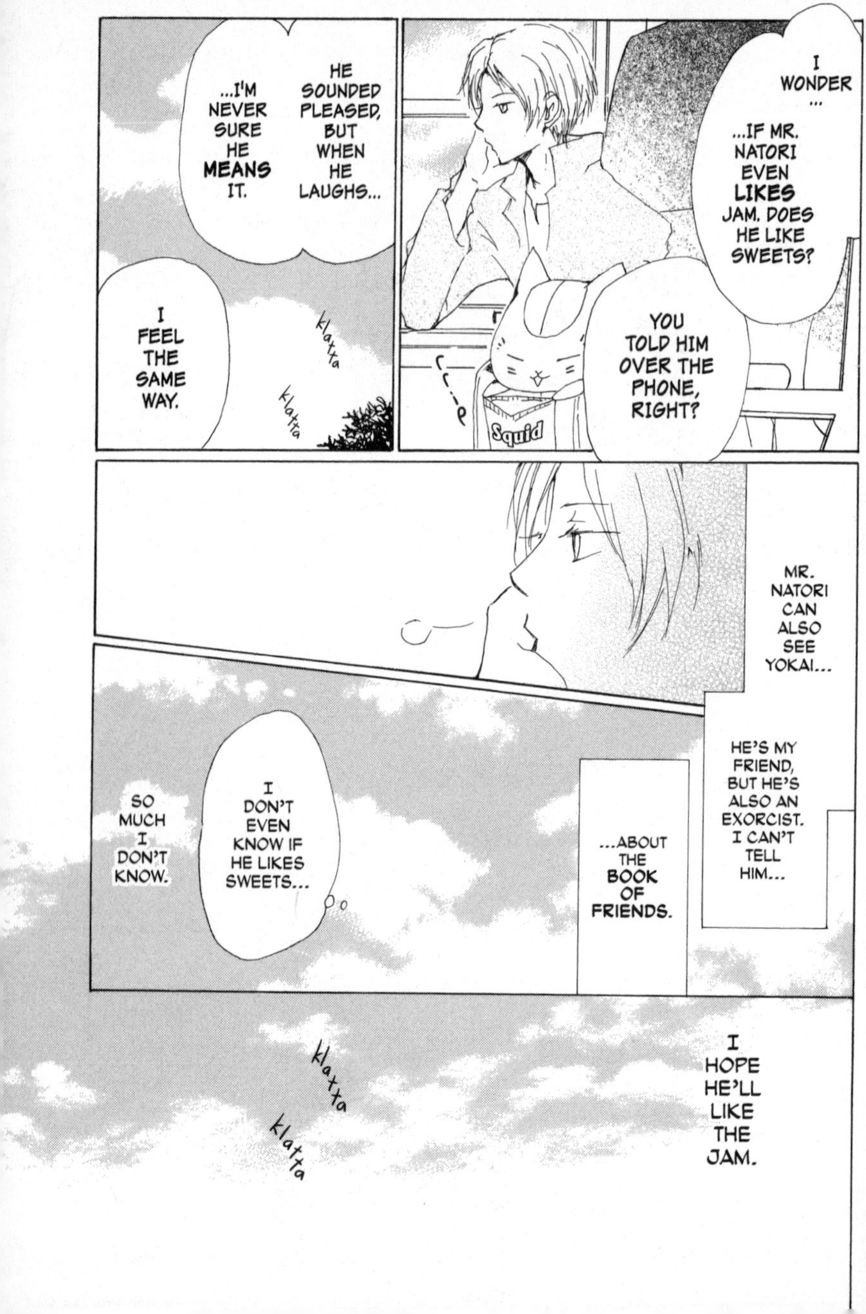
I WONDER...
...IF MR. NATORI EVEN LIKES JAM. DOES HE LIKE SWEETS?
YOU TOLD HIM OVER THE PHONE, RIGHT?
Squid
HE SOUNDED PLEASED, BUT WHEN HE LAUGHS...
...I'M NEVER SURE HE MEANS IT.
I FEEL THE SAME WAY.
klatta
klatta
MR. NATORI CAN ALSO SEE YOKAI...
HE'S MY FRIEND, BUT HE'S ALSO AN EXORCIST. I CAN'T TELL HIM...
...ABOUT THE BOOK OF FRIENDS.
I DON'T EVEN KNOW IF HE LIKES SWEETS...
SO MUCH I DON'T KNOW.
I HOPE HE'LL LIKE THE JAM.
klatta
klatta

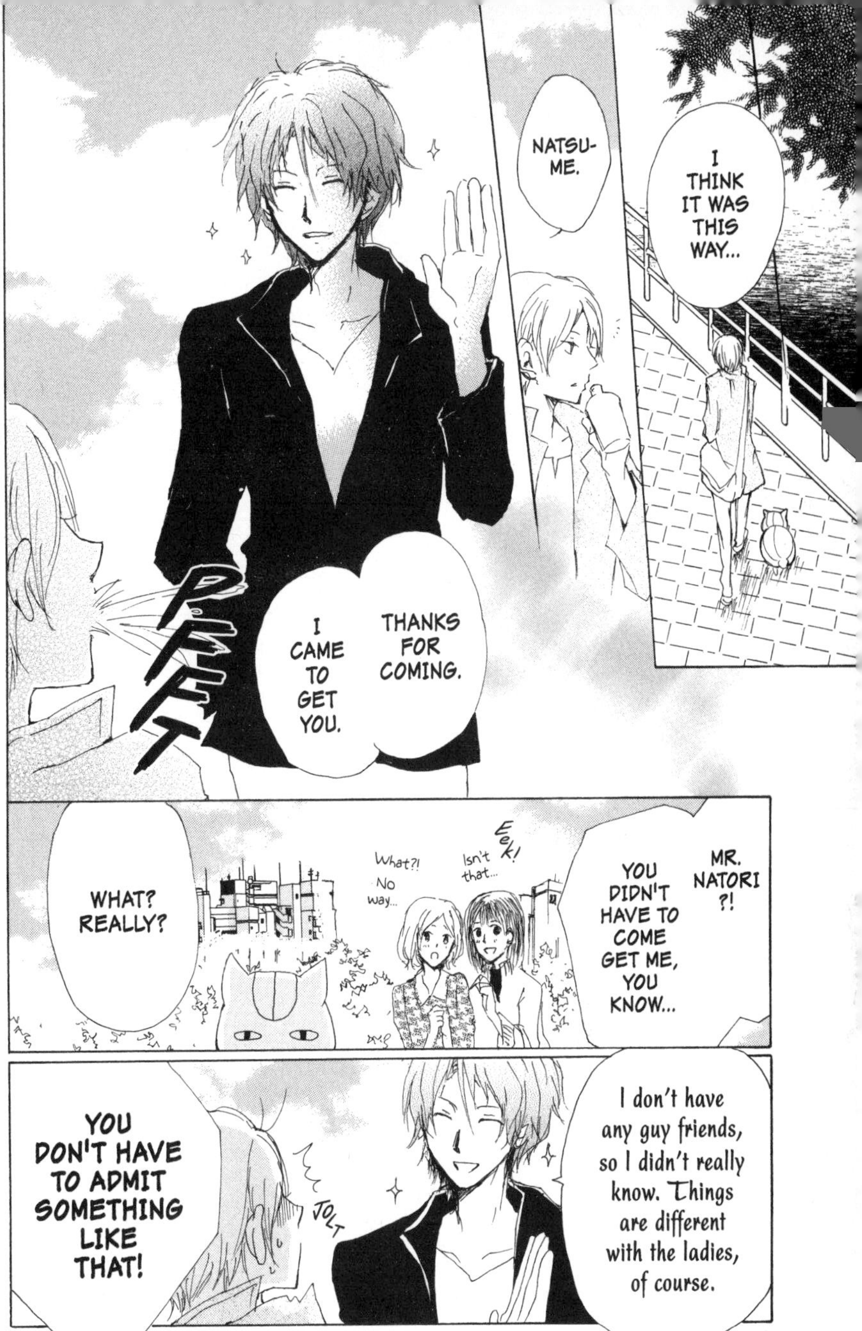
I THINK IT WAS THIS WAY...
NATSU-ME.
THANKS FOR COMING.
I CAME TO GET YOU.
PIFFT
MR. NATORI ?!
YOU DIDN'T HAVE TO COME GET ME, YOU KNOW...
Eek!
Isn't that...
What?!
No way...
WHAT? REALLY?
I don't have any guy friends, so I didn't really know. Things are different with the ladies, of course.
JOLT
YOU DON'T HAVE TO ADMIT SOMETHING LIKE THAT!

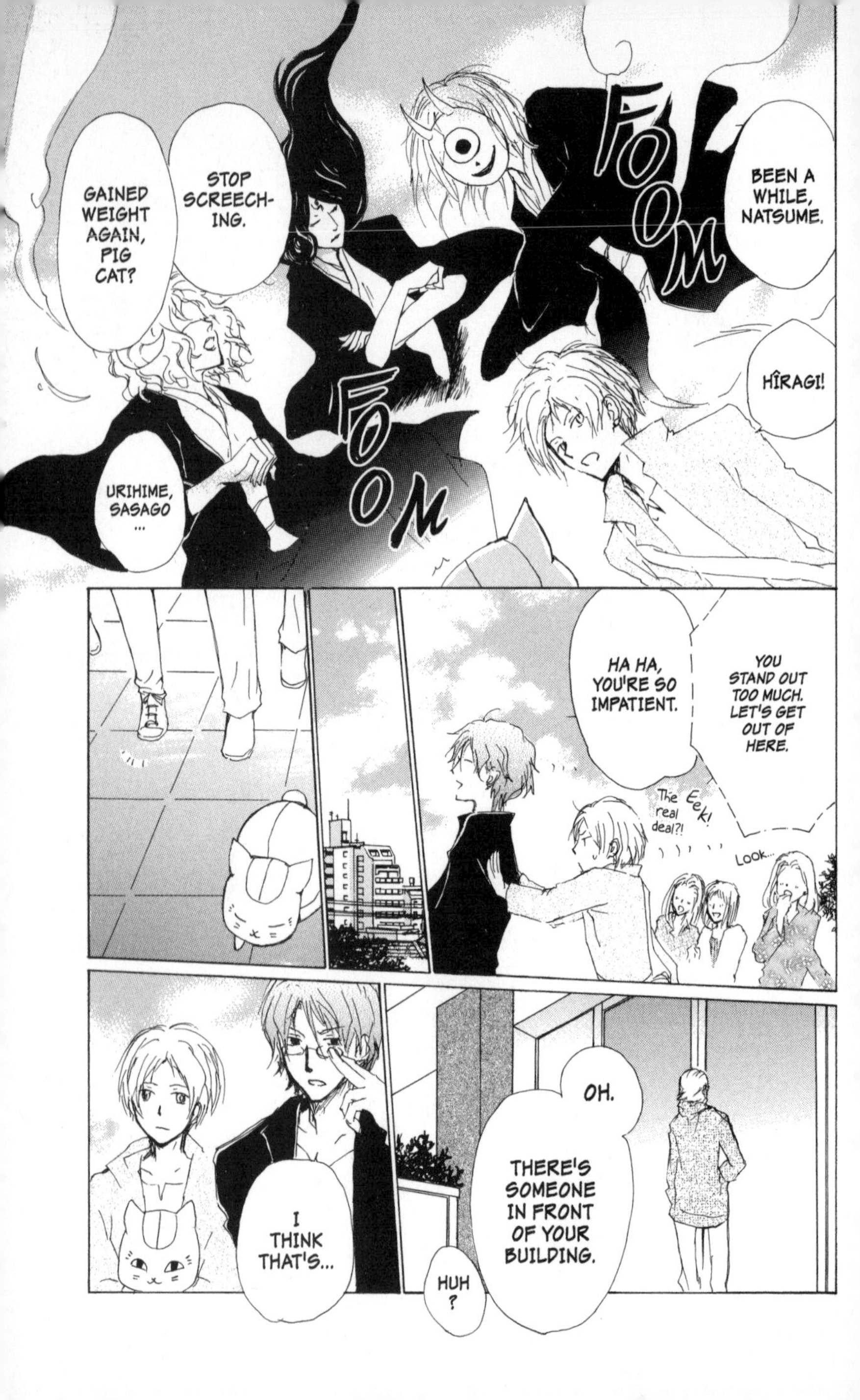
BEEN A WHILE, NATSUME.
FOOM
HÎRAGI!
STOP SCREECHING.
GAINED WEIGHT AGAIN, PIG CAT?
FOOM
URIHIME, SASAGO...
YOU STAND OUT TOO MUCH. LET'S GET OUT OF HERE.
HA HA, YOU'RE SO IMPATIENT.
Eek!
The real deal?!
Look...
OH.
THERE'S SOMEONE IN FRONT OF YOUR BUILDING.
HUH?
I THINK THAT'S...

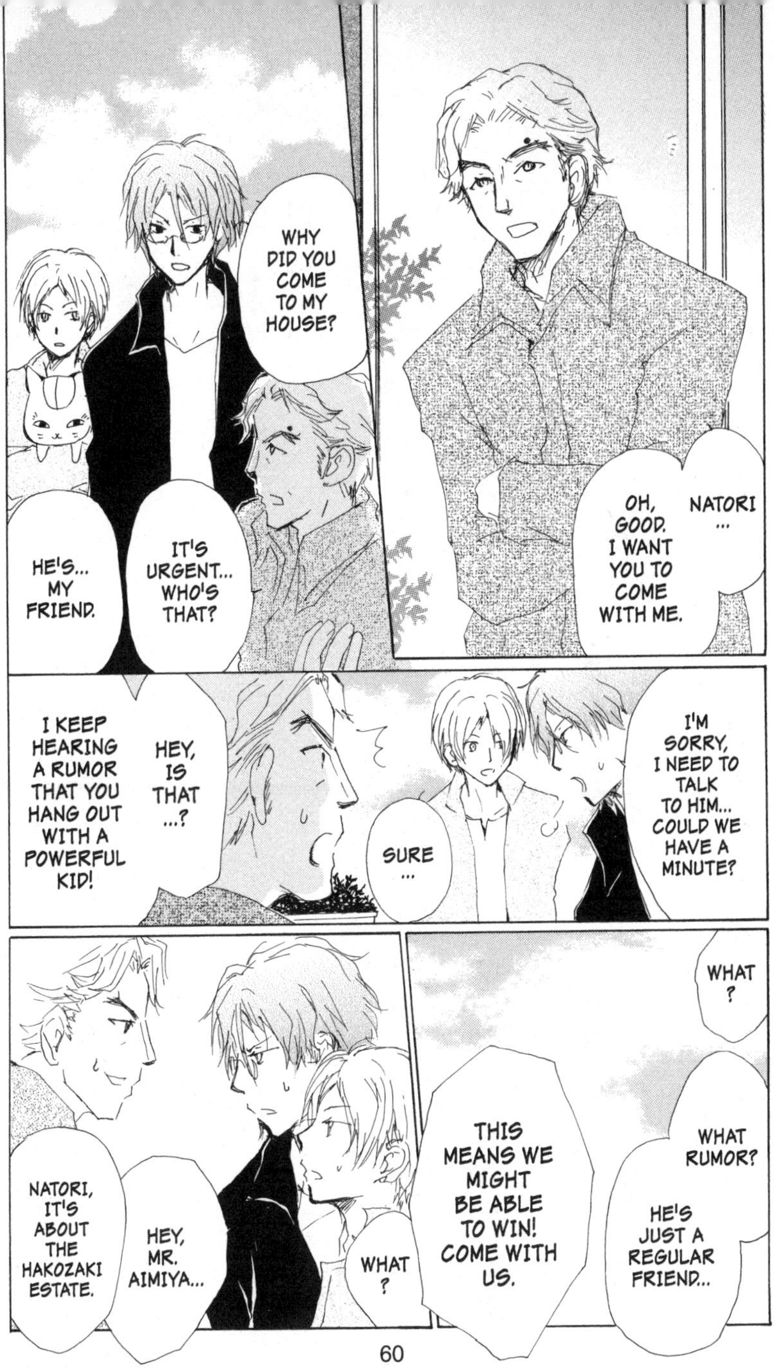
NATORI ...
OH, GOOD. I WANT YOU TO COME WITH ME.
WHY DID YOU COME TO MY HOUSE?
IT'S URGENT... WHO'S THAT?
HE'S... MY FRIEND.
I'M SORRY, I NEED TO TALK TO HIM... COULD WE HAVE A MINUTE?
SURE ...
HEY, IS THAT ...?
I KEEP HEARING A RUMOR THAT YOU HANG OUT WITH A POWERFUL KID!
WHAT ?
WHAT RUMOR?
HE'S JUST A REGULAR FRIEND...
THIS MEANS WE MIGHT BE ABLE TO WIN! COME WITH US.
WHAT ?
HEY, MR. AIMIYA...
NATORI, IT'S ABOUT THE HAKOZAKI ESTATE.

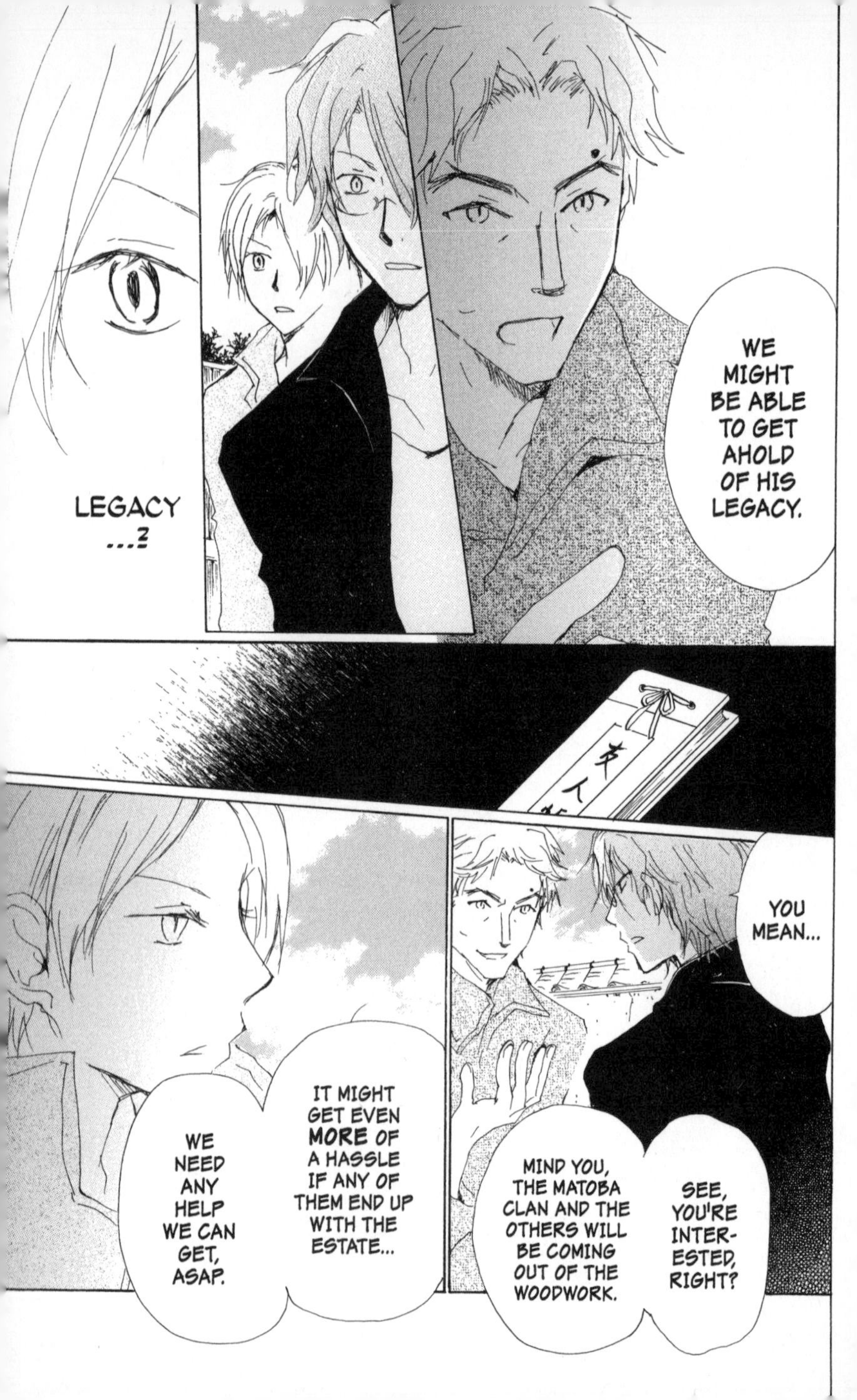
WE MIGHT BE ABLE TO GET AHOLD OF HIS LEGACY.
LEGACY ...?
YOU MEAN...
SEE, YOU'RE INTER-ESTED, RIGHT?
MIND YOU, THE MATOBA CLAN AND THE OTHERS WILL BE COMING OUT OF THE WOODWORK.
IT MIGHT GET EVEN MORE OF A HASSLE IF ANY OF THEM END UP WITH THE ESTATE...
WE NEED ANY HELP WE CAN GET, ASAP.

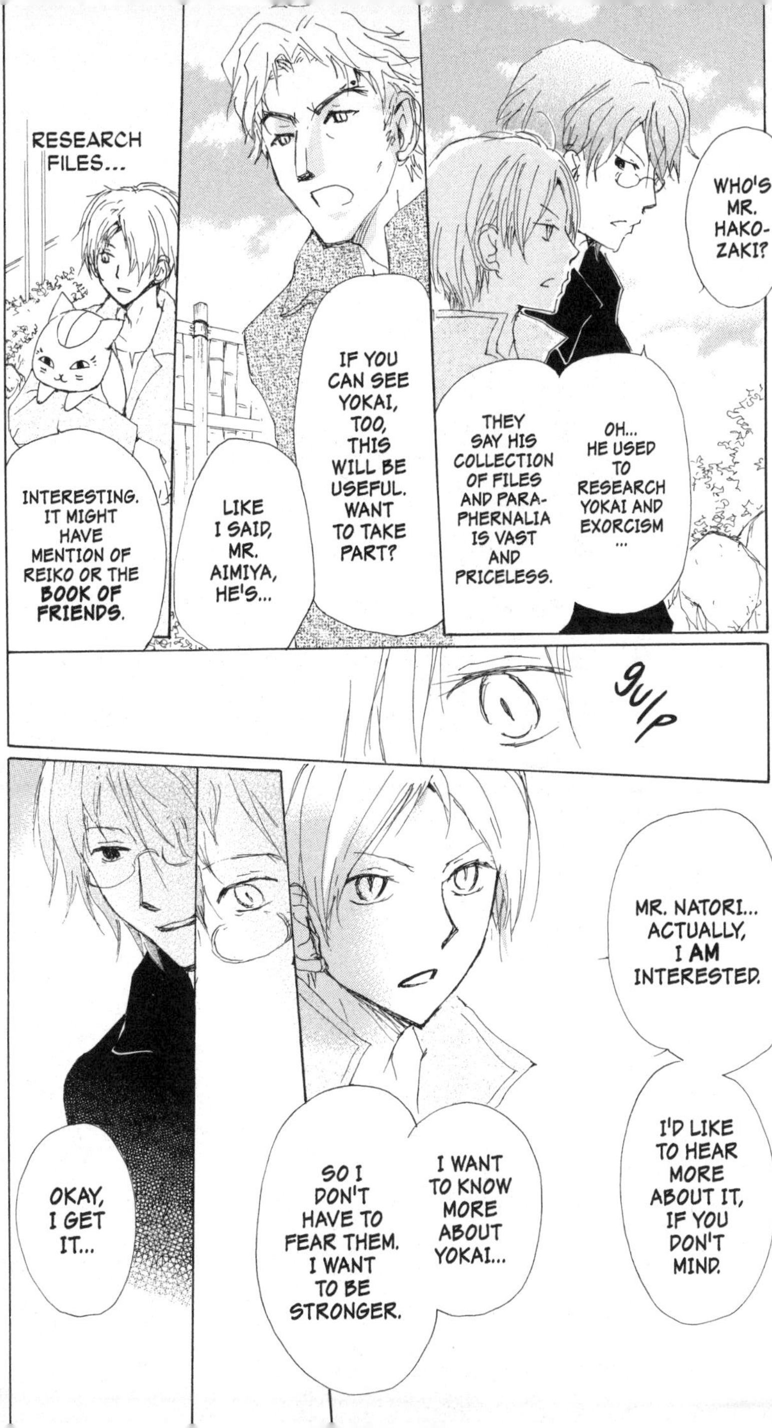
WHO'S MR. HAKO-ZAKI?
OH... HE USED TO RESEARCH YOKAI AND EXORCISM...
THEY SAY HIS COLLECTION OF FILES AND PARA-PHERNALIA IS VAST AND PRICELESS.
IF YOU CAN SEE YOKAI, TOO, THIS WILL BE USEFUL. WANT TO TAKE PART?
LIKE I SAID, MR. AIMIYA, HE'S...
RESEARCH FILES...
INTERESTING. IT MIGHT HAVE MENTION OF REIKO OR THE BOOK OF FRIENDS.
gulp
MR. NATORI... ACTUALLY, I AM INTERESTED.
I'D LIKE TO HEAR MORE ABOUT IT, IF YOU DON'T MIND.
I WANT TO KNOW MORE ABOUT YOKAI...
SO I DON'T HAVE TO FEAR THEM. I WANT TO BE STRONGER.
OKAY, I GET IT...

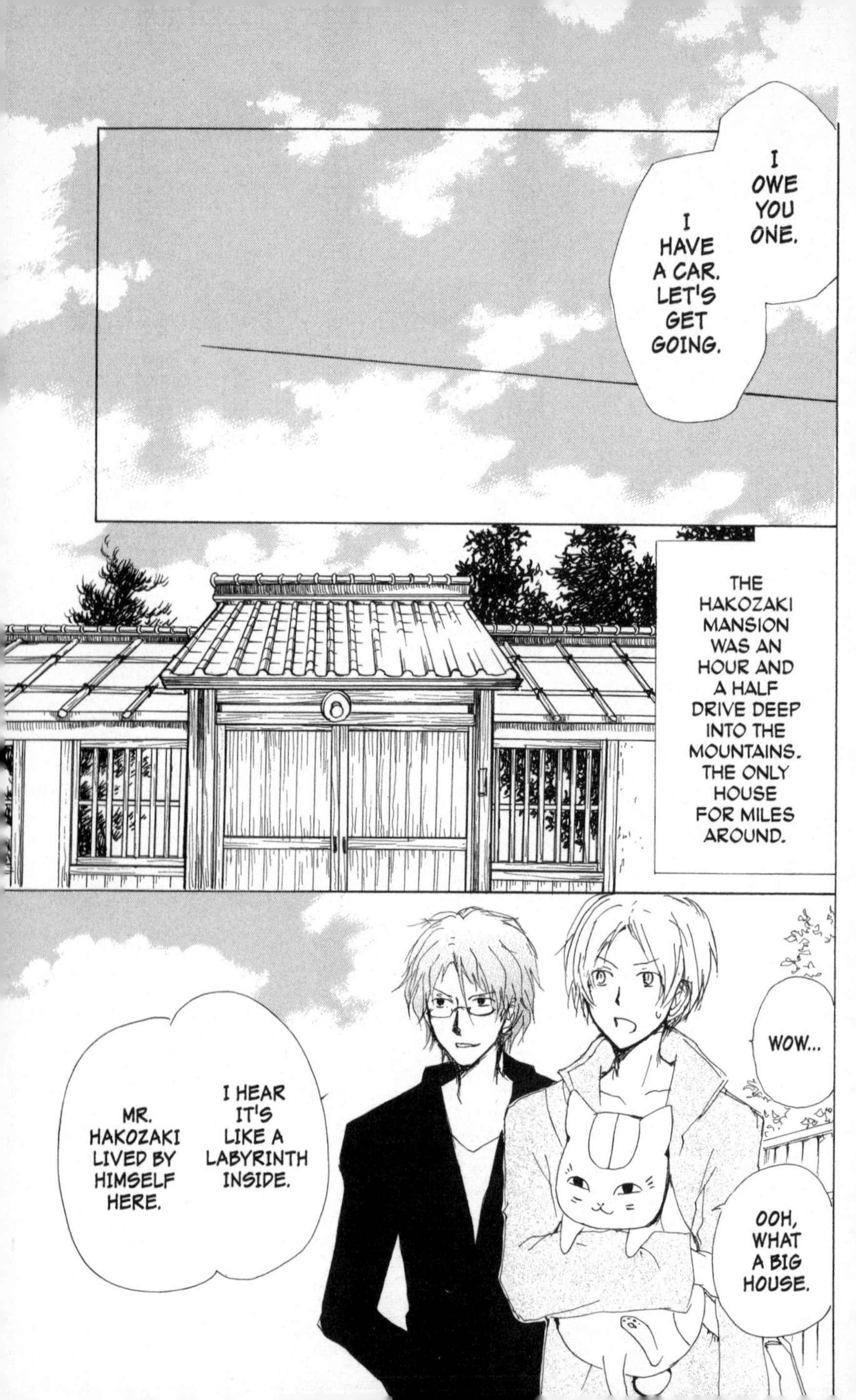
I OWE YOU ONE.
I HAVE A CAR. LET'S GET GOING.
THE HAKOZAKI MANSION WAS AN HOUR AND A HALF DRIVE DEEP INTO THE MOUNTAINS. THE ONLY HOUSE FOR MILES AROUND.
WOW...
I HEAR IT'S LIKE A LABYRINTH INSIDE.
MR. HAKOZAKI LIVED BY HIMSELF HERE.
OOH, WHAT A BIG HOUSE.

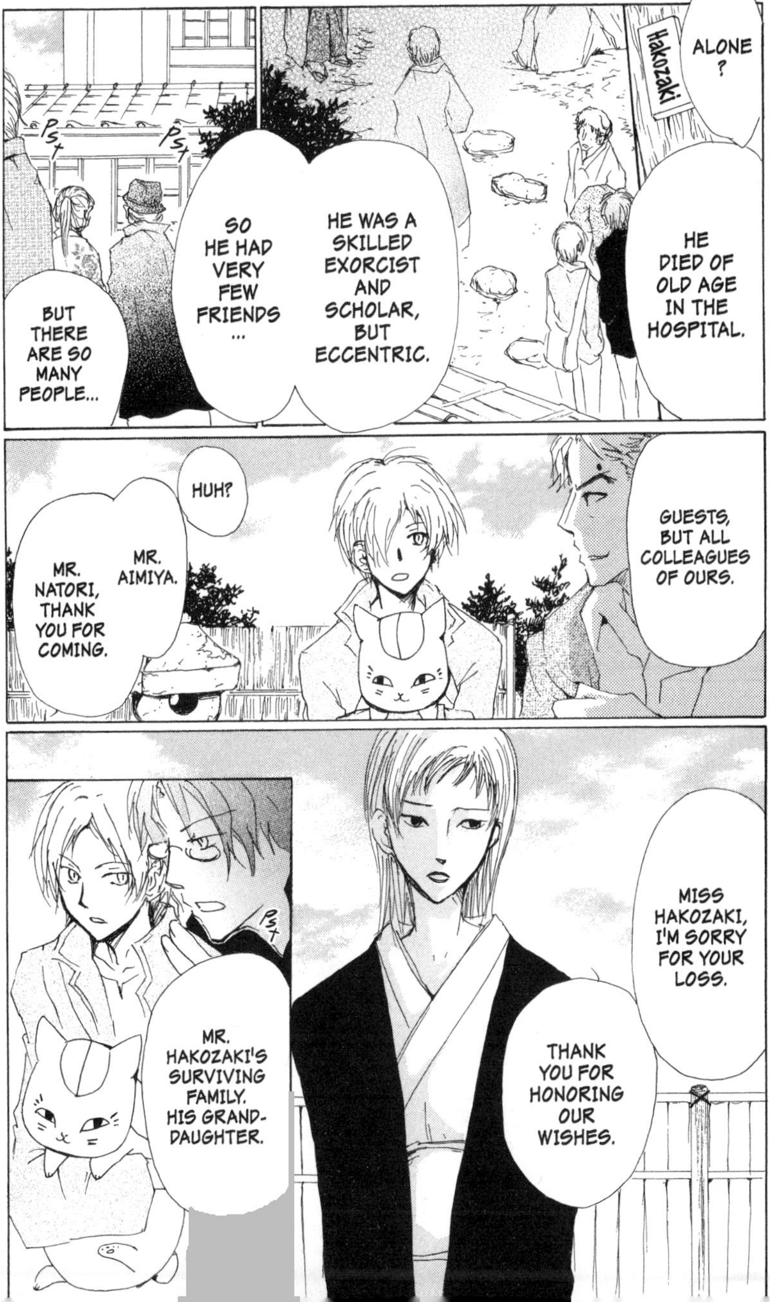
Hakozaki
ALONE?
HE DIED OF OLD AGE IN THE HOSPITAL.
HE WAS A SKILLED EXORCIST AND SCHOLAR, BUT ECCENTRIC.
SO HE HAD VERY FEW FRIENDS...
Pst
Pst
BUT THERE ARE SO MANY PEOPLE...
GUESTS, BUT ALL COLLEAGUES OF OURS.
HUH?
MR. AIMIYA.
MR. NATORI, THANK YOU FOR COMING.
MISS HAKOZAKI, I'M SORRY FOR YOUR LOSS.
THANK YOU FOR HONORING OUR WISHES.
Pst
MR. HAKOZAKI'S SURVIVING FAMILY. HIS GRAND-DAUGHTER.

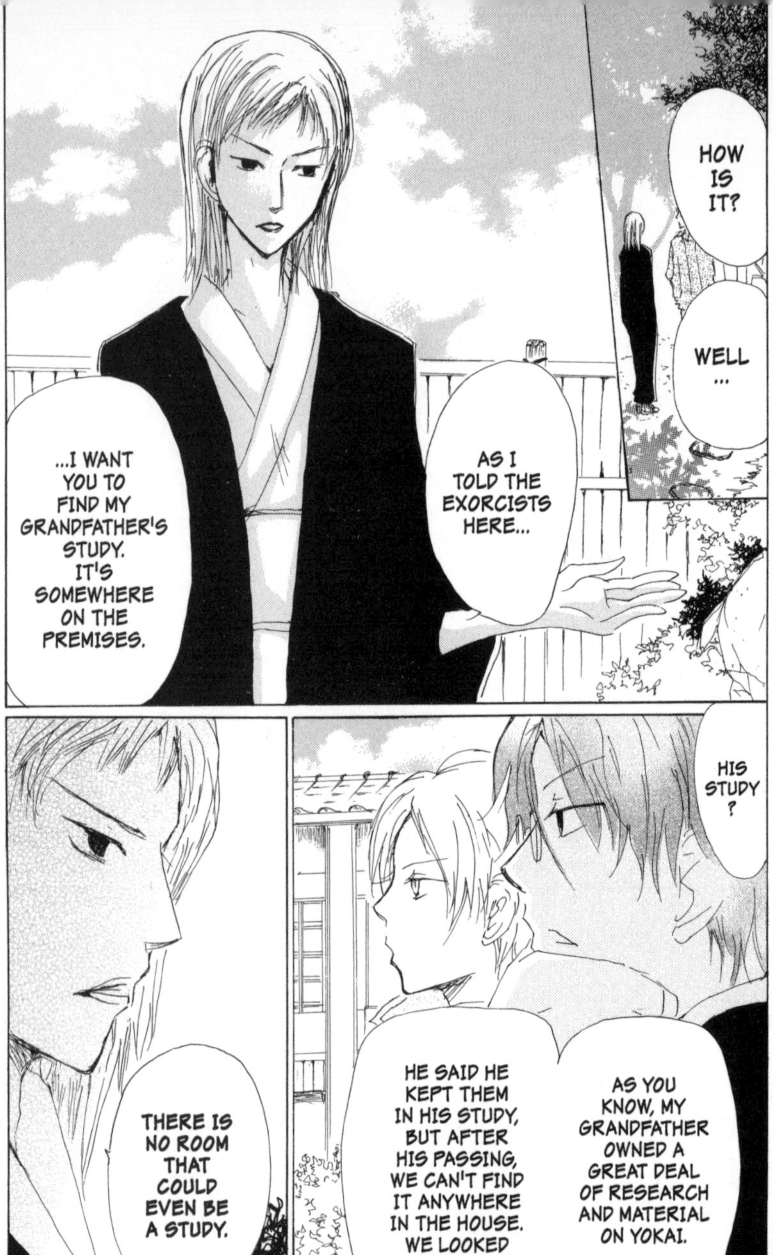
HOW IS IT?
WELL ...
AS I TOLD THE EXORCISTS HERE...
...I WANT YOU TO FIND MY GRANDFATHER'S STUDY. IT'S SOMEWHERE ON THE PREMISES.
HIS STUDY?
AS YOU KNOW, MY GRANDFATHER OWNED A GREAT DEAL OF RESEARCH AND MATERIAL ON YOKAI.
HE SAID HE KEPT THEM IN HIS STUDY, BUT AFTER HIS PASSING, WE CAN'T FIND IT ANYWHERE IN THE HOUSE. WE LOOKED EVERYWHERE.
THERE IS NO ROOM THAT COULD EVEN BE A STUDY.

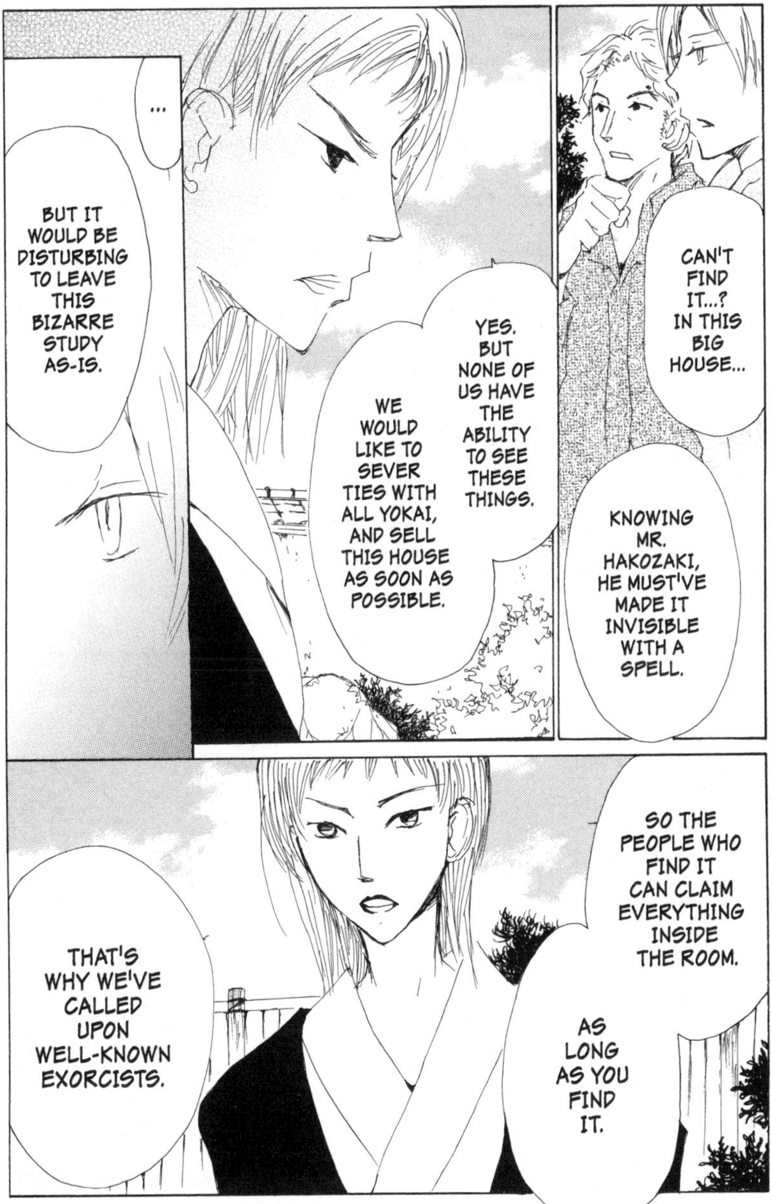
CAN'T FIND IT...? IN THIS BIG HOUSE...
KNOWING MR. HAKOZAKI, HE MUST'VE MADE IT INVISIBLE WITH A SPELL.
YES. BUT NONE OF US HAVE THE ABILITY TO SEE THESE THINGS.
WE WOULD LIKE TO SEVER TIES WITH ALL YOKAI, AND SELL THIS HOUSE AS SOON AS POSSIBLE.
...
BUT IT WOULD BE DISTURBING TO LEAVE THIS BIZARRE STUDY AS-IS.
SO THE PEOPLE WHO FIND IT CAN CLAIM EVERYTHING INSIDE THE ROOM.
AS LONG AS YOU FIND IT.
THAT'S WHY WE'VE CALLED UPON WELL-KNOWN EXORCISTS.

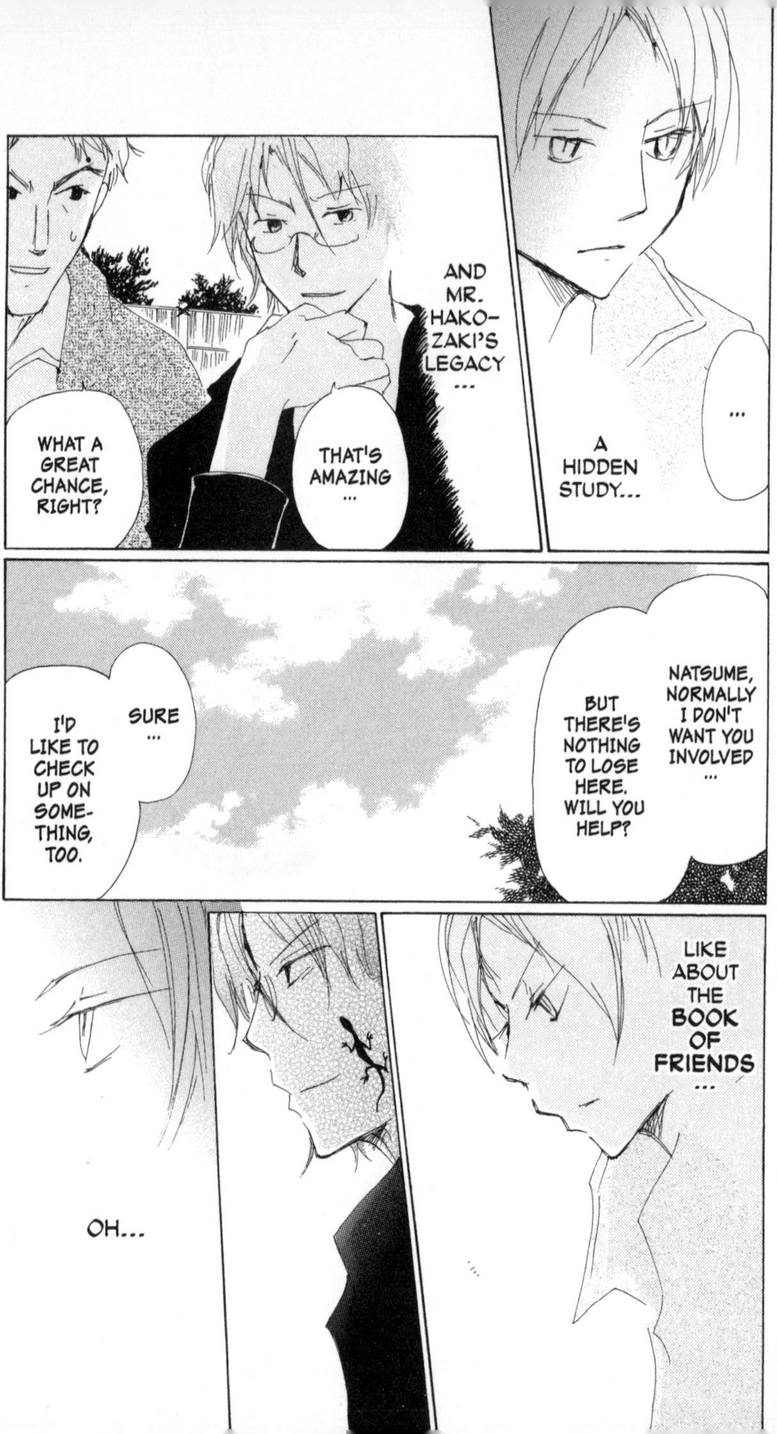
...
A HIDDEN STUDY...
AND MR. HAKOZAKI'S LEGACY...
THAT'S AMAZING...
WHAT A GREAT CHANCE, RIGHT?
NATSUME, NORMALLY I DON'T WANT YOU INVOLVED...
BUT THERE'S NOTHING TO LOSE HERE. WILL YOU HELP?
SURE...
I'D LIKE TO CHECK UP ON SOMETHING, TOO.
LIKE ABOUT THE BOOK OF FRIENDS...
OH...

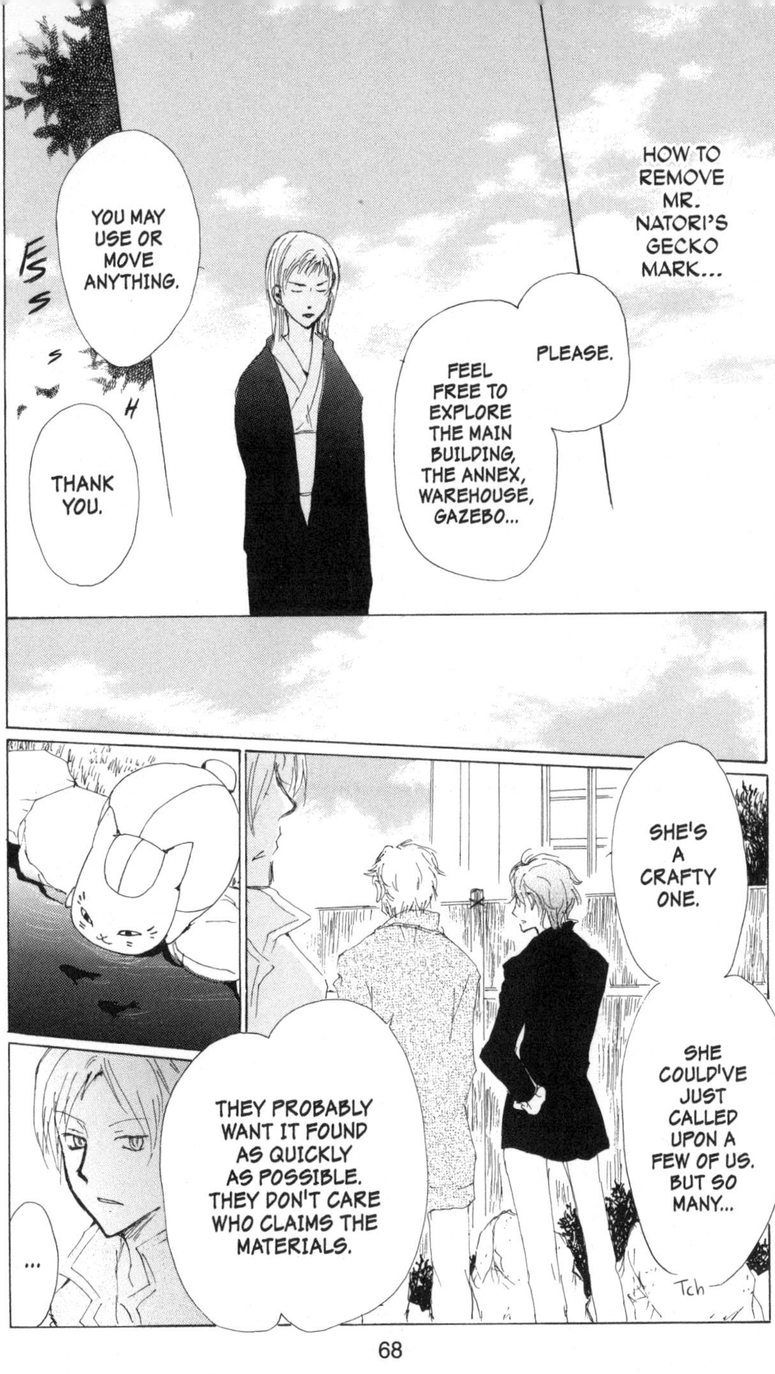
HOW TO REMOVE MR. NATORI'S GECKO MARK...
PLEASE.
FEEL FREE TO EXPLORE THE MAIN BUILDING, THE ANNEX, WAREHOUSE, GAZEBO...
YOU MAY USE OR MOVE ANYTHING.
FSSSH
THANK YOU.
SHE'S A CRAFTY ONE.
SHE COULD'VE JUST CALLED UPON A FEW OF US. BUT SO MANY...
Tch
THEY PROBABLY WANT IT FOUND AS QUICKLY AS POSSIBLE. THEY DON'T CARE WHO CLAIMS THE MATERIALS.
...

04

❋ Here comes Nyanko Sensei

Miss Junko Kanechiku is drawing a cute and fun comic strip based on Natsume's Book of Friends on the Lala Melody Online website. The characters who are usually serene or naïve are drawn so adorably and playfully, sometimes transforming into bold and expressive imps. It makes you chuckle and provides a welcome relief in your day. Also unexpected fun sides to Shigeru, Matoba, Taki, and Tanuma! Mr. Natori isn't very different from his usual self, but that's what makes it funnier. Please check it out.

http://www.lala-melody-online.com

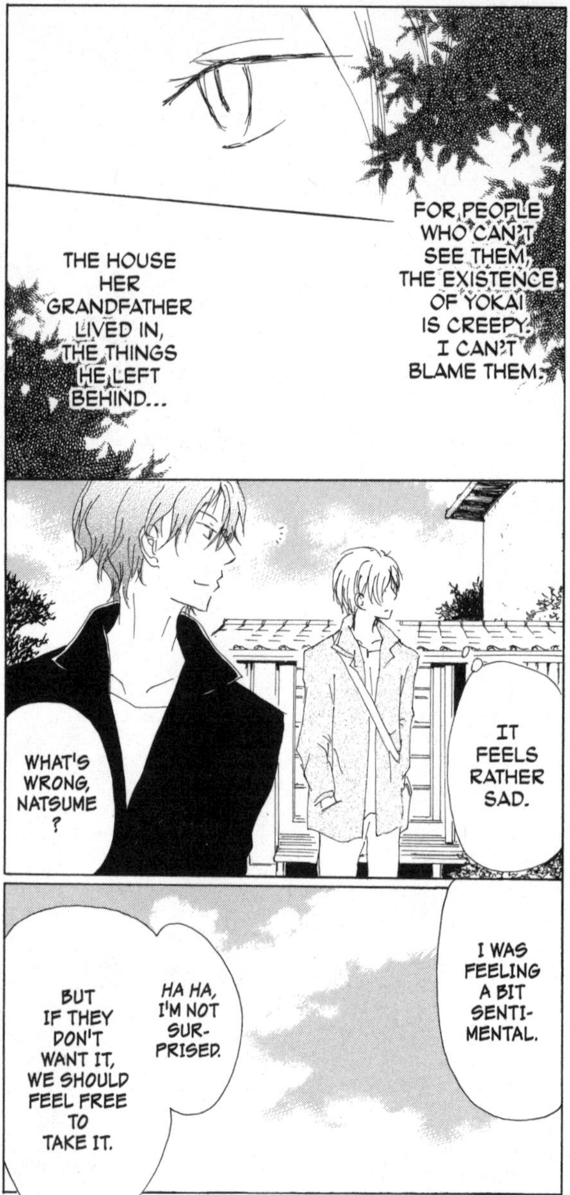
FOR PEOPLE WHO CAN'T SEE THEM, THE EXISTENCE OF YOKAI IS CREEPY. I CAN'T BLAME THEM.
THE HOUSE HER GRANDFATHER LIVED IN, THE THINGS HE LEFT BEHIND...
IT FEELS RATHER SAD.
WHAT'S WRONG, NATSUME?
I WAS FEELING A BIT SENTIMENTAL.
HA HA, I'M NOT SURPRISED.
BUT IF THEY DON'T WANT IT, WE SHOULD FEEL FREE TO TAKE IT.

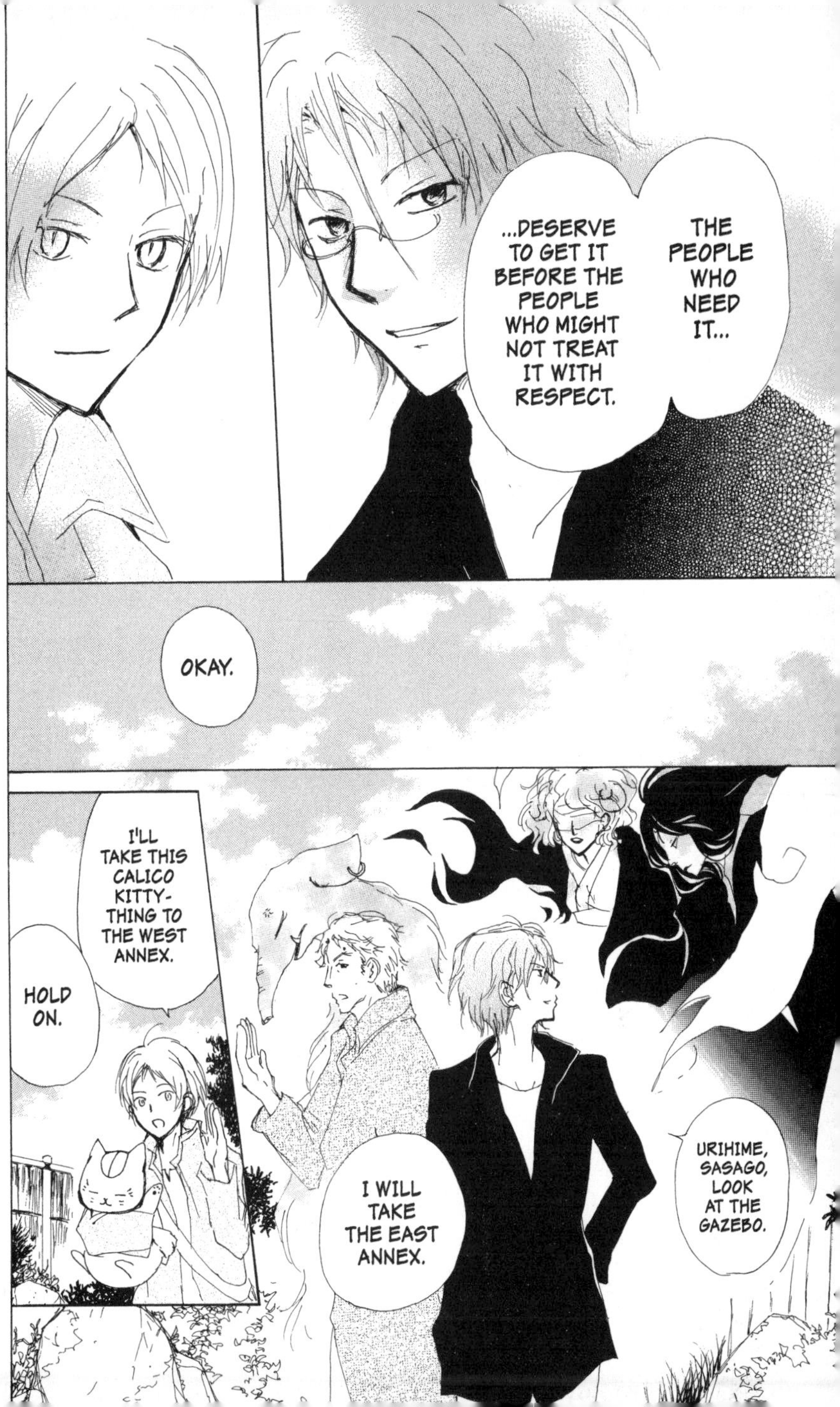
THE PEOPLE WHO NEED IT...
...DESERVE TO GET IT BEFORE THE PEOPLE WHO MIGHT NOT TREAT IT WITH RESPECT.
OKAY.
URIHIME, SASAGO, LOOK AT THE GAZEBO.
I WILL TAKE THE EAST ANNEX.
I'LL TAKE THIS CALICO KITTY-THING TO THE WEST ANNEX.
HOLD ON.

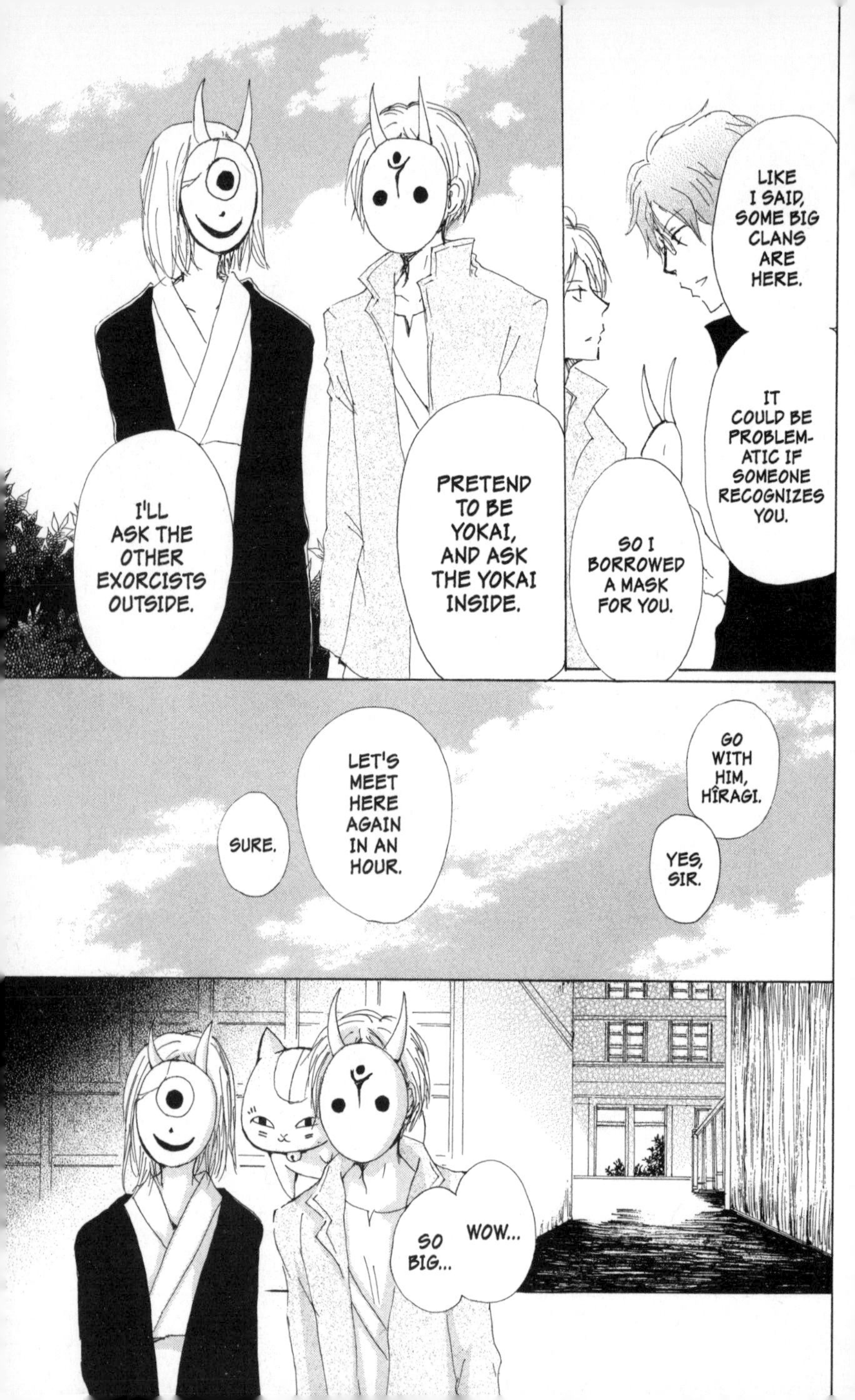
LIKE I SAID, SOME BIG CLANS ARE HERE.
IT COULD BE PROBLEMATIC IF SOMEONE RECOGNIZES YOU.
SO I BORROWED A MASK FOR YOU.
PRETEND TO BE YOKAI, AND ASK THE YOKAI INSIDE.
I'LL ASK THE OTHER EXORCISTS OUTSIDE.
GO WITH HIM, HÎRAGI.
YES, SIR.
LET'S MEET HERE AGAIN IN AN HOUR.
SURE.
WOW...
SO BIG...

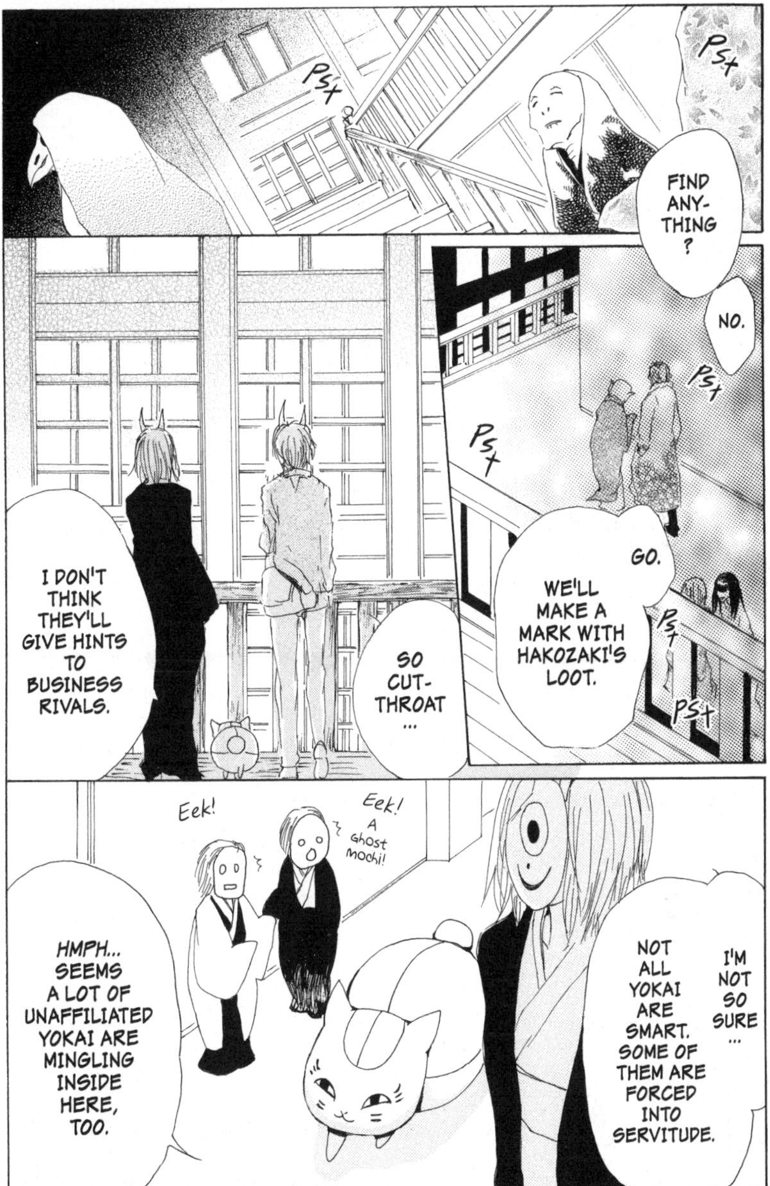

Pst
FIND ANY-THING?
Pst
NO.
Pst
Pst
GO.
WE'LL MAKE A MARK WITH HAKOZAKI'S LOOT.
Pst
Pst
SO CUT-THROAT...
I DON'T THINK THEY'LL GIVE HINTS TO BUSINESS RIVALS.
I'M NOT SO SURE...
NOT ALL YOKAI ARE SMART. SOME OF THEM ARE FORCED INTO SERVITUDE.
Eek! A Ghost mochi!
Eek!
HMPH... SEEMS A LOT OF UNAFFILIATED YOKAI ARE MINGLING INSIDE HERE, TOO.

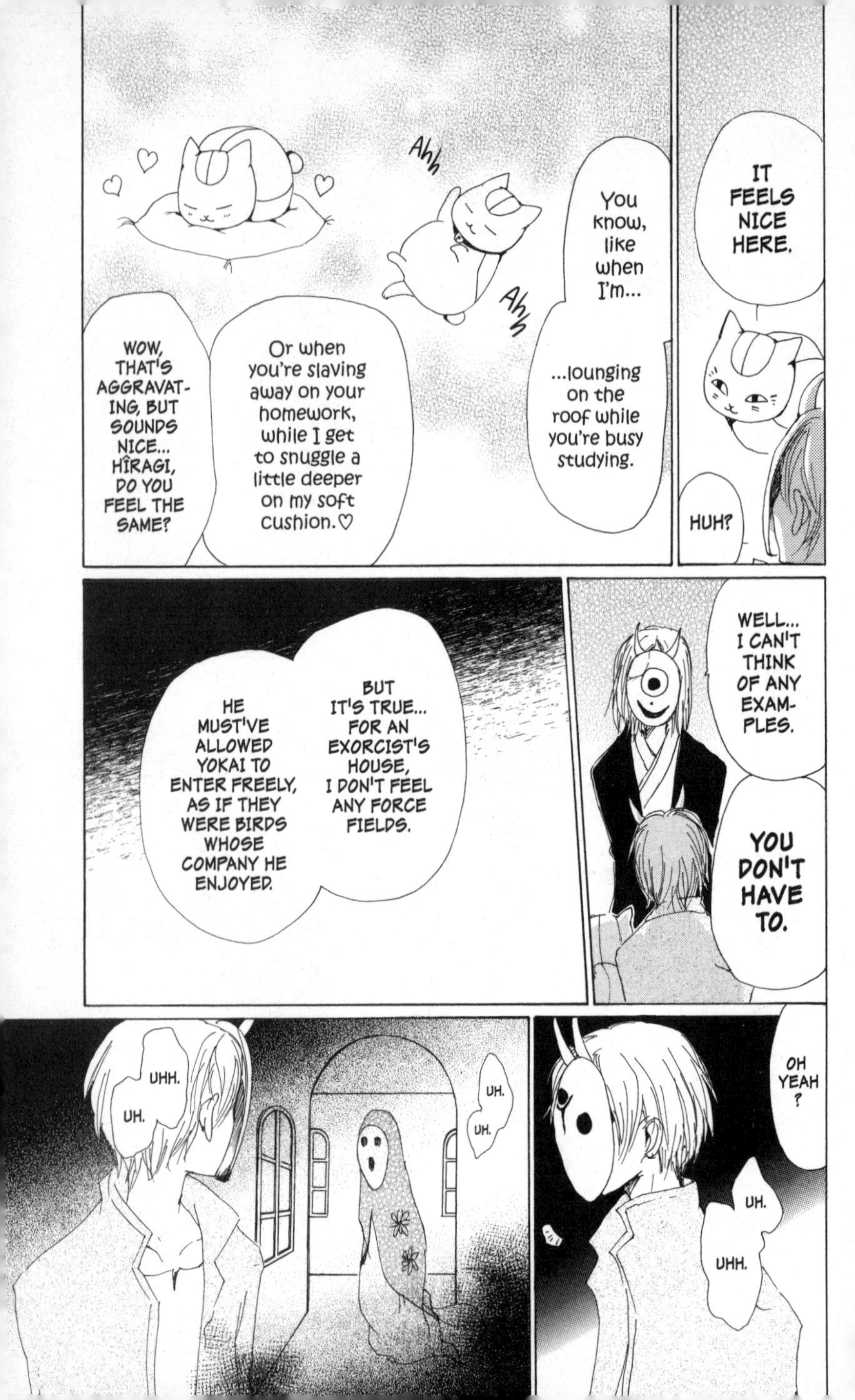
IT FEELS NICE HERE.
HUH?
You know, like when I'm...
...lounging on the roof while you're busy studying.
Ahh
Ahh
Or when you're slaving away on your homework, while I get to snuggle a little deeper on my soft cushion.♡
WOW, THAT'S AGGRAVAT-ING, BUT SOUNDS NICE... HÎRAGI, DO YOU FEEL THE SAME?
WELL... I CAN'T THINK OF ANY EXAM-PLES.
YOU DON'T HAVE TO.
BUT IT'S TRUE... FOR AN EXORCIST'S HOUSE, I DON'T FEEL ANY FORCE FIELDS.
HE MUST'VE ALLOWED YOKAI TO ENTER FREELY, AS IF THEY WERE BIRDS WHOSE COMPANY HE ENJOYED.
OH YEAH?
UH.
UHH.
UH.
UH.
UHH.
UH.

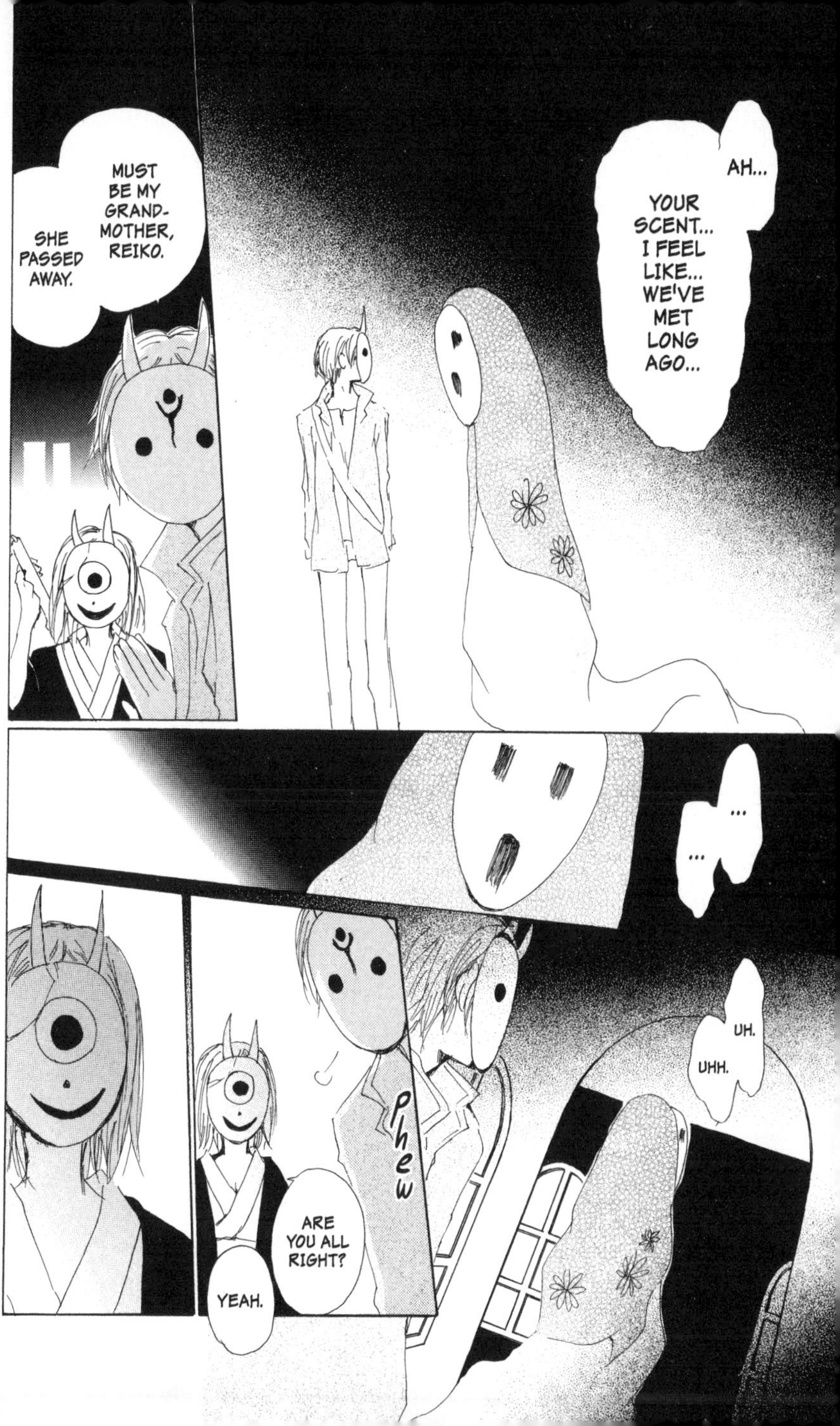
AH... YOUR SCENT... I FEEL LIKE... WE'VE MET LONG AGO...
MUST BE MY GRAND-MOTHER, REIKO.
SHE PASSED AWAY.
...
...
UH.
UHH.
Phew
ARE YOU ALL RIGHT?
YEAH.

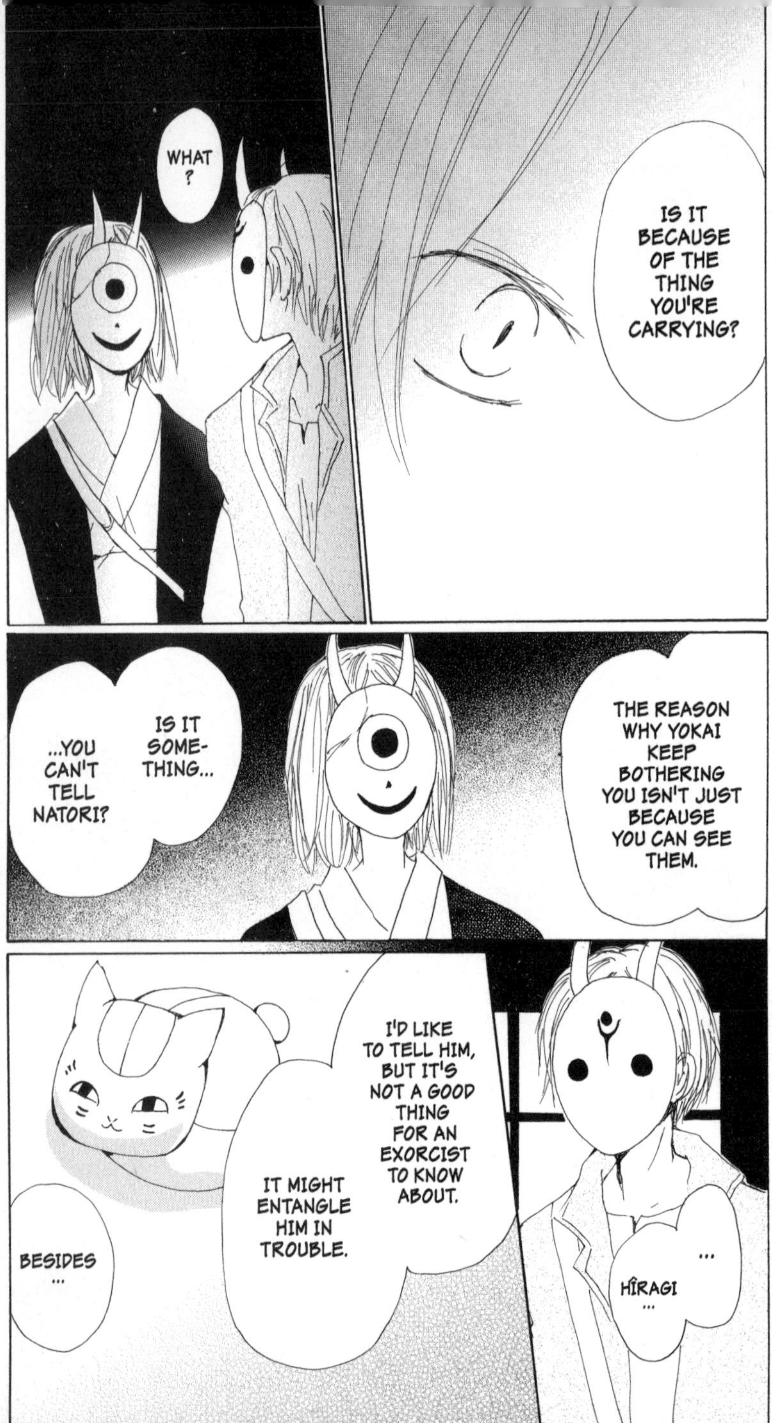
IS IT BECAUSE OF THE THING YOU'RE CARRYING?
WHAT?
THE REASON WHY YOKAI KEEP BOTHERING YOU ISN'T JUST BECAUSE YOU CAN SEE THEM.
IS IT SOMETHING...
...YOU CAN'T TELL NATORI?
... HÎRAGI ...
I'D LIKE TO TELL HIM, BUT IT'S NOT A GOOD THING FOR AN EXORCIST TO KNOW ABOUT.
IT MIGHT ENTANGLE HIM IN TROUBLE.
BESIDES ...

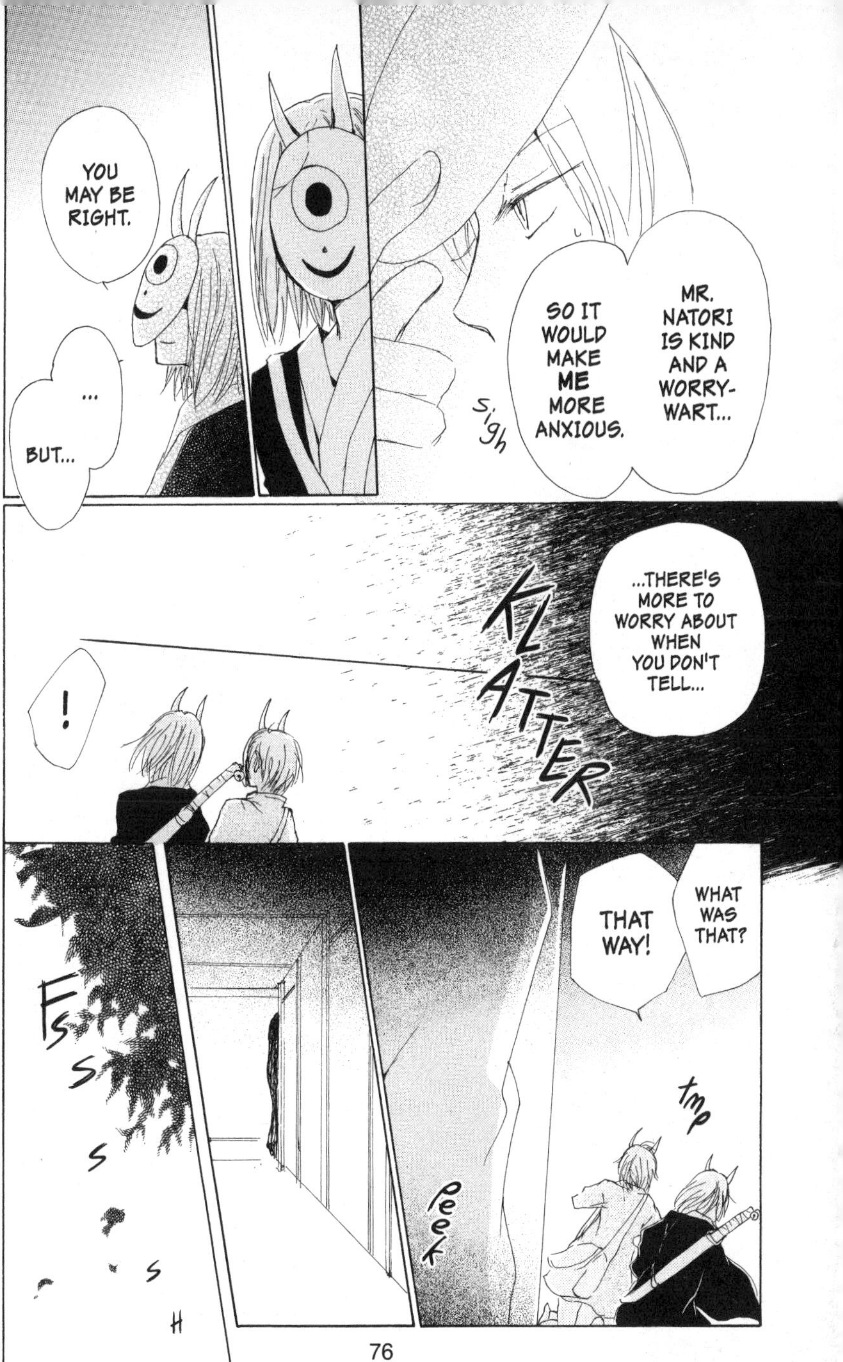
MR. NATORI IS KIND AND A WORRY-WART...
SO IT WOULD MAKE **ME** MORE ANXIOUS.
sigh
YOU MAY BE RIGHT.
... BUT...
...THERE'S MORE TO WORRY ABOUT WHEN YOU DON'T TELL...
KLATTER
!
WHAT WAS THAT?
THAT WAY!
tmp
peek
FSSSSH

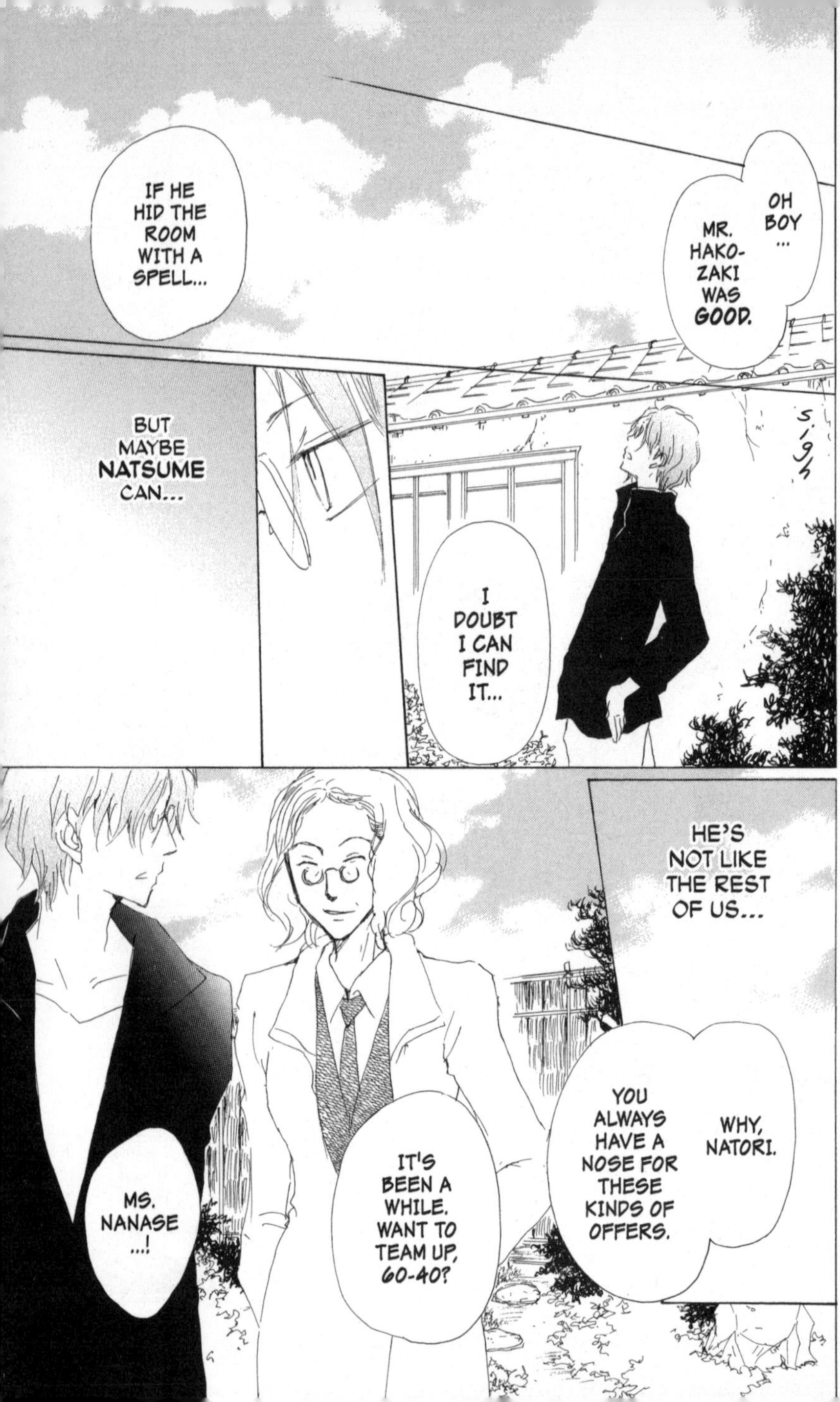
OH BOY ...
MR. HAKOZAKI WAS GOOD.
IF HE HID THE ROOM WITH A SPELL...
sigh
I DOUBT I CAN FIND IT...
BUT MAYBE NATSUME CAN...
HE'S NOT LIKE THE REST OF US...
WHY, NATORI.
YOU ALWAYS HAVE A NOSE FOR THESE KINDS OF OFFERS.
IT'S BEEN A WHILE. WANT TO TEAM UP, 60-40?
MS. NANASE ...!

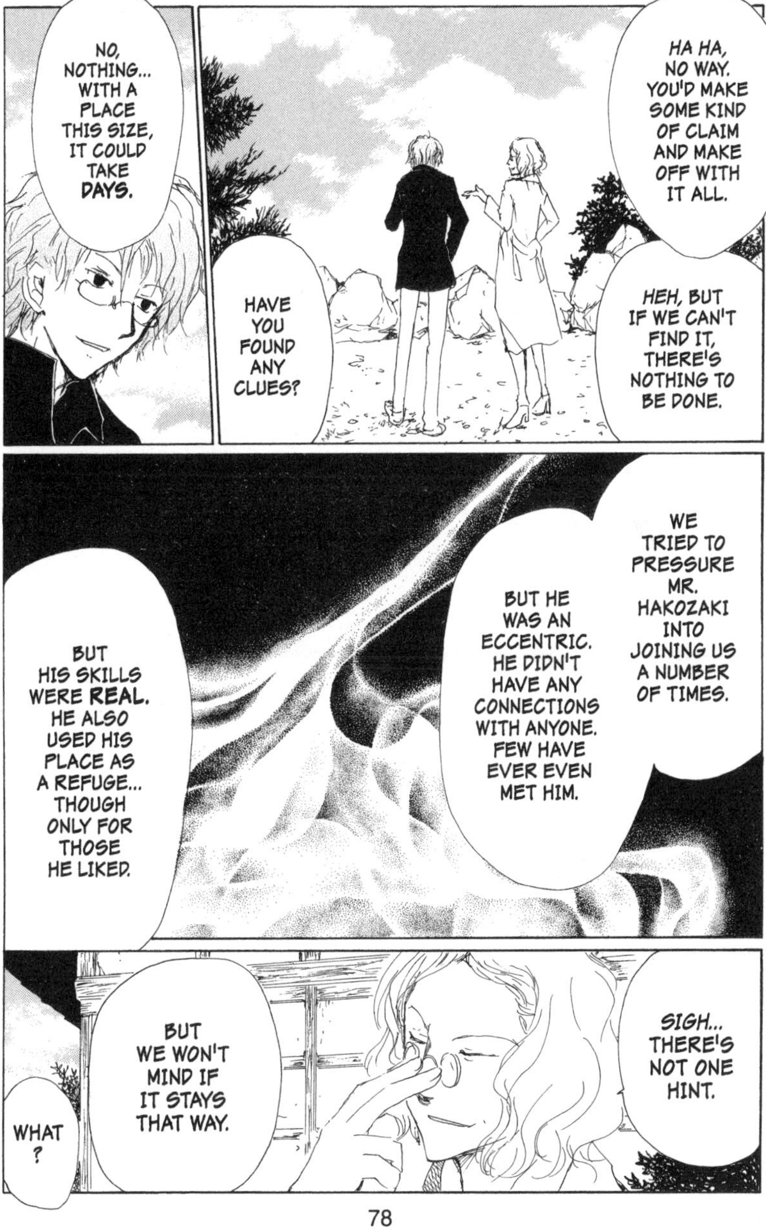
HA HA, NO WAY. YOU'D MAKE SOME KIND OF CLAIM AND MAKE OFF WITH IT ALL.
HEH, BUT IF WE CAN'T FIND IT, THERE'S NOTHING TO BE DONE.
HAVE YOU FOUND ANY CLUES?
NO, NOTHING... WITH A PLACE THIS SIZE, IT COULD TAKE DAYS.
WE TRIED TO PRESSURE MR. HAKOZAKI INTO JOINING US A NUMBER OF TIMES.
BUT HE WAS AN ECCENTRIC. HE DIDN'T HAVE ANY CONNECTIONS WITH ANYONE. FEW HAVE EVER EVEN MET HIM.
BUT HIS SKILLS WERE REAL. HE ALSO USED HIS PLACE AS A REFUGE... THOUGH ONLY FOR THOSE HE LIKED.
SIGH... THERE'S NOT ONE HINT.
BUT WE WON'T MIND IF IT STAYS THAT WAY.
WHAT?

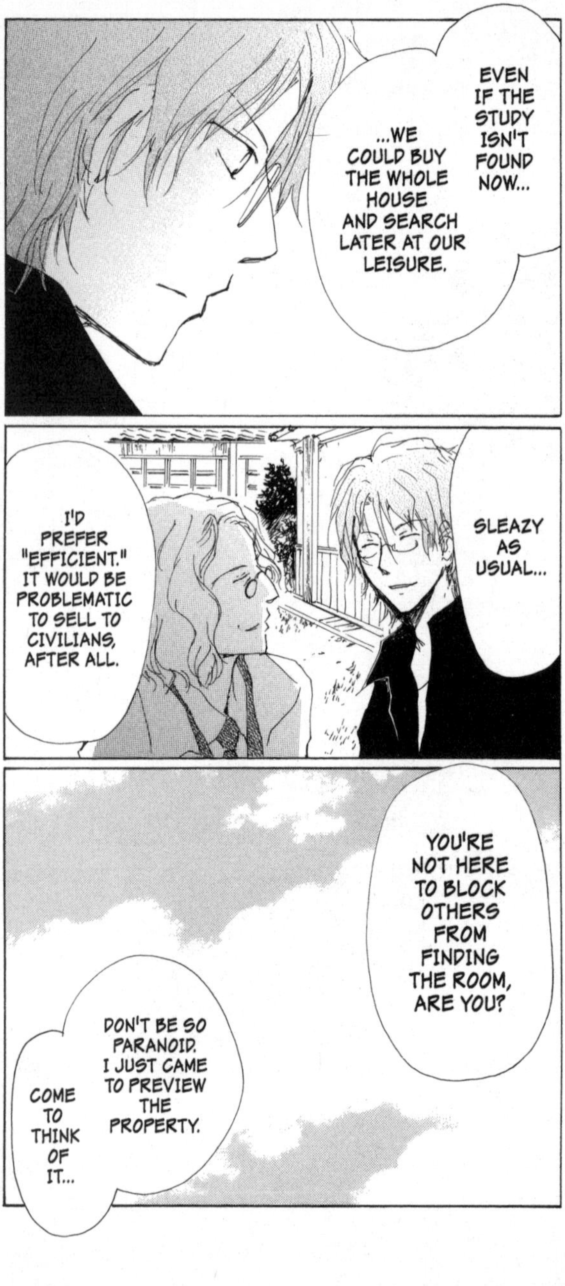
EVEN IF THE STUDY ISN'T FOUND NOW...
...WE COULD BUY THE WHOLE HOUSE AND SEARCH LATER AT OUR LEISURE.
SLEAZY AS USUAL...
I'D PREFER "EFFICIENT." IT WOULD BE PROBLEMATIC TO SELL TO CIVILIANS, AFTER ALL.
YOU'RE NOT HERE TO BLOCK OTHERS FROM FINDING THE ROOM, ARE YOU?
DON'T BE SO PARANOID. I JUST CAME TO PREVIEW THE PROPERTY.
COME TO THINK OF IT...

05

On the Hakusensha Novels site, Mr. Sadayuki Murai is writing a novel for Natsume's Book of Friends. Mr. Murai was the series editor and wrote the original scripts for the third and fourth seasons of the anime. The story is quietly beautiful, a little mysterious, and it comes together in soft bittersweet echoes. It contains elements best enjoyed in novel form. Please check it out.

http://www.hakusensha.co.jp/novels/

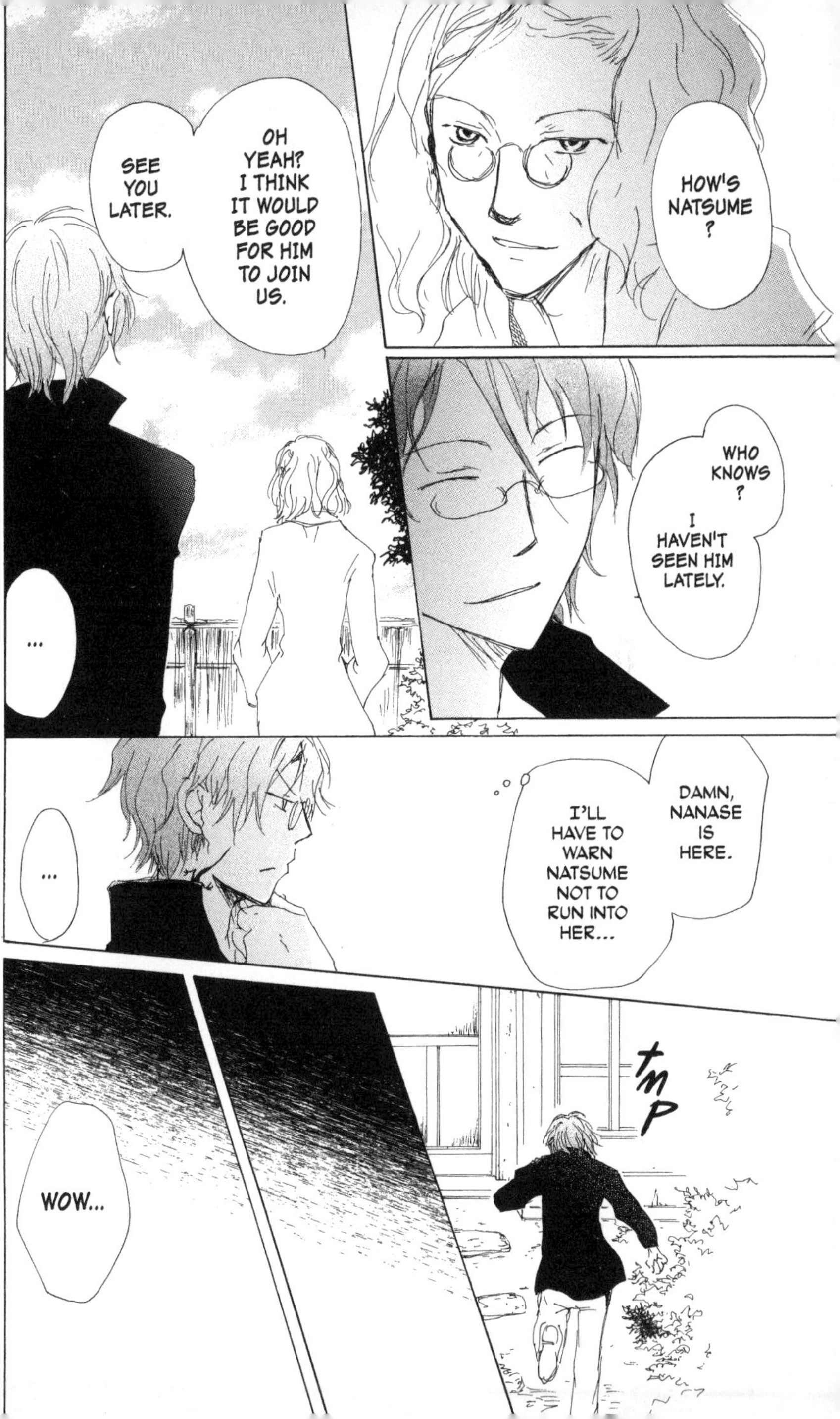
HOW'S NATSUME?
WHO KNOWS?
I HAVEN'T SEEN HIM LATELY.
OH YEAH? I THINK IT WOULD BE GOOD FOR HIM TO JOIN US.
SEE YOU LATER.
...
DAMN, NANASE IS HERE.
I'LL HAVE TO WARN NATSUME NOT TO RUN INTO HER...
...
TMP
WOW...

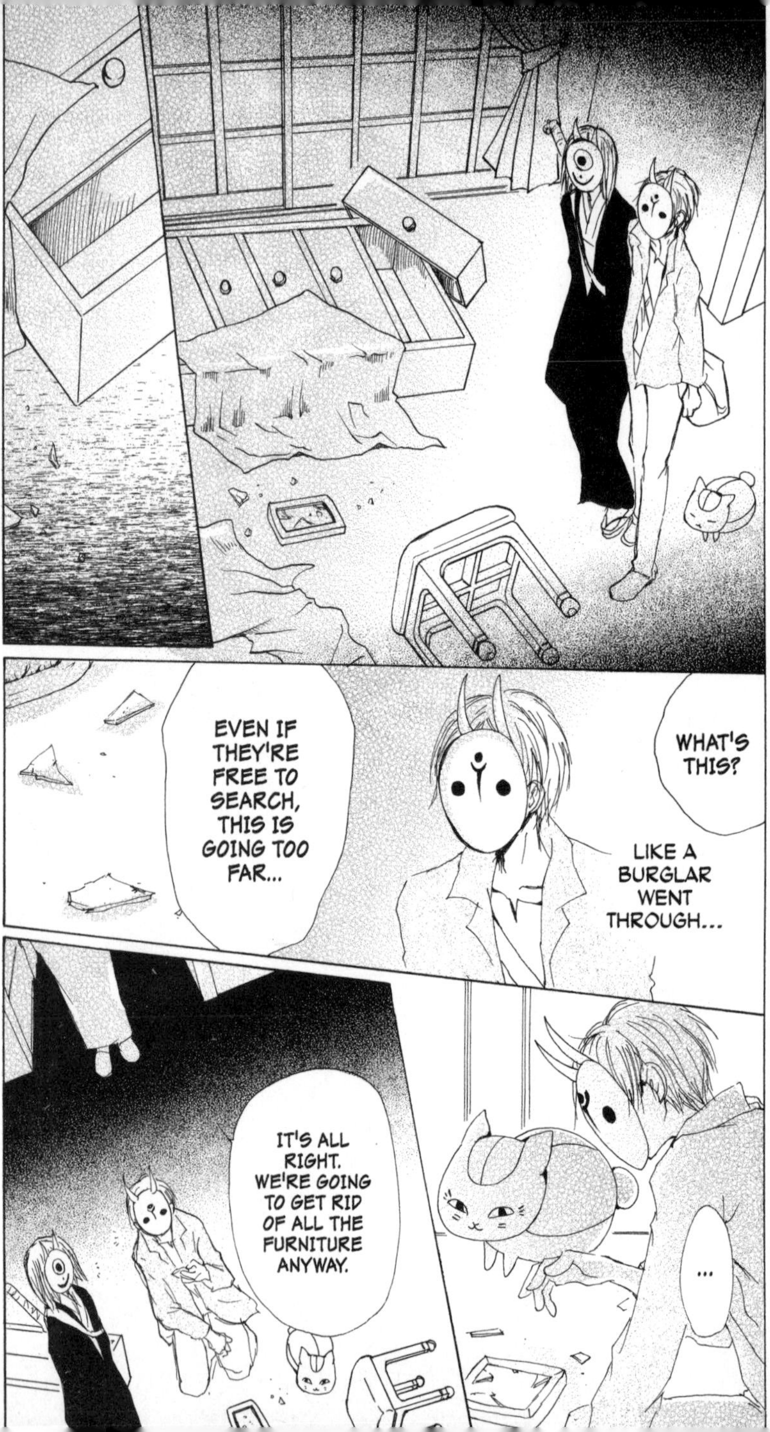
WHAT'S THIS?
LIKE A BURGLAR WENT THROUGH...
EVEN IF THEY'RE FREE TO SEARCH, THIS IS GOING TOO FAR...
...
IT'S ALL RIGHT. WE'RE GOING TO GET RID OF ALL THE FURNITURE ANYWAY.

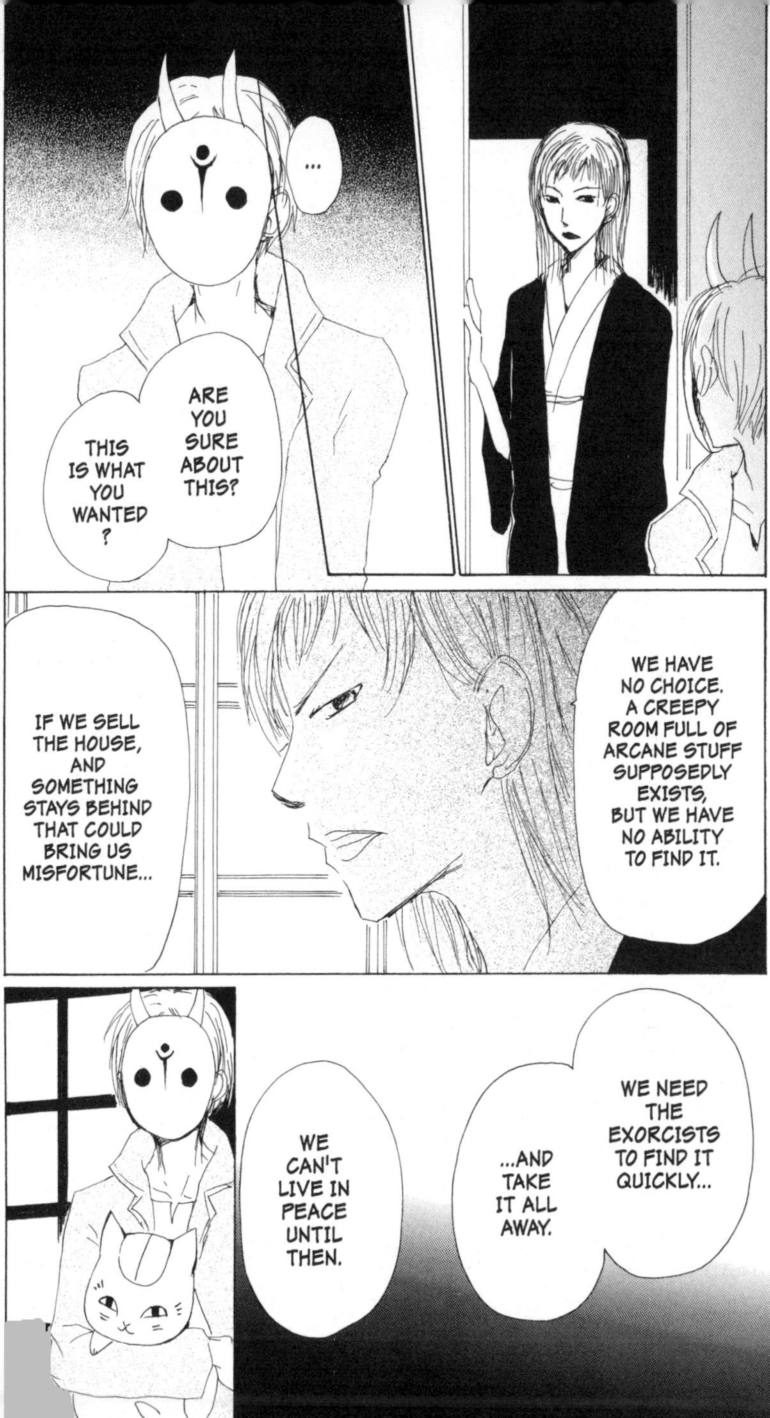
...
ARE YOU SURE ABOUT THIS?
THIS IS WHAT YOU WANTED?
WE HAVE NO CHOICE. A CREEPY ROOM FULL OF ARCANE STUFF SUPPOSEDLY EXISTS, BUT WE HAVE NO ABILITY TO FIND IT.
IF WE SELL THE HOUSE, AND SOMETHING STAYS BEHIND THAT COULD BRING US MISFORTUNE...
WE NEED THE EXORCISTS TO FIND IT QUICKLY...
...AND TAKE IT ALL AWAY.
WE CAN'T LIVE IN PEACE UNTIL THEN.

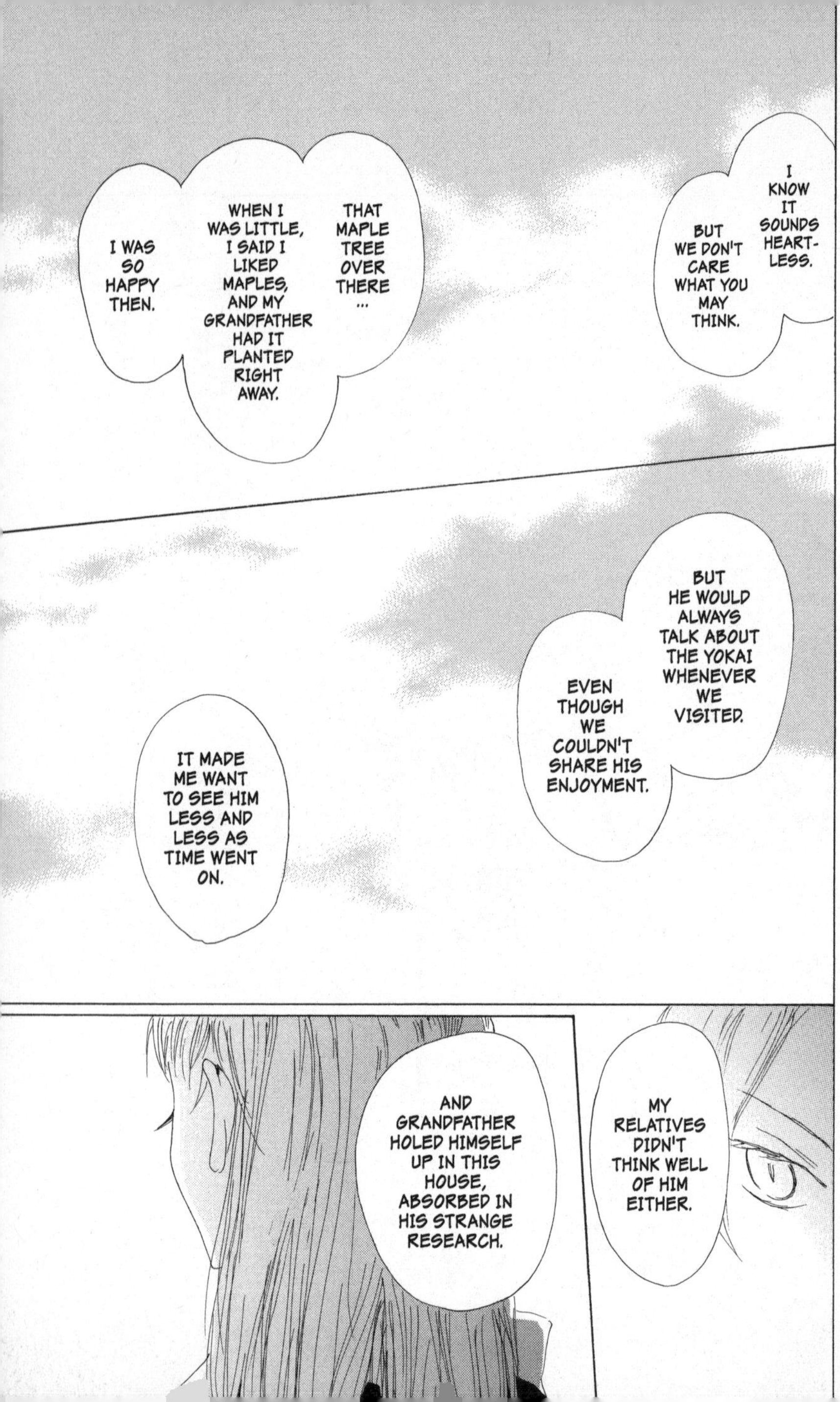
I KNOW IT SOUNDS HEART-LESS.
BUT WE DON'T CARE WHAT YOU MAY THINK.
THAT MAPLE TREE OVER THERE ...
WHEN I WAS LITTLE, I SAID I LIKED MAPLES, AND MY GRANDFATHER HAD IT PLANTED RIGHT AWAY.
I WAS SO HAPPY THEN.
BUT HE WOULD ALWAYS TALK ABOUT THE YOKAI WHENEVER WE VISITED.
EVEN THOUGH WE COULDN'T SHARE HIS ENJOYMENT.
IT MADE ME WANT TO SEE HIM LESS AND LESS AS TIME WENT ON.
MY RELATIVES DIDN'T THINK WELL OF HIM EITHER.
AND GRANDFATHER HOLED HIMSELF UP IN THIS HOUSE, ABSORBED IN HIS STRANGE RESEARCH.

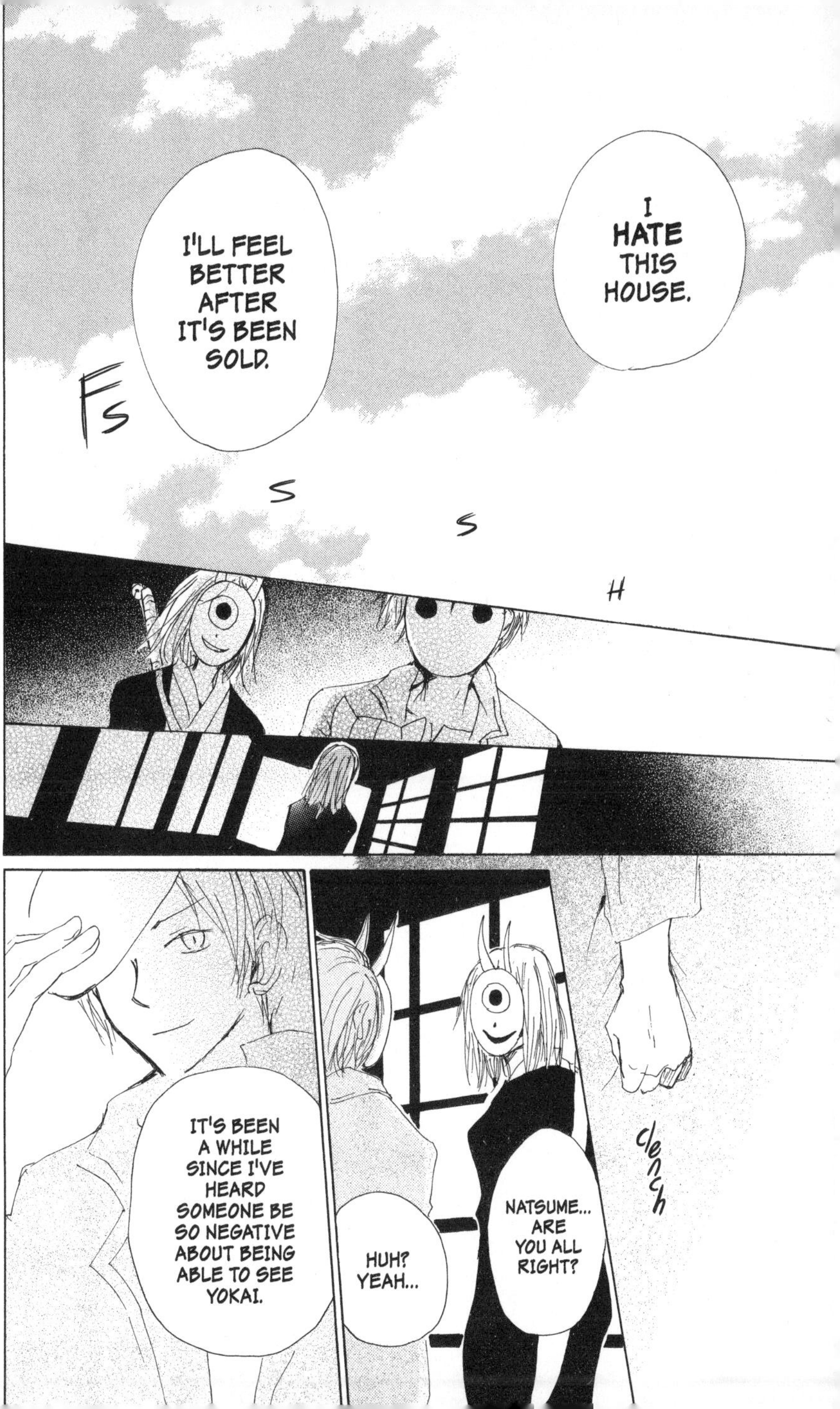
I HATE THIS HOUSE.
I'LL FEEL BETTER AFTER IT'S BEEN SOLD.
Fs
S
S
H
clench
NATSUME... ARE YOU ALL RIGHT?
HUH? YEAH...
IT'S BEEN A WHILE SINCE I'VE HEARD SOMEONE BE SO NEGATIVE ABOUT BEING ABLE TO SEE YOKAI.

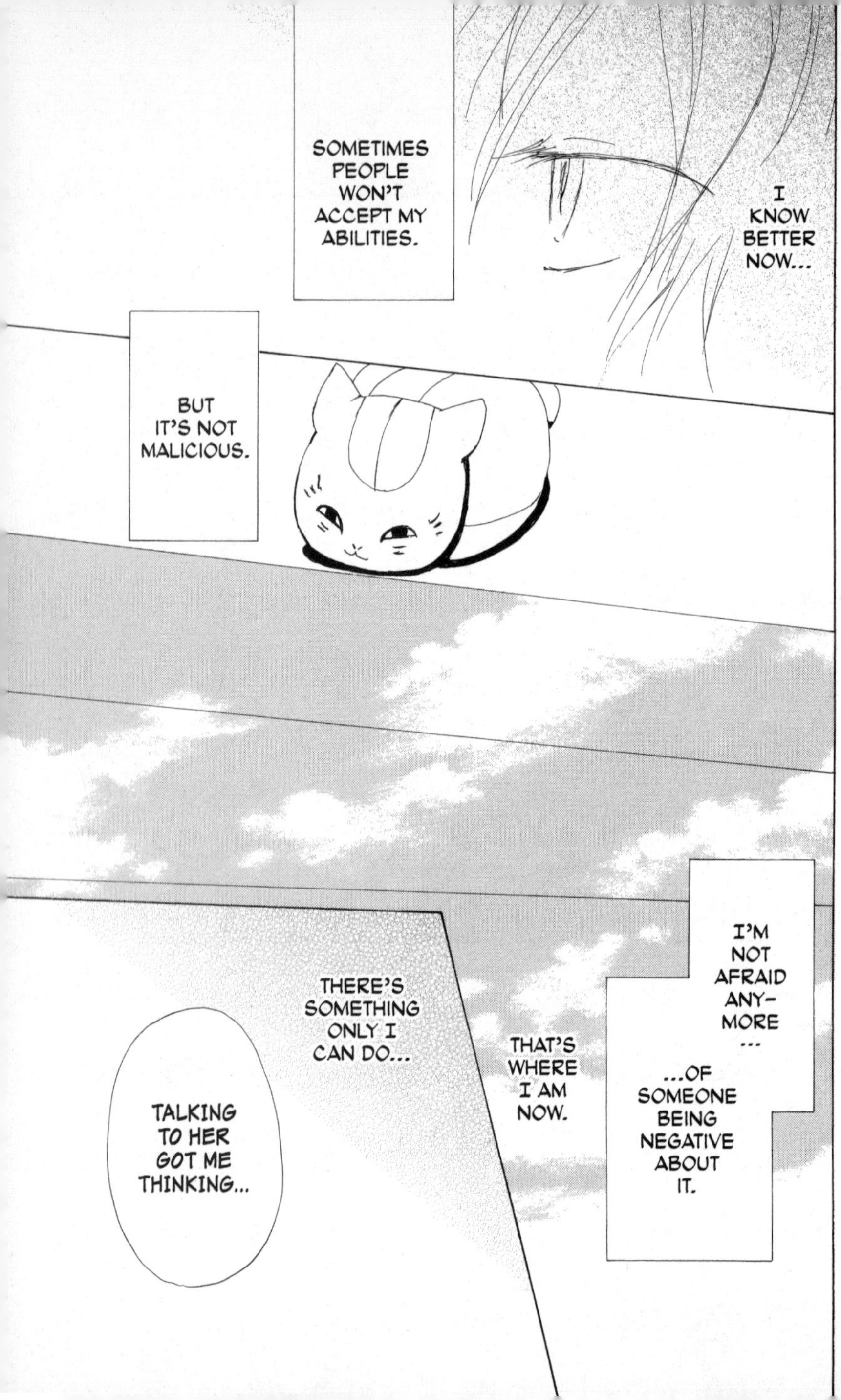
I KNOW BETTER NOW...
SOMETIMES PEOPLE WON'T ACCEPT MY ABILITIES.
BUT IT'S NOT MALICIOUS.
I'M NOT AFRAID ANYMORE...
...OF SOMEONE BEING NEGATIVE ABOUT IT.
THAT'S WHERE I AM NOW.
THERE'S SOMETHING ONLY I CAN DO...
TALKING TO HER GOT ME THINKING...

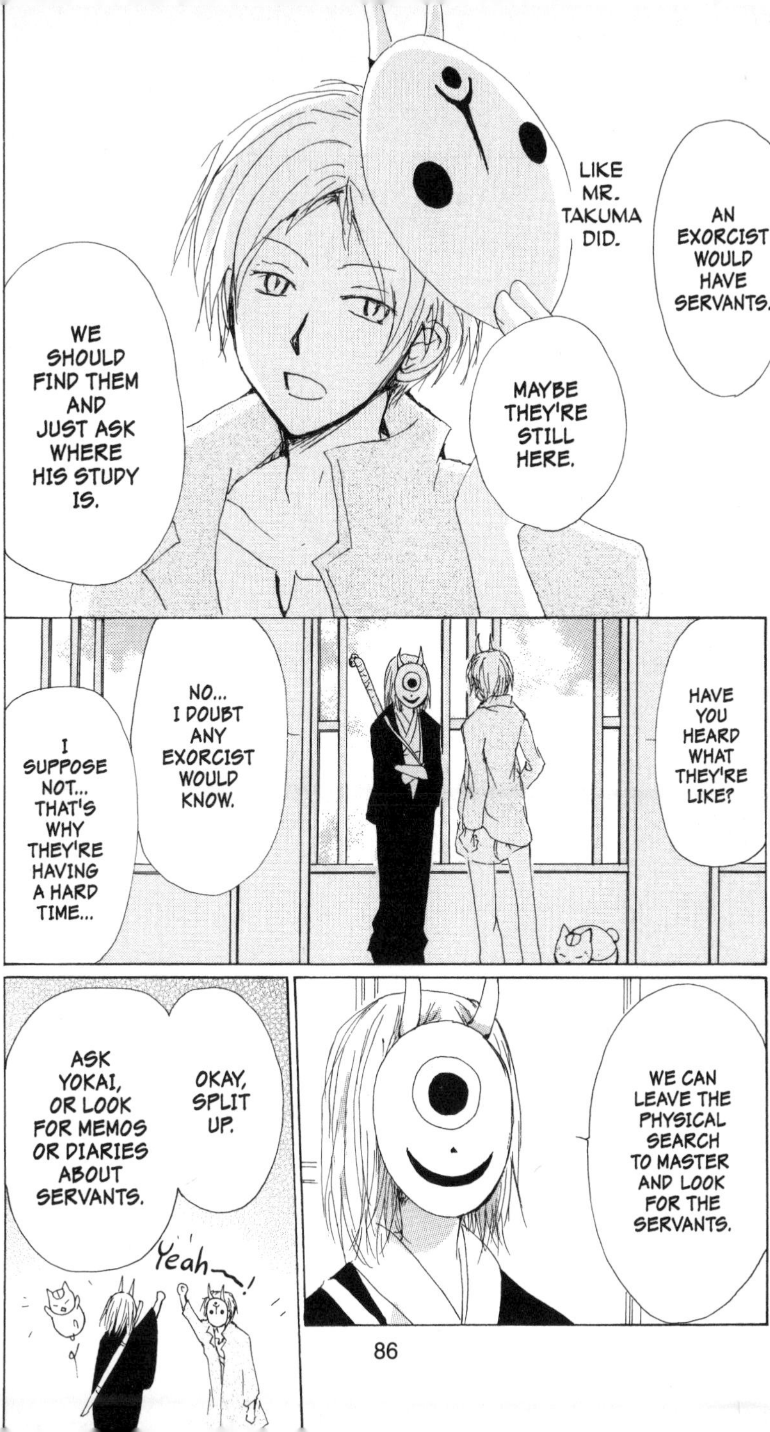
AN EXORCIST WOULD HAVE SERVANTS.
LIKE MR. TAKUMA DID.
MAYBE THEY'RE STILL HERE.
WE SHOULD FIND THEM AND JUST ASK WHERE HIS STUDY IS.
HAVE YOU HEARD WHAT THEY'RE LIKE?
NO... I DOUBT ANY EXORCIST WOULD KNOW.
I SUPPOSE NOT... THAT'S WHY THEY'RE HAVING A HARD TIME...
WE CAN LEAVE THE PHYSICAL SEARCH TO MASTER AND LOOK FOR THE SERVANTS.
OKAY, SPLIT UP.
ASK YOKAI, OR LOOK FOR MEMOS OR DIARIES ABOUT SERVANTS.
Yeah~!

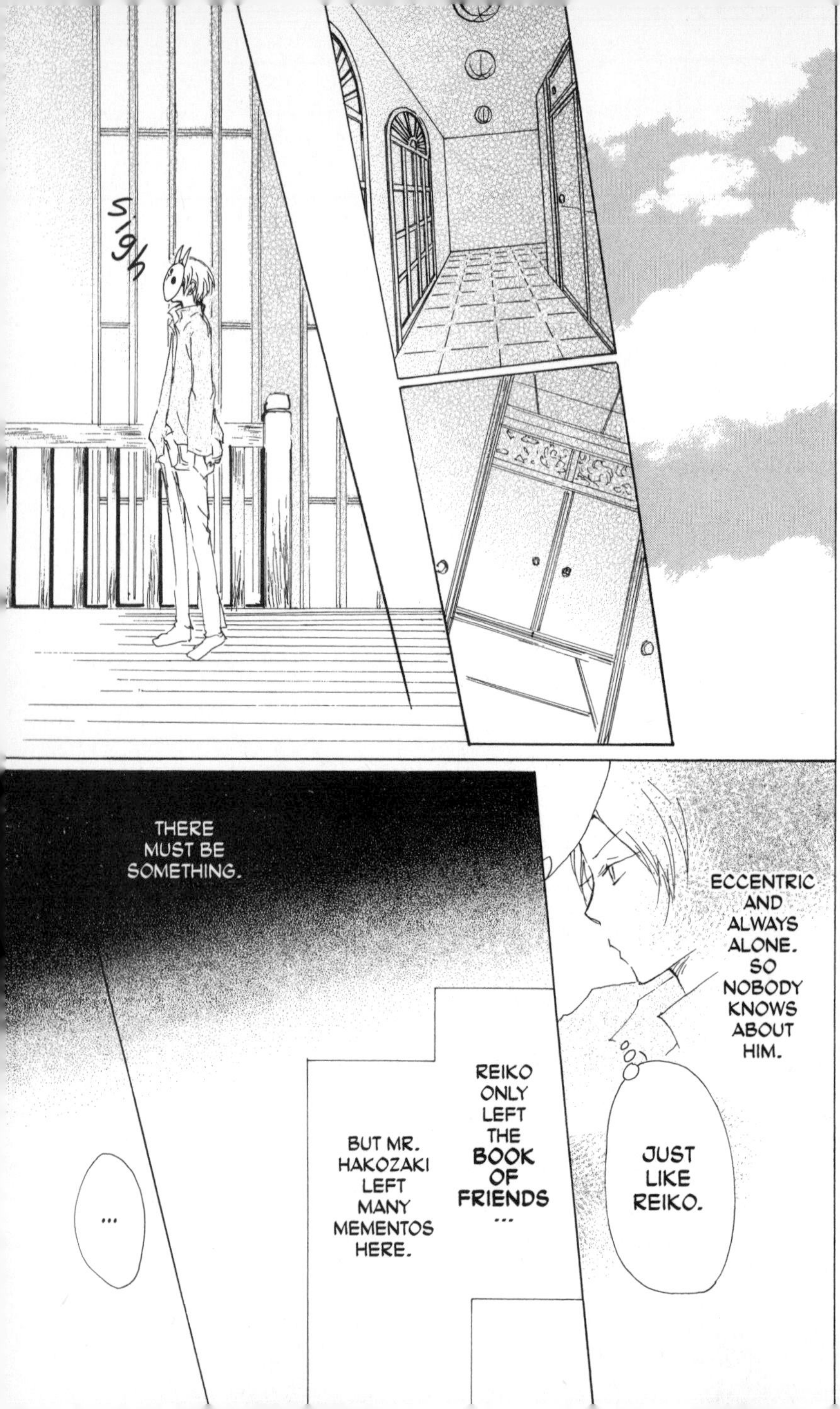
sigh
ECCENTRIC AND ALWAYS ALONE. SO NOBODY KNOWS ABOUT HIM.
JUST LIKE REIKO.
REIKO ONLY LEFT THE BOOK OF FRIENDS...
BUT MR. HAKOZAKI LEFT MANY MEMENTOS HERE.
THERE MUST BE SOMETHING.
...

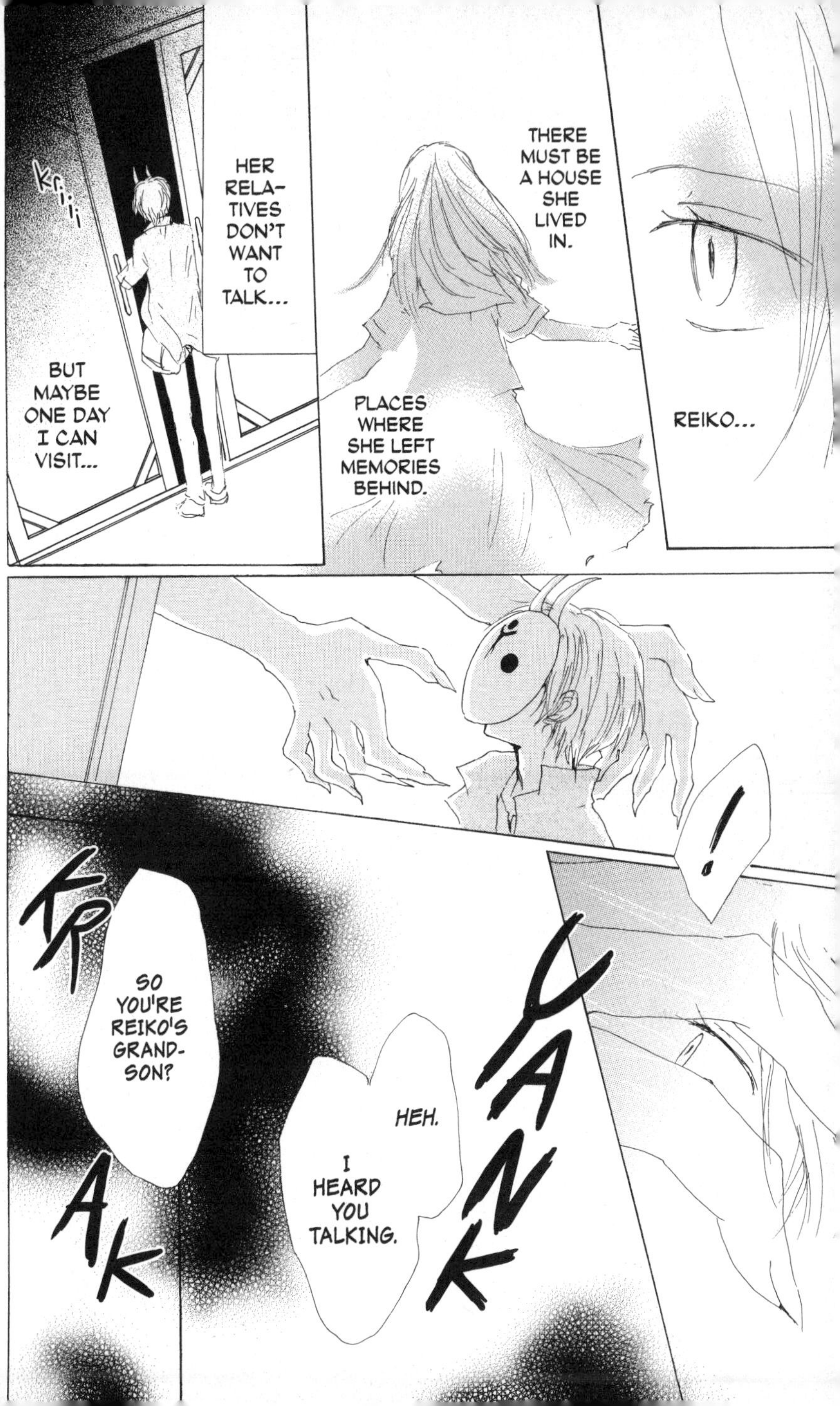
REIKO...
THERE MUST BE A HOUSE SHE LIVED IN.
PLACES WHERE SHE LEFT MEMORIES BEHIND.
HER RELATIVES DON'T WANT TO TALK...
Kriii
BUT MAYBE ONE DAY I CAN VISIT...
!
YANK
HEH.
I HEARD YOU TALKING.
KRAK
SO YOU'RE REIKO'S GRANDSON?

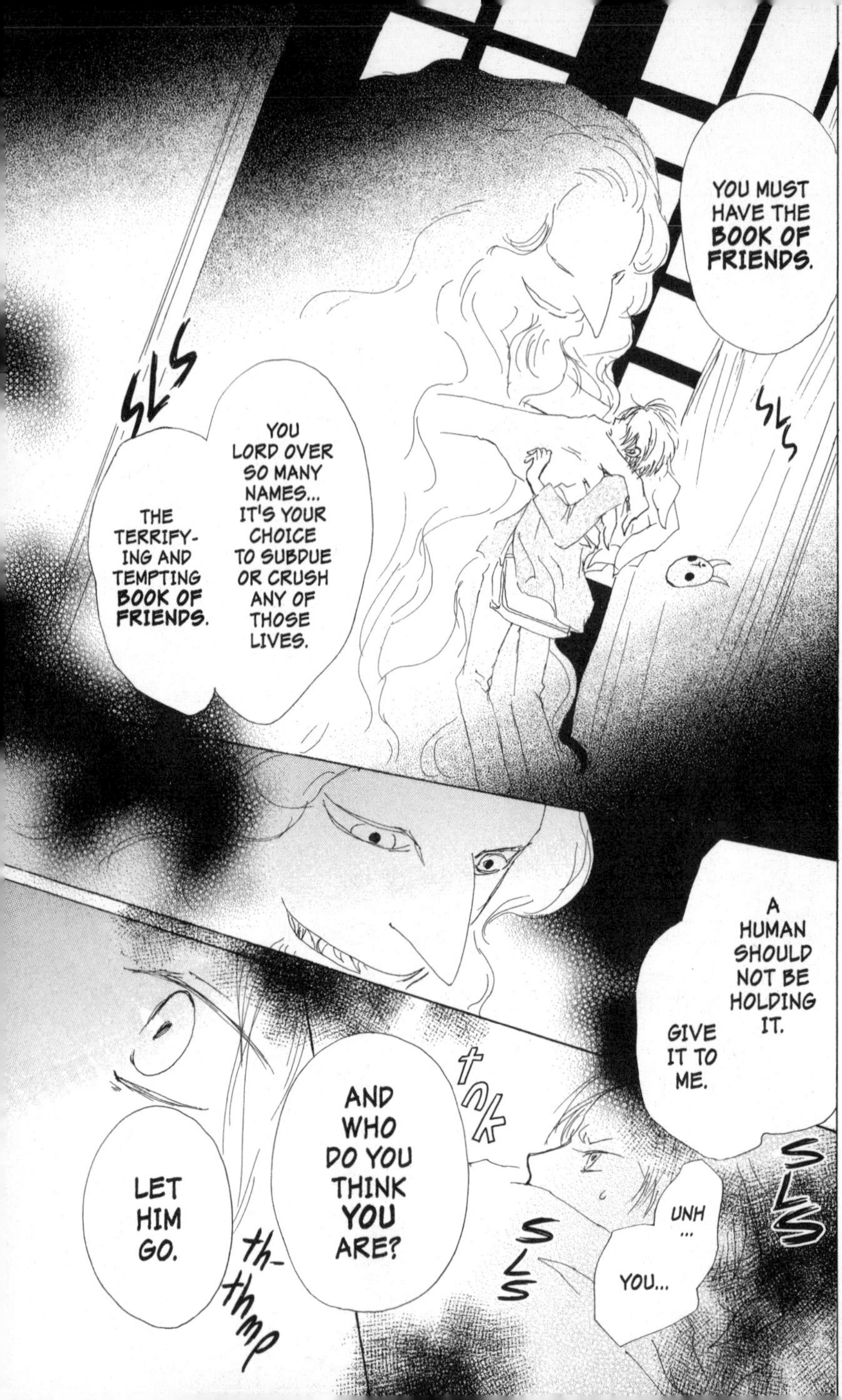
YOU MUST HAVE THE BOOK OF FRIENDS.
SLS
YOU LORD OVER SO MANY NAMES... IT'S YOUR CHOICE TO SUBDUE OR CRUSH ANY OF THOSE LIVES.
THE TERRIFYING AND TEMPTING BOOK OF FRIENDS.
SLS
A HUMAN SHOULD NOT BE HOLDING IT.
GIVE IT TO ME.
SLS
UNH...
YOU...
SLS
tnk
AND WHO DO YOU THINK YOU ARE?
LET HIM GO.
th-thmp

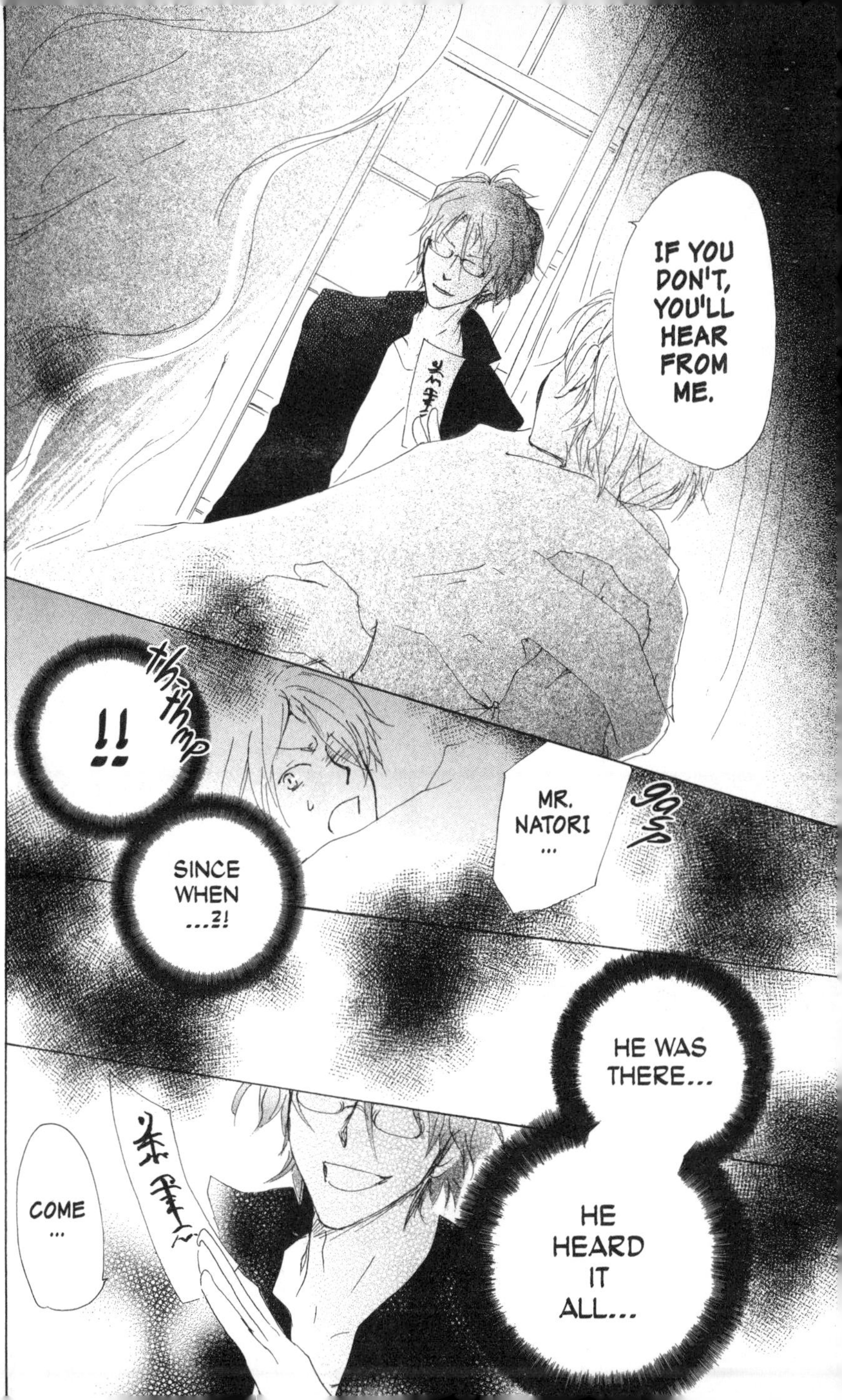
IF YOU DON'T, YOU'LL HEAR FROM ME.
!!
thmp thmp
gasp
MR. NATORI ...
SINCE WHEN ...?!
HE WAS THERE...
HE HEARD IT ALL...
COME ...

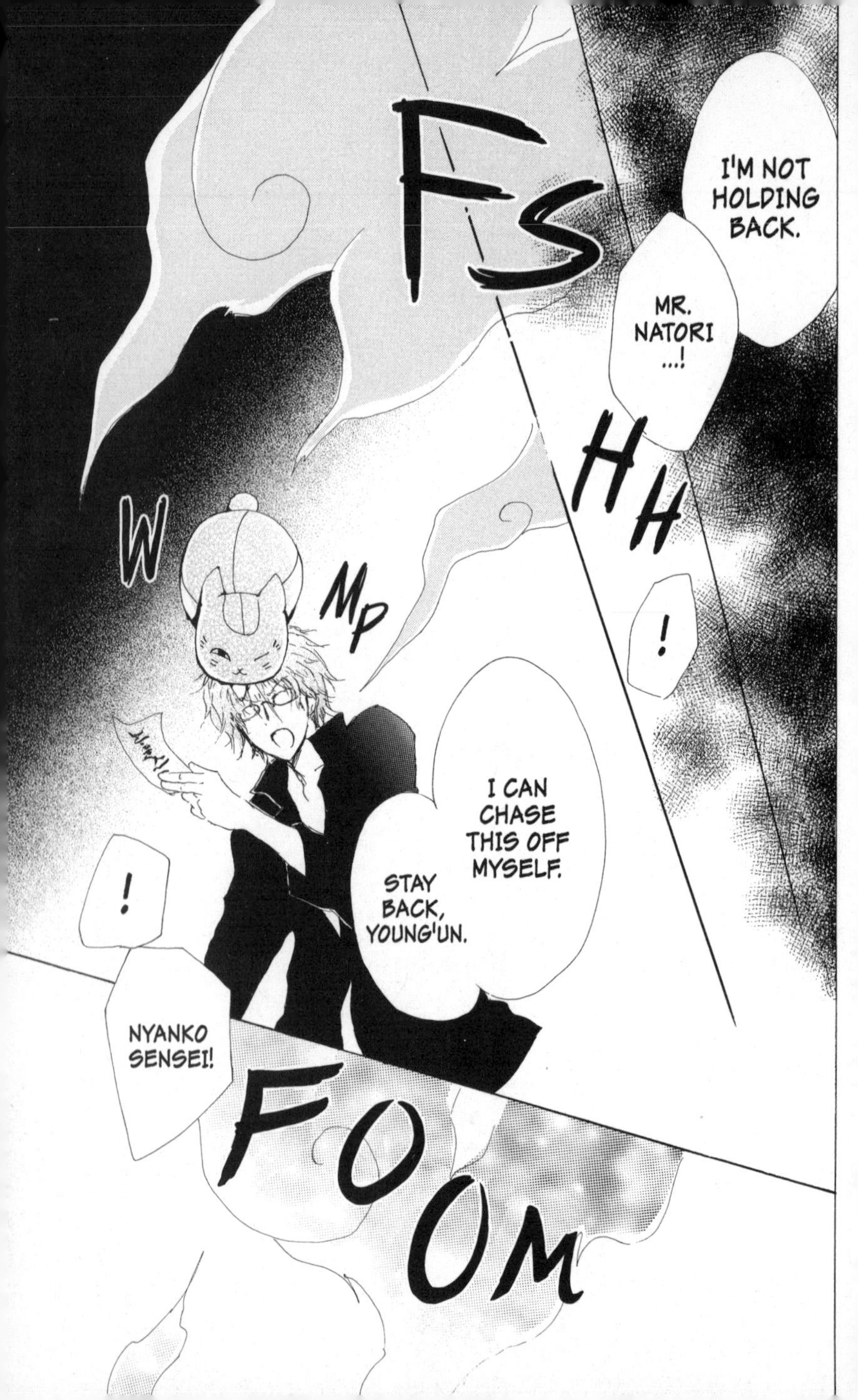
I'M NOT HOLDING BACK.
MR. NATORI ...!
FSHH
!
I CAN CHASE THIS OFF MYSELF.
STAY BACK, YOUNG'UN.
WMP
!
NYANKO SENSEI!
FOOM

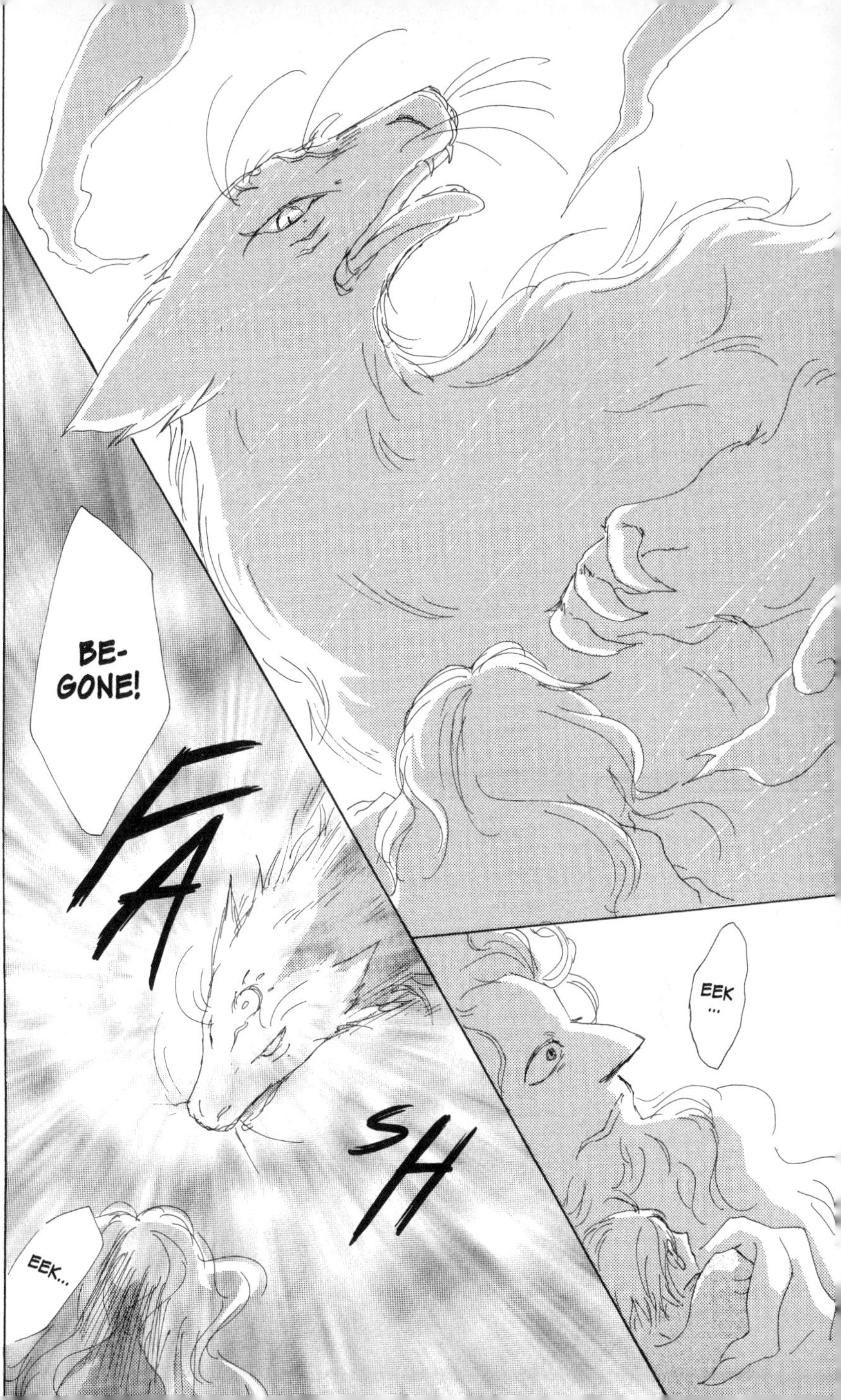
BE-GONE!
FA
SH
EEK ...
EEK...

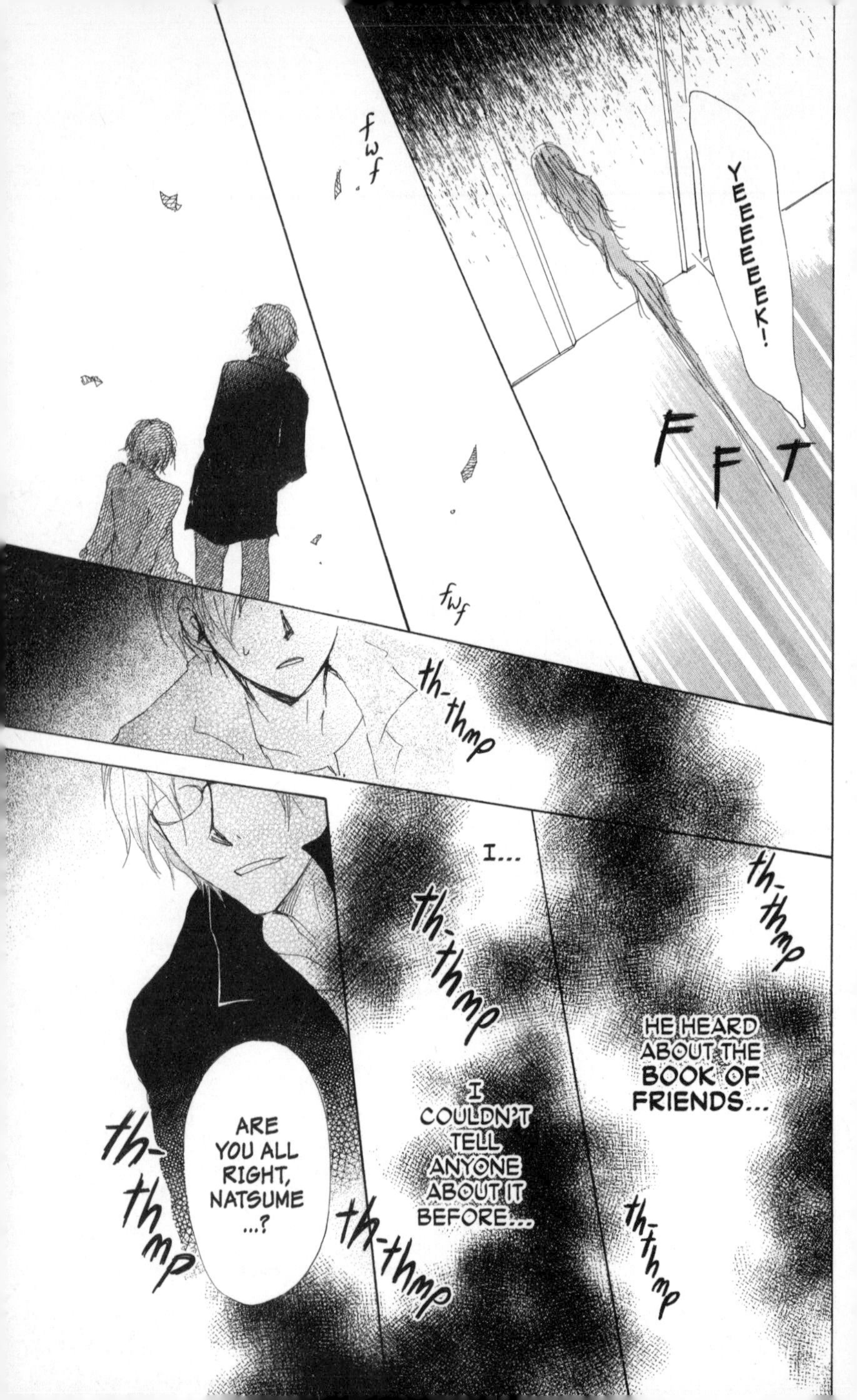
YEEEEEEK!
FFT
fwf
fwf
th-thmp
th-thmp
HE HEARD ABOUT THE BOOK OF FRIENDS...
th-thmp
I...
th-thmp
I COULDN'T TELL ANYONE ABOUT IT BEFORE...
th-thmp
ARE YOU ALL RIGHT, NATSUME ...?
th-thmp

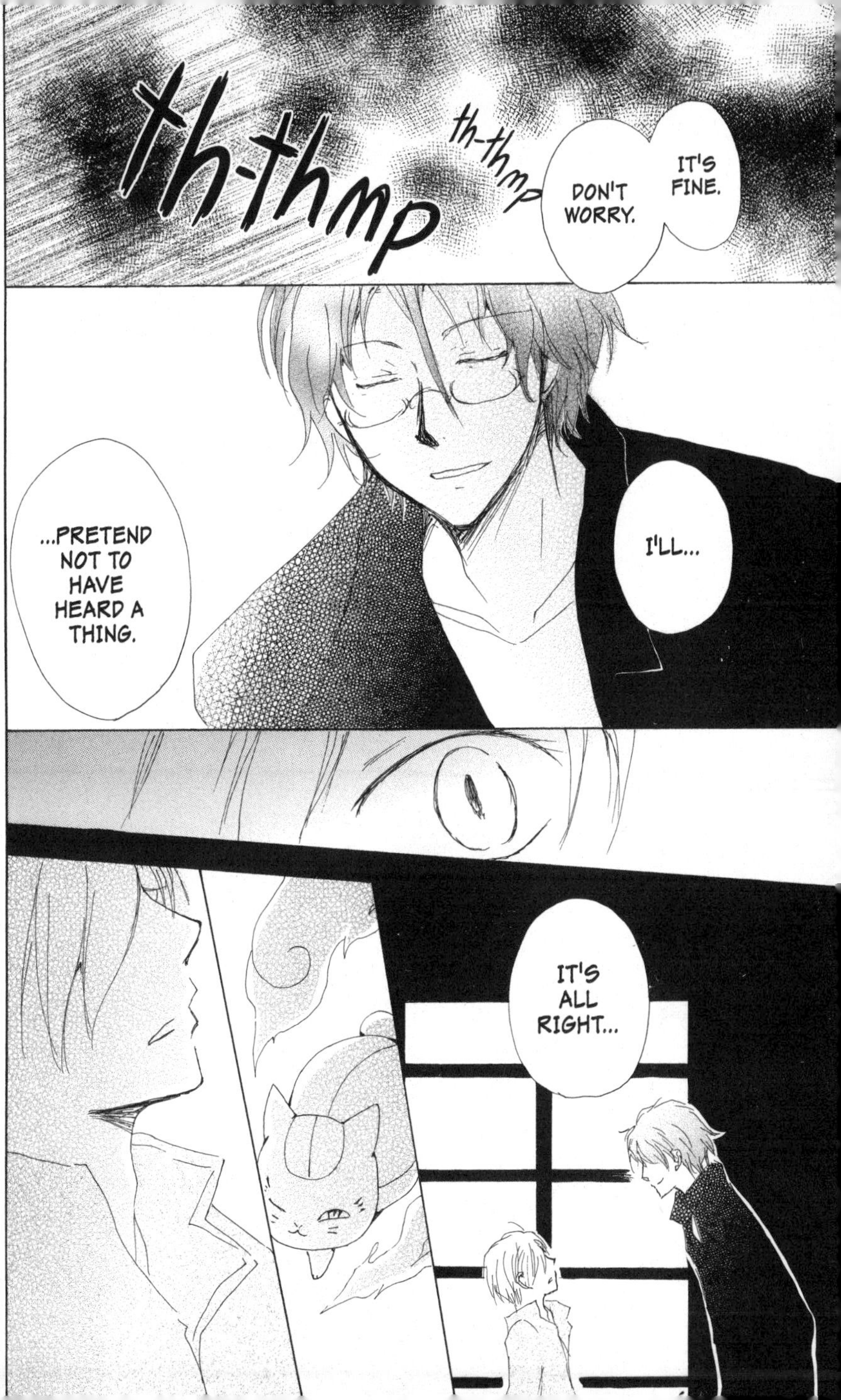
IT'S FINE.
DON'T WORRY.
th-thmp
th-thmp
I'LL...
...PRETEND NOT TO HAVE HEARD A THING.
IT'S ALL RIGHT...

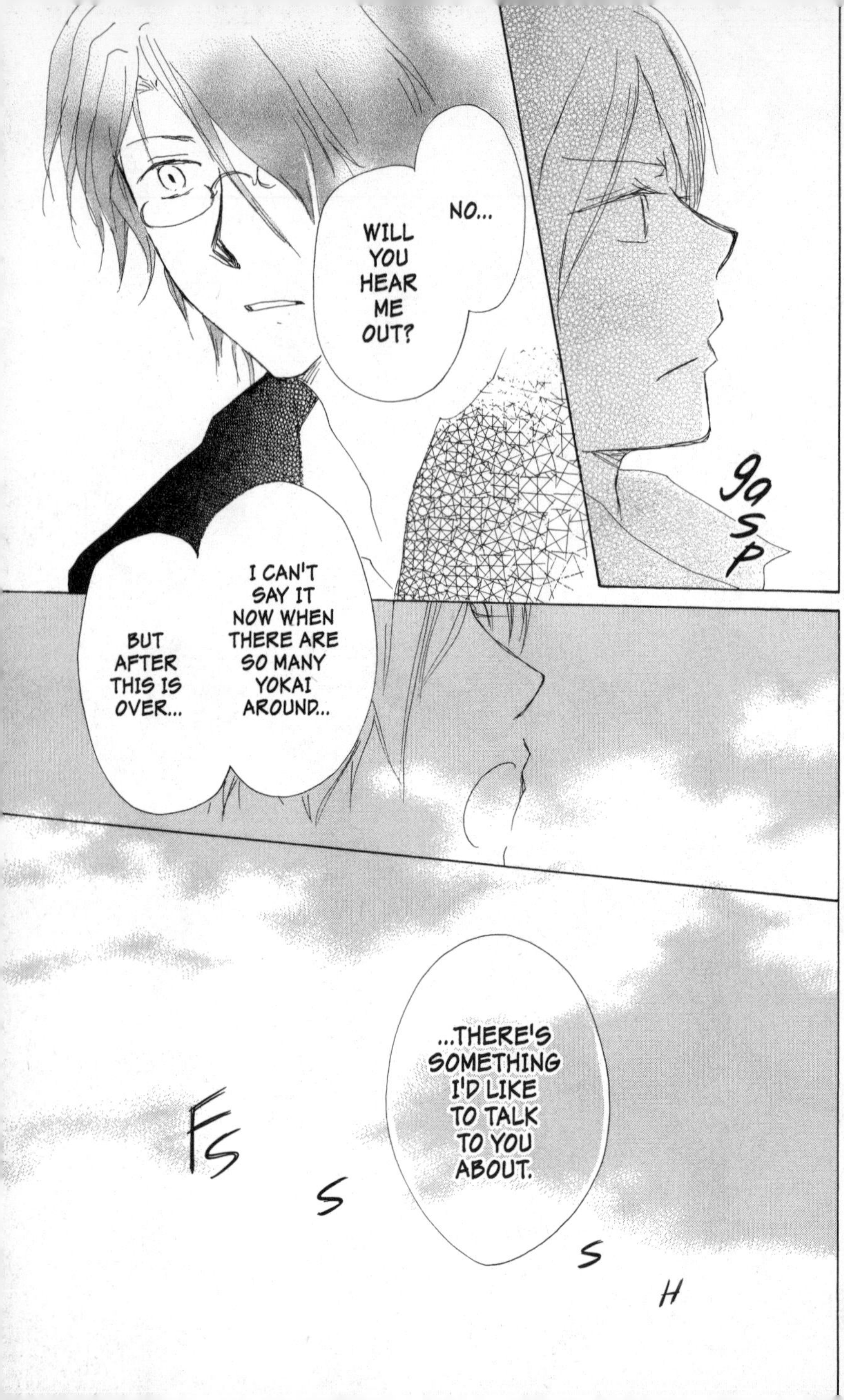
gasp
NO... WILL YOU HEAR ME OUT?
I CAN'T SAY IT NOW WHEN THERE ARE SO MANY YOKAI AROUND... BUT AFTER THIS IS OVER...
...THERE'S SOMETHING I'D LIKE TO TALK TO YOU ABOUT.
FSSSH

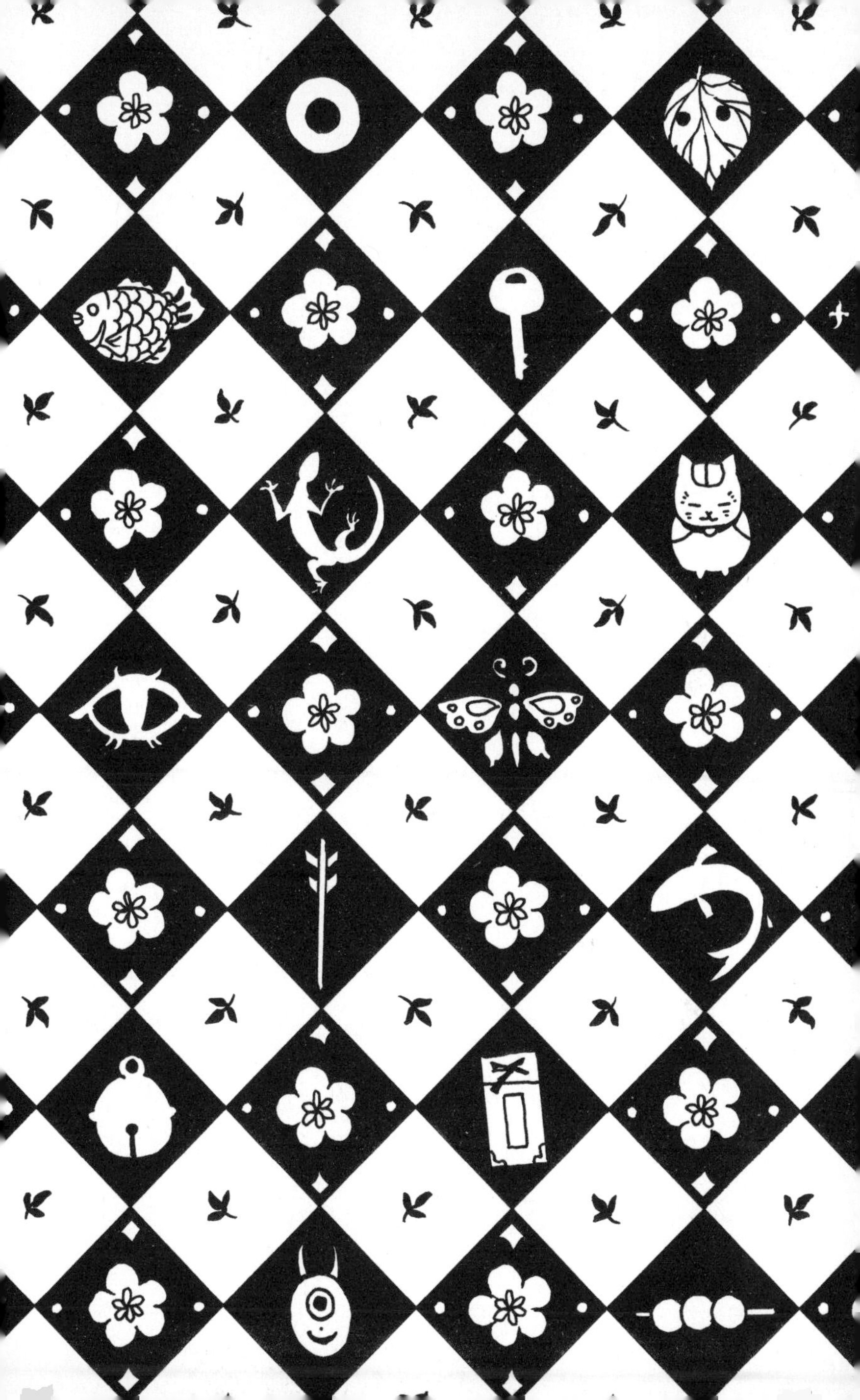

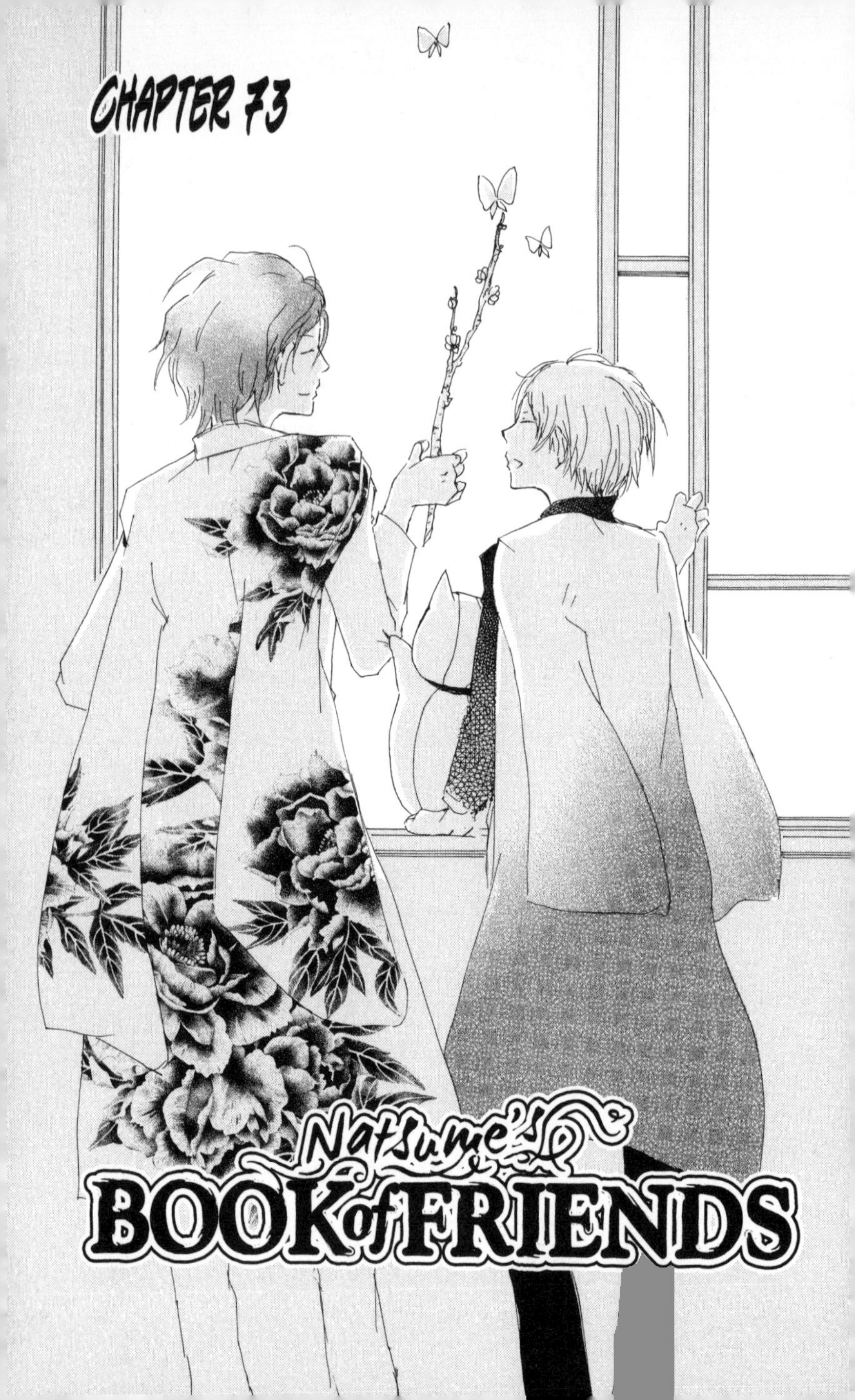
CHAPTER 73
Natsume's
BOOK of FRIENDS

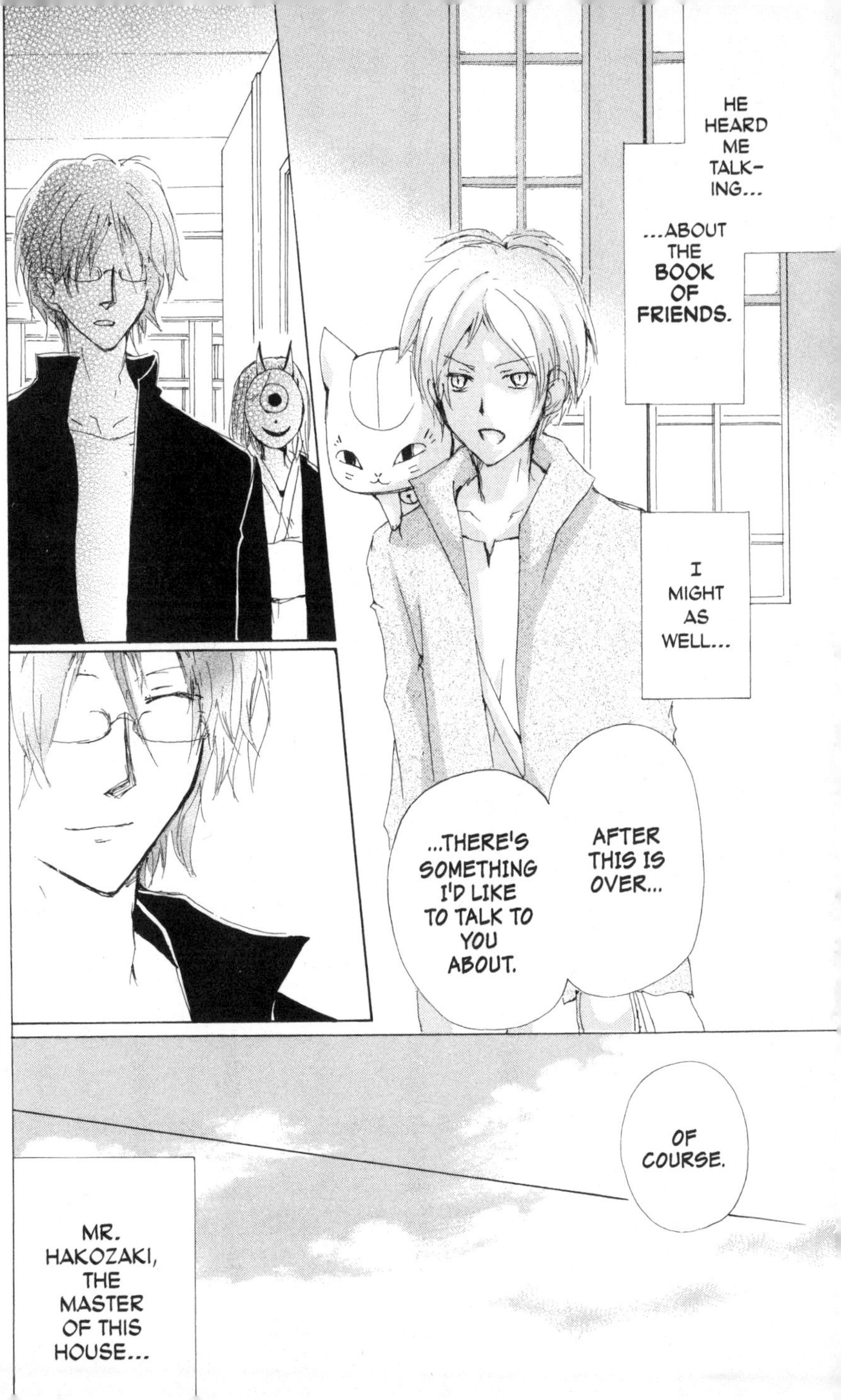
HE HEARD ME TALKING...
...ABOUT THE BOOK OF FRIENDS.
I MIGHT AS WELL...
AFTER THIS IS OVER... ...THERE'S SOMETHING I'D LIKE TO TALK TO YOU ABOUT.
OF COURSE.
MR. HAKOZAKI, THE MASTER OF THIS HOUSE...

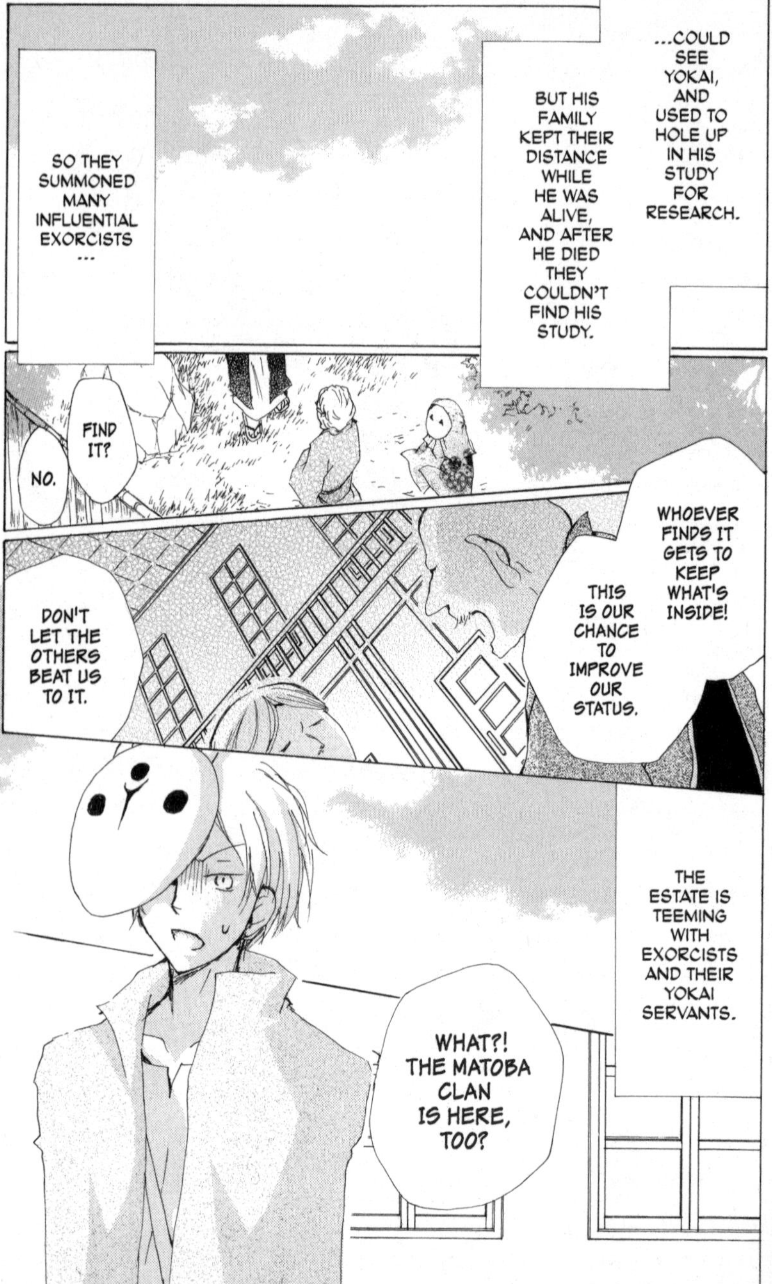
...COULD SEE YOKAI, AND USED TO HOLE UP IN HIS STUDY FOR RESEARCH.
BUT HIS FAMILY KEPT THEIR DISTANCE WHILE HE WAS ALIVE, AND AFTER HE DIED THEY COULDN'T FIND HIS STUDY.
SO THEY SUMMONED MANY INFLUENTIAL EXORCISTS ...
FIND IT?
NO.
WHOEVER FINDS IT GETS TO KEEP WHAT'S INSIDE!
THIS IS OUR CHANCE TO IMPROVE OUR STATUS.
DON'T LET THE OTHERS BEAT US TO IT.
THE ESTATE IS TEEMING WITH EXORCISTS AND THEIR YOKAI SERVANTS.
WHAT?! THE MATOBA CLAN IS HERE, TOO?

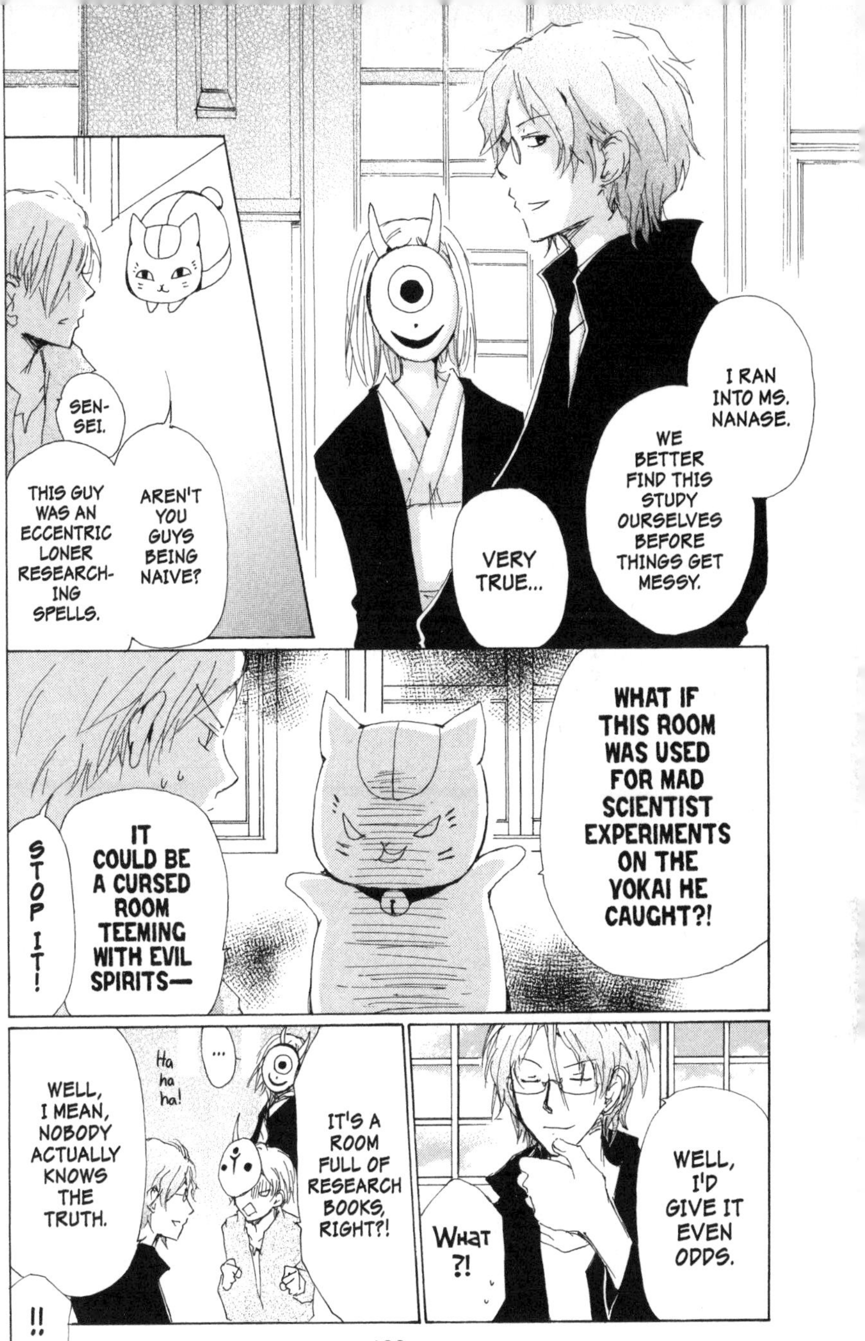
I RAN INTO MS. NANASE.
WE BETTER FIND THIS STUDY OURSELVES BEFORE THINGS GET MESSY.
VERY TRUE...
SEN-SEI.
AREN'T YOU GUYS BEING NAIVE?
THIS GUY WAS AN ECCENTRIC LONER RESEARCH-ING SPELLS.
WHAT IF THIS ROOM WAS USED FOR MAD SCIENTIST EXPERIMENTS ON THE YOKAI HE CAUGHT?!
IT COULD BE A CURSED ROOM TEEMING WITH EVIL SPIRITS—
STOP IT!
WELL, I'D GIVE IT EVEN ODDS.
WHAT ?!
IT'S A ROOM FULL OF RESEARCH BOOKS, RIGHT?!
...
Ha ha ha!
WELL, I MEAN, NOBODY ACTUALLY KNOWS THE TRUTH.
!!

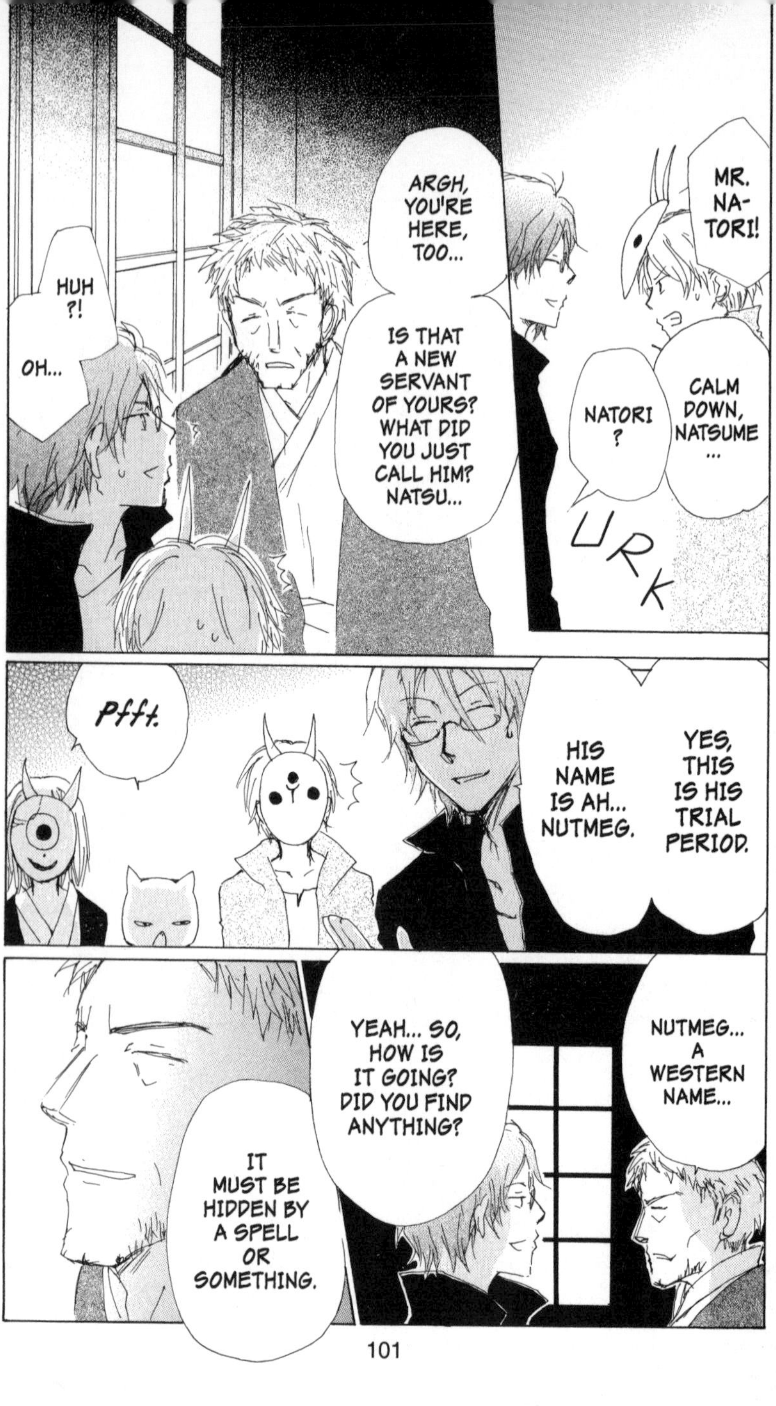
MR. NATORI!
CALM DOWN, NATSUME...
NATORI?
URK
ARGH, YOU'RE HERE, TOO...
IS THAT A NEW SERVANT OF YOURS? WHAT DID YOU JUST CALL HIM? NATSU...
HUH?!
OH...
YES, THIS IS HIS TRIAL PERIOD.
HIS NAME IS AH... NUTMEG.
Pfft.
NUTMEG... A WESTERN NAME...
YEAH... SO, HOW IS IT GOING? DID YOU FIND ANYTHING?
IT MUST BE HIDDEN BY A SPELL OR SOMETHING.

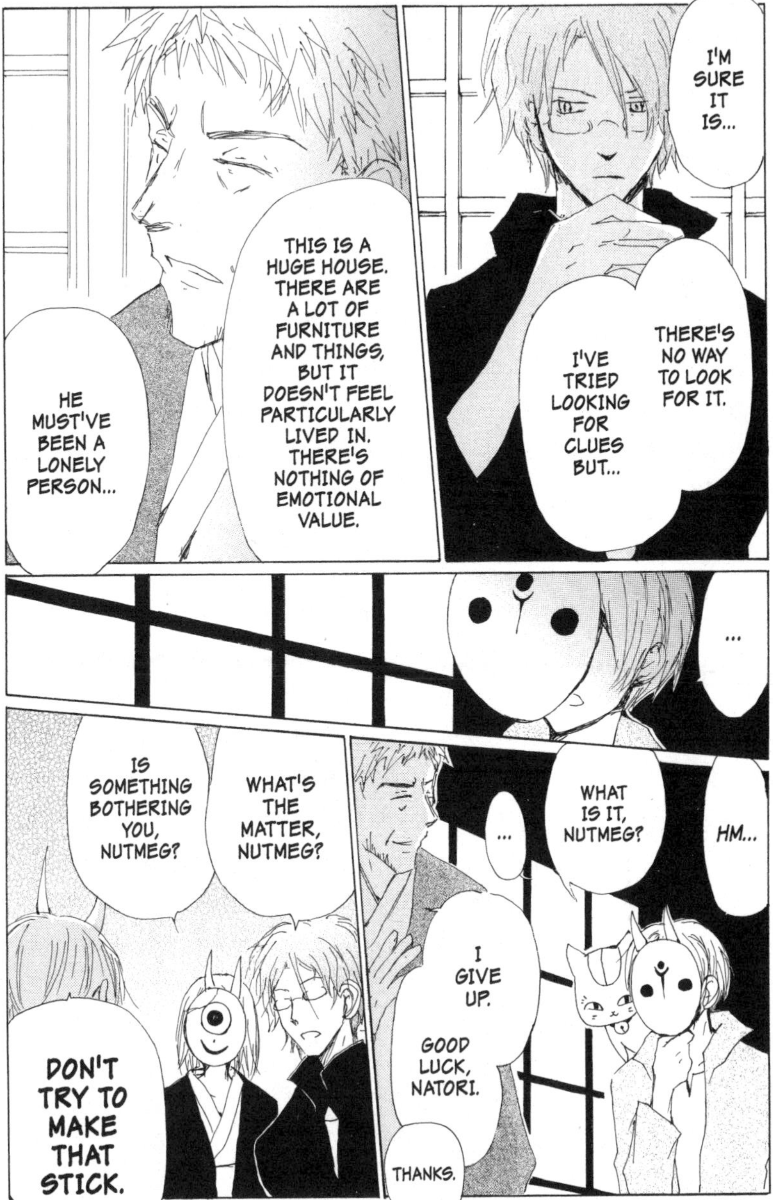

I'M SURE IT IS...
THERE'S NO WAY TO LOOK FOR IT.
I'VE TRIED LOOKING FOR CLUES BUT...
THIS IS A HUGE HOUSE. THERE ARE A LOT OF FURNITURE AND THINGS, BUT IT DOESN'T FEEL PARTICULARLY LIVED IN. THERE'S NOTHING OF EMOTIONAL VALUE.
HE MUST'VE BEEN A LONELY PERSON...
...
HM...
WHAT IS IT, NUTMEG?
...
I GIVE UP.
GOOD LUCK, NATORI.
THANKS.
WHAT'S THE MATTER, NUTMEG?
IS SOMETHING BOTHERING YOU, NUTMEG?
DON'T TRY TO MAKE THAT STICK.

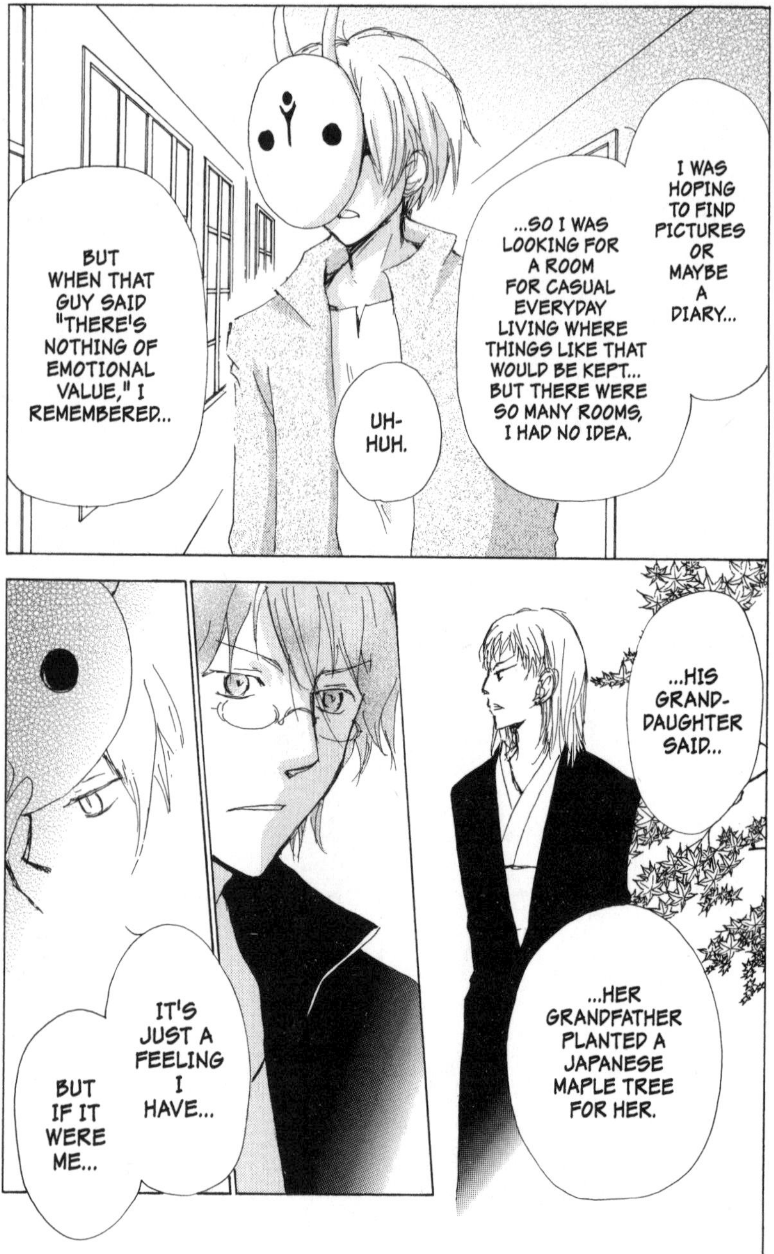
I WAS HOPING TO FIND PICTURES OR MAYBE A DIARY...
...SO I WAS LOOKING FOR A ROOM FOR CASUAL EVERYDAY LIVING WHERE THINGS LIKE THAT WOULD BE KEPT... BUT THERE WERE SO MANY ROOMS, I HAD NO IDEA.
UH-HUH.
BUT WHEN THAT GUY SAID "THERE'S NOTHING OF EMOTIONAL VALUE," I REMEMBERED...
...HIS GRAND-DAUGHTER SAID...
...HER GRANDFATHER PLANTED A JAPANESE MAPLE TREE FOR HER.
IT'S JUST A FEELING I HAVE...
BUT IF IT WERE ME...

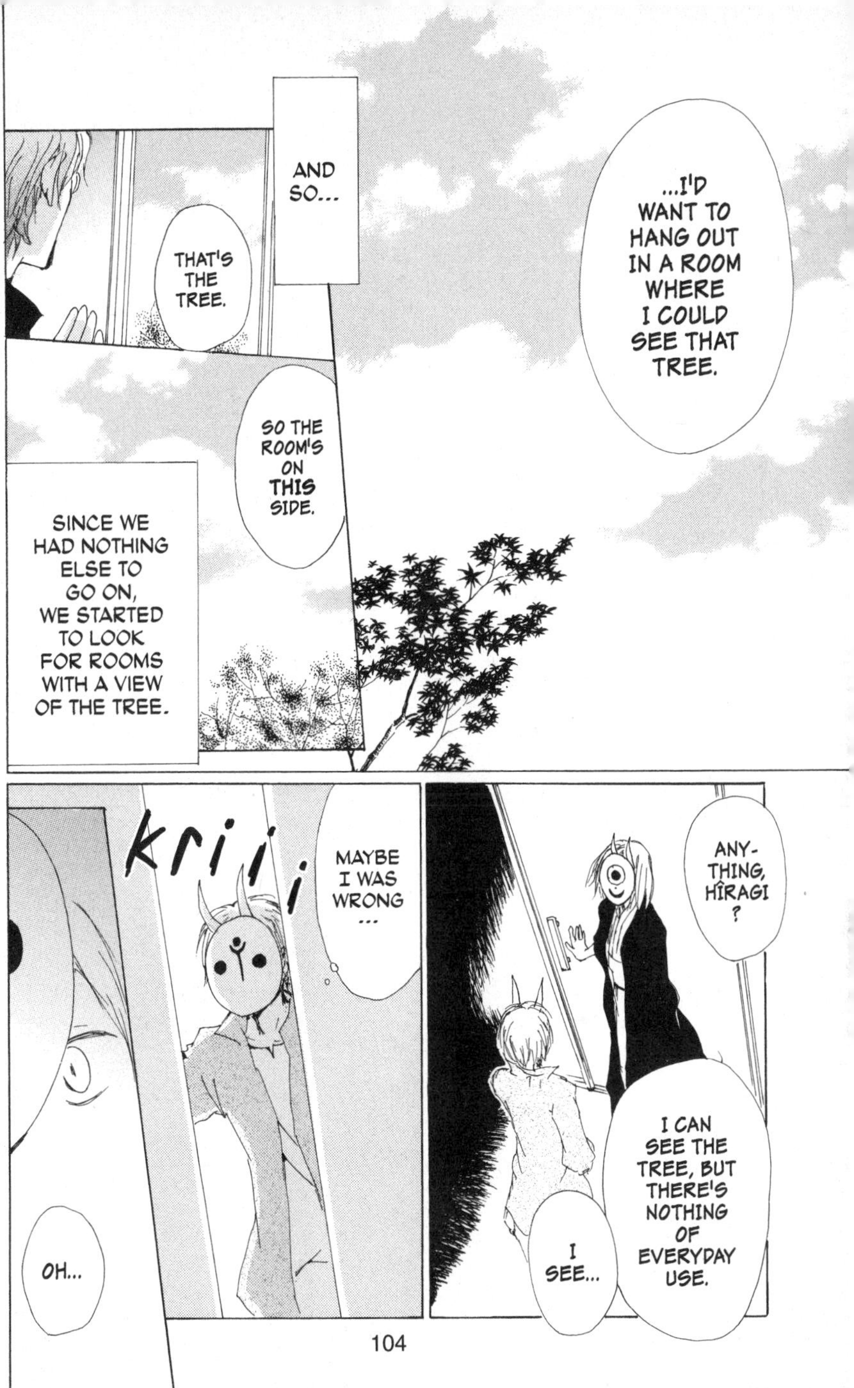
...I'D WANT TO HANG OUT IN A ROOM WHERE I COULD SEE THAT TREE.
AND SO...
THAT'S THE TREE.
SO THE ROOM'S ON THIS SIDE.
SINCE WE HAD NOTHING ELSE TO GO ON, WE STARTED TO LOOK FOR ROOMS WITH A VIEW OF THE TREE.
ANY-THING, HÎRAGI?
I CAN SEE THE TREE, BUT THERE'S NOTHING OF EVERYDAY USE.
I SEE...
kriii
MAYBE I WAS WRONG...
OH...

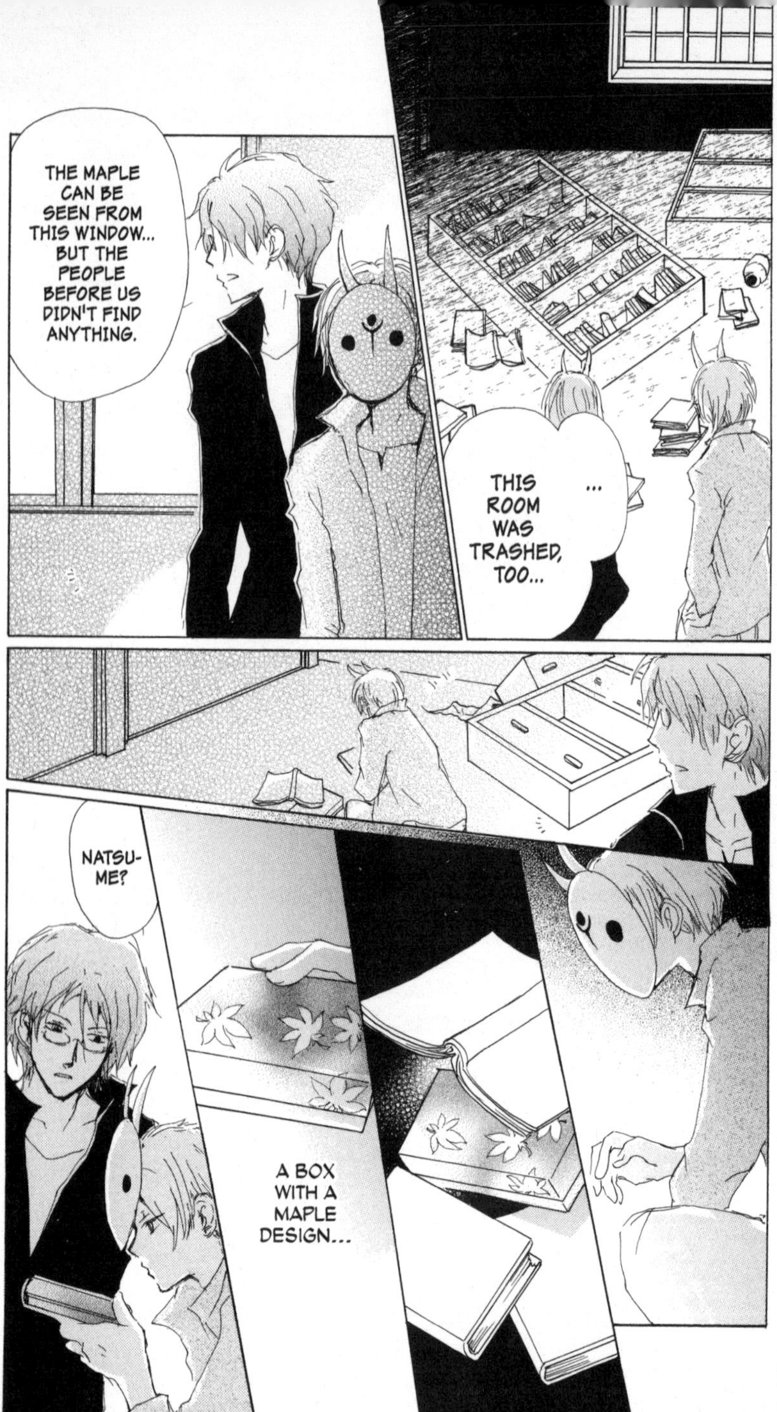
...
THIS ROOM WAS TRASHED, TOO...
THE MAPLE CAN BE SEEN FROM THIS WINDOW... BUT THE PEOPLE BEFORE US DIDN'T FIND ANYTHING.
A BOX WITH A MAPLE DESIGN...
NATSU-ME?

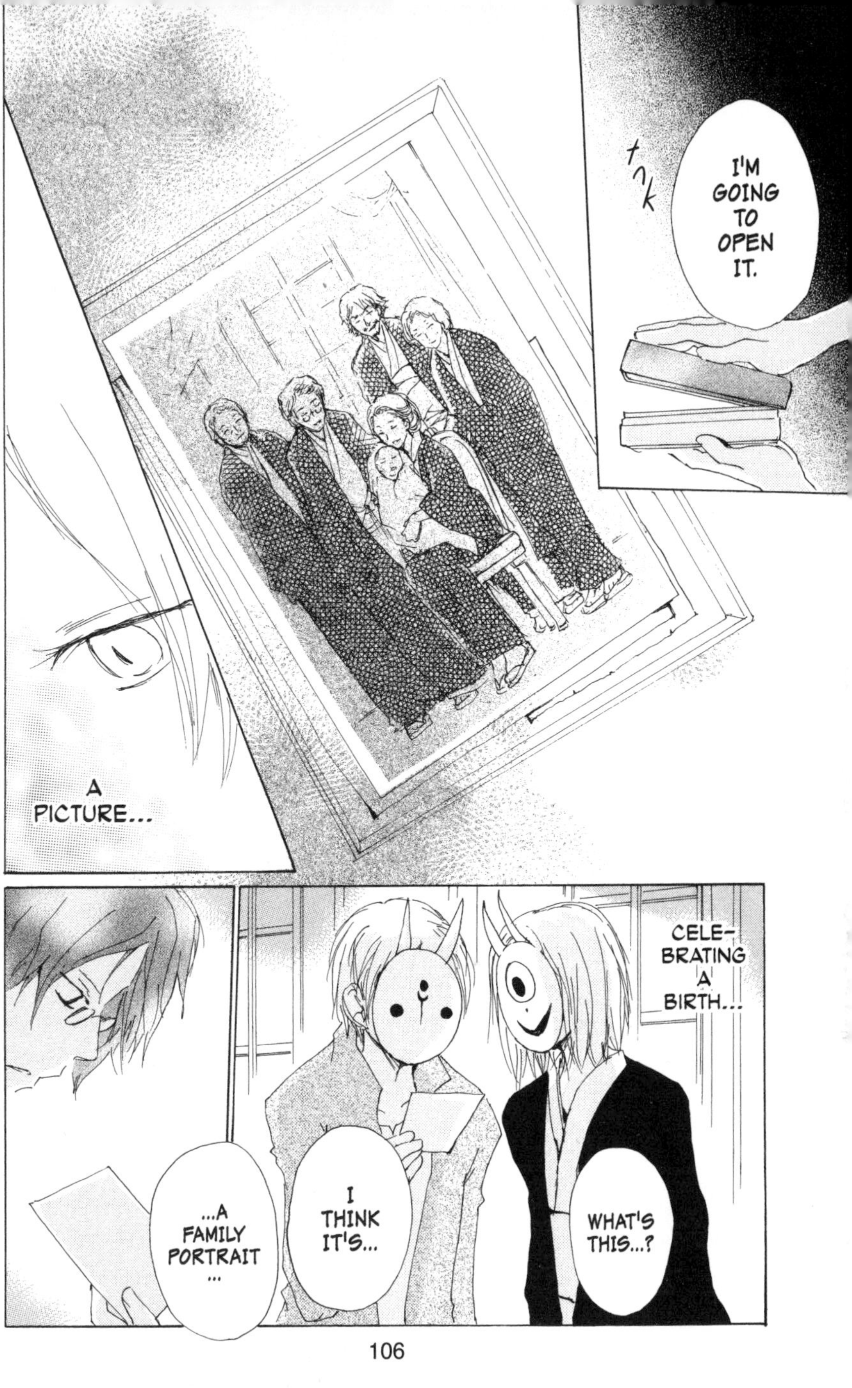
tak
I'M GOING TO OPEN IT.
A PICTURE...
CELE-BRATING A BIRTH...
WHAT'S THIS...?
I THINK IT'S...
...A FAMILY PORTRAIT ...

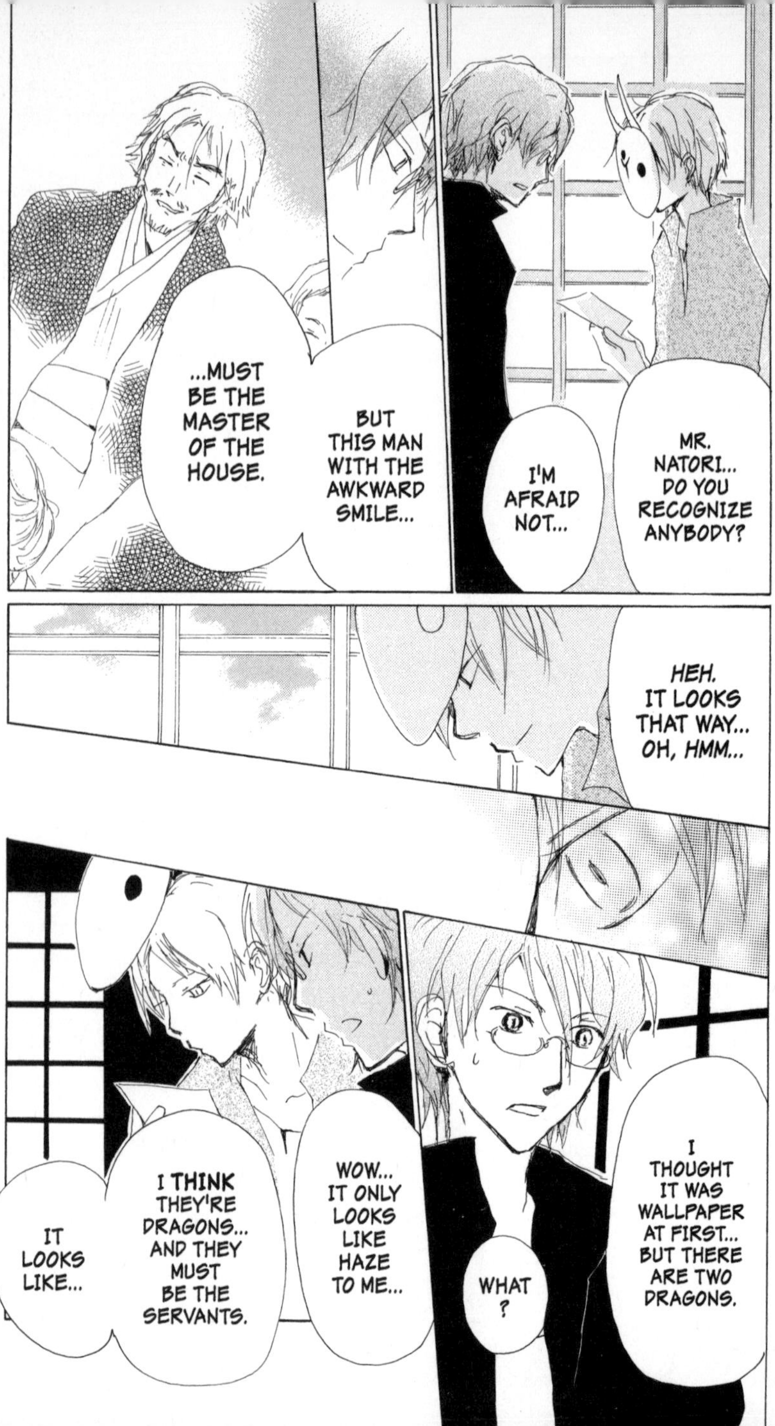
MR. NATORI... DO YOU RECOGNIZE ANYBODY?
I'M AFRAID NOT...
BUT THIS MAN WITH THE AWKWARD SMILE...
...MUST BE THE MASTER OF THE HOUSE.
HEH. IT LOOKS THAT WAY... OH, HMM...
I THOUGHT IT WAS WALLPAPER AT FIRST... BUT THERE ARE TWO DRAGONS.
WHAT?
WOW... IT ONLY LOOKS LIKE HAZE TO ME...
I THINK THEY'RE DRAGONS... AND THEY MUST BE THE SERVANTS.
IT LOOKS LIKE...

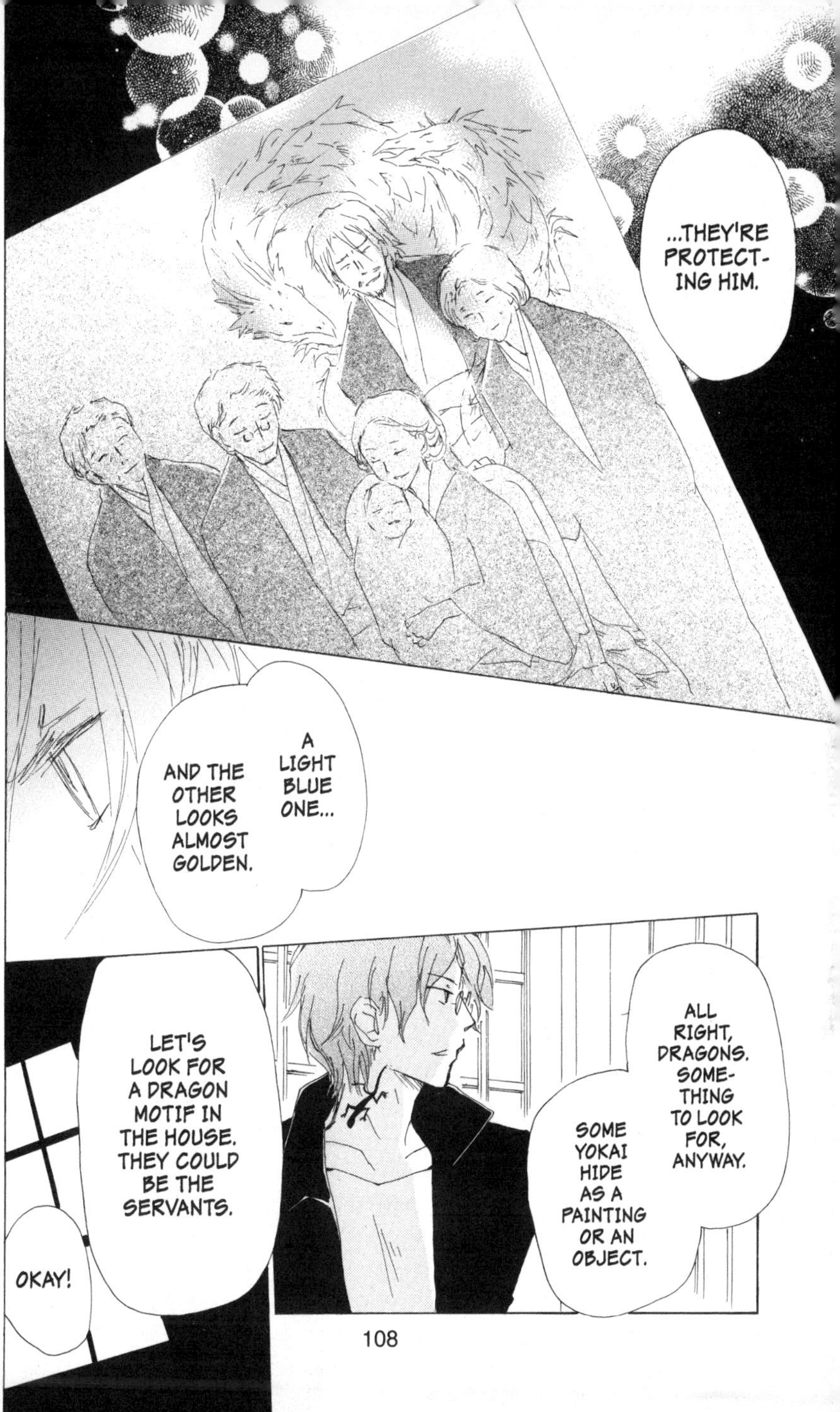
...THEY'RE PROTECTING HIM.
A LIGHT BLUE ONE...
AND THE OTHER LOOKS ALMOST GOLDEN.
ALL RIGHT, DRAGONS. SOMETHING TO LOOK FOR, ANYWAY.
SOME YOKAI HIDE AS A PAINTING OR AN OBJECT.
LET'S LOOK FOR A DRAGON MOTIF IN THE HOUSE. THEY COULD BE THE SERVANTS.
OKAY!

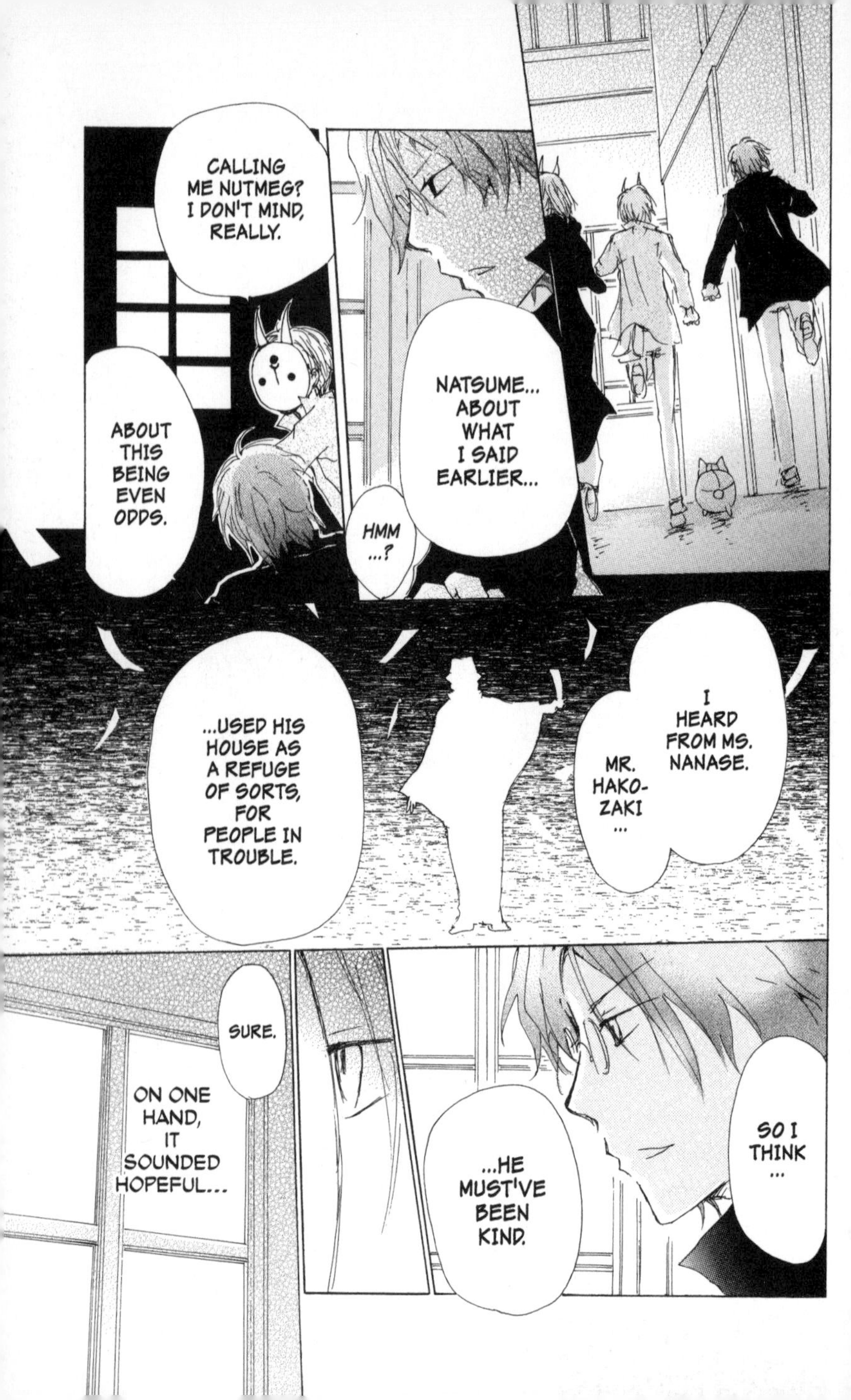
NATSUME... ABOUT WHAT I SAID EARLIER...
HMM ...?
CALLING ME NUTMEG? I DON'T MIND, REALLY.
ABOUT THIS BEING EVEN ODDS.
I HEARD FROM MS. NANASE.
MR. HAKOZAKI ...
...USED HIS HOUSE AS A REFUGE OF SORTS, FOR PEOPLE IN TROUBLE.
SO I THINK ...
...HE MUST'VE BEEN KIND.
SURE.
ON ONE HAND, IT SOUNDED HOPEFUL...

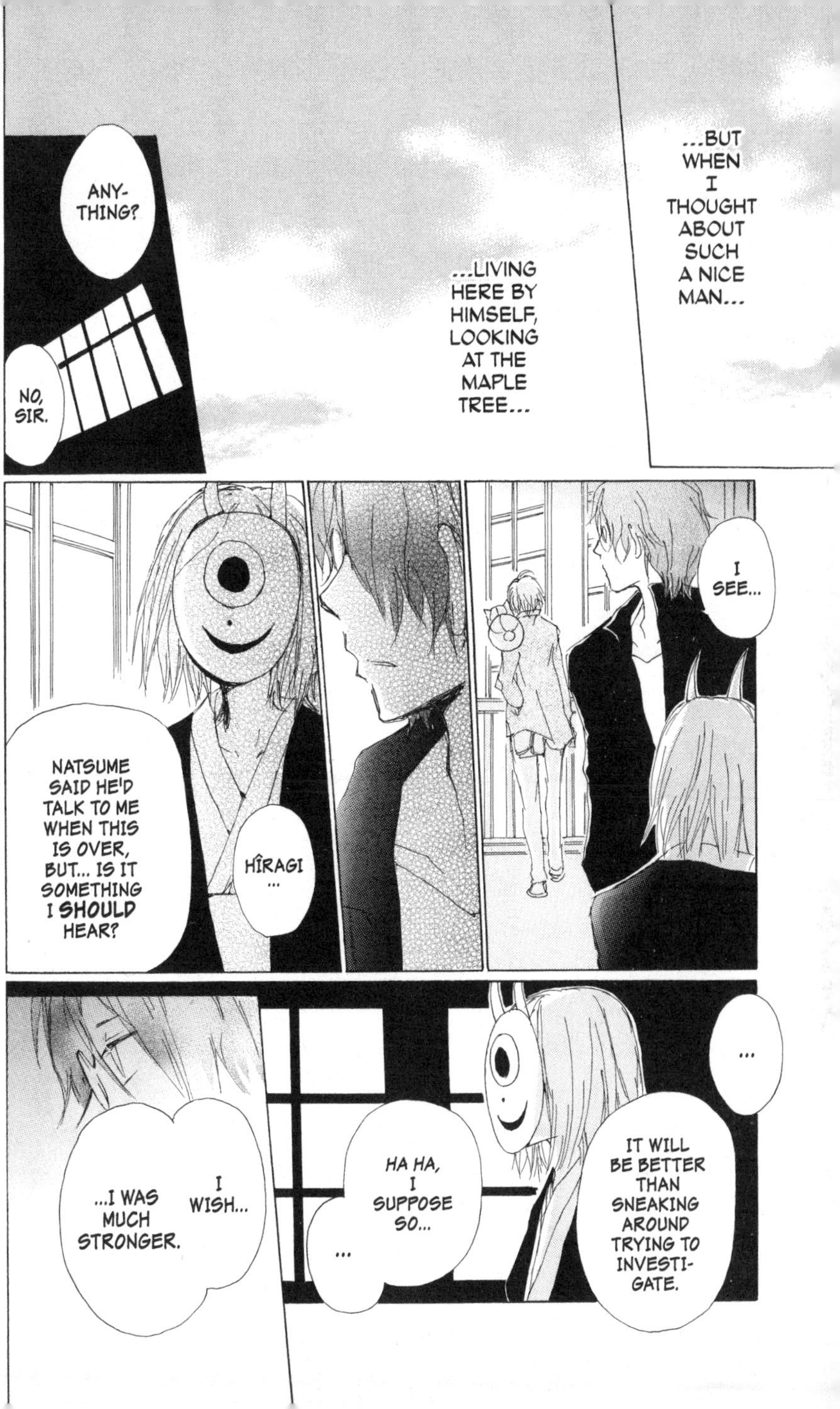
...BUT WHEN I THOUGHT ABOUT SUCH A NICE MAN...
...LIVING HERE BY HIMSELF, LOOKING AT THE MAPLE TREE...
ANY-THING?
NO, SIR.
I SEE...
HÎRAGI ...
NATSUME SAID HE'D TALK TO ME WHEN THIS IS OVER, BUT... IS IT SOMETHING I **SHOULD** HEAR?
...
IT WILL BE BETTER THAN SNEAKING AROUND TRYING TO INVESTI-GATE.
HA HA, I SUPPOSE SO...
...
I WISH...
...I WAS MUCH STRONGER.

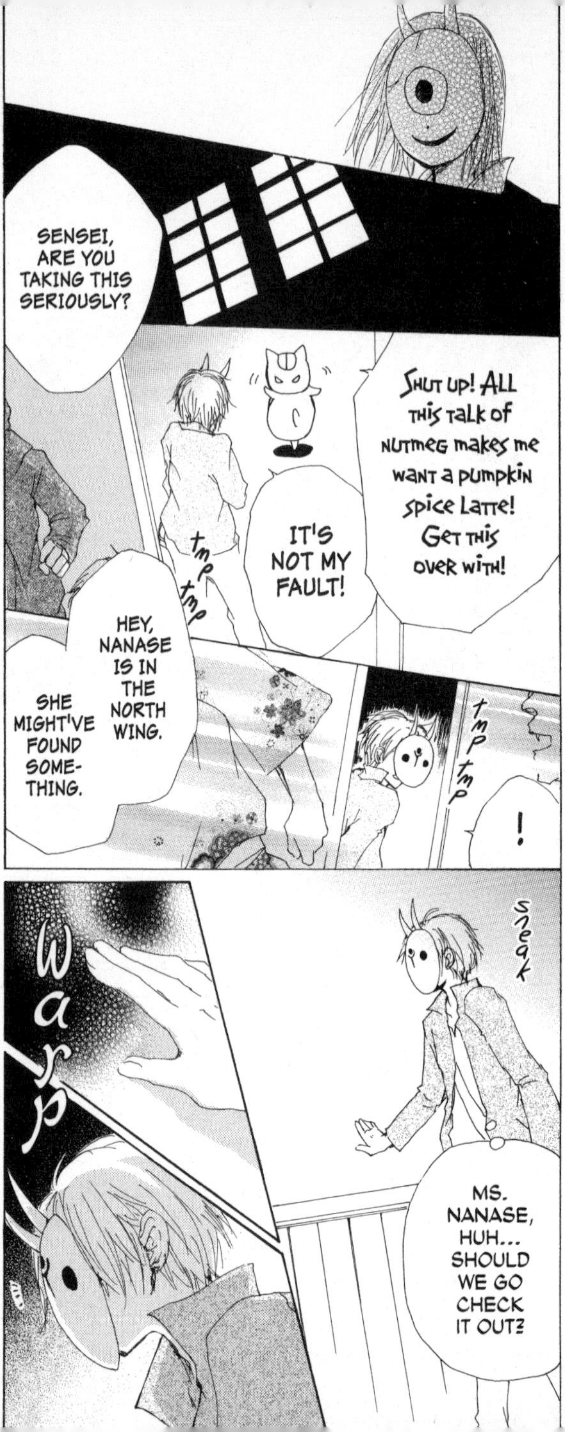
SENSEI, ARE YOU TAKING THIS SERIOUSLY?
SHUT UP! ALL THIS TALK OF NUTMEG MAKES ME WANT A PUMPKIN SPICE LATTE! GET THIS OVER WITH!
IT'S NOT MY FAULT!
tmp tmp
tmp tmp
!
HEY, NANASE IS IN THE NORTH WING.
SHE MIGHT'VE FOUND SOMETHING.
sneak
MS. NANASE, HUH... SHOULD WE GO CHECK IT OUT?
warp

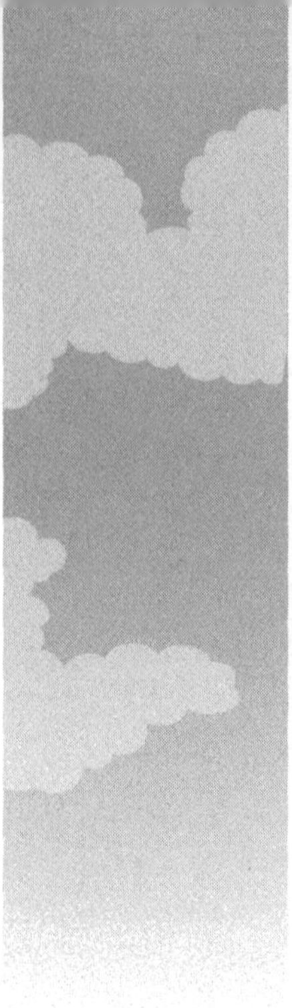

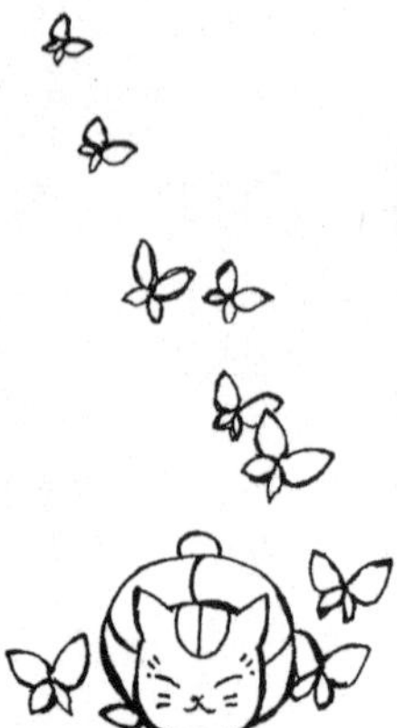

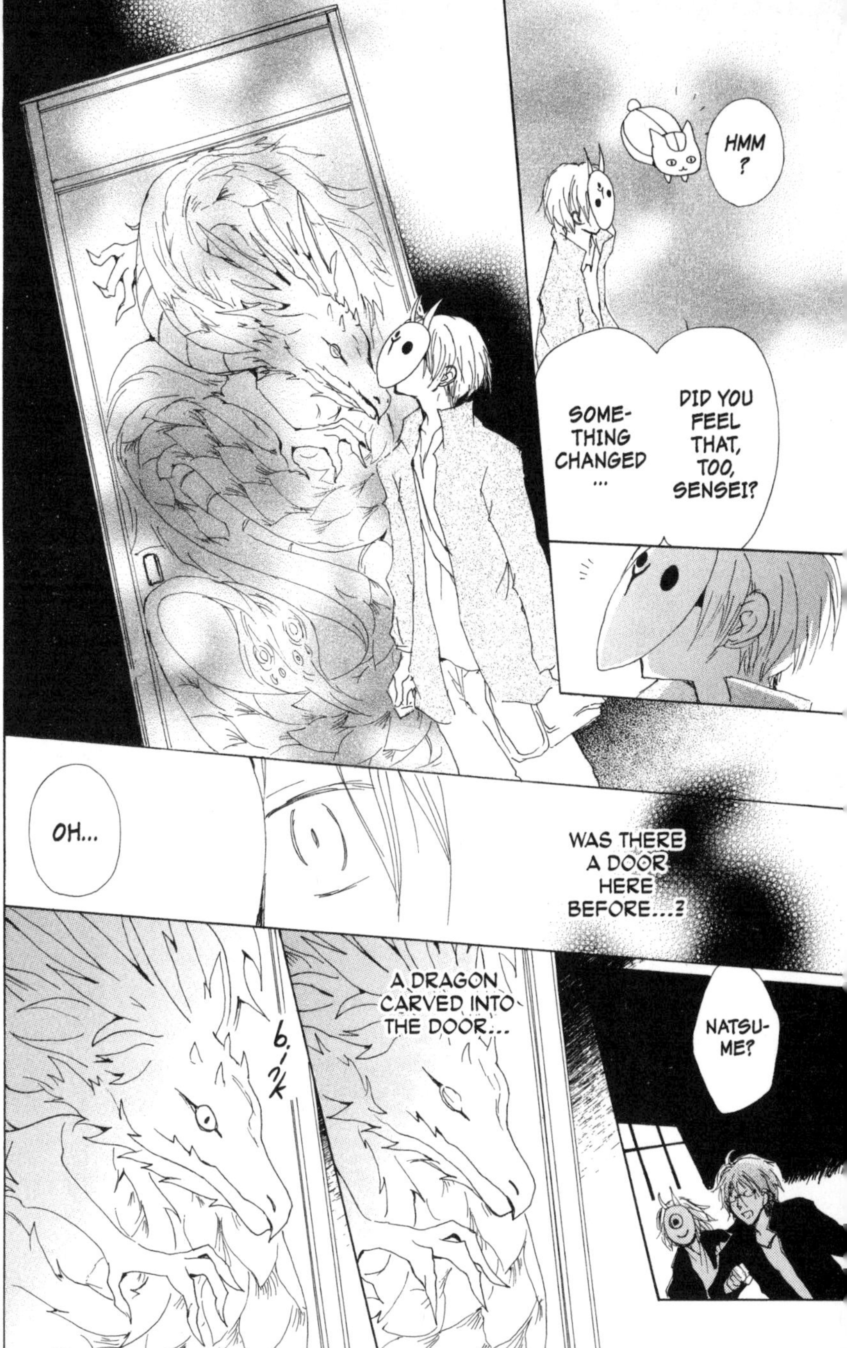
HMM?
DID YOU FEEL THAT, TOO, SENSEI?
SOMETHING CHANGED...
WAS THERE A DOOR HERE BEFORE...?
OH...
NATSUME?
A DRAGON CARVED INTO THE DOOR...
blink

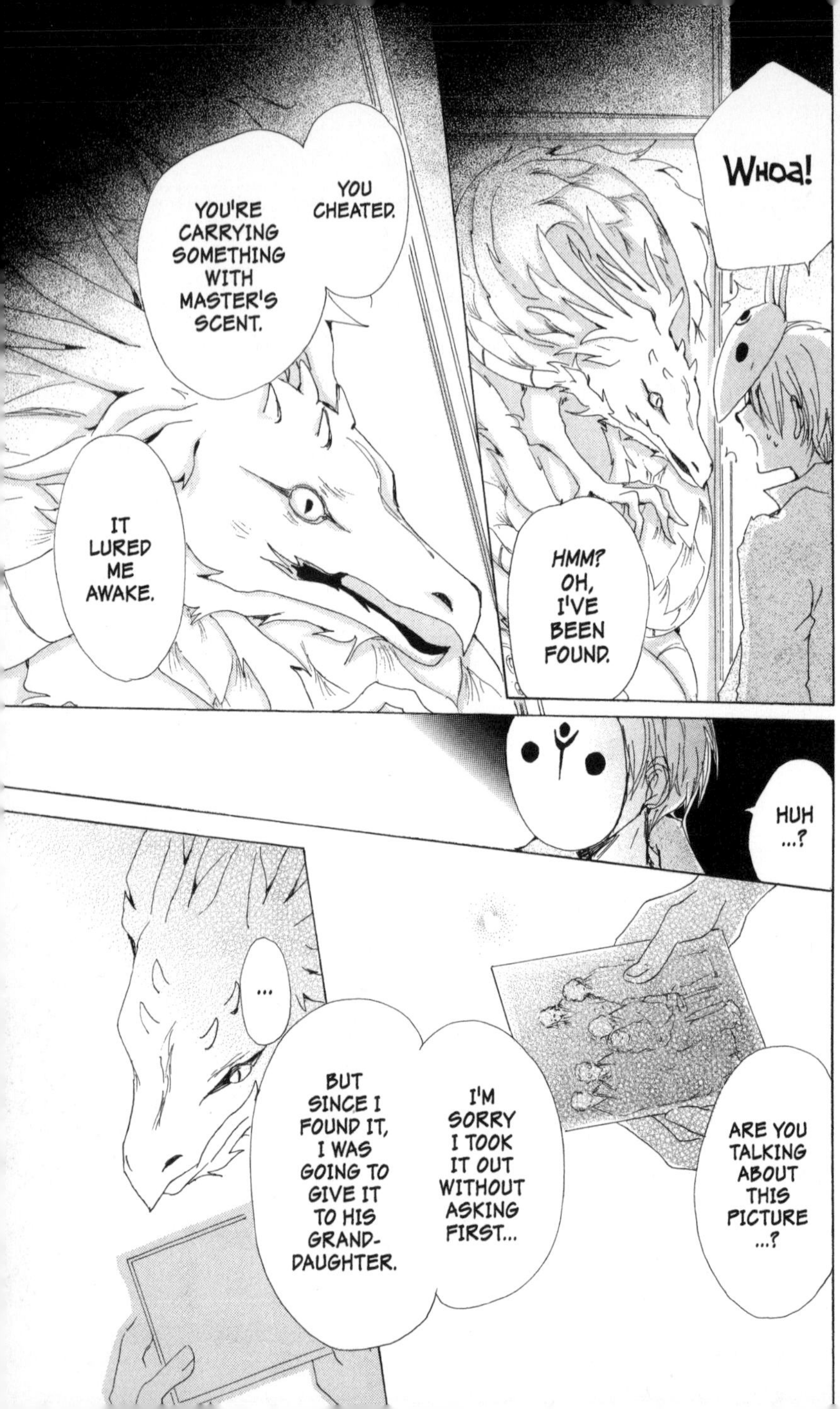
WHOA!
HMM? OH, I'VE BEEN FOUND.
YOU CHEATED.
YOU'RE CARRYING SOMETHING WITH MASTER'S SCENT.
IT LURED ME AWAKE.
HUH ...?
ARE YOU TALKING ABOUT THIS PICTURE ...?
I'M SORRY I TOOK IT OUT WITHOUT ASKING FIRST...
BUT SINCE I FOUND IT, I WAS GOING TO GIVE IT TO HIS GRAND-DAUGHTER.
...

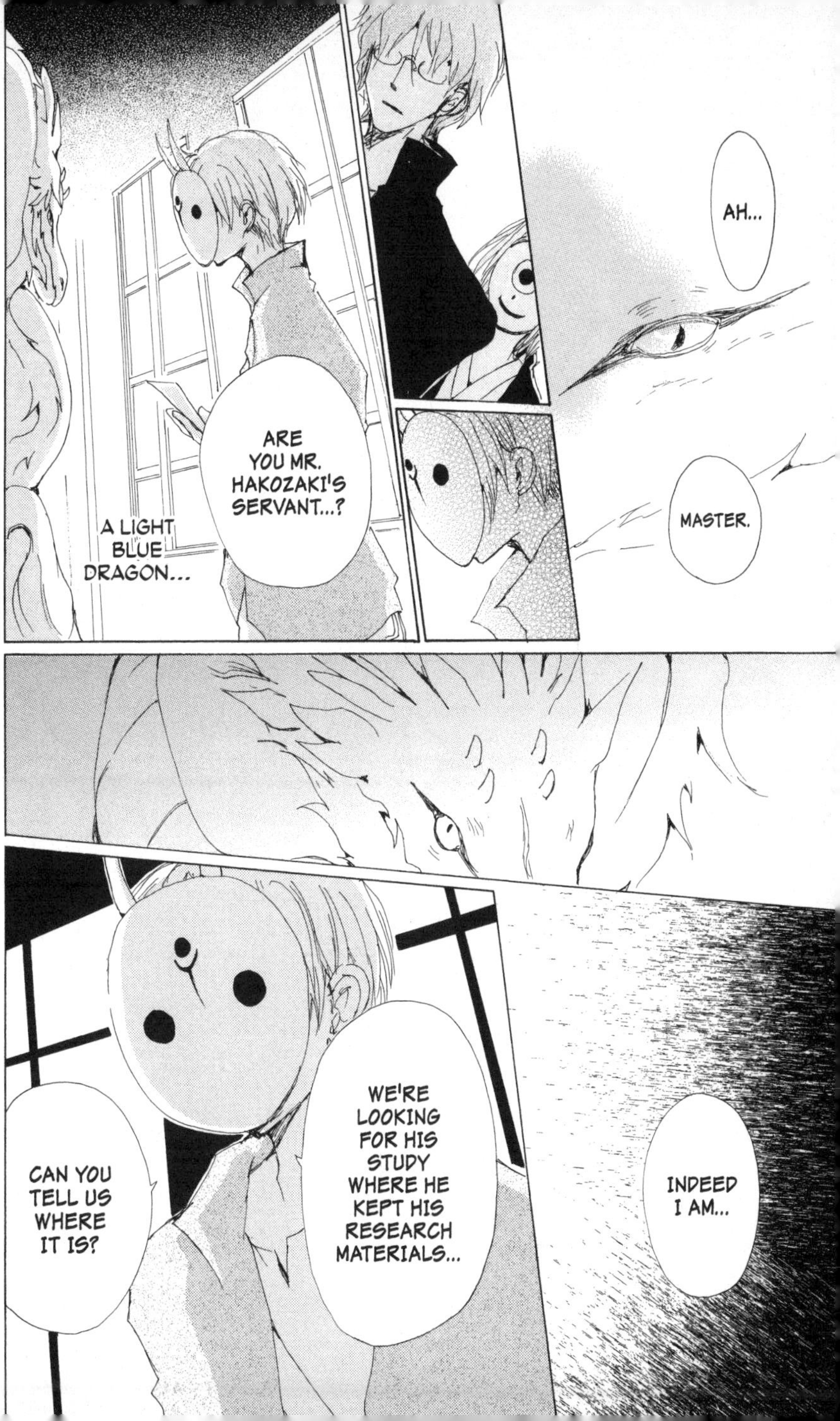
AH...
MASTER.
ARE YOU MR. HAKOZAKI'S SERVANT...?
A LIGHT BLUE DRAGON...
INDEED I AM...
WE'RE LOOKING FOR HIS STUDY WHERE HE KEPT HIS RESEARCH MATERIALS...
CAN YOU TELL US WHERE IT IS?

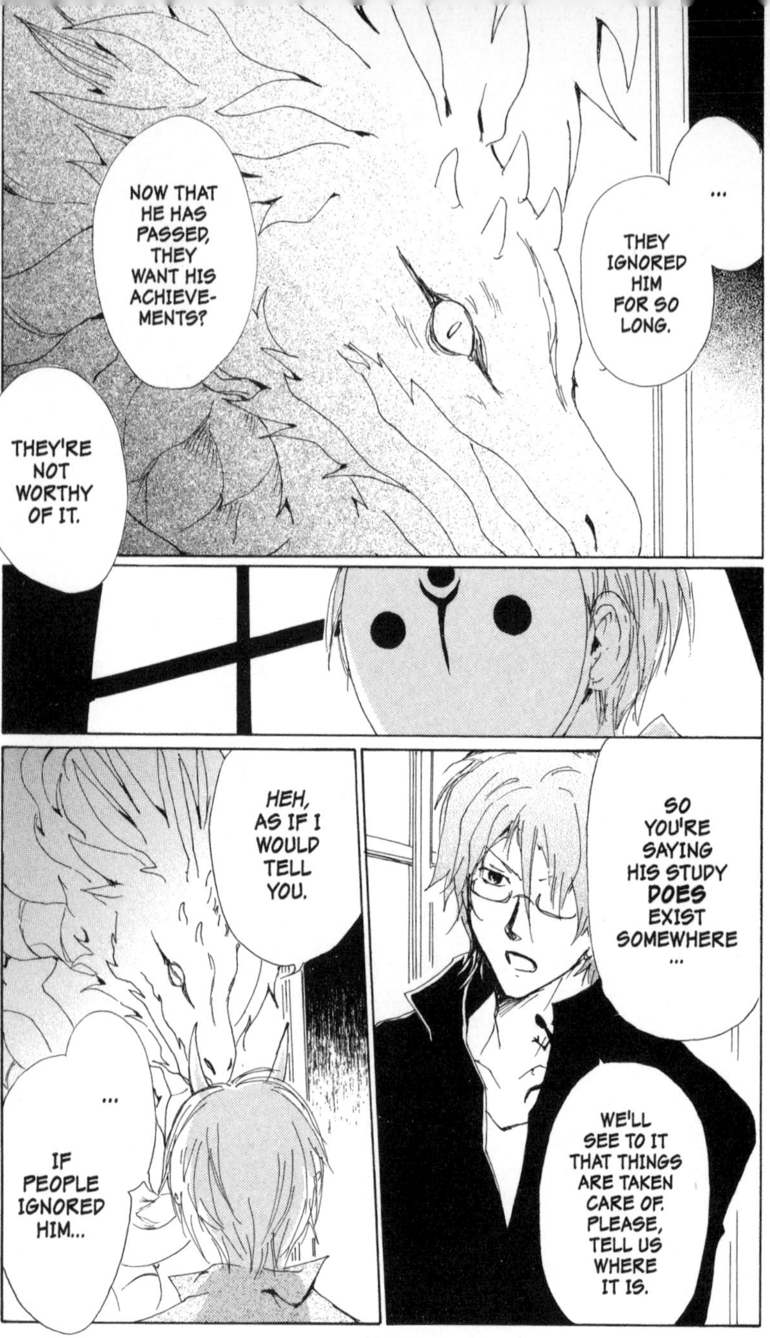
... THEY IGNORED HIM FOR SO LONG.
NOW THAT HE HAS PASSED, THEY WANT HIS ACHIEVEMENTS?
THEY'RE NOT WORTHY OF IT.
SO YOU'RE SAYING HIS STUDY DOES EXIST SOMEWHERE...
WE'LL SEE TO IT THAT THINGS ARE TAKEN CARE OF. PLEASE, TELL US WHERE IT IS.
HEH, AS IF I WOULD TELL YOU.
... IF PEOPLE IGNORED HIM...

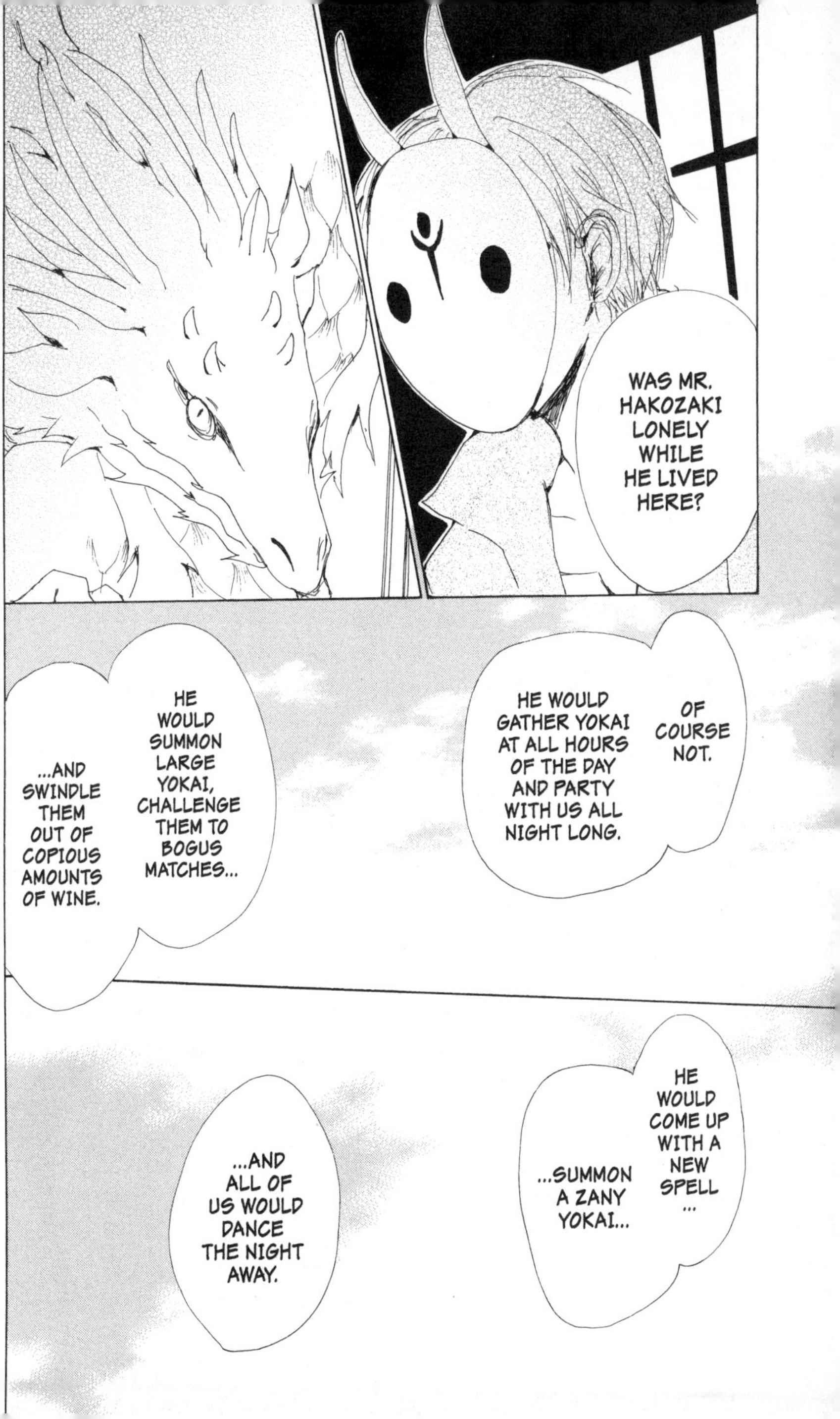
WAS MR. HAKOZAKI LONELY WHILE HE LIVED HERE?
OF COURSE NOT.
HE WOULD GATHER YOKAI AT ALL HOURS OF THE DAY AND PARTY WITH US ALL NIGHT LONG.
HE WOULD SUMMON LARGE YOKAI, CHALLENGE THEM TO BOGUS MATCHES...
...AND SWINDLE THEM OUT OF COPIOUS AMOUNTS OF WINE.
HE WOULD COME UP WITH A NEW SPELL ...
...SUMMON A ZANY YOKAI...
...AND ALL OF US WOULD DANCE THE NIGHT AWAY.

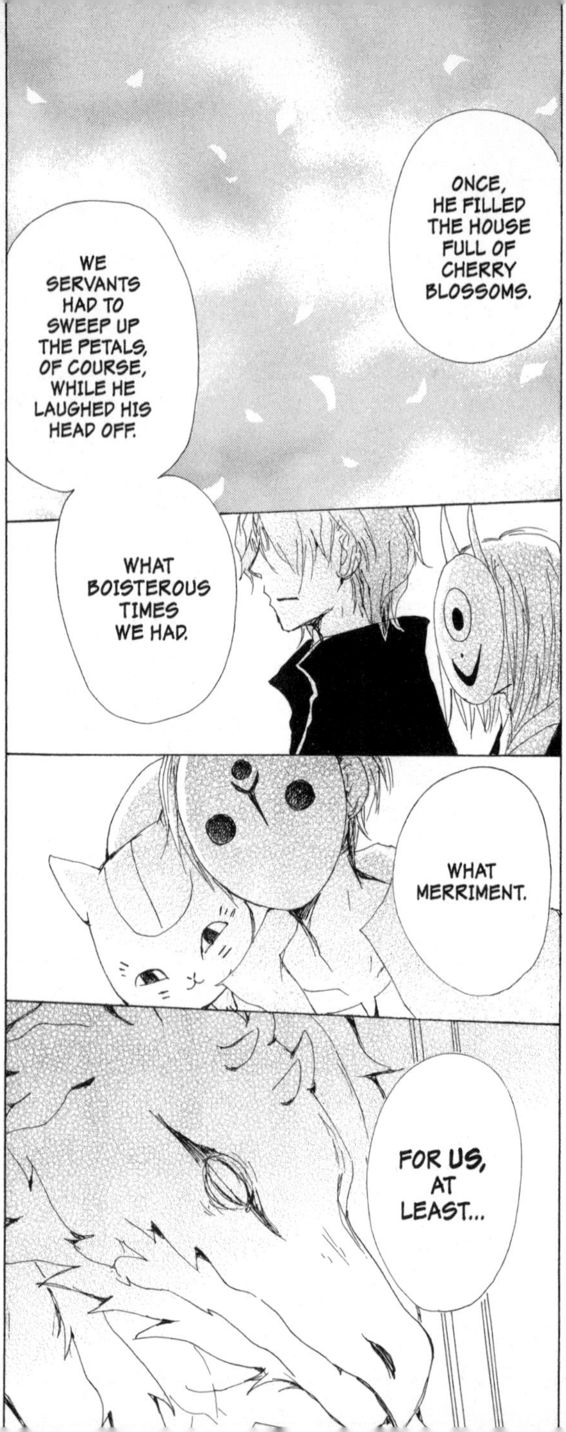
ONCE, HE FILLED THE HOUSE FULL OF CHERRY BLOSSOMS.
WE SERVANTS HAD TO SWEEP UP THE PETALS, OF COURSE, WHILE HE LAUGHED HIS HEAD OFF.
WHAT BOISTEROUS TIMES WE HAD.
WHAT MERRIMENT.
FOR US, AT LEAST...
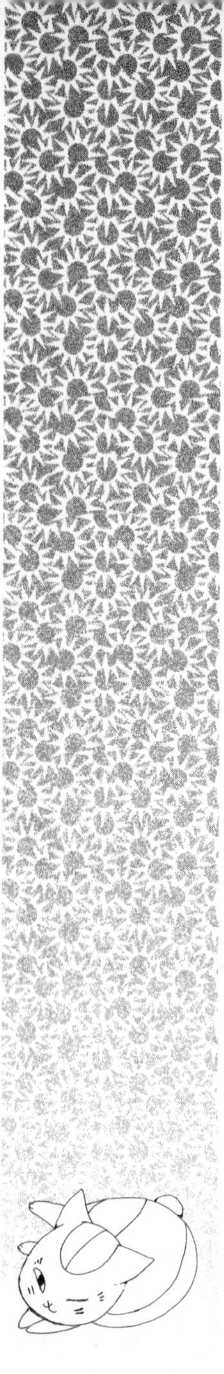

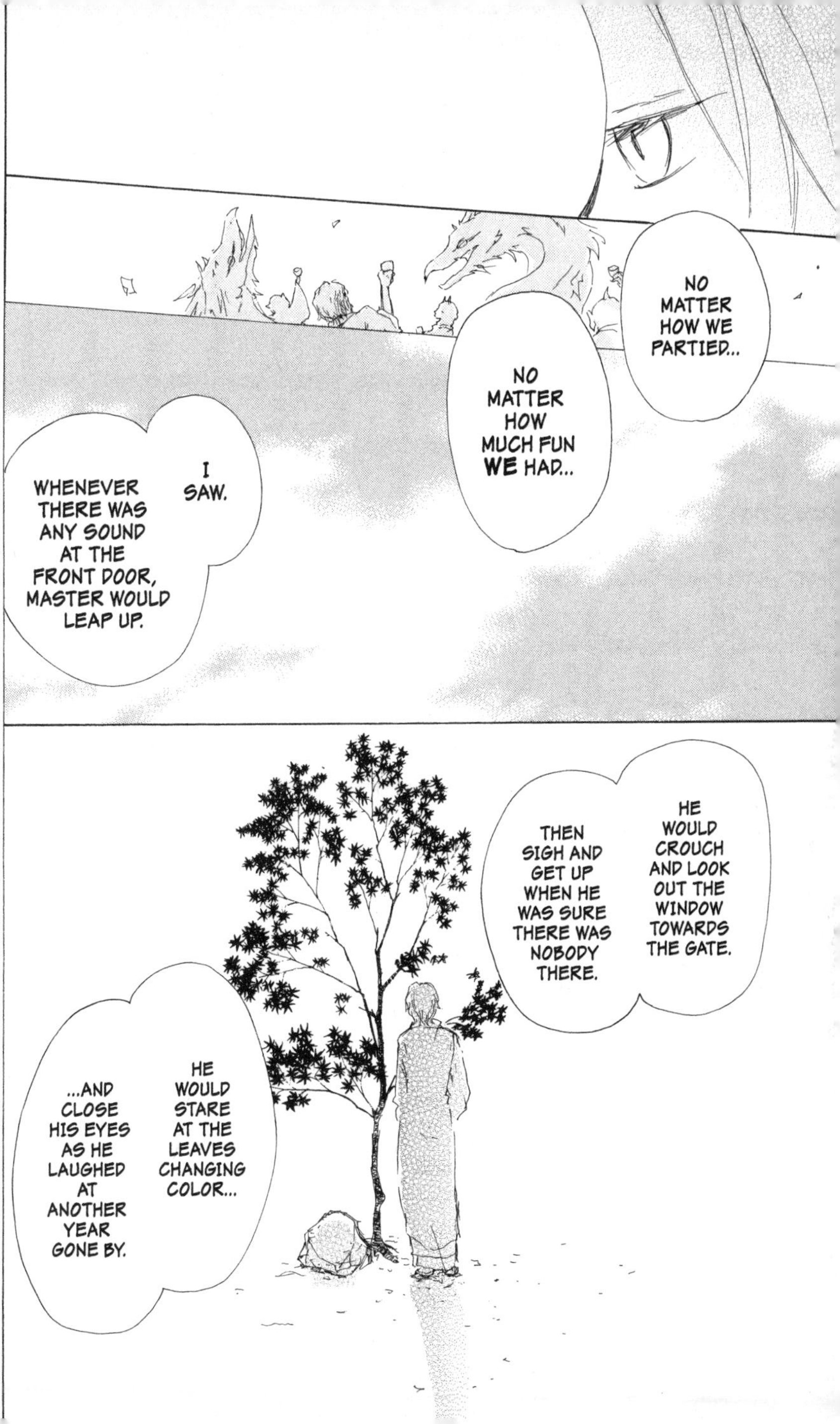
NO MATTER HOW WE PARTIED...
NO MATTER HOW MUCH FUN **WE** HAD...
I SAW.
WHENEVER THERE WAS ANY SOUND AT THE FRONT DOOR, MASTER WOULD LEAP UP.
HE WOULD CROUCH AND LOOK OUT THE WINDOW TOWARDS THE GATE.
THEN SIGH AND GET UP WHEN HE WAS SURE THERE WAS NOBODY THERE.
HE WOULD STARE AT THE LEAVES CHANGING COLOR...
...AND CLOSE HIS EYES AS HE LAUGHED AT ANOTHER YEAR GONE BY.

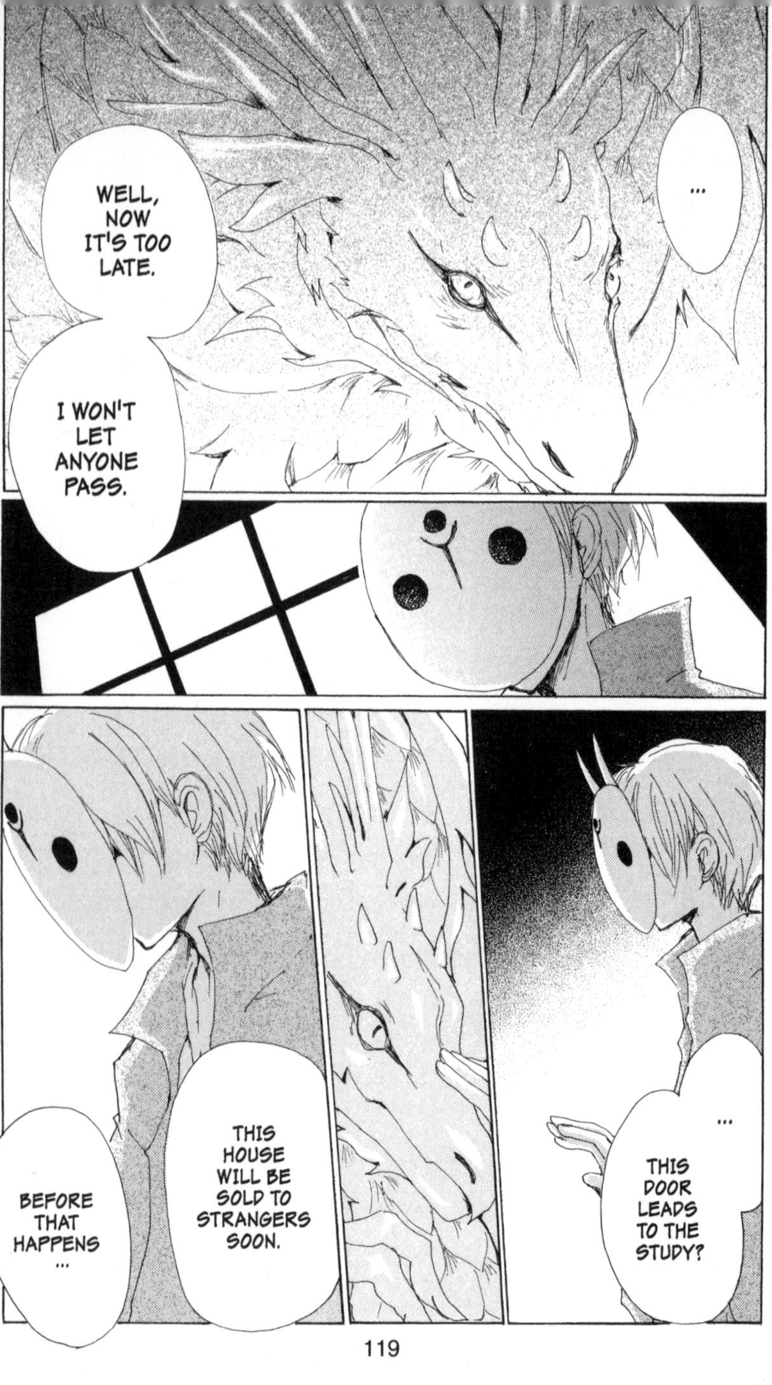
...
WELL, NOW IT'S TOO LATE.
I WON'T LET ANYONE PASS.
...
THIS DOOR LEADS TO THE STUDY?
THIS HOUSE WILL BE SOLD TO STRANGERS SOON.
BEFORE THAT HAPPENS ...

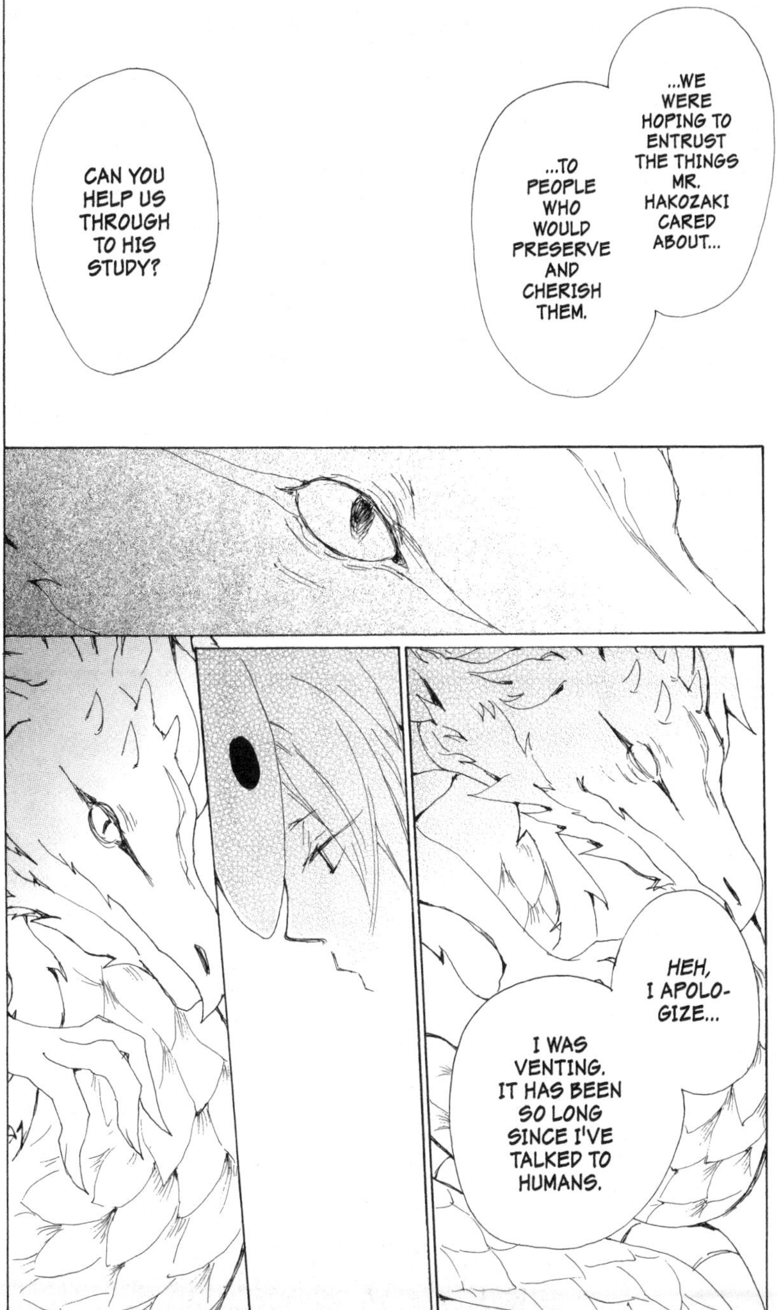
...WE WERE HOPING TO ENTRUST THE THINGS MR. HAKOZAKI CARED ABOUT...
...TO PEOPLE WHO WOULD PRESERVE AND CHERISH THEM.
CAN YOU HELP US THROUGH TO HIS STUDY?
HEH, I APOLO-GIZE...
I WAS VENTING. IT HAS BEEN SO LONG SINCE I'VE TALKED TO HUMANS.

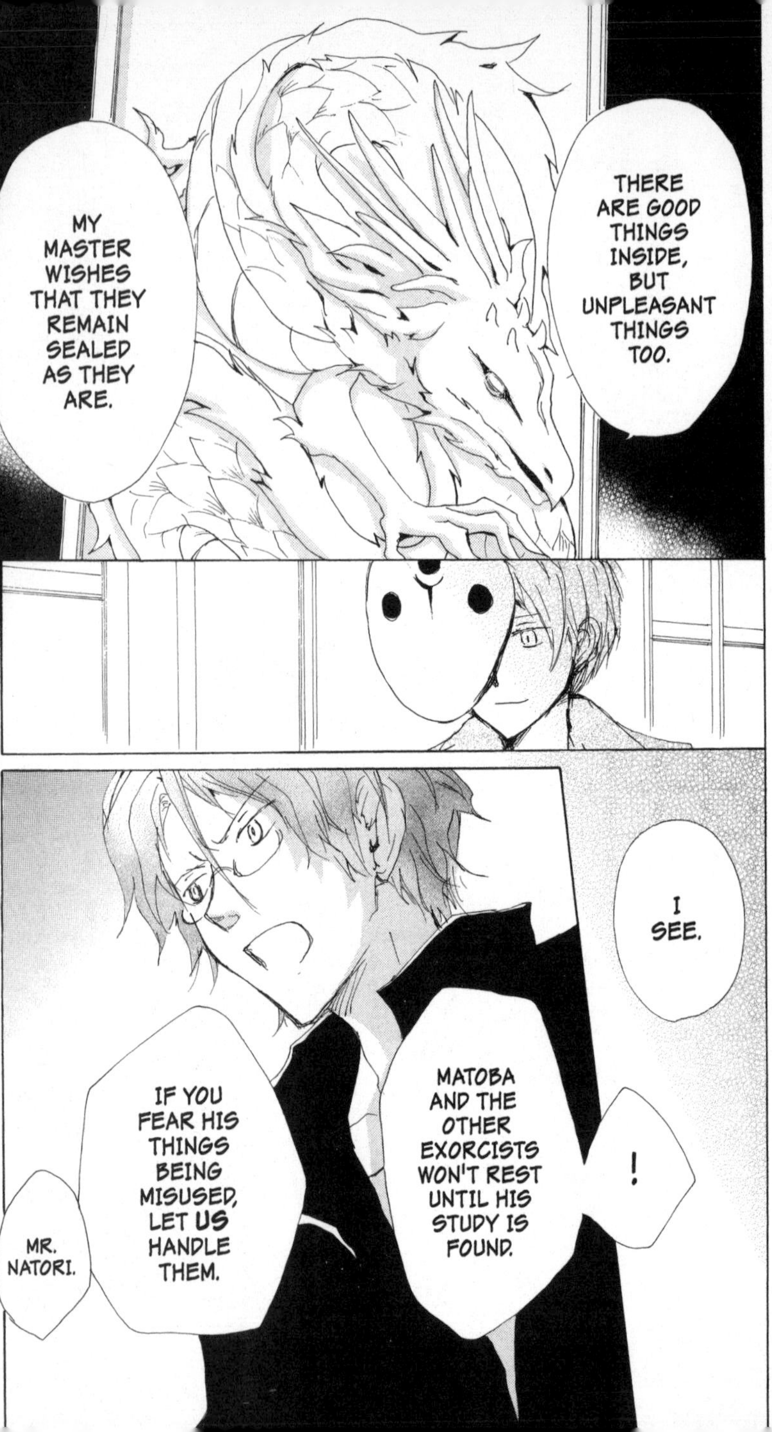
THERE ARE GOOD THINGS INSIDE, BUT UNPLEASANT THINGS TOO.
MY MASTER WISHES THAT THEY REMAIN SEALED AS THEY ARE.
I SEE.
!
MATOBA AND THE OTHER EXORCISTS WON'T REST UNTIL HIS STUDY IS FOUND.
IF YOU FEAR HIS THINGS BEING MISUSED, LET US HANDLE THEM.
MR. NATORI.

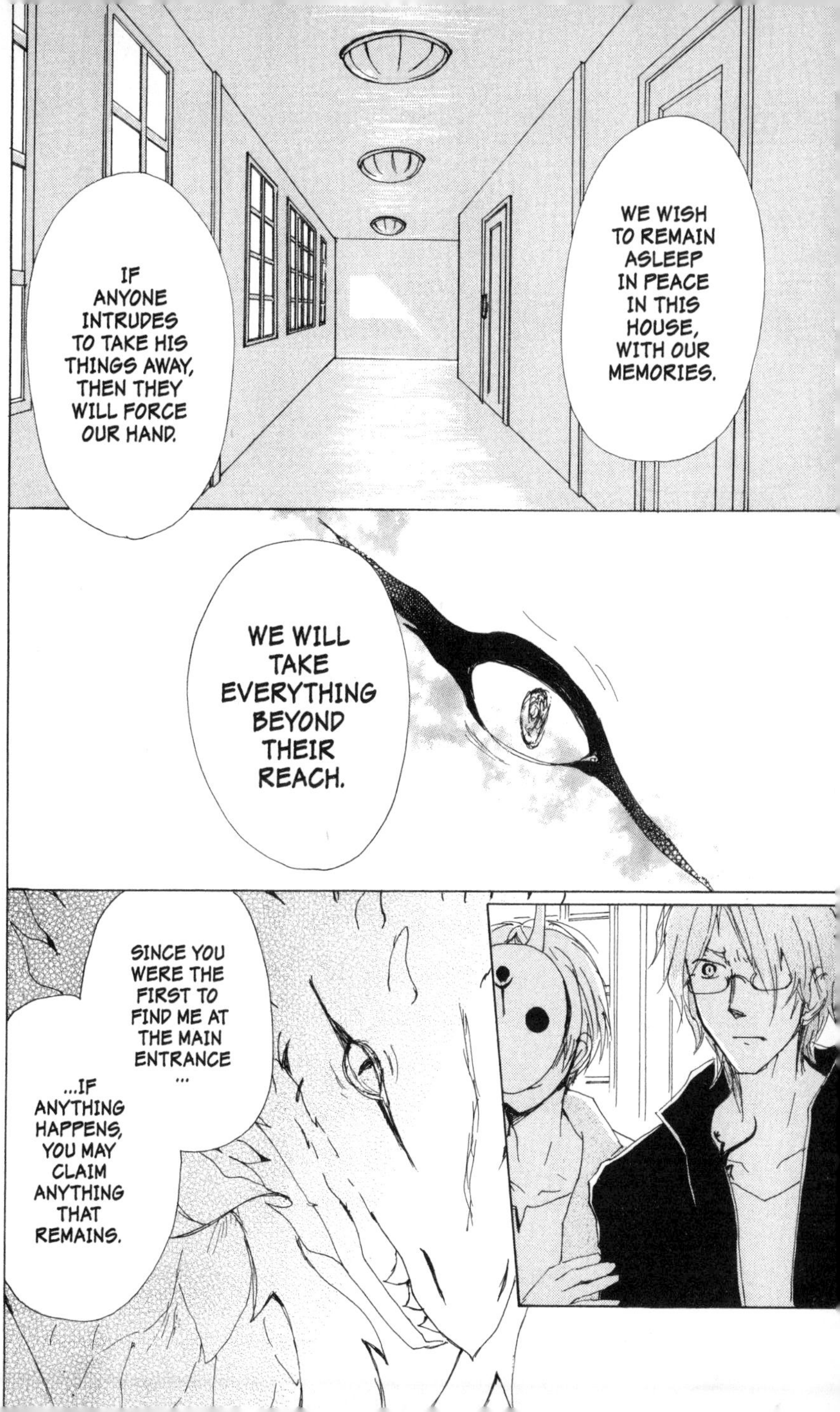
WE WISH TO REMAIN ASLEEP IN PEACE IN THIS HOUSE, WITH OUR MEMORIES.
IF ANYONE INTRUDES TO TAKE HIS THINGS AWAY, THEN THEY WILL FORCE OUR HAND.
WE WILL TAKE EVERYTHING BEYOND THEIR REACH.
SINCE YOU WERE THE FIRST TO FIND ME AT THE MAIN ENTRANCE...
...IF ANYTHING HAPPENS, YOU MAY CLAIM ANYTHING THAT REMAINS.

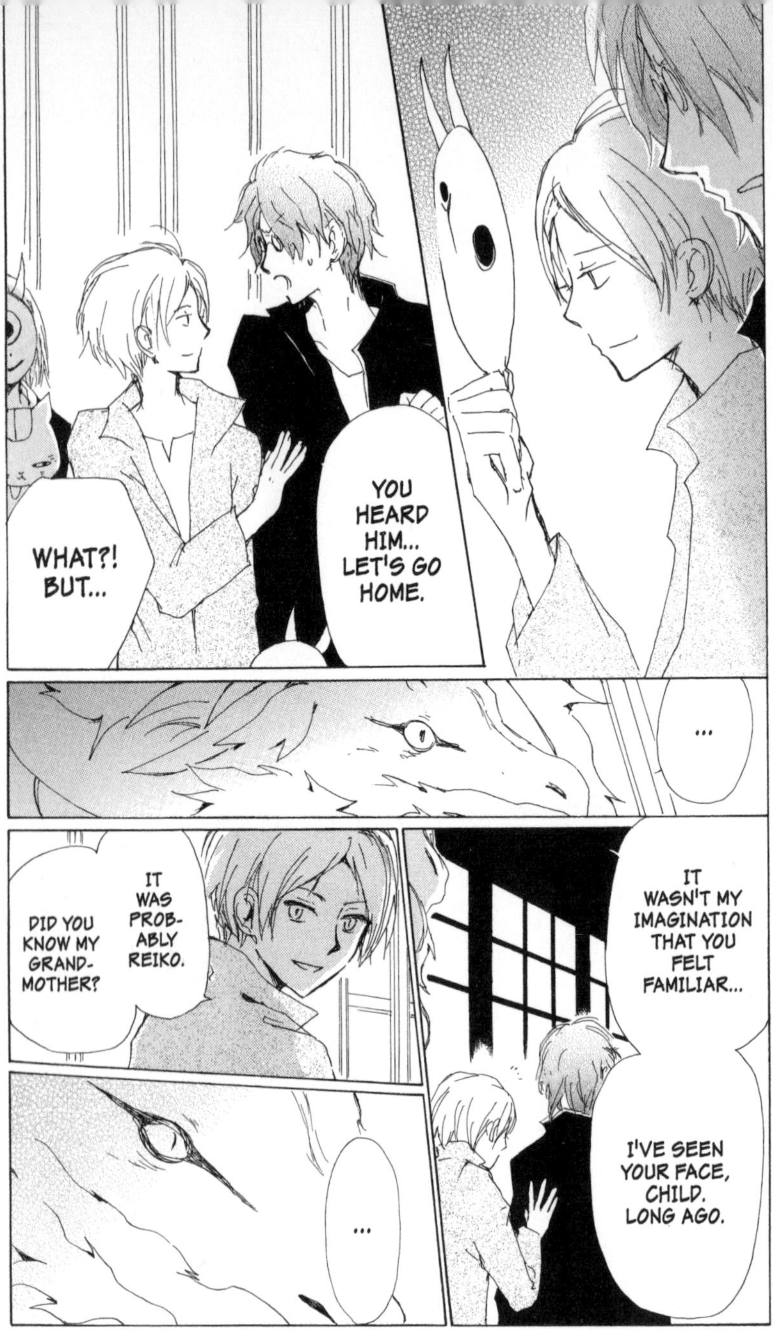
YOU HEARD HIM... LET'S GO HOME.
WHAT?! BUT...
...
IT WASN'T MY IMAGINATION THAT YOU FELT FAMILIAR...
I'VE SEEN YOUR FACE, CHILD. LONG AGO.
IT WAS PROB-ABLY REIKO.
DID YOU KNOW MY GRAND-MOTHER?
...

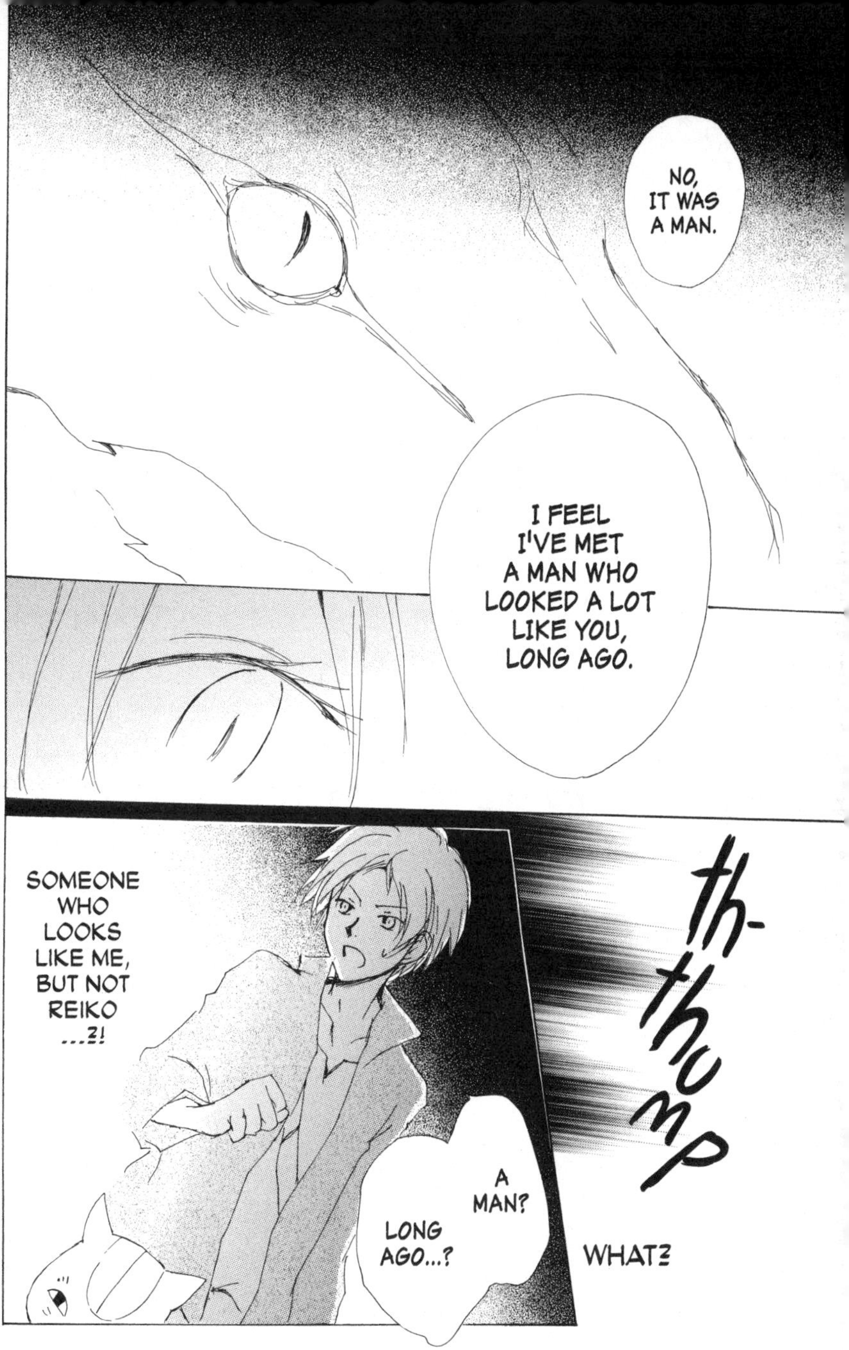
NO, IT WAS A MAN.
I FEEL I'VE MET A MAN WHO LOOKED A LOT LIKE YOU, LONG AGO.
th-thump
WHAT?
A MAN?
LONG AGO...?
SOMEONE WHO LOOKS LIKE ME, BUT NOT REIKO ...?!

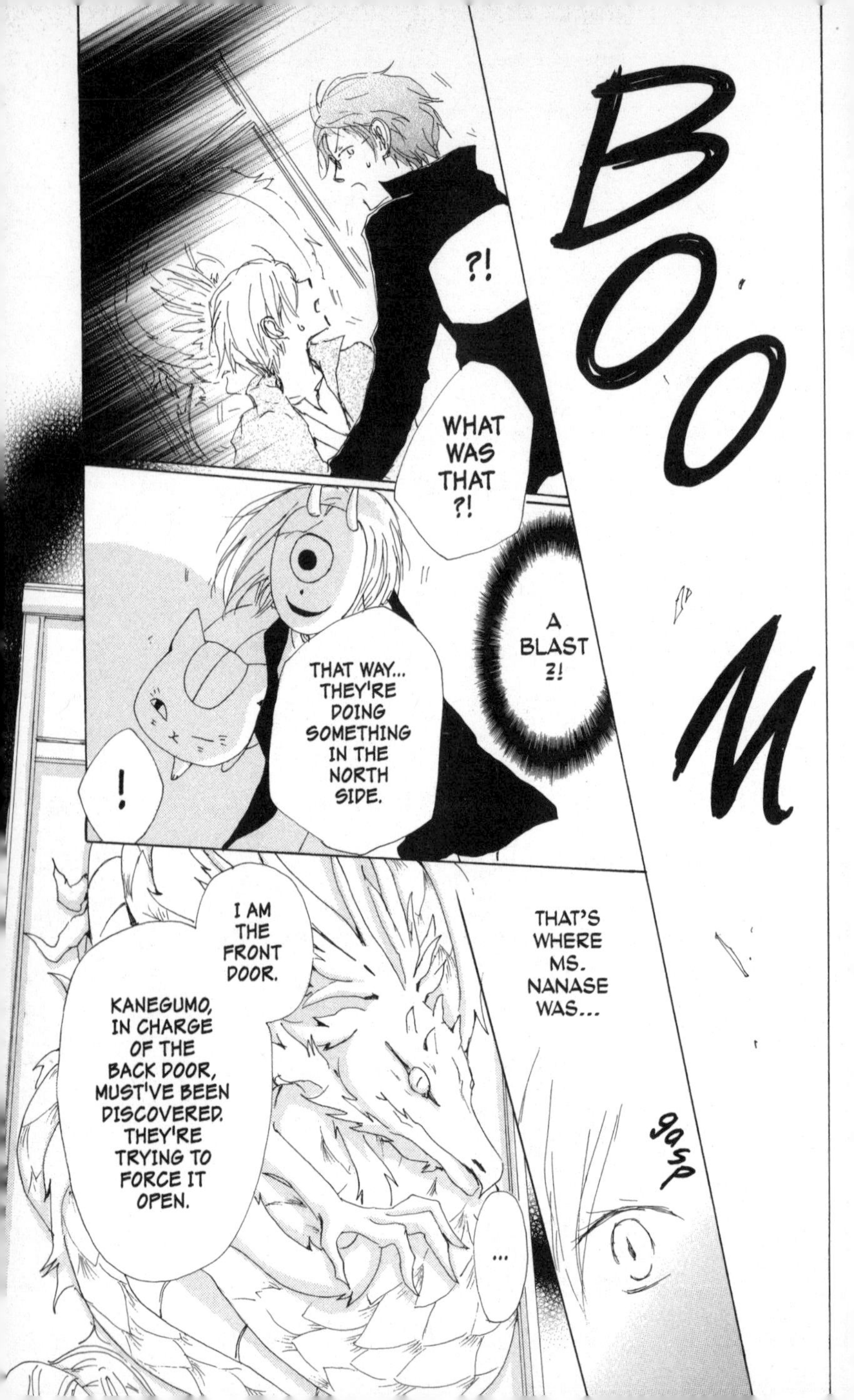
BOOOM
?!
WHAT WAS THAT ?!
A BLAST ?!
THAT WAY... THEY'RE DOING SOMETHING IN THE NORTH SIDE.
!
THAT'S WHERE MS. NANASE WAS...
gasp
I AM THE FRONT DOOR.
KANEGUMO, IN CHARGE OF THE BACK DOOR, MUST'VE BEEN DISCOVERED. THEY'RE TRYING TO FORCE IT OPEN.
...

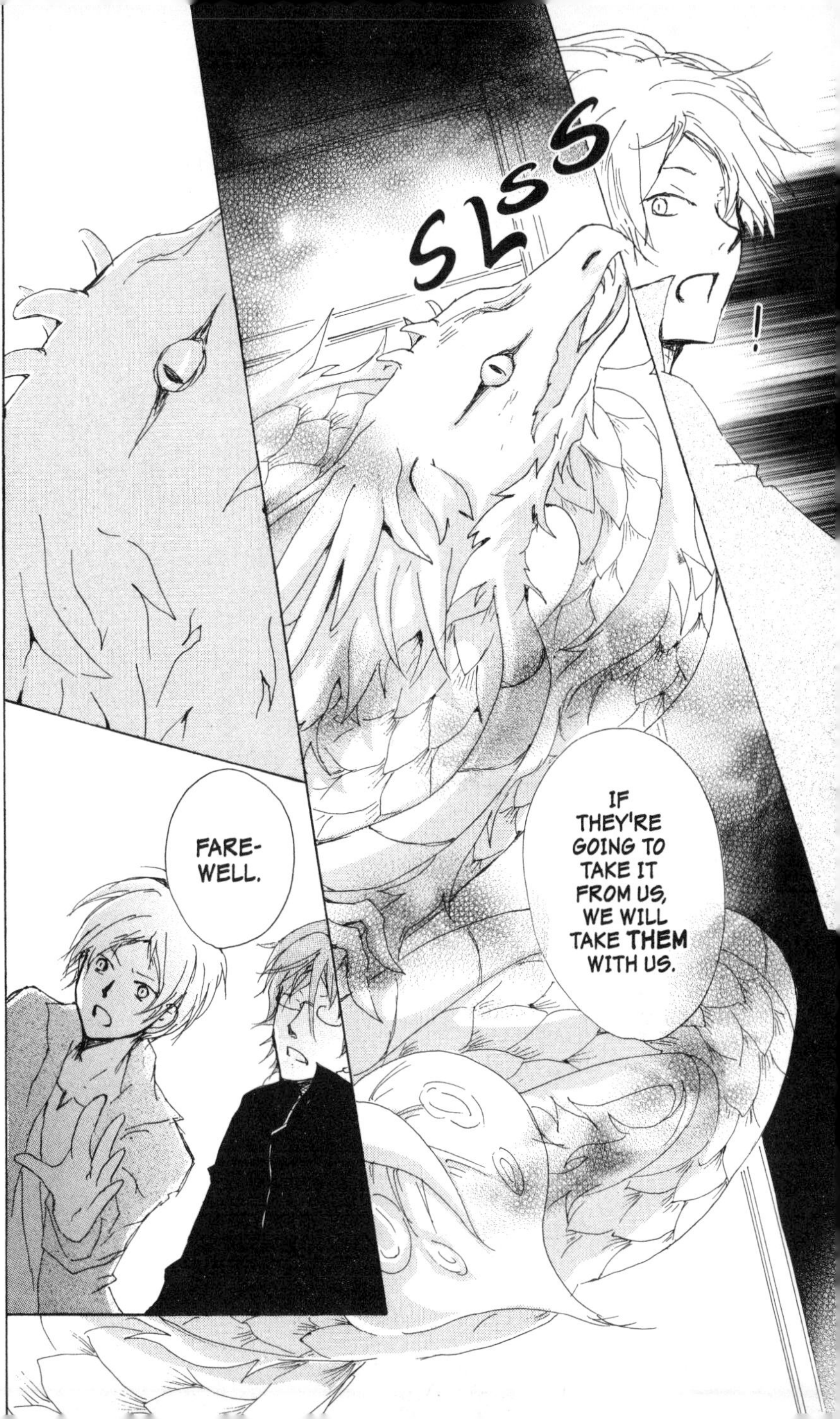
SLSS
!
IF THEY'RE GOING TO TAKE IT FROM US, WE WILL TAKE THEM WITH US.
FARE-WELL.

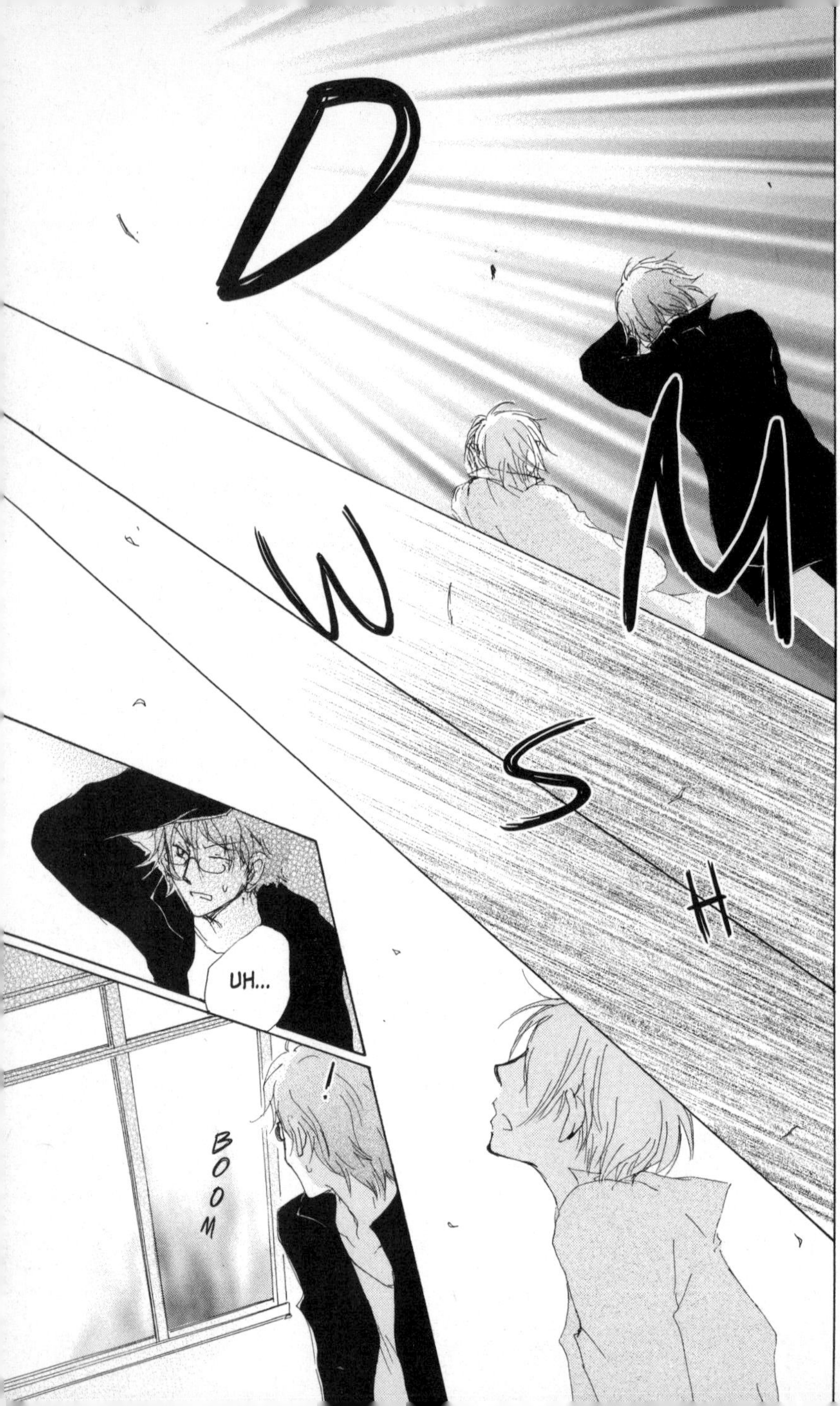
D
M
W
S
H
UH...
!
BOOM

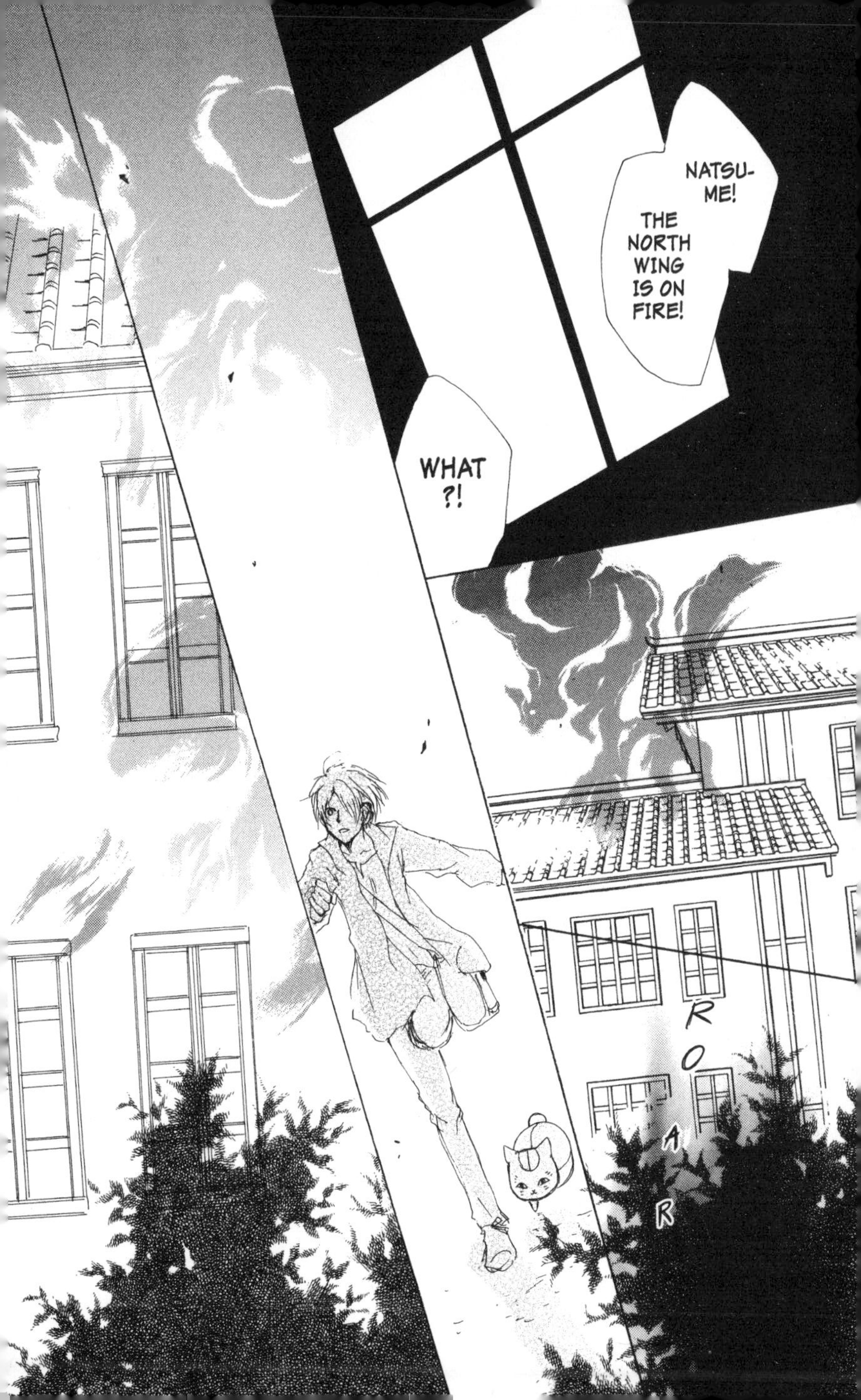
NATSU-ME!
THE NORTH WING IS ON FIRE!
WHAT ?!
ROAR

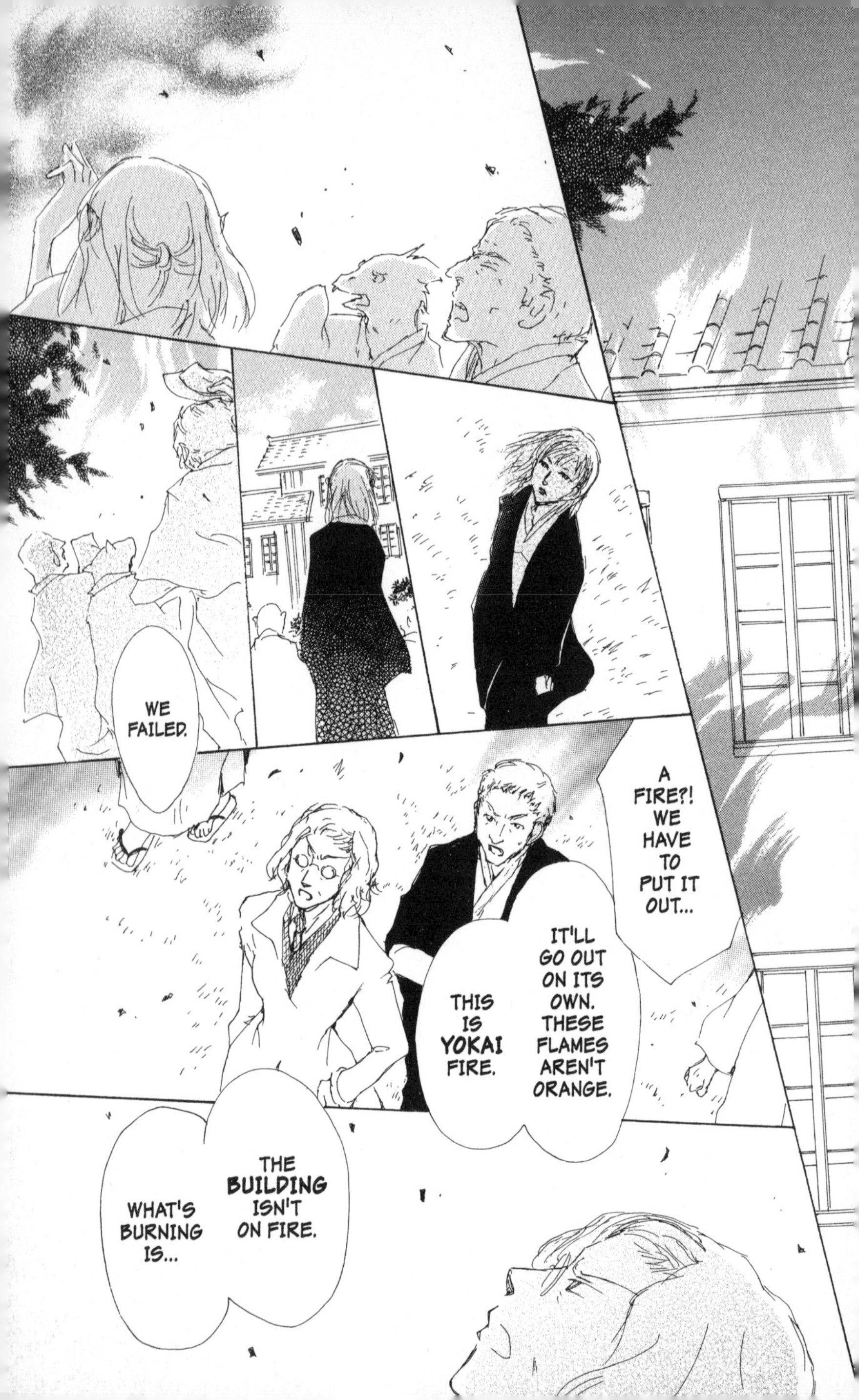
WE FAILED.
A FIRE?! WE HAVE TO PUT IT OUT...
IT'LL GO OUT ON ITS OWN. THESE FLAMES AREN'T ORANGE.
THIS IS YOKAI FIRE.
THE BUILDING ISN'T ON FIRE.
WHAT'S BURNING IS...

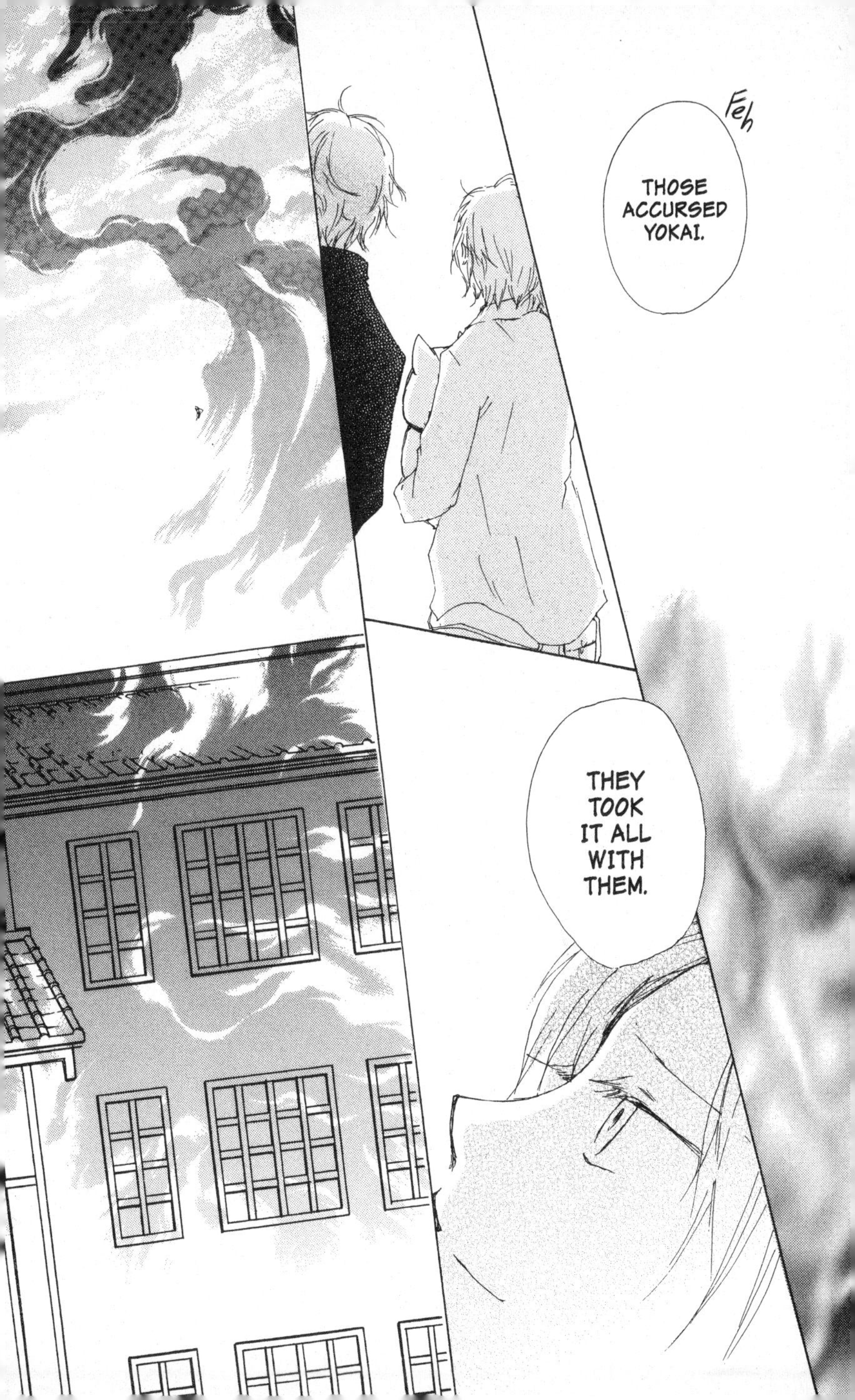
Feh
THOSE ACCURSED YOKAI.
THEY TOOK IT ALL WITH THEM.

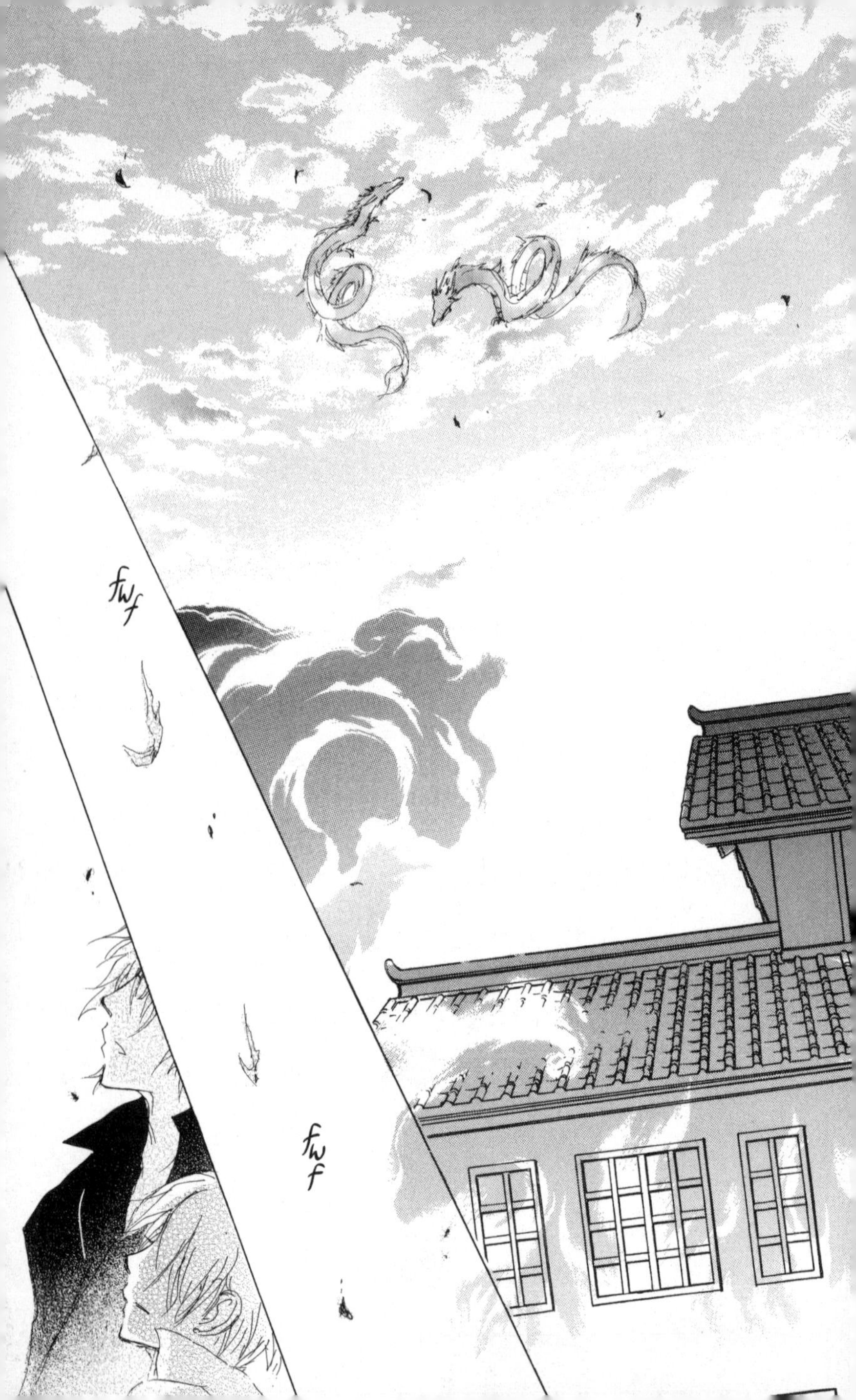
fwf
fwf

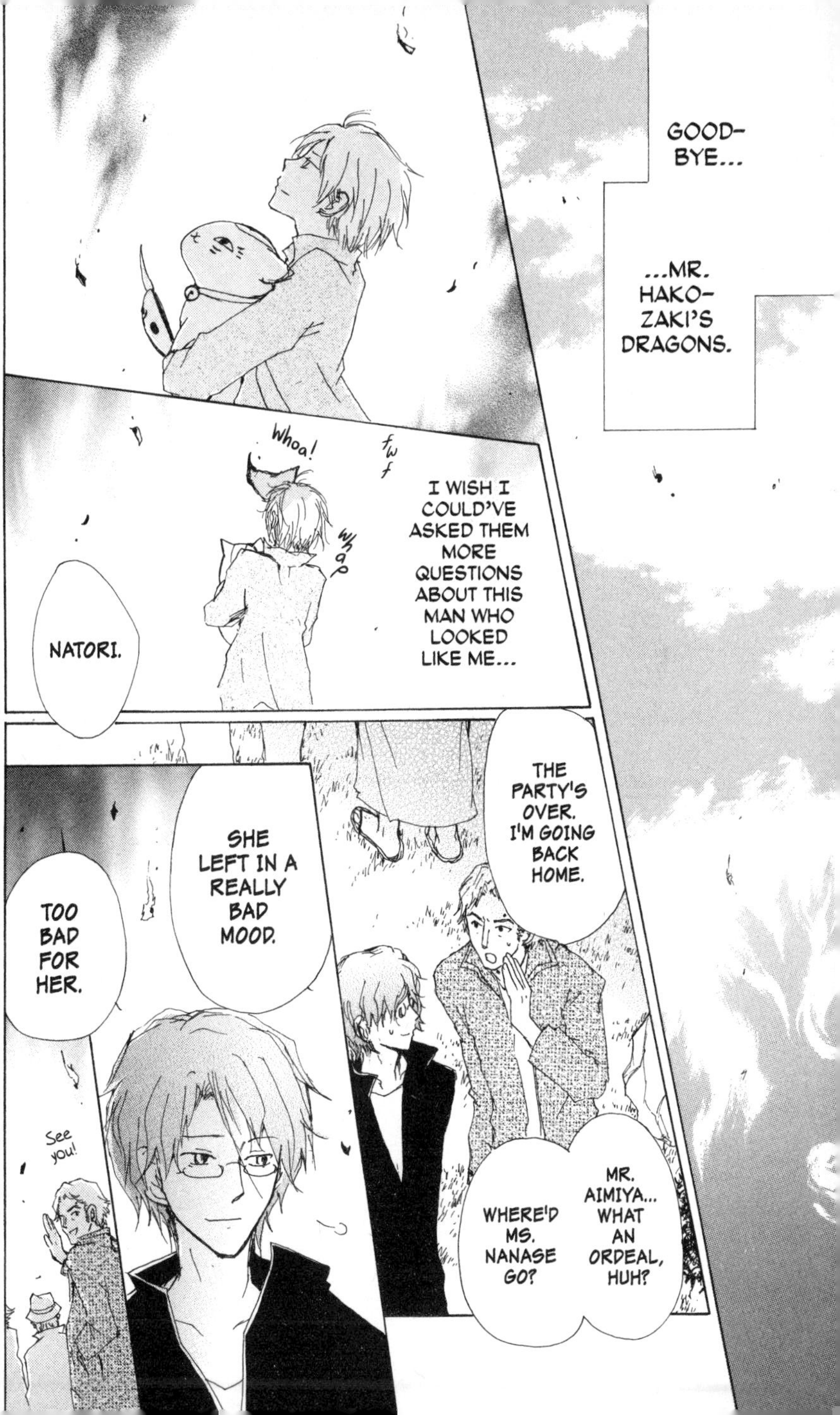
GOOD-BYE...
...MR. HAKO-ZAKI'S DRAGONS.
fwf
Whoa!
I WISH I COULD'VE ASKED THEM MORE QUESTIONS ABOUT THIS MAN WHO LOOKED LIKE ME...
whap
NATORI.
THE PARTY'S OVER. I'M GOING BACK HOME.
MR. AIMIYA... WHAT AN ORDEAL, HUH?
WHERE'D MS. NANASE GO?
SHE LEFT IN A REALLY BAD MOOD.
TOO BAD FOR HER.
See you!

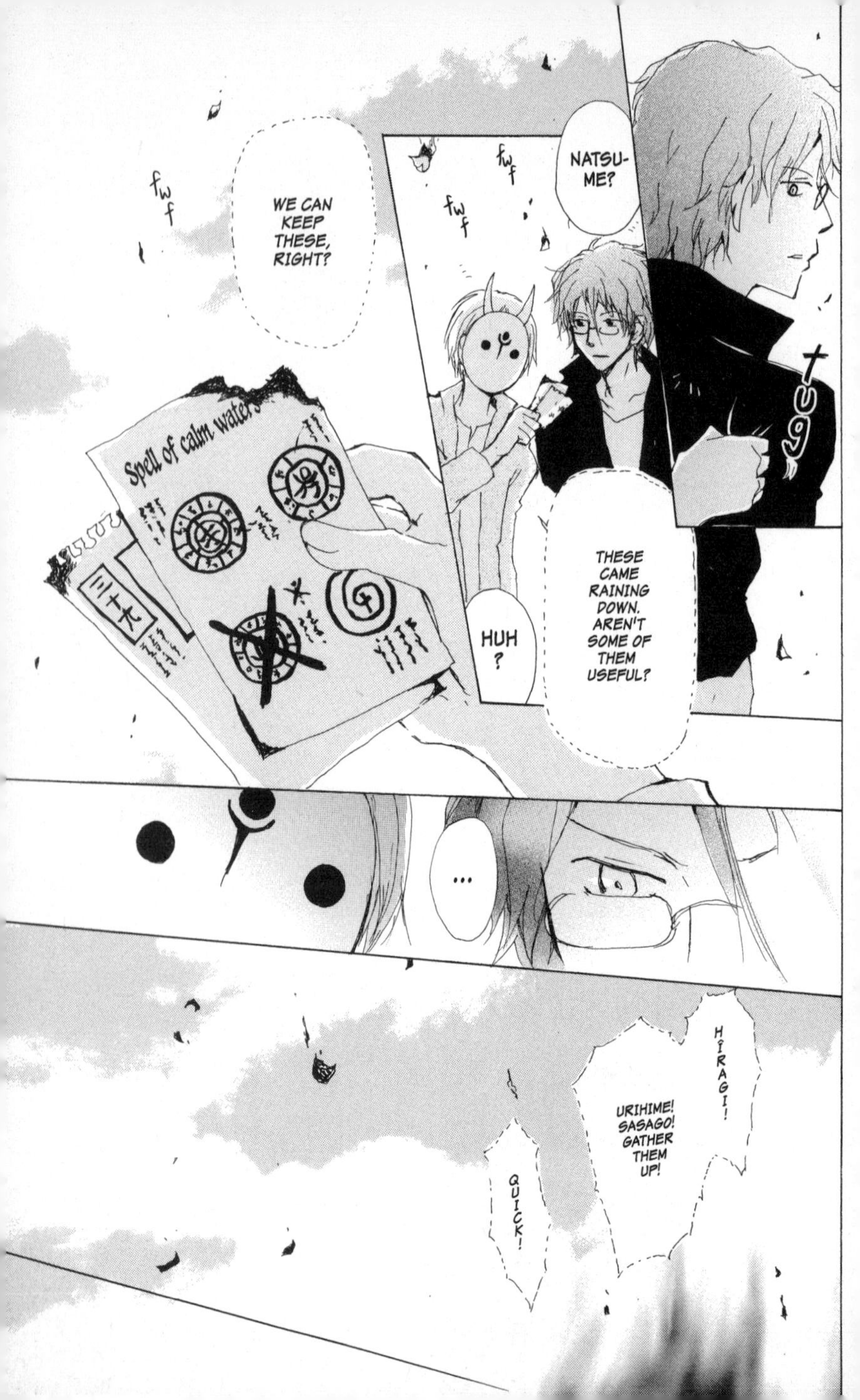
NATSU-ME?
tug
fwf
fwf
THESE CAME RAINING DOWN. AREN'T SOME OF THEM USEFUL?
HUH?
WE CAN KEEP THESE, RIGHT?
fwf
Spell of calm waters
...
HÎRAGI!
URIHIME! SASAGO! GATHER THEM UP!
QUICK!

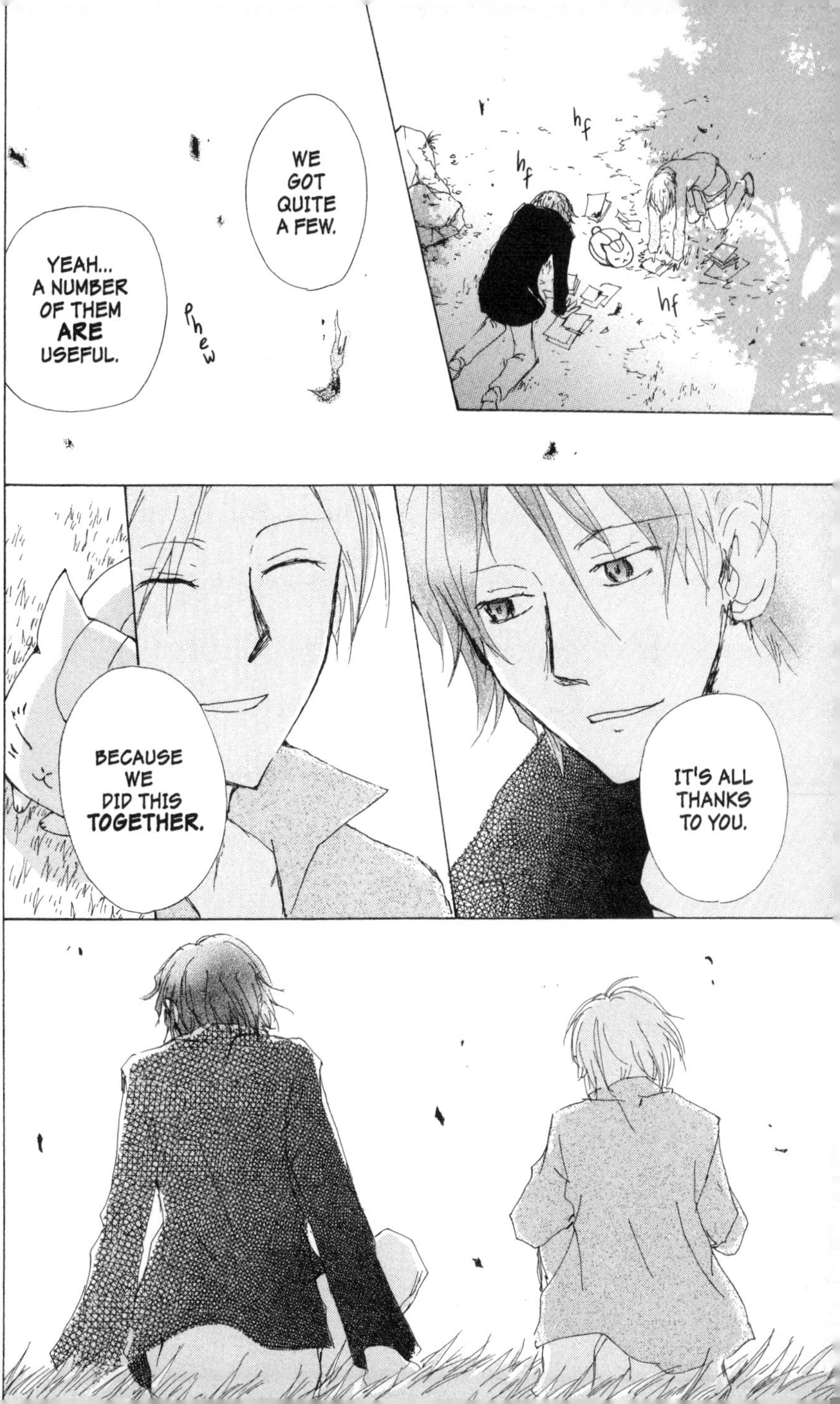
hf
hf
hf
WE GOT QUITE A FEW.
phew
YEAH... A NUMBER OF THEM **ARE** USEFUL.
IT'S ALL THANKS TO YOU.
BECAUSE WE DID THIS **TOGETHER.**

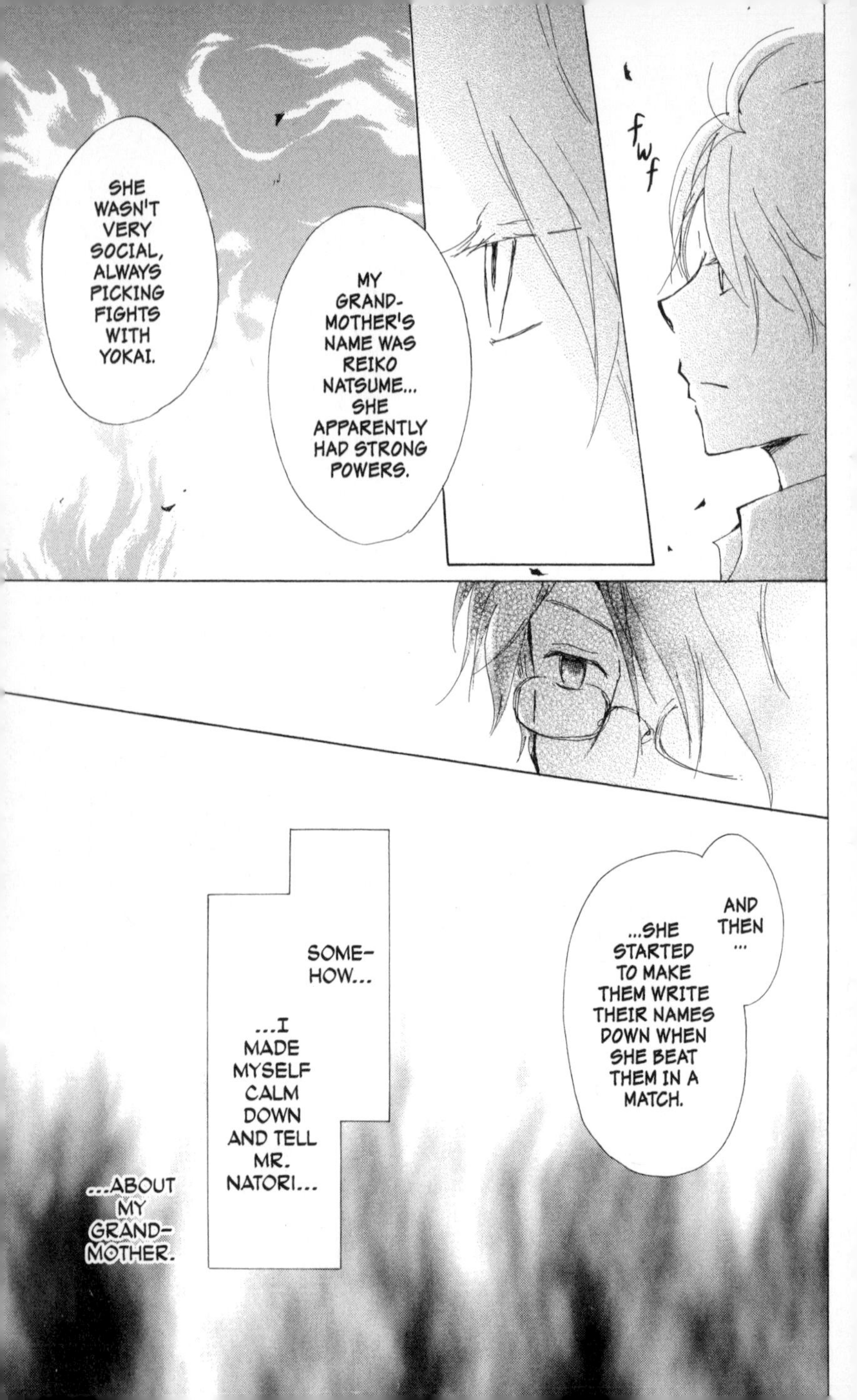
fwf
MY GRANDMOTHER'S NAME WAS REIKO NATSUME... SHE APPARENTLY HAD STRONG POWERS.
SHE WASN'T VERY SOCIAL, ALWAYS PICKING FIGHTS WITH YOKAI.
AND THEN...
...SHE STARTED TO MAKE THEM WRITE THEIR NAMES DOWN WHEN SHE BEAT THEM IN A MATCH.
SOME-HOW...
...I MADE MYSELF CALM DOWN AND TELL MR. NATORI...
...ABOUT MY GRAND-MOTHER.

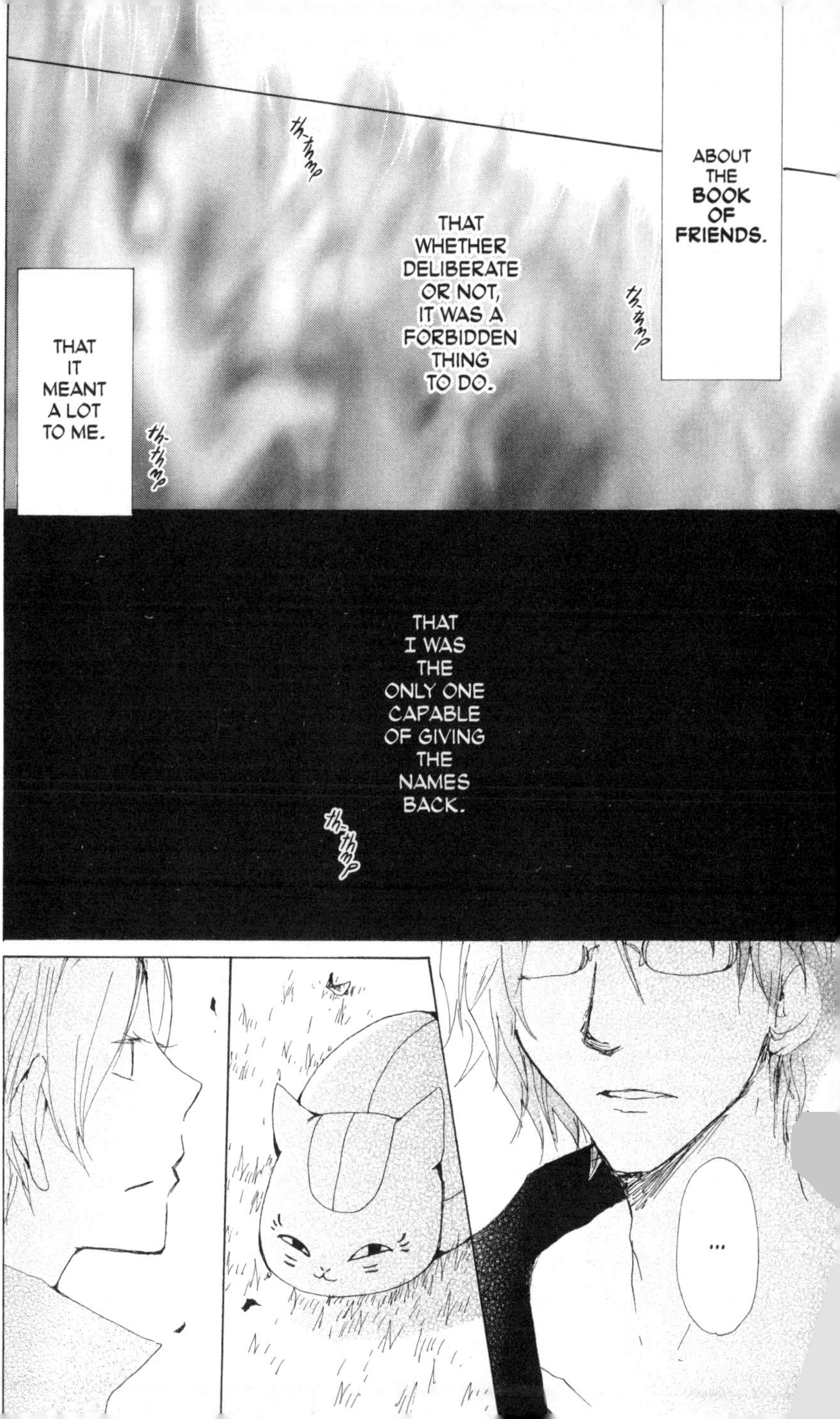
ABOUT THE BOOK OF FRIENDS.
th-thmp
THAT WHETHER DELIBERATE OR NOT, IT WAS A FORBIDDEN THING TO DO.
th-thmp
THAT IT MEANT A LOT TO ME.
th-thmp
THAT I WAS THE ONLY ONE CAPABLE OF GIVING THE NAMES BACK.
th-thmp
...

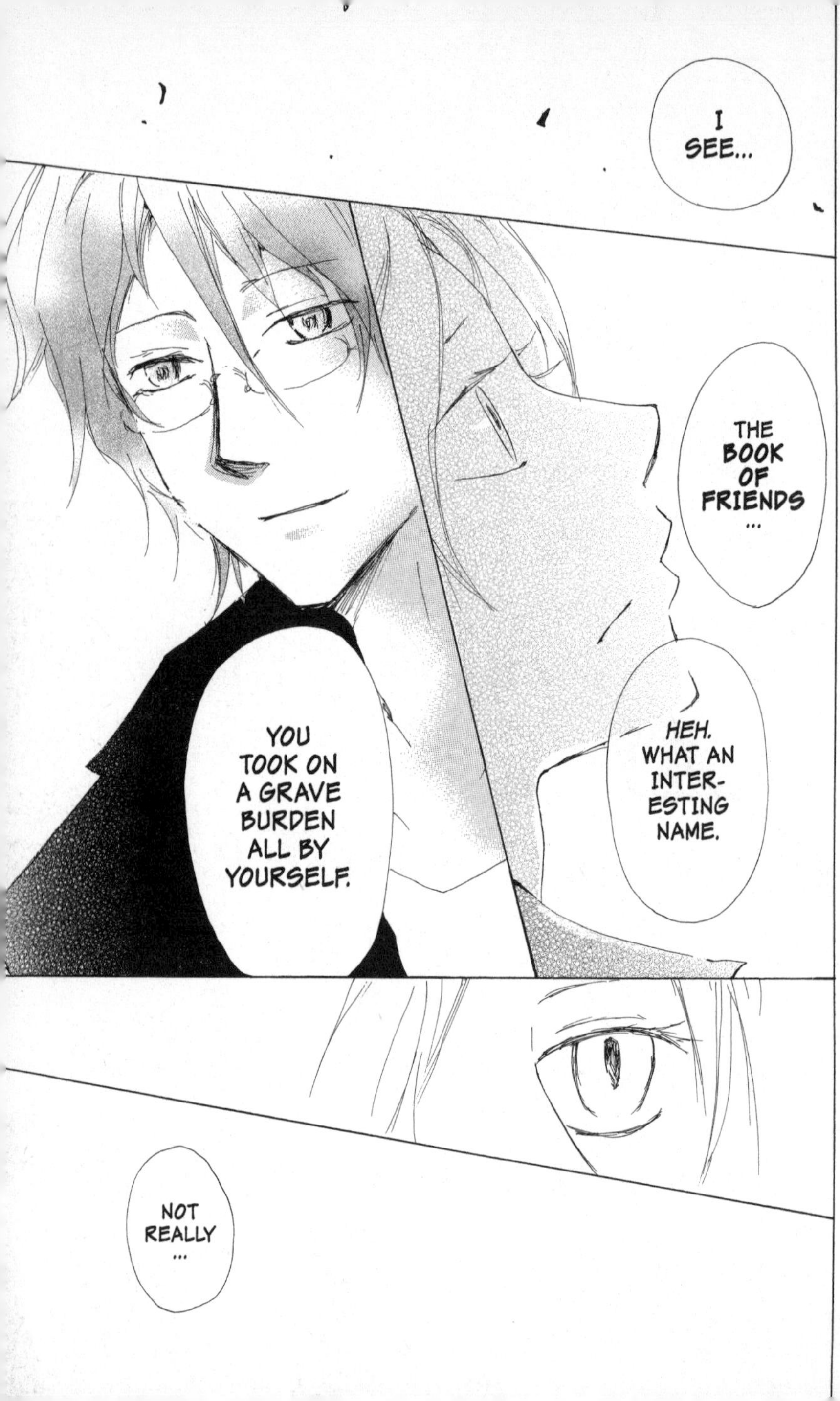
I SEE...
THE BOOK OF FRIENDS...
HEH. WHAT AN INTER-ESTING NAME.
YOU TOOK ON A GRAVE BURDEN ALL BY YOURSELF.
NOT REALLY...

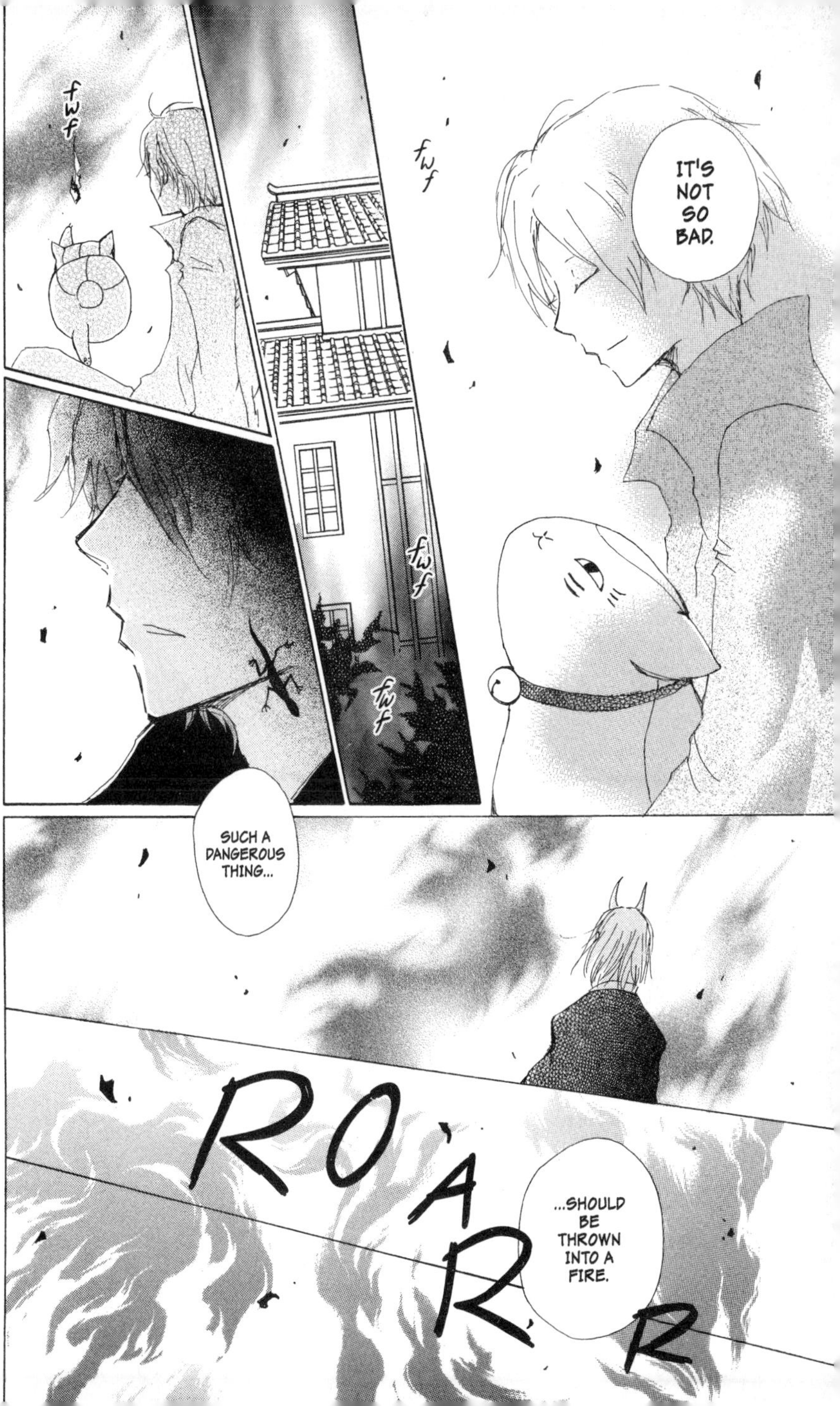
IT'S NOT SO BAD.
fwf
fwf
fwf
fwf
SUCH A DANGEROUS THING...
ROARR
...SHOULD BE THROWN INTO A FIRE.

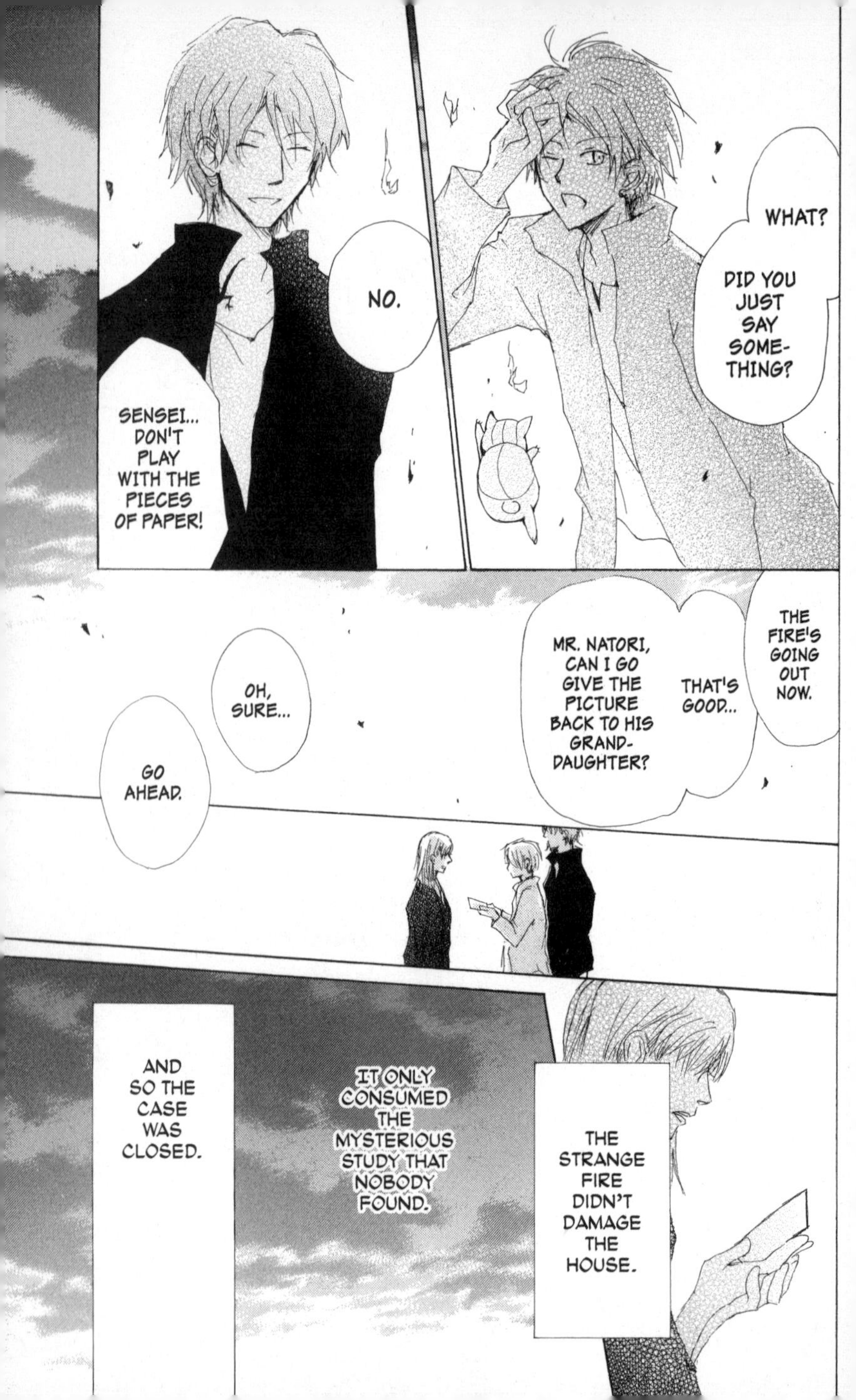
WHAT?
DID YOU JUST SAY SOME-THING?
NO.
SENSEI... DON'T PLAY WITH THE PIECES OF PAPER!
THE FIRE'S GOING OUT NOW.
THAT'S GOOD...
MR. NATORI, CAN I GO GIVE THE PICTURE BACK TO HIS GRAND-DAUGHTER?
OH, SURE...
GO AHEAD.
THE STRANGE FIRE DIDN'T DAMAGE THE HOUSE.
IT ONLY CONSUMED THE MYSTERIOUS STUDY THAT NOBODY FOUND.
AND SO THE CASE WAS CLOSED.

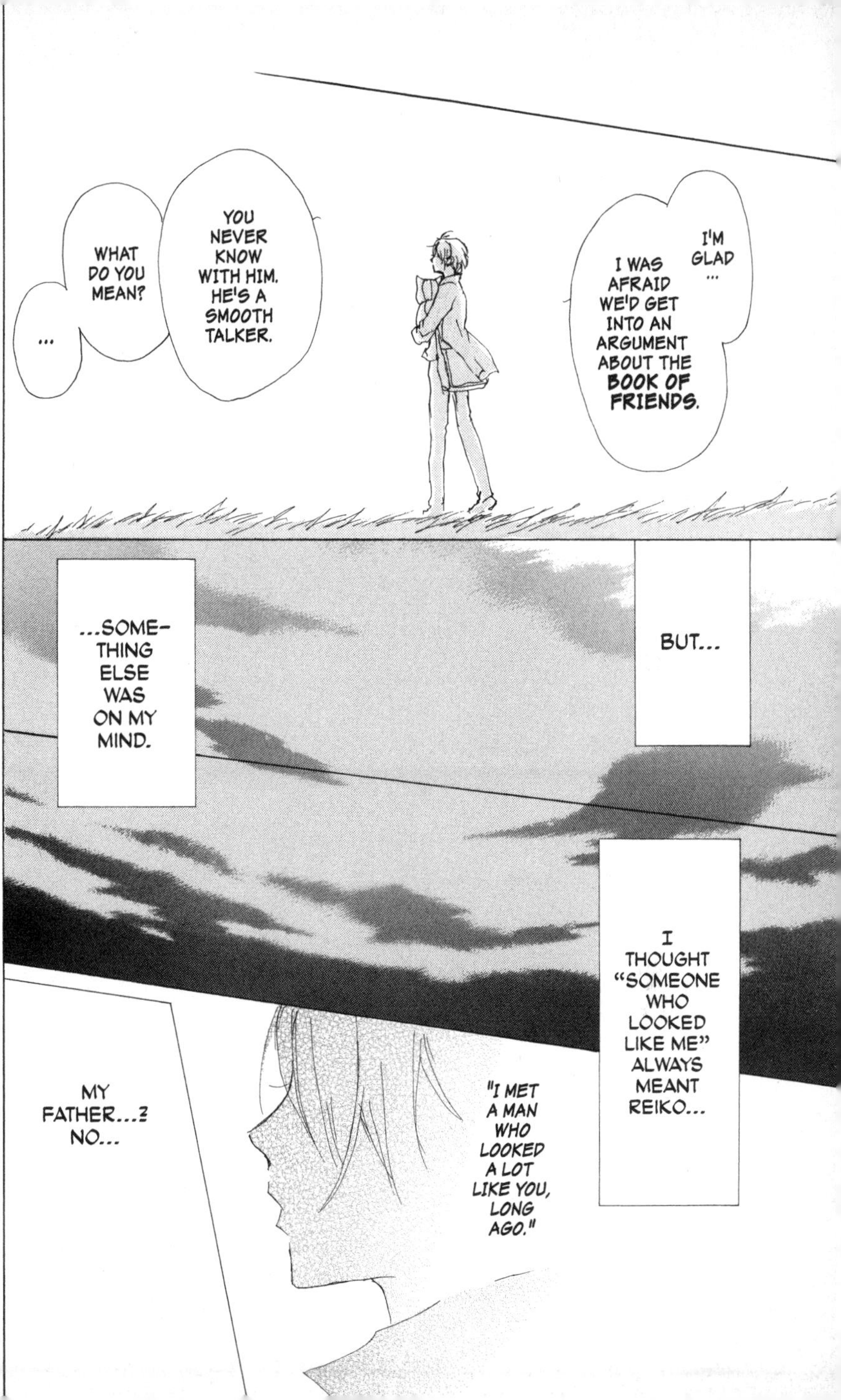
I'M GLAD...
I WAS AFRAID WE'D GET INTO AN ARGUMENT ABOUT THE BOOK OF FRIENDS.
YOU NEVER KNOW WITH HIM. HE'S A SMOOTH TALKER.
WHAT DO YOU MEAN?
...
BUT...
...SOME-THING ELSE WAS ON MY MIND.
I THOUGHT "SOMEONE WHO LOOKED LIKE ME" ALWAYS MEANT REIKO...
"I MET A MAN WHO LOOKED A LOT LIKE YOU, LONG AGO."
MY FATHER...? NO...

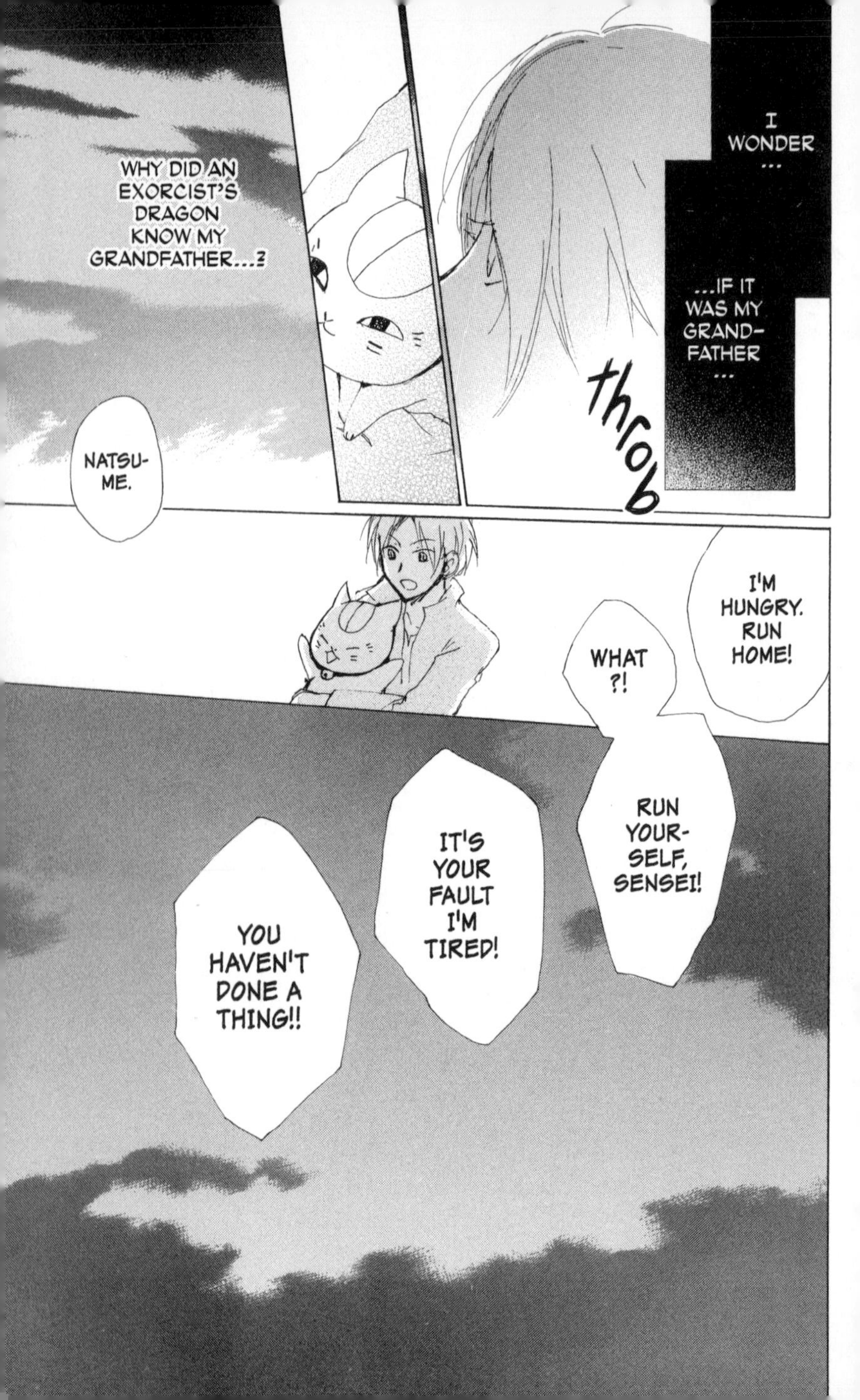
I WONDER...
...IF IT WAS MY GRAND-FATHER...
throb
WHY DID AN EXORCIST'S DRAGON KNOW MY GRANDFATHER...?
NATSU-ME.
I'M HUNGRY. RUN HOME!
WHAT?!
RUN YOUR-SELF, SENSEI!
IT'S YOUR FAULT I'M TIRED!
YOU HAVEN'T DONE A THING!!

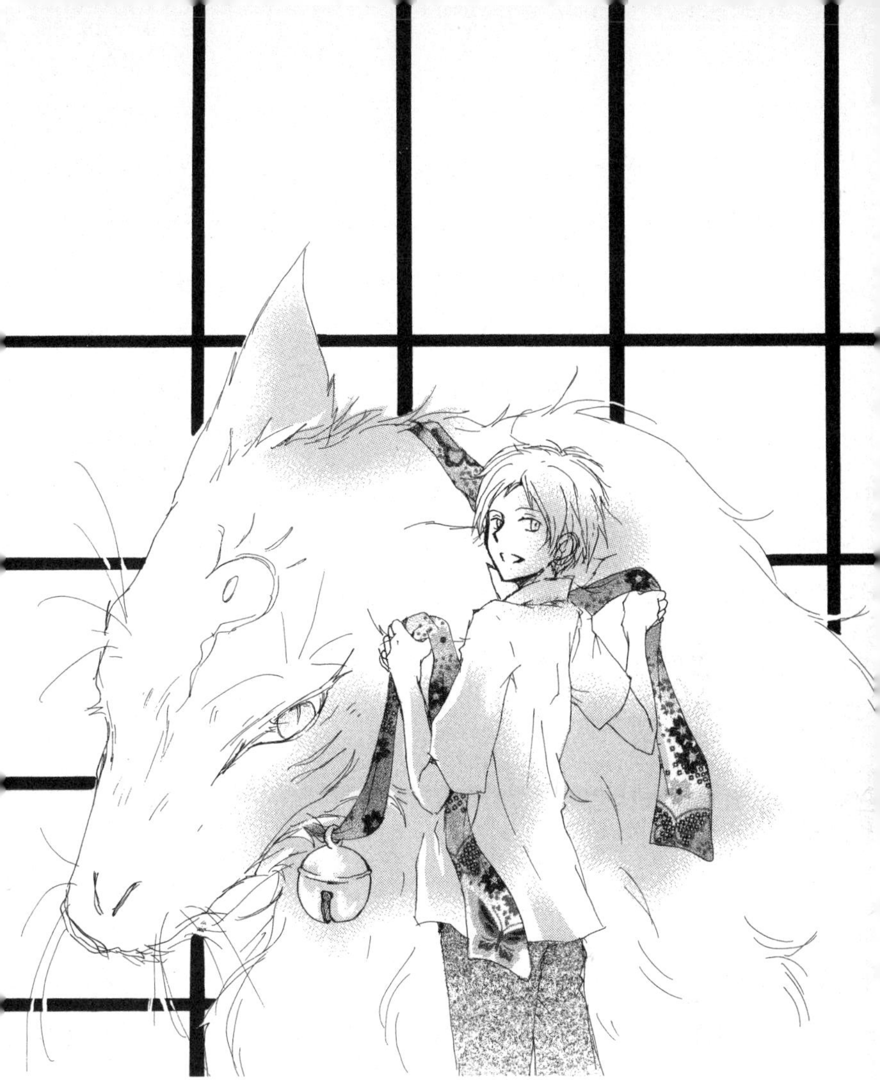

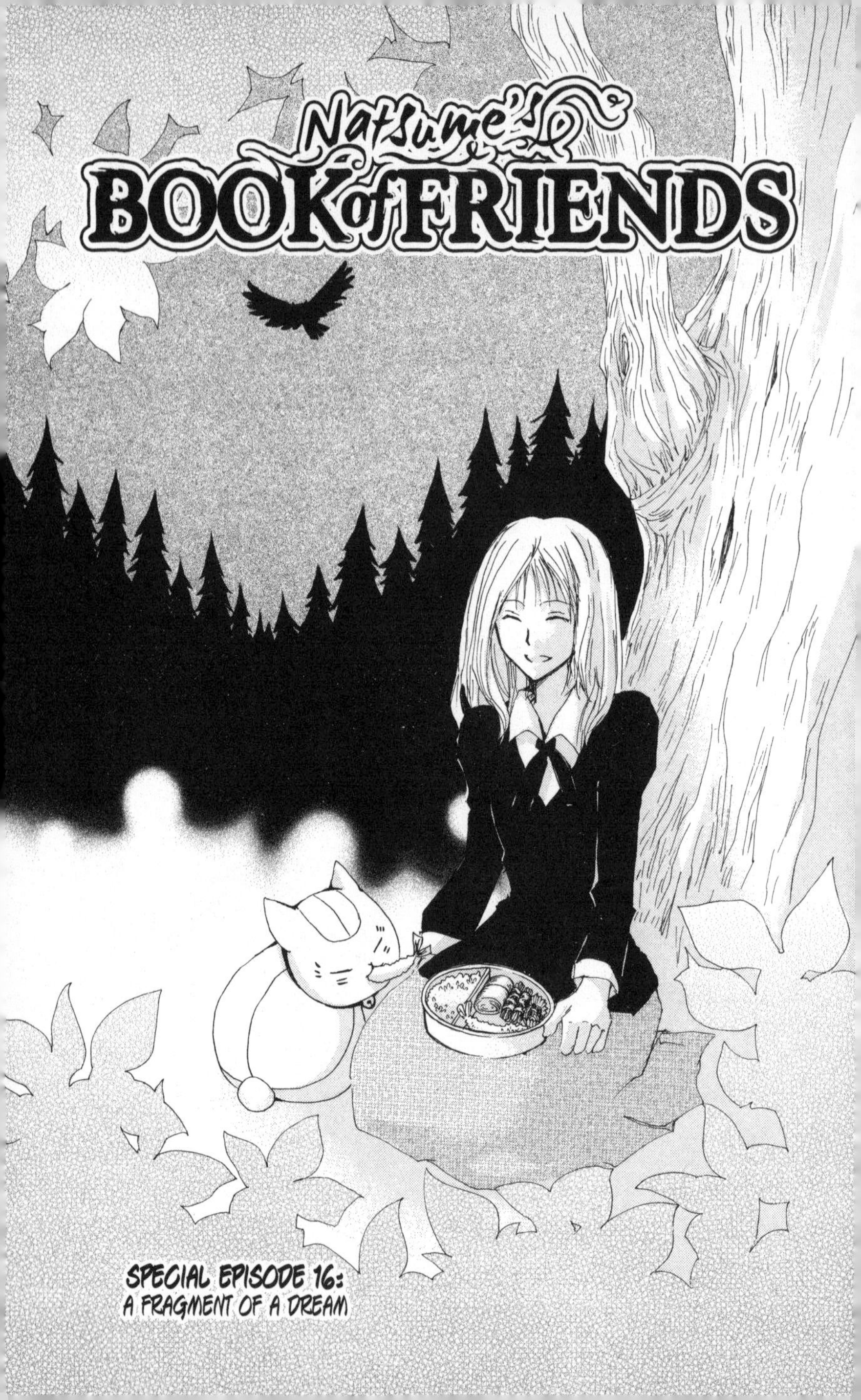
Natsume's
BOOK of FRIENDS
SPECIAL EPISODE 16:
A FRAGMENT OF A DREAM

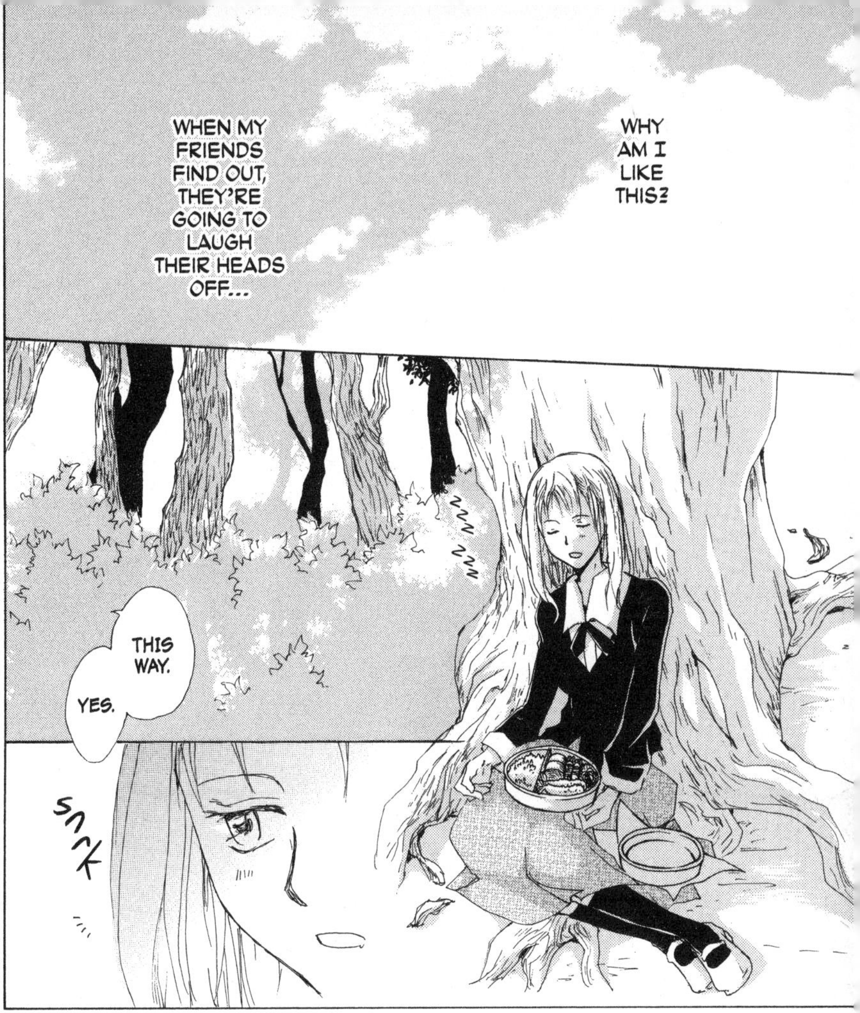
WHY AM I LIKE THIS?
WHEN MY FRIENDS FIND OUT, THEY'RE GOING TO LAUGH THEIR HEADS OFF...
ZZZ
ZZZ
THIS WAY.
YES.
SNRK

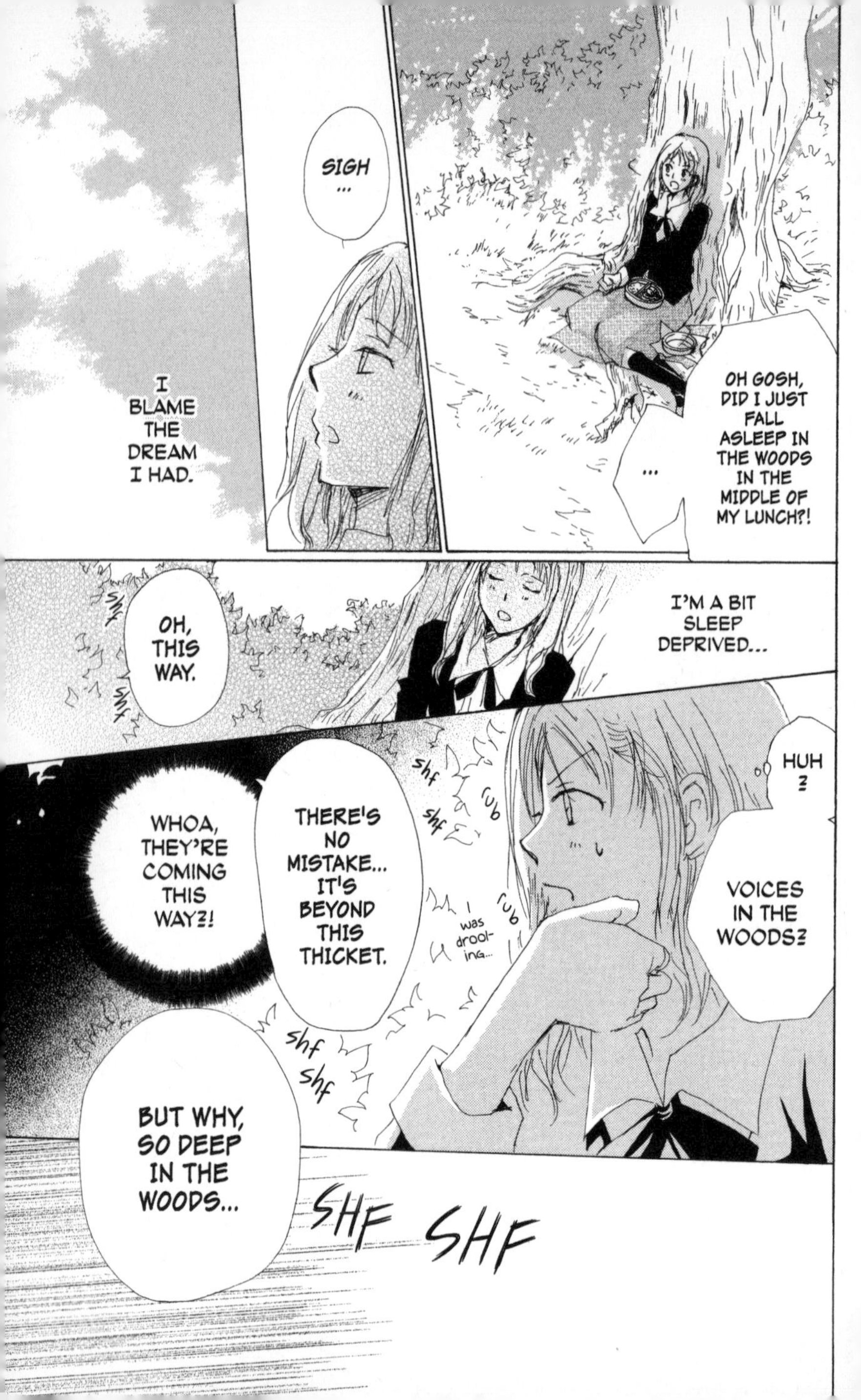
OH GOSH, DID I JUST FALL ASLEEP IN THE WOODS IN THE MIDDLE OF MY LUNCH?!
...
SIGH ...
I BLAME THE DREAM I HAD.
I'M A BIT SLEEP DEPRIVED...
OH, THIS WAY.
shf
shf
HUH?
VOICES IN THE WOODS?
rub
rub
I was drooling...
shf
shf
THERE'S NO MISTAKE... IT'S BEYOND THIS THICKET.
WHOA, THEY'RE COMING THIS WAY?!
shf
shf
BUT WHY, SO DEEP IN THE WOODS...
SHF SHF

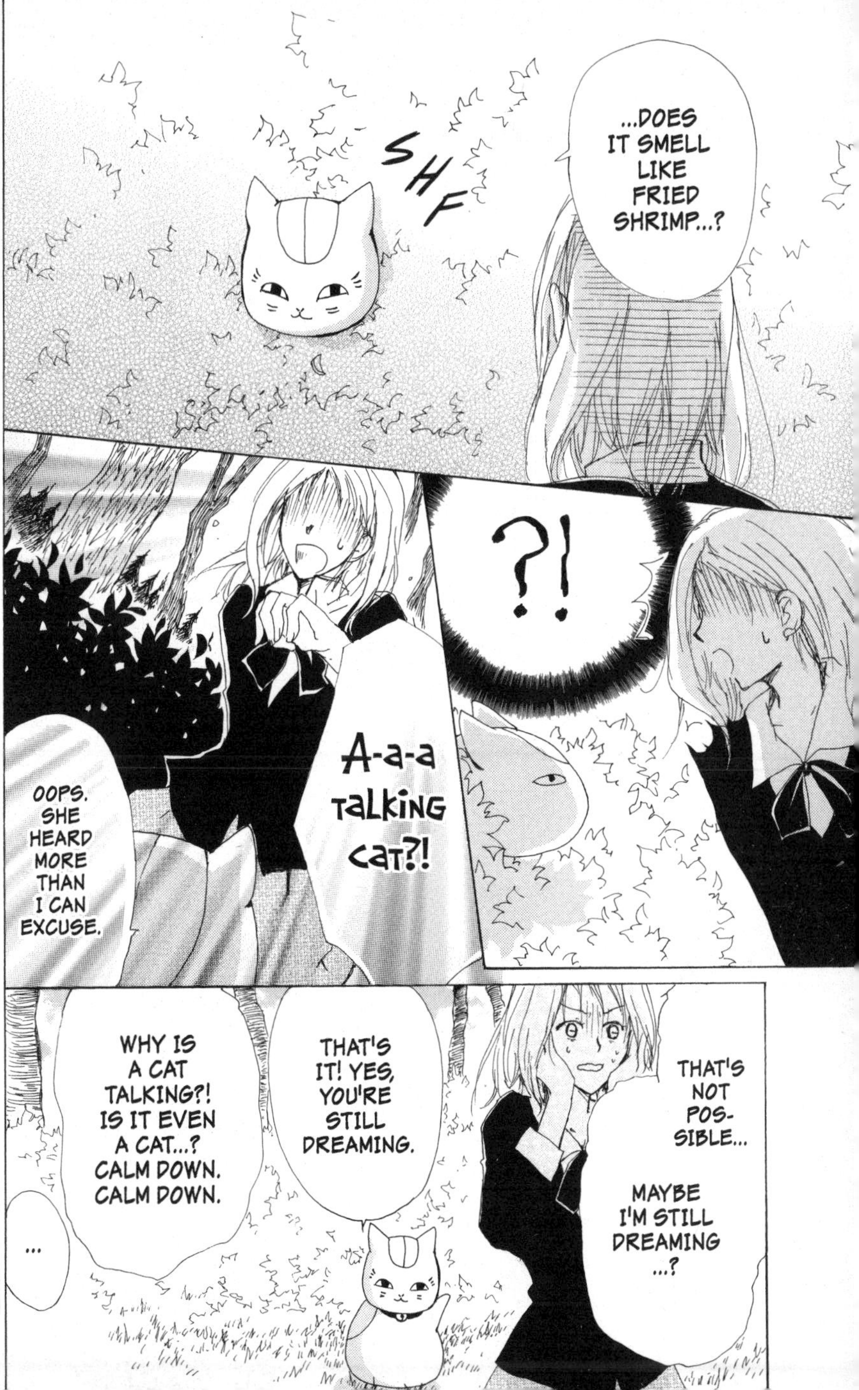
...DOES IT SMELL LIKE FRIED SHRIMP...?
SHF
?!
A-a-a talking cat?!
OOPS. SHE HEARD MORE THAN I CAN EXCUSE.
THAT'S NOT POS-SIBLE...
MAYBE I'M STILL DREAMING ...?
THAT'S IT! YES, YOU'RE STILL DREAMING.
WHY IS A CAT TALKING?! IS IT EVEN A CAT...? CALM DOWN. CALM DOWN.
...

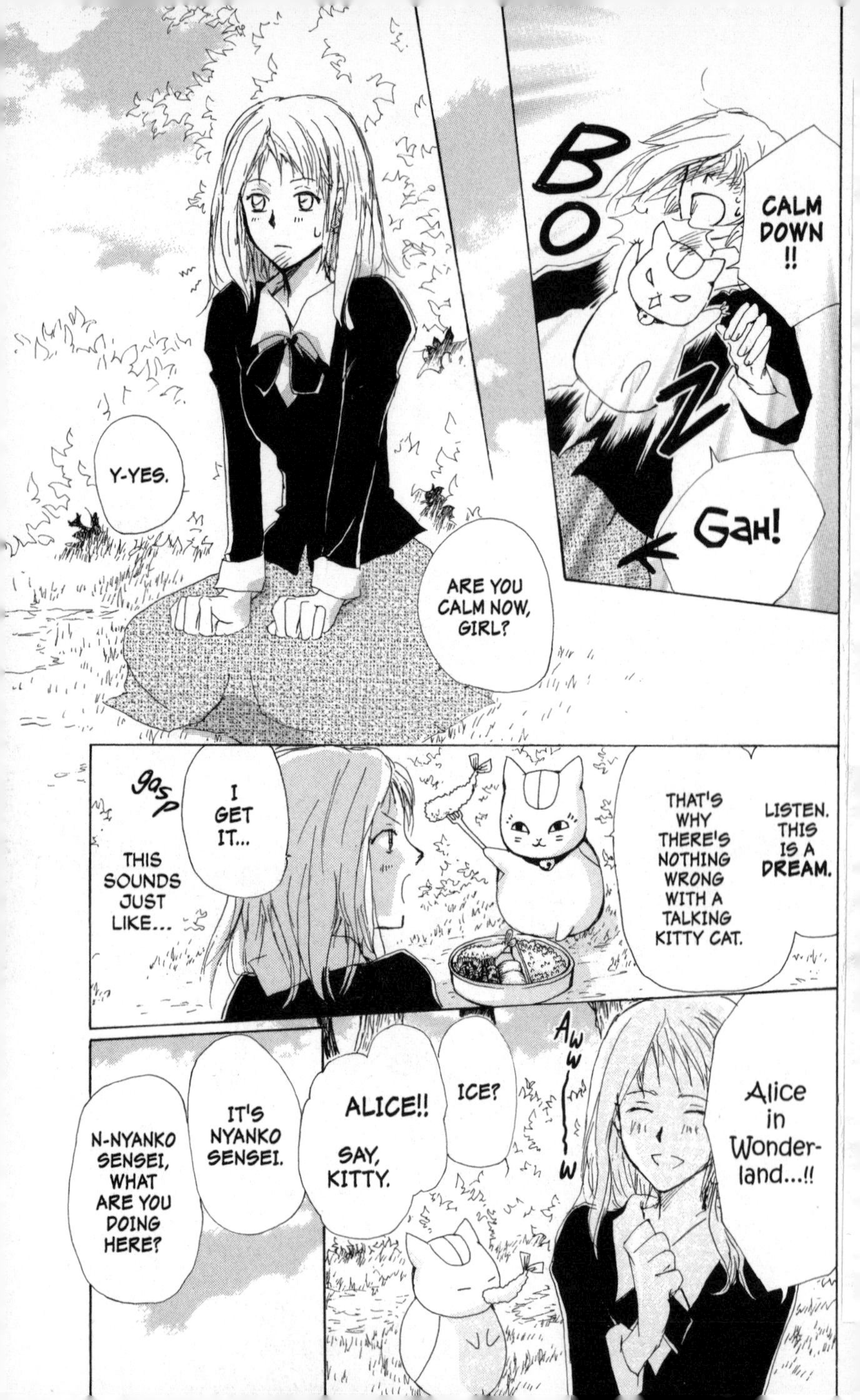
BO
CALM DOWN !!
GAH!
ARE YOU CALM NOW, GIRL?
Y-YES.
LISTEN. THIS IS A DREAM.
THAT'S WHY THERE'S NOTHING WRONG WITH A TALKING KITTY CAT.
I GET IT...
gasp
THIS SOUNDS JUST LIKE...
Alice in Wonder-land...!!
ICE?
ALICE!!
SAY, KITTY.
IT'S NYANKO SENSEI.
N-NYANKO SENSEI, WHAT ARE YOU DOING HERE?

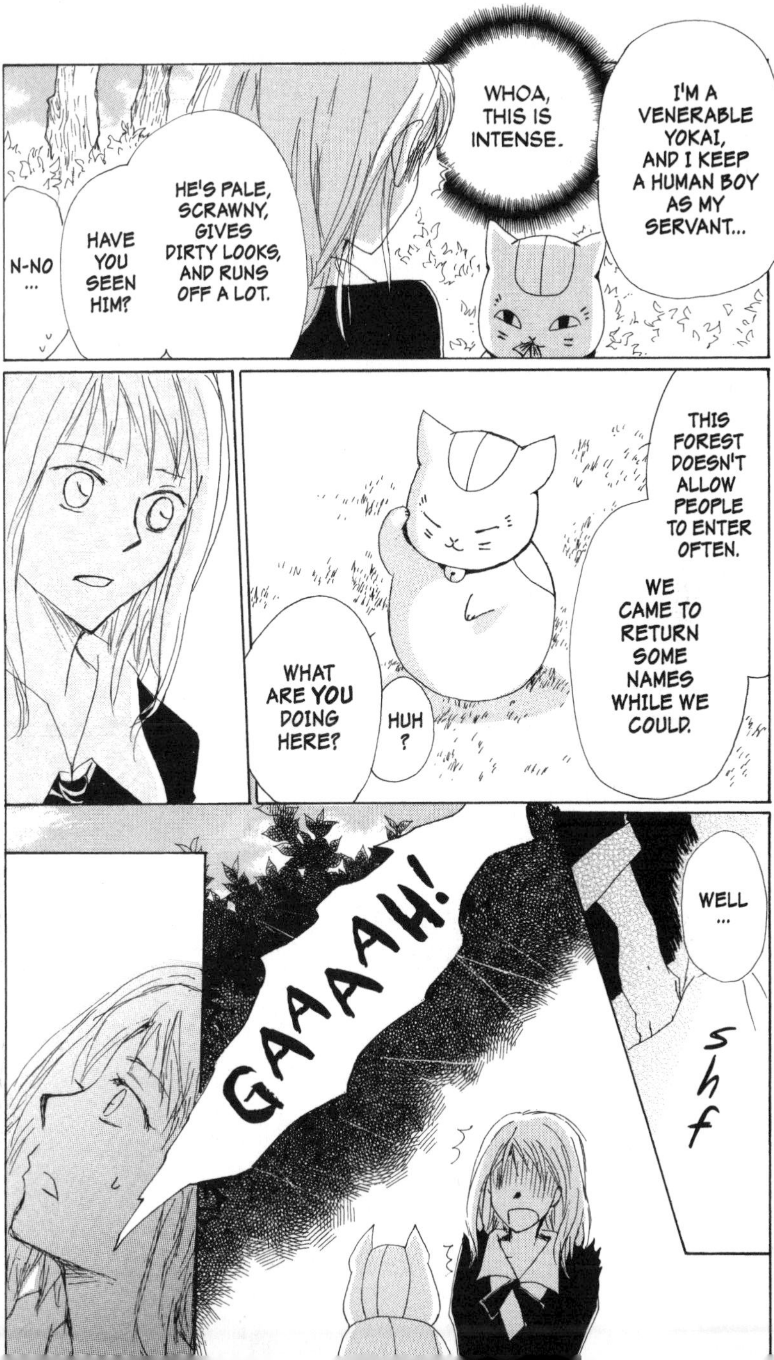
I'M A VENERABLE YOKAI, AND I KEEP A HUMAN BOY AS MY SERVANT...
WHOA, THIS IS INTENSE.
HE'S PALE, SCRAWNY, GIVES DIRTY LOOKS, AND RUNS OFF A LOT.
HAVE YOU SEEN HIM?
N-NO ...
THIS FOREST DOESN'T ALLOW PEOPLE TO ENTER OFTEN.
WE CAME TO RETURN SOME NAMES WHILE WE COULD.
HUH ?
WHAT ARE YOU DOING HERE?
WELL ...
shf
GAAAAH!

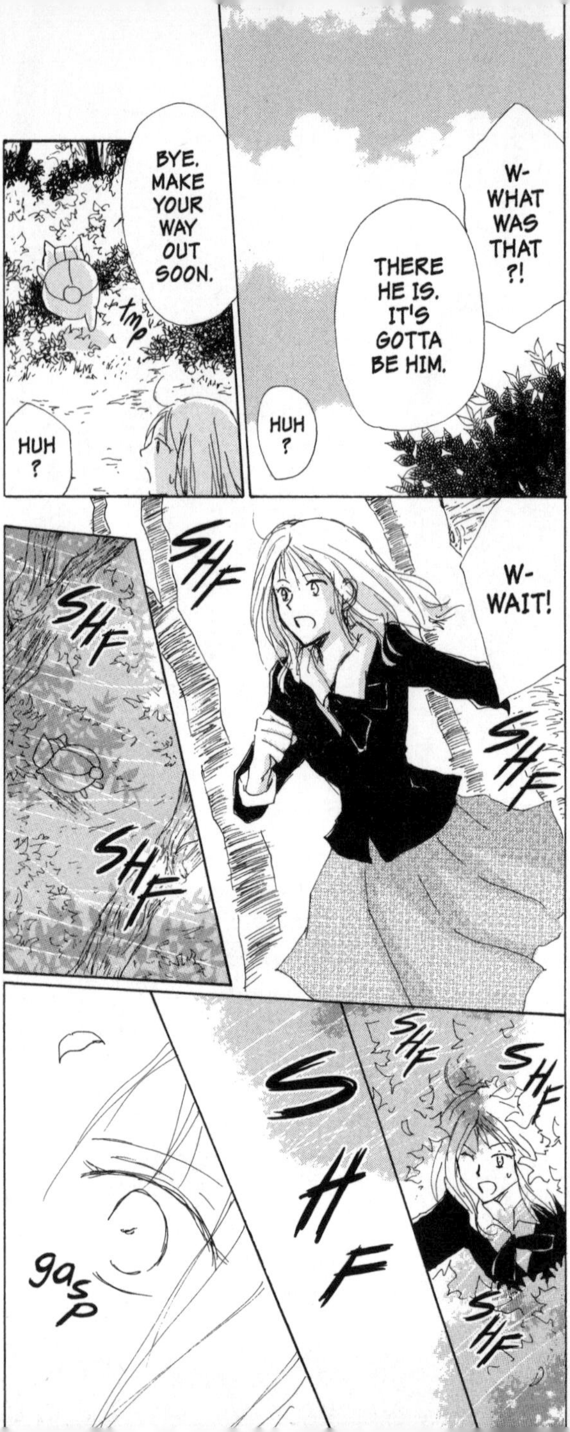
W- WHAT WAS THAT?!
THERE HE IS. IT'S GOTTA BE HIM.
HUH?
BYE. MAKE YOUR WAY OUT SOON.
tmp
HUH?
W- WAIT!
SHF
SHF
SHF
SHF
SHF
SHF
SHF
SHF
SHF
gasp

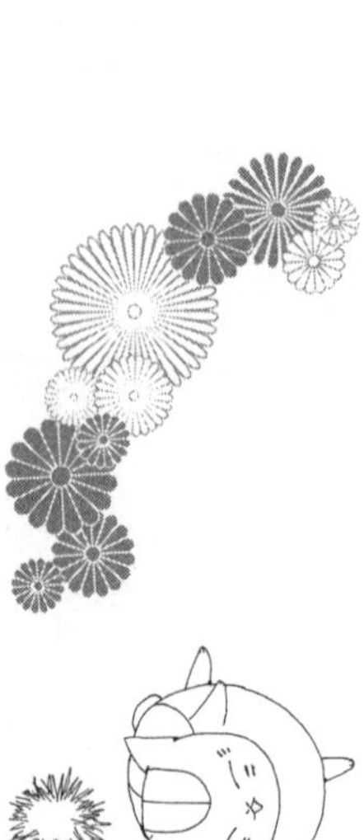

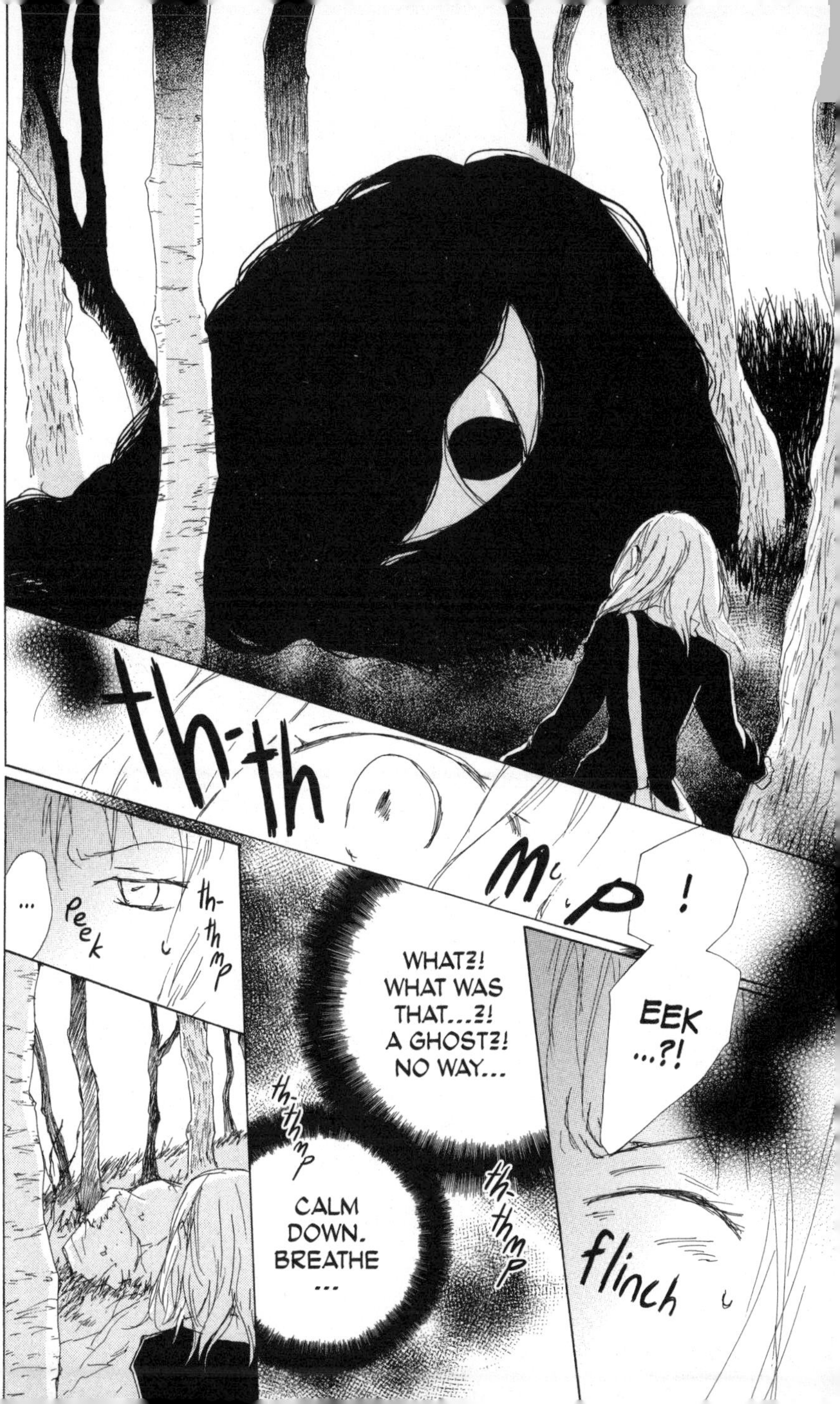
th-thump!
EEK ...?!
flinch
WHAT?! WHAT WAS THAT...?! A GHOST?! NO WAY...
th-thump
th-thump
CALM DOWN. BREATHE ...
...
peek
th-thump

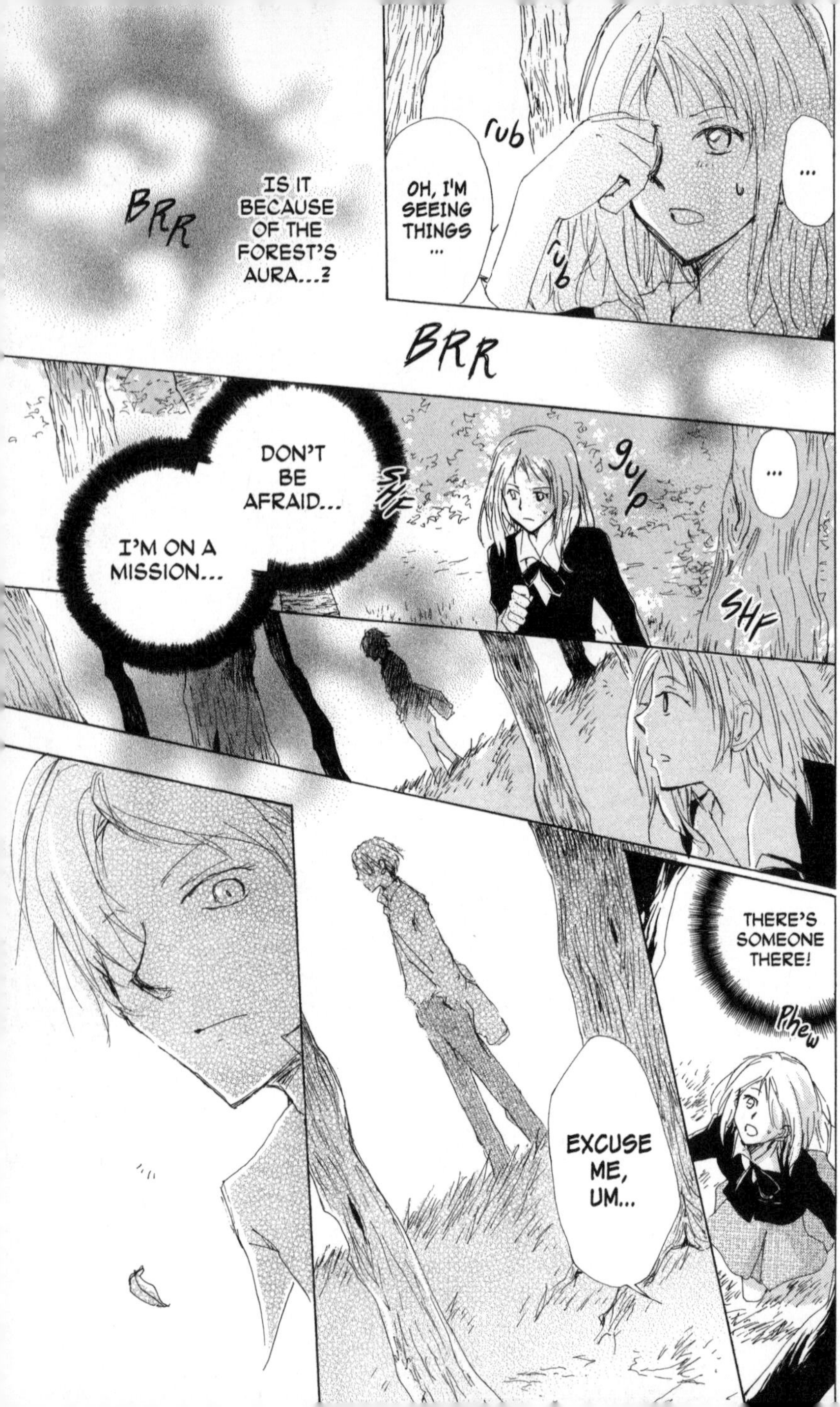
...
rub
OH, I'M SEEING THINGS ...
rub
IS IT BECAUSE OF THE FOREST'S AURA...?
BRR
BRR
...
gulp
SHF
DON'T BE AFRAID...
I'M ON A MISSION...
SHF
THERE'S SOMEONE THERE!
Phew
EXCUSE ME, UM...

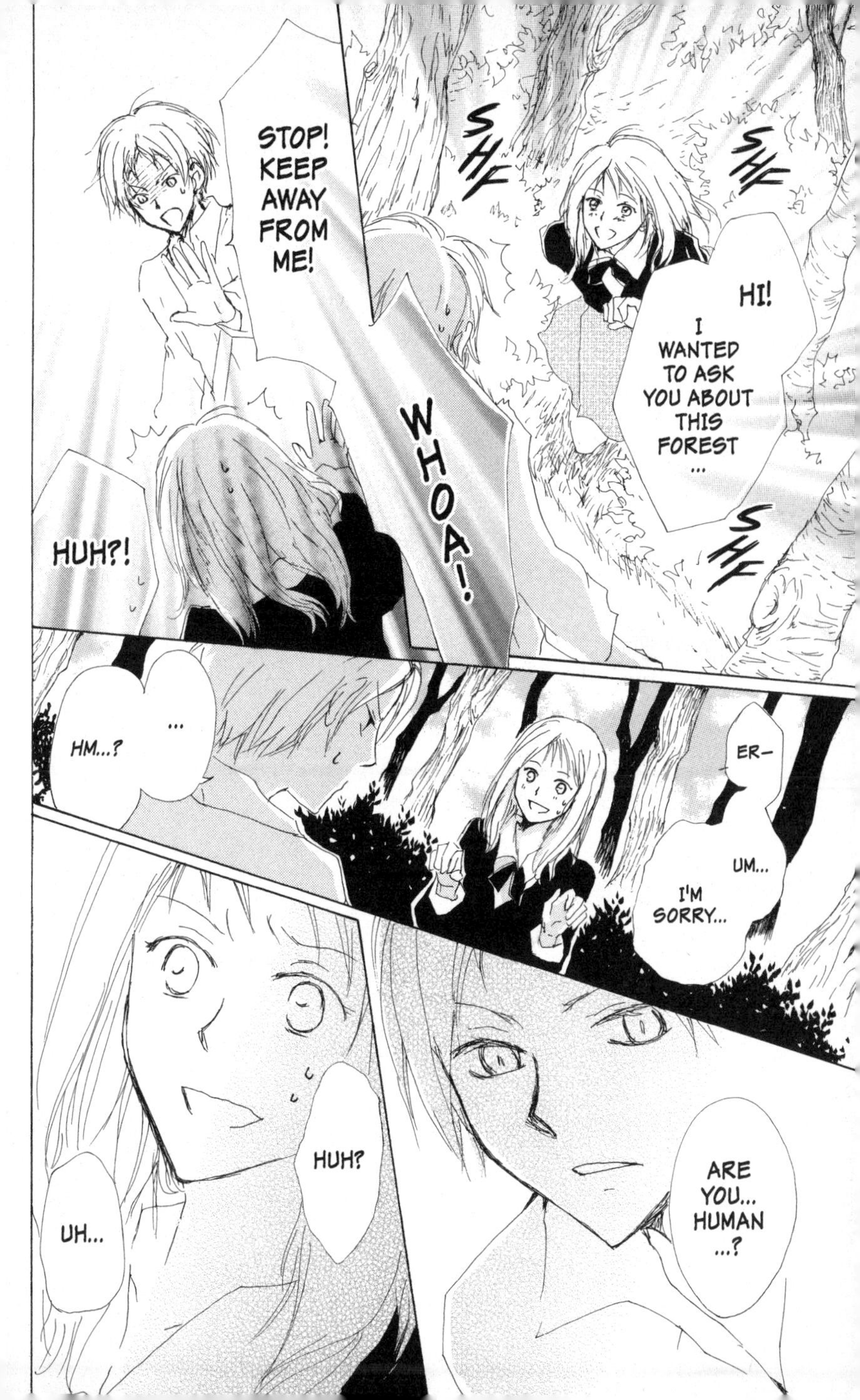
SHH
SHH
HI!
I WANTED TO ASK YOU ABOUT THIS FOREST...
SHH
STOP! KEEP AWAY FROM ME!
WHOA!
HUH?!
ER—
UM...
I'M SORRY...
...
HM...?
ARE YOU... HUMAN...?
HUH?
UH...

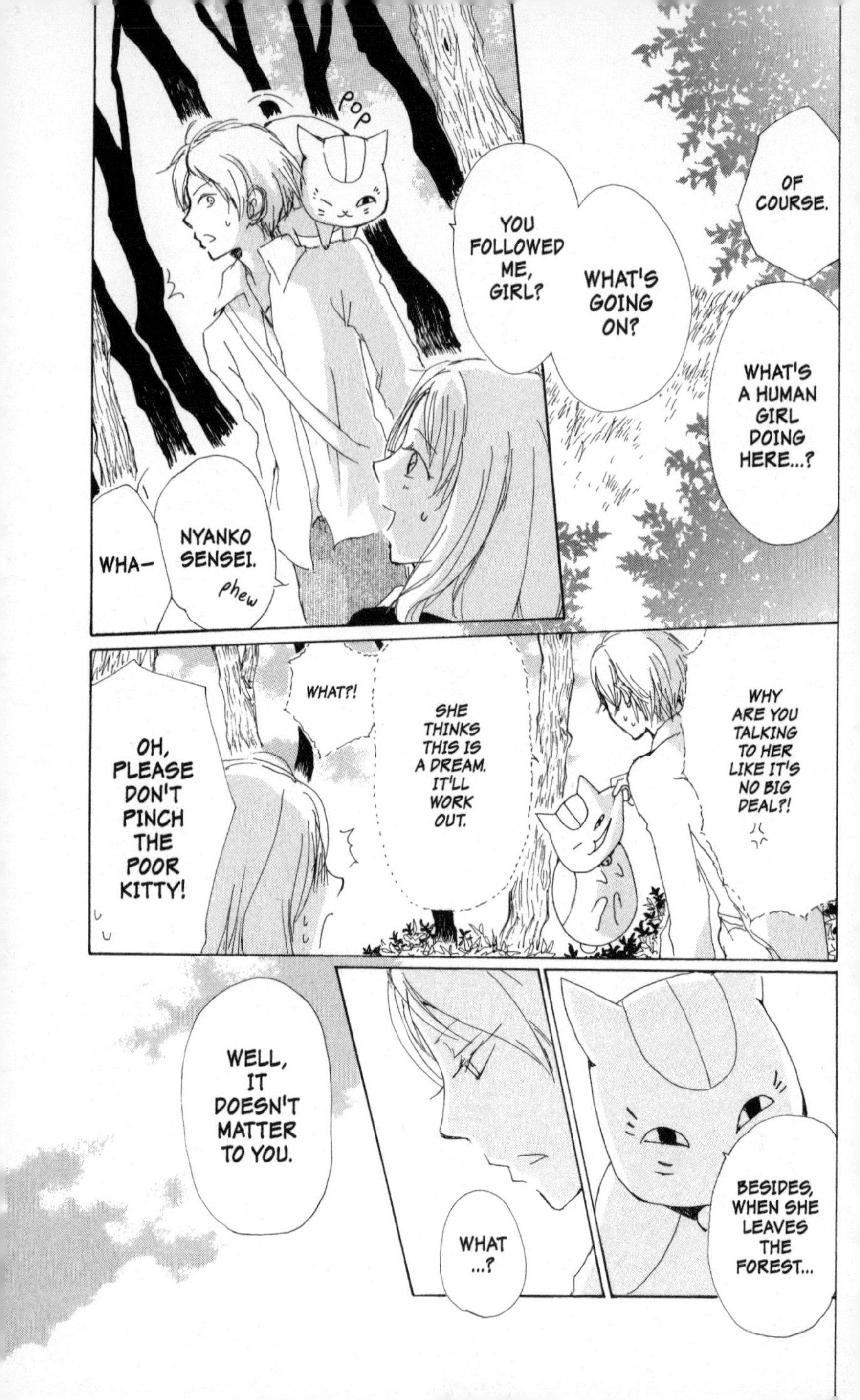
OF COURSE.
YOU FOLLOWED ME, GIRL?
WHAT'S GOING ON?
WHAT'S A HUMAN GIRL DOING HERE...?
POP
NYANKO SENSEI.
phew
WHA-
WHY ARE YOU TALKING TO HER LIKE IT'S NO BIG DEAL?!
SHE THINKS THIS IS A DREAM. IT'LL WORK OUT.
WHAT?!
OH, PLEASE DON'T PINCH THE POOR KITTY!
BESIDES, WHEN SHE LEAVES THE FOREST...
WHAT ...?
WELL, IT DOESN'T MATTER TO YOU.

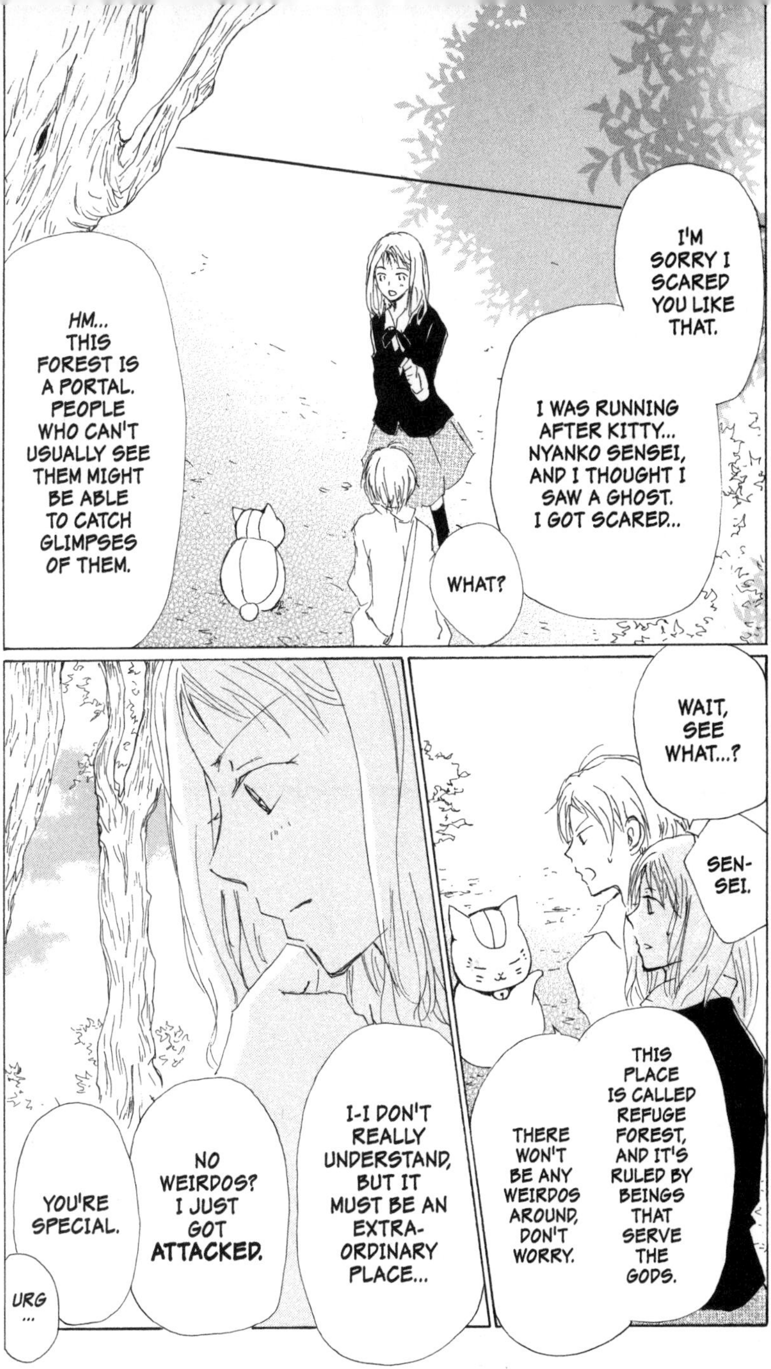
I'M SORRY I SCARED YOU LIKE THAT.
I WAS RUNNING AFTER KITTY... NYANKO SENSEI, AND I THOUGHT I SAW A GHOST. I GOT SCARED...
WHAT?
HM... THIS FOREST IS A PORTAL. PEOPLE WHO CAN'T USUALLY SEE THEM MIGHT BE ABLE TO CATCH GLIMPSES OF THEM.
WAIT, SEE WHAT...?
SEN-SEI.
THIS PLACE IS CALLED REFUGE FOREST, AND IT'S RULED BY BEINGS THAT SERVE THE GODS.
THERE WON'T BE ANY WEIRDOS AROUND, DON'T WORRY.
I-I DON'T REALLY UNDERSTAND, BUT IT MUST BE AN EXTRA-ORDINARY PLACE...
NO WEIRDOS? I JUST GOT **ATTACKED.**
YOU'RE SPECIAL.
URG...

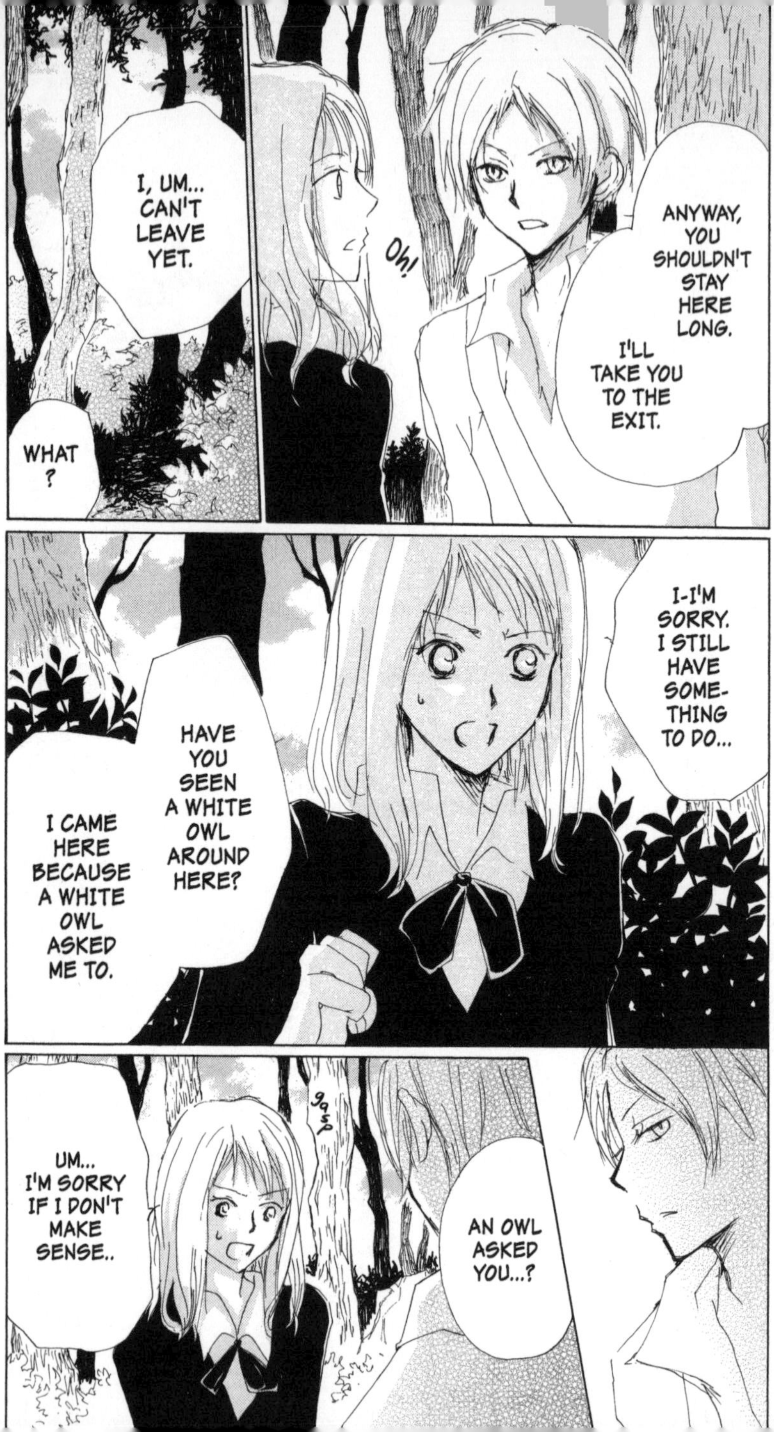
ANYWAY, YOU SHOULDN'T STAY HERE LONG.
Oh!
I'LL TAKE YOU TO THE EXIT.
I, UM... CAN'T LEAVE YET.
WHAT?
I-I'M SORRY. I STILL HAVE SOME-THING TO DO...
HAVE YOU SEEN A WHITE OWL AROUND HERE?
I CAME HERE BECAUSE A WHITE OWL ASKED ME TO.
AN OWL ASKED YOU...?
gasp
UM... I'M SORRY IF I DON'T MAKE SENSE..

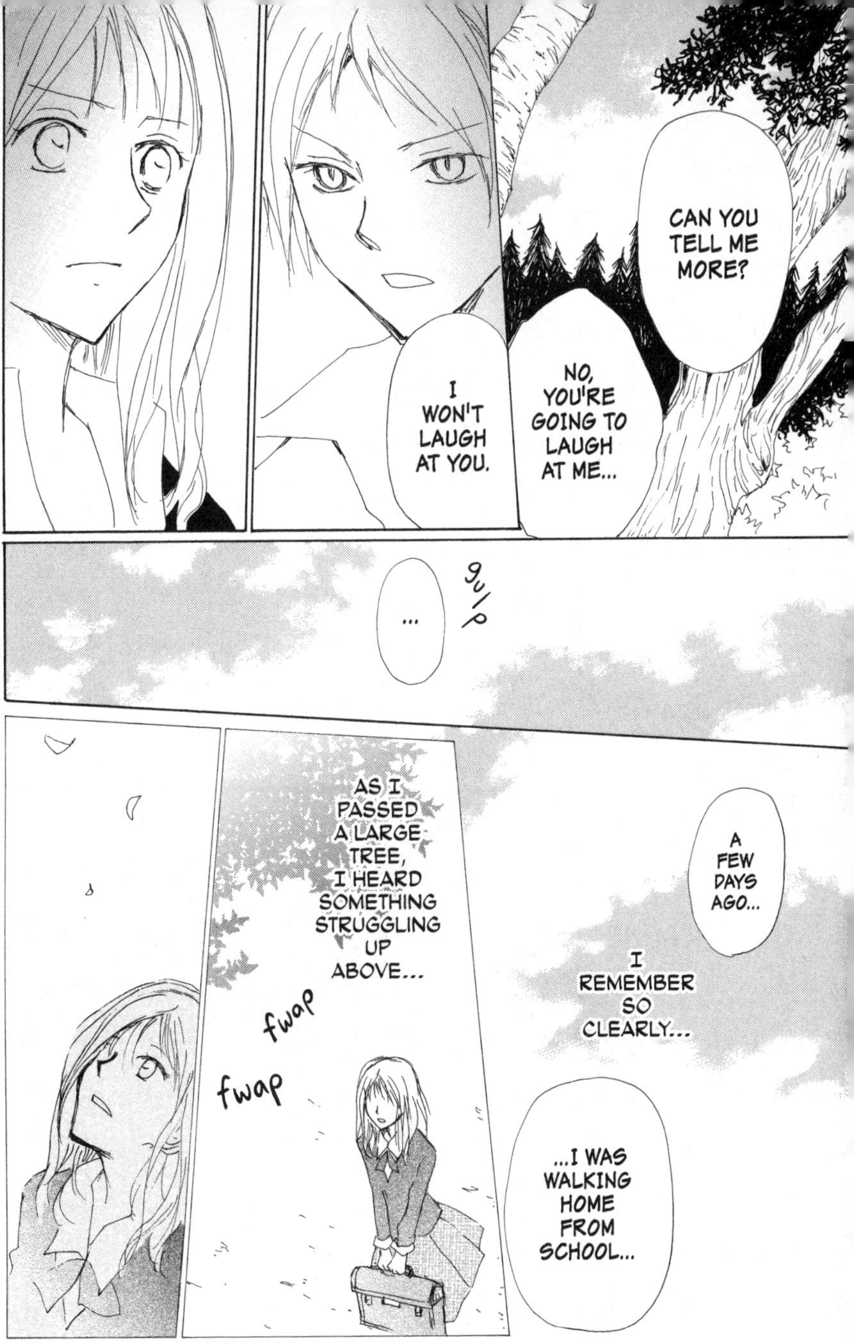
CAN YOU TELL ME MORE?
NO, YOU'RE GOING TO LAUGH AT ME...
I WON'T LAUGH AT YOU.
...
gulp
A FEW DAYS AGO...
I REMEMBER SO CLEARLY...
...I WAS WALKING HOME FROM SCHOOL...
AS I PASSED A LARGE TREE, I HEARD SOMETHING STRUGGLING UP ABOVE...
fwap
fwap

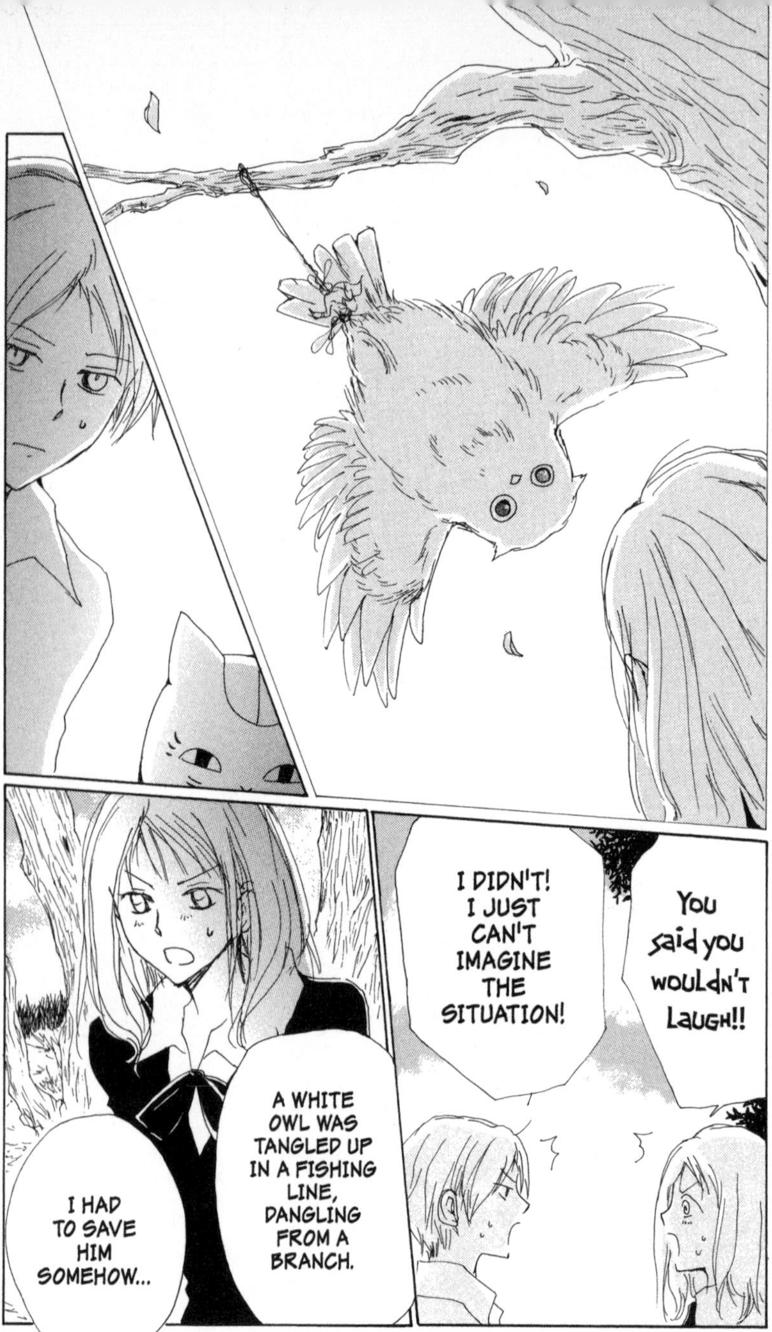
You said you wouldn't laugh!!
I DIDN'T! I JUST CAN'T IMAGINE THE SITUATION!
A WHITE OWL WAS TANGLED UP IN A FISHING LINE, DANGLING FROM A BRANCH.
I HAD TO SAVE HIM SOMEHOW...

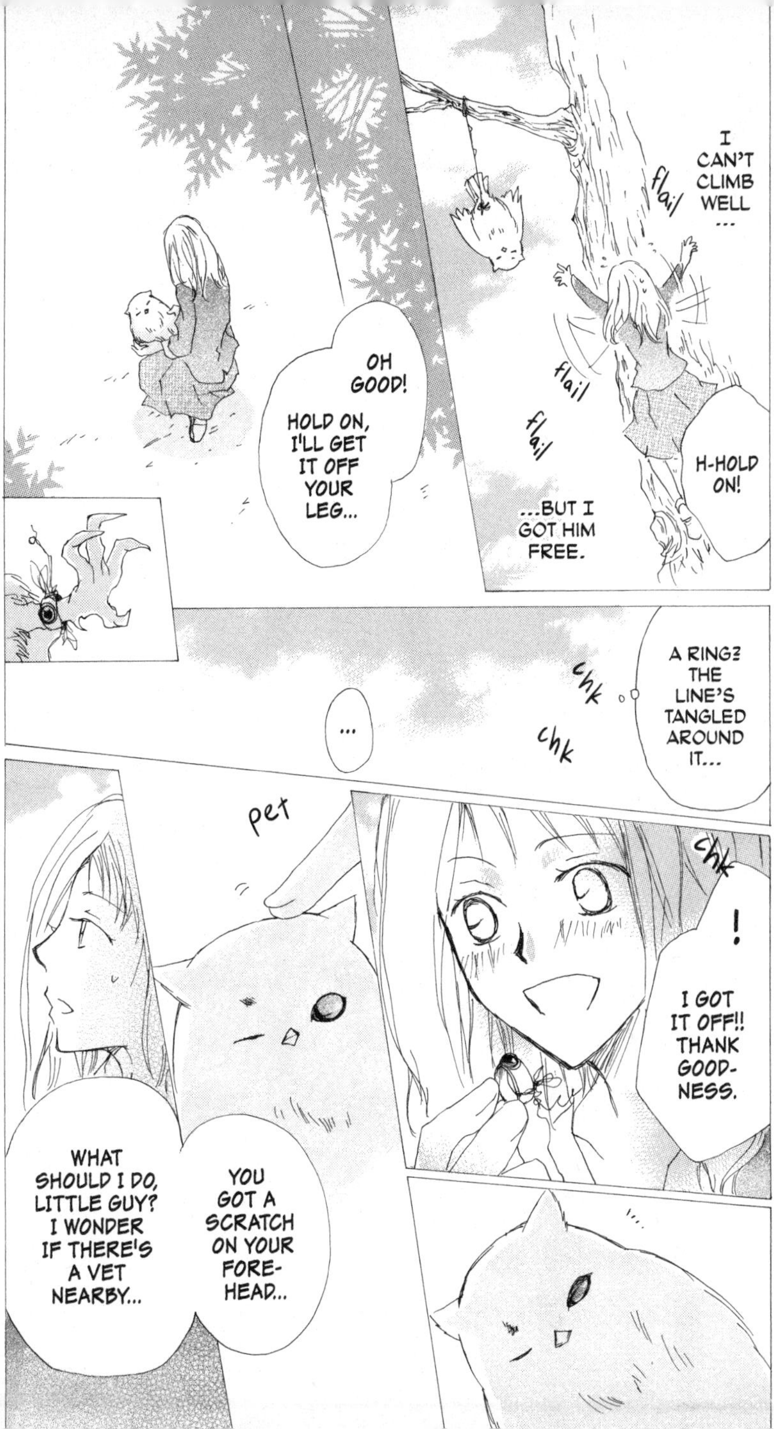

I CAN'T CLIMB WELL...
flail
flail
flail
H-HOLD ON!
...BUT I GOT HIM FREE.
OH GOOD!
HOLD ON, I'LL GET IT OFF YOUR LEG...
A RING? THE LINE'S TANGLED AROUND IT...
chk
chk
...
chk
!
I GOT IT OFF!! THANK GOOD-NESS.
pet
YOU GOT A SCRATCH ON YOUR FORE-HEAD...
WHAT SHOULD I DO, LITTLE GUY? I WONDER IF THERE'S A VET NEARBY...

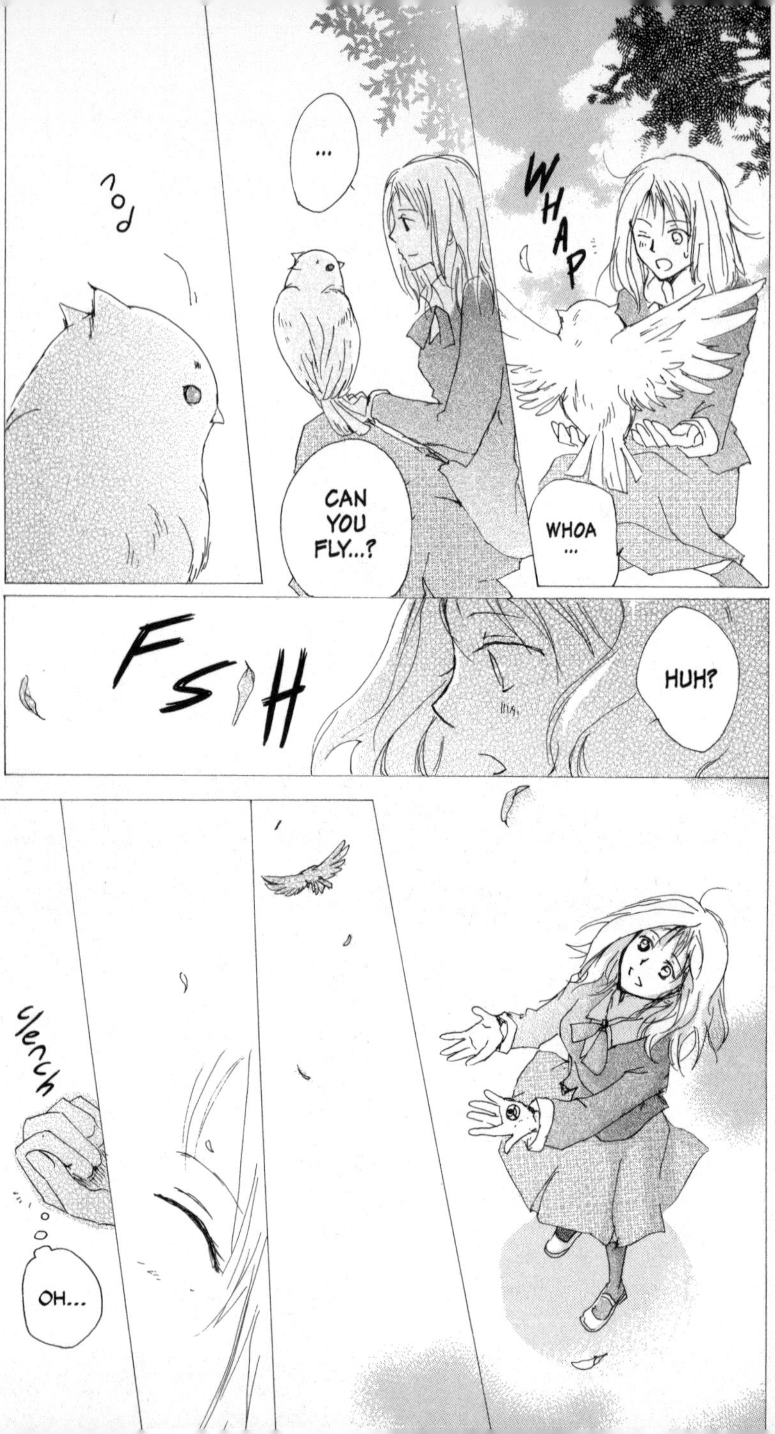

WHAP
WHOA...
...
CAN YOU FLY...?
pou
HUH?
FSH
clench
OH...

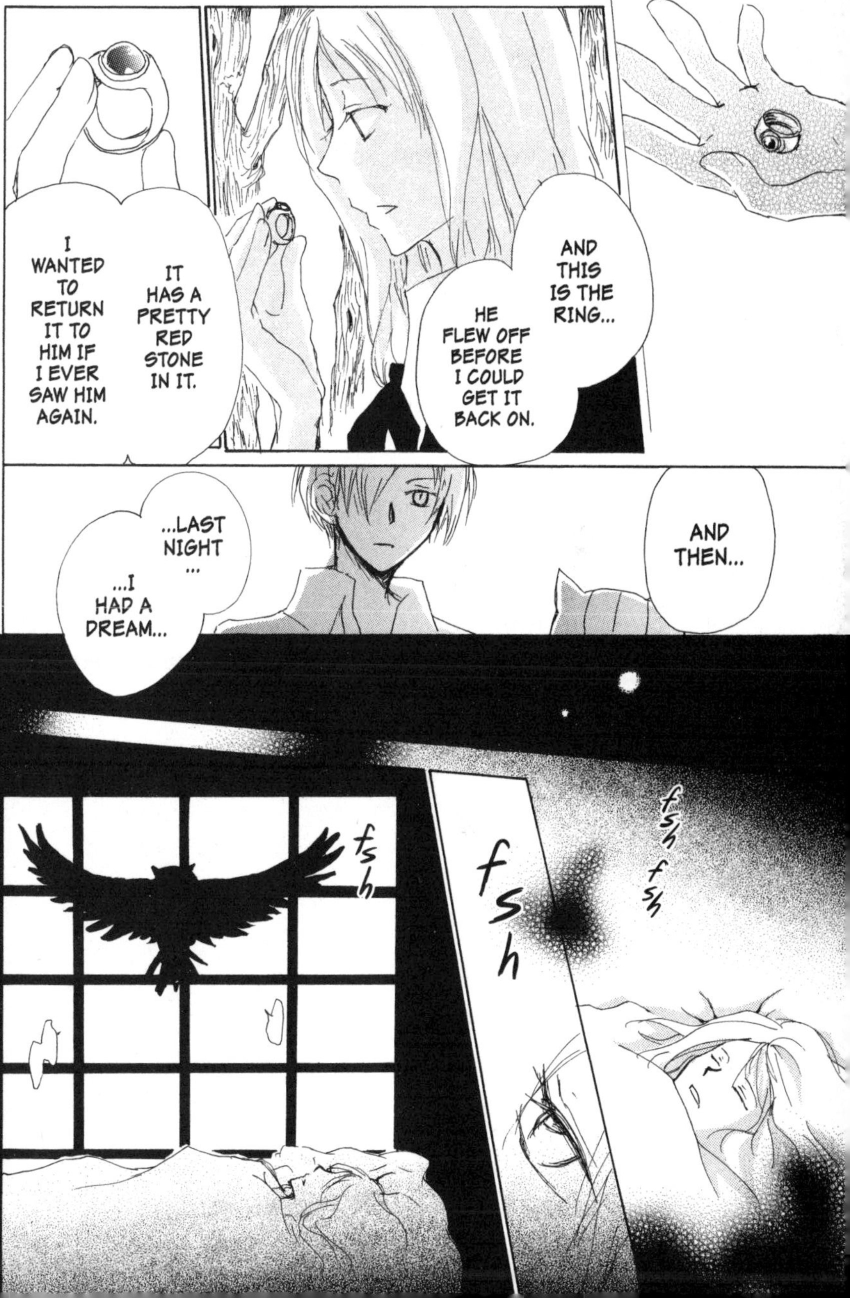
AND THIS IS THE RING...
HE FLEW OFF BEFORE I COULD GET IT BACK ON.
IT HAS A PRETTY RED STONE IN IT.
I WANTED TO RETURN IT TO HIM IF I EVER SAW HIM AGAIN.
AND THEN...
...LAST NIGHT ...
...I HAD A DREAM...
fsh fsh
fsh
fsh

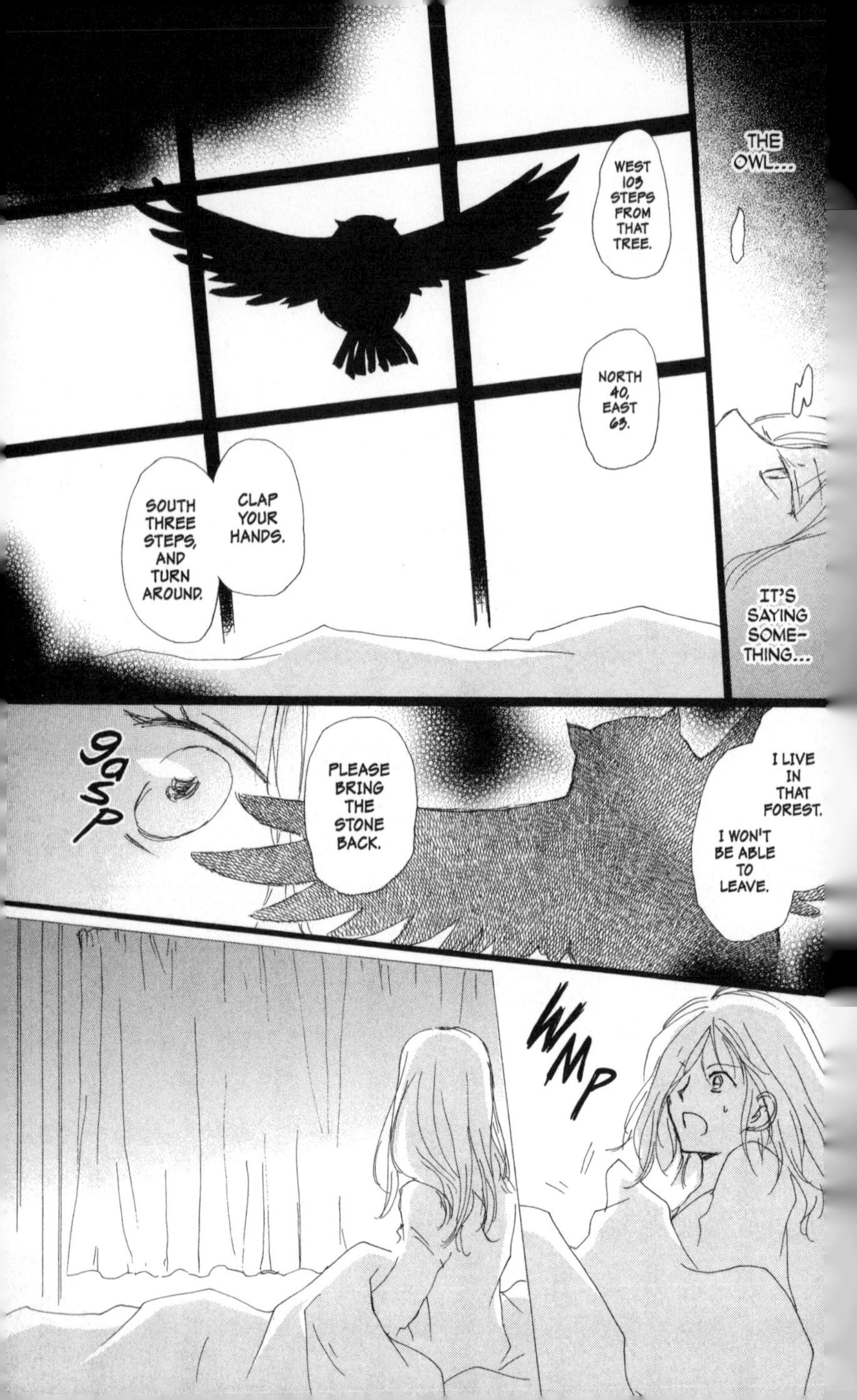
THE OWL...
IT'S SAYING SOME-THING...
WEST 103 STEPS FROM THAT TREE.
NORTH 40, EAST 63.
CLAP YOUR HANDS.
SOUTH THREE STEPS, AND TURN AROUND.
I LIVE IN THAT FOREST.
I WON'T BE ABLE TO LEAVE.
PLEASE BRING THE STONE BACK.
gasp
WMP

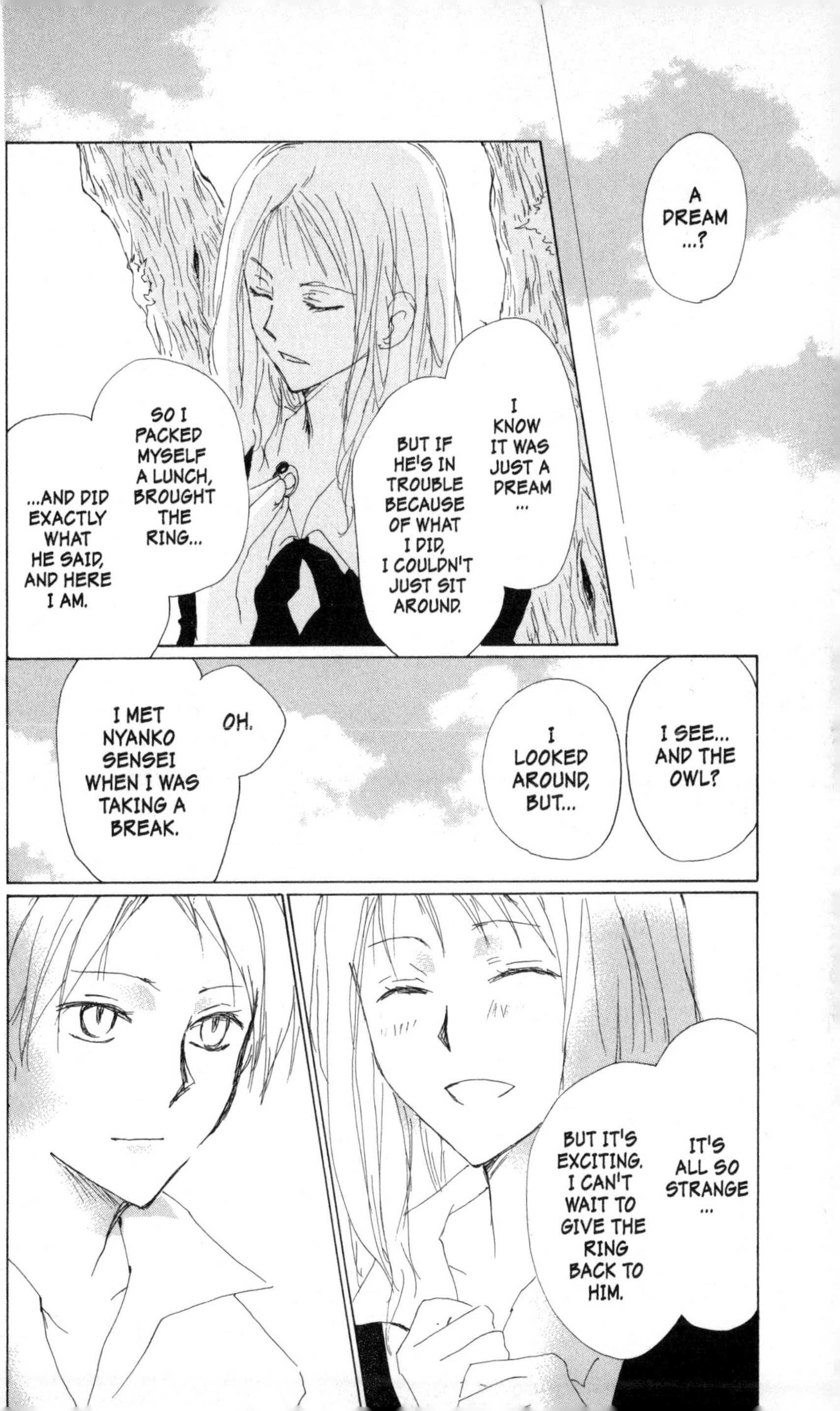
A DREAM ...?
I KNOW IT WAS JUST A DREAM ...
BUT IF HE'S IN TROUBLE BECAUSE OF WHAT I DID, I COULDN'T JUST SIT AROUND.
SO I PACKED MYSELF A LUNCH, BROUGHT THE RING...
...AND DID EXACTLY WHAT HE SAID, AND HERE I AM.
I SEE... AND THE OWL?
I LOOKED AROUND, BUT...
OH.
I MET NYANKO SENSEI WHEN I WAS TAKING A BREAK.
IT'S ALL SO STRANGE ...
BUT IT'S EXCITING. I CAN'T WAIT TO GIVE THE RING BACK TO HIM.

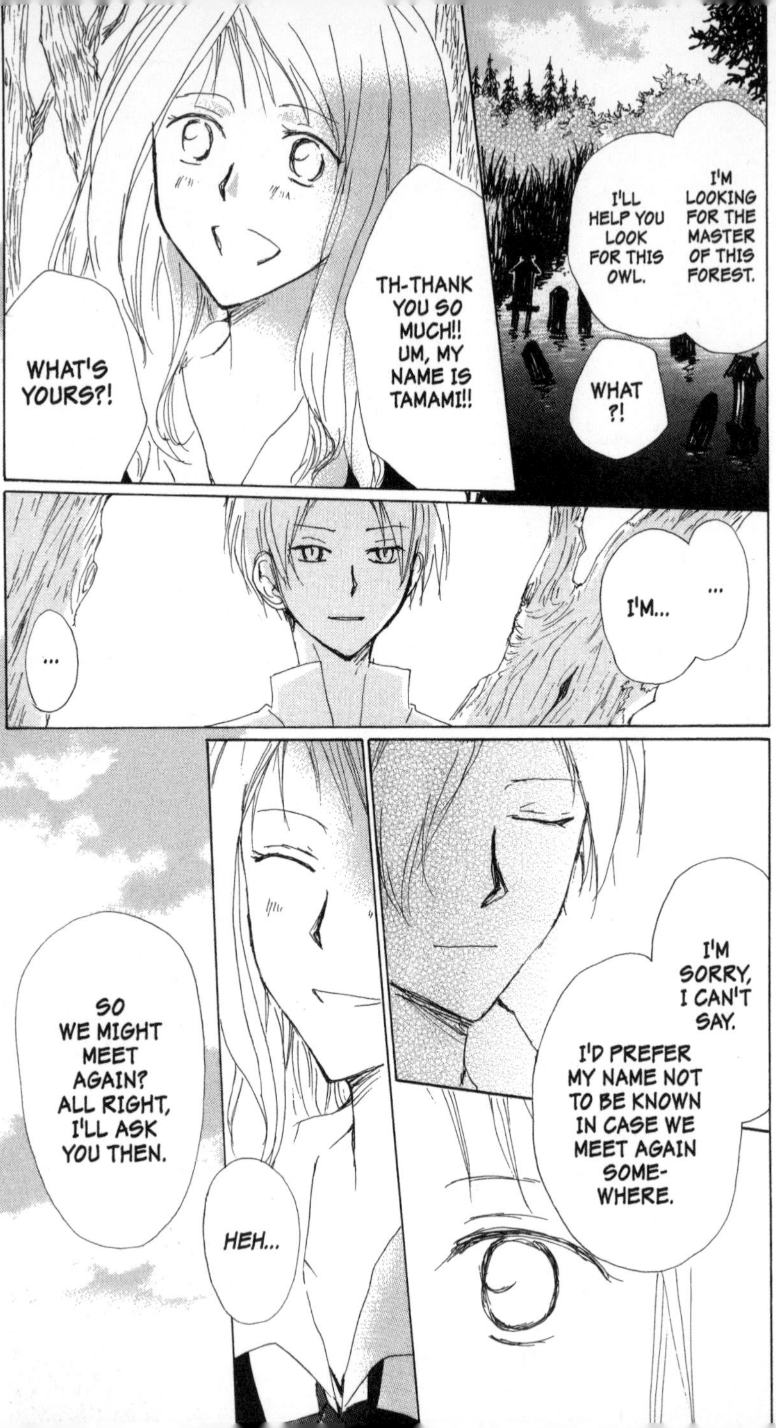
I'M LOOKING FOR THE MASTER OF THIS FOREST.
I'LL HELP YOU LOOK FOR THIS OWL.
WHAT?!
TH-THANK YOU SO MUCH!! UM, MY NAME IS TAMAMI!!
WHAT'S YOURS?!
...
I'M...
...
I'M SORRY, I CAN'T SAY.
I'D PREFER MY NAME NOT TO BE KNOWN IN CASE WE MEET AGAIN SOME-WHERE.
SO WE MIGHT MEET AGAIN? ALL RIGHT, I'LL ASK YOU THEN.
HEH...

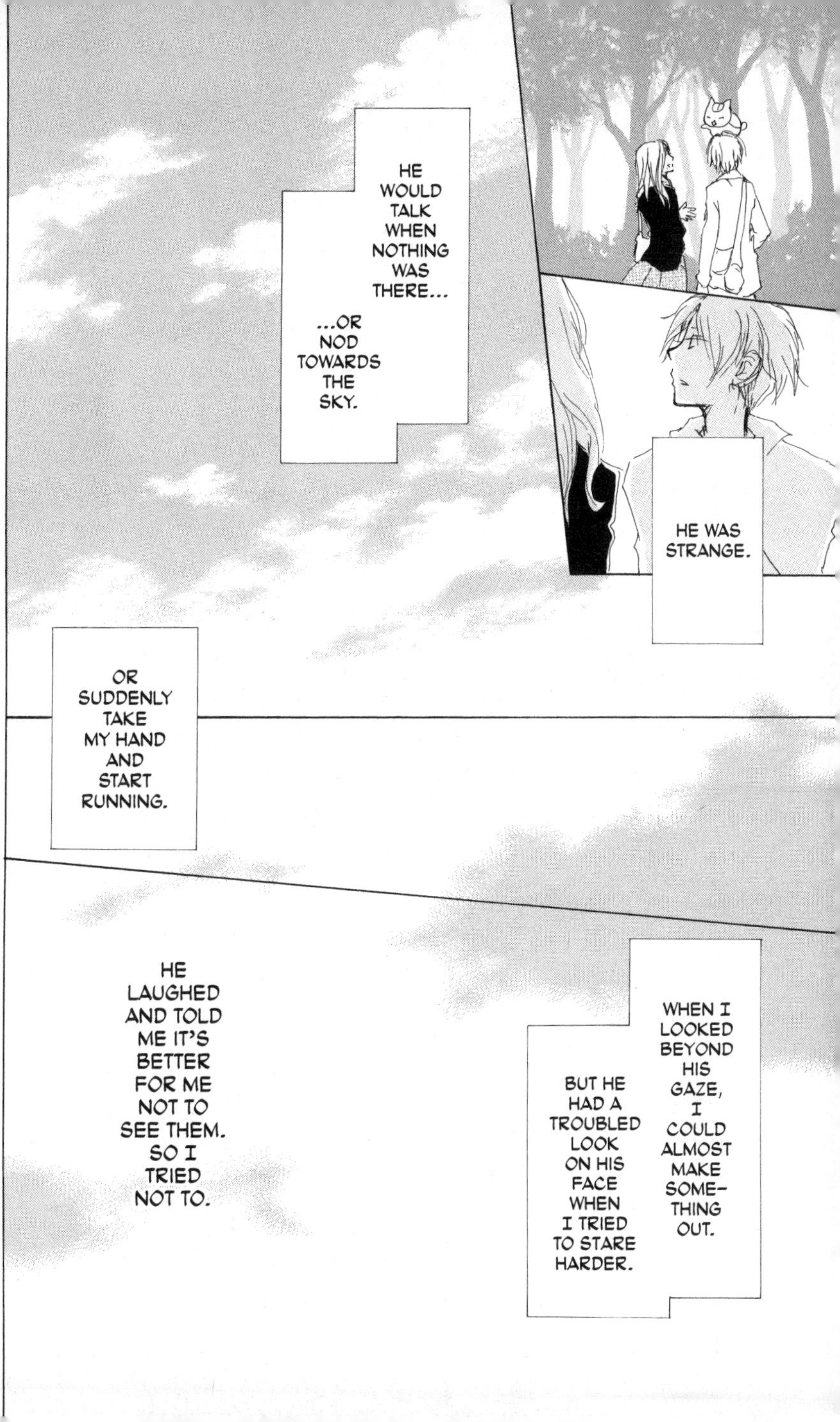
HE WAS STRANGE.
HE WOULD TALK WHEN NOTHING WAS THERE...
...OR NOD TOWARDS THE SKY.
OR SUDDENLY TAKE MY HAND AND START RUNNING.
WHEN I LOOKED BEYOND HIS GAZE, I COULD ALMOST MAKE SOME-THING OUT.
BUT HE HAD A TROUBLED LOOK ON HIS FACE WHEN I TRIED TO STARE HARDER.
HE LAUGHED AND TOLD ME IT'S BETTER FOR ME NOT TO SEE THEM. SO I TRIED NOT TO.

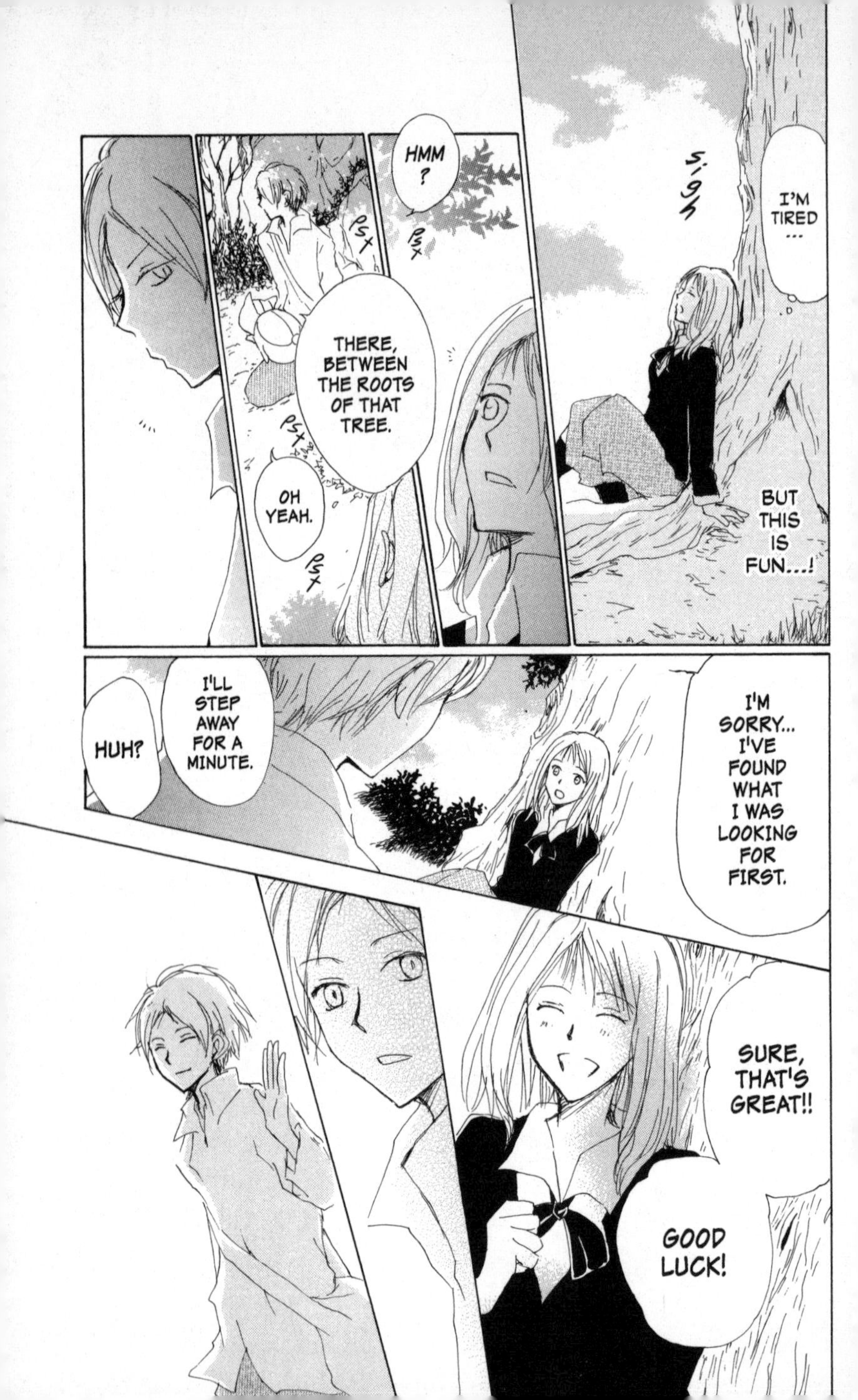
sigh
I'M TIRED...
BUT THIS IS FUN...!
HMM?
pst
pst
THERE, BETWEEN THE ROOTS OF THAT TREE.
pst
OH YEAH.
pst
I'M SORRY... I'VE FOUND WHAT I WAS LOOKING FOR FIRST.
I'LL STEP AWAY FOR A MINUTE.
HUH?
SURE, THAT'S GREAT!!
GOOD LUCK!

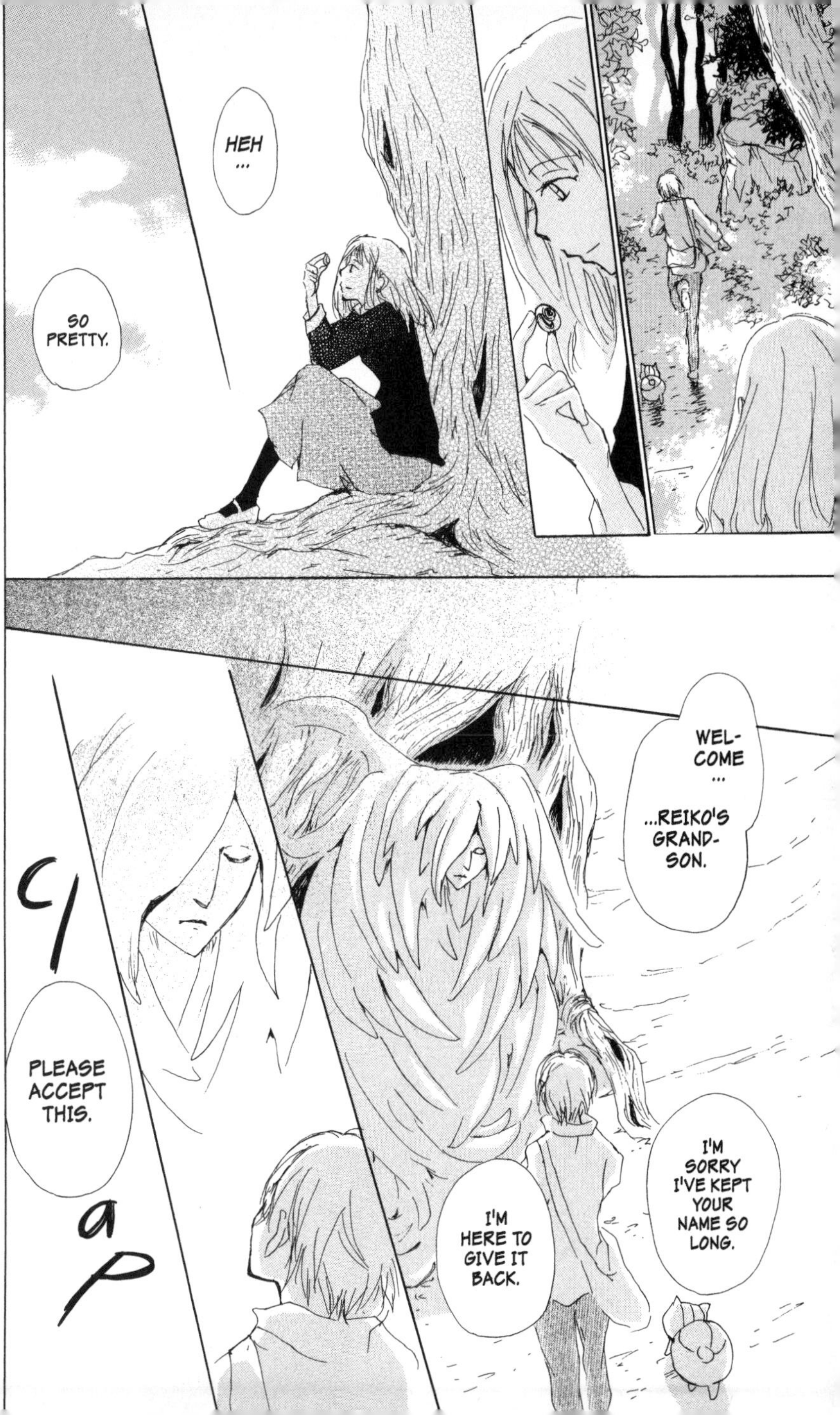
HEH ...
SO PRETTY.
WEL-COME ...
...REIKO'S GRAND-SON.
I'M SORRY I'VE KEPT YOUR NAME SO LONG.
I'M HERE TO GIVE IT BACK.
PLEASE ACCEPT THIS.
Clap

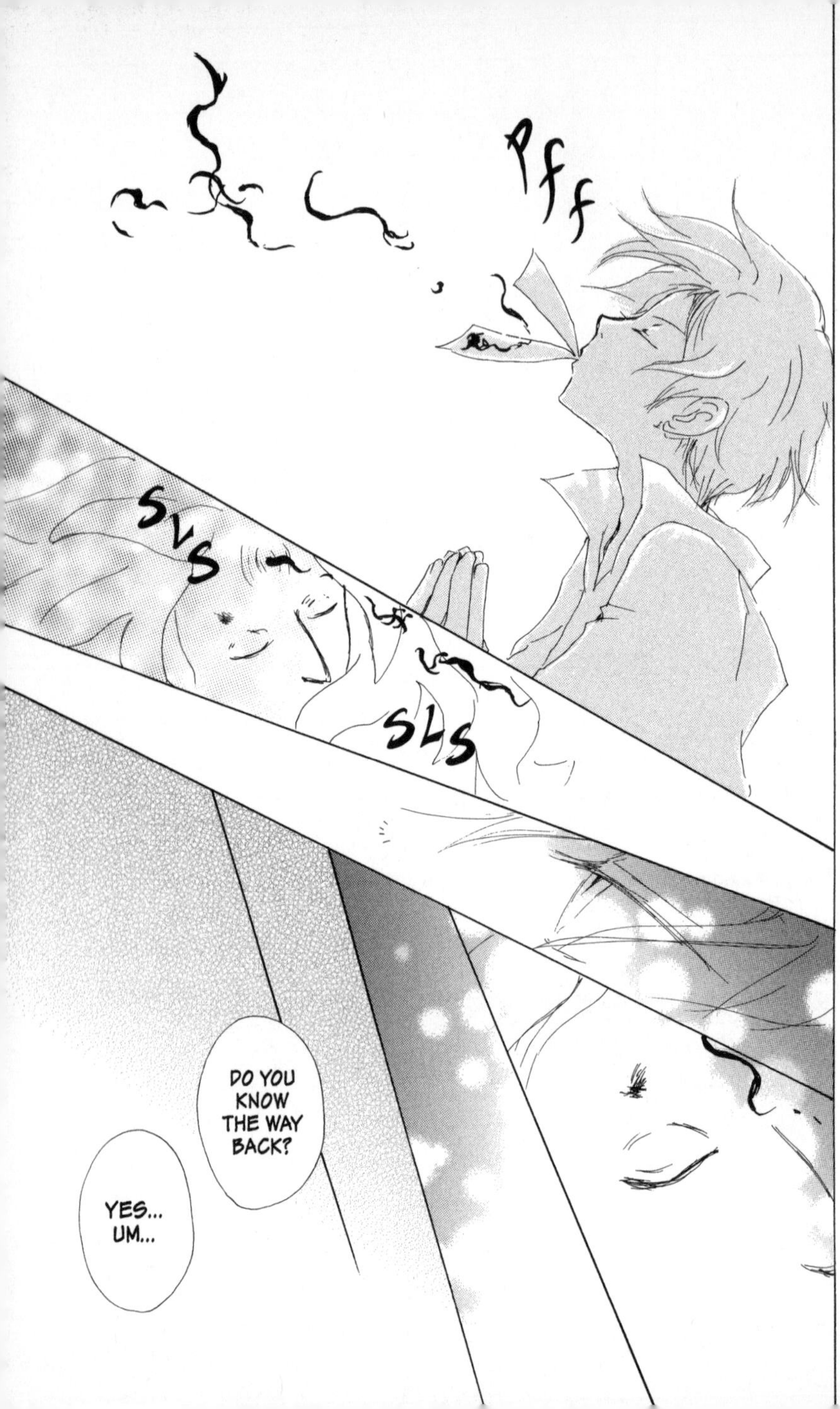
Pff
SVS
SLS
DO YOU KNOW THE WAY BACK?
YES... UM...

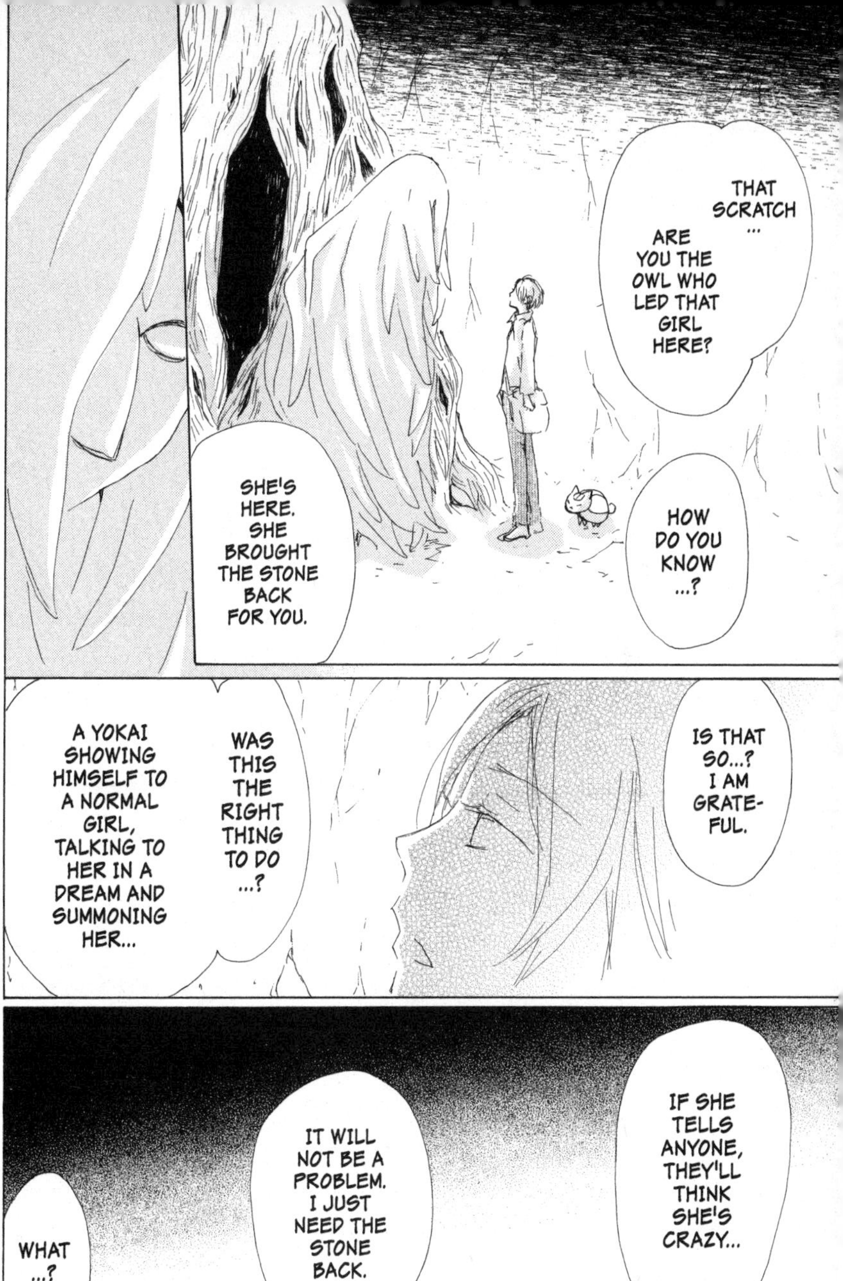
THAT SCRATCH ...
ARE YOU THE OWL WHO LED THAT GIRL HERE?
HOW DO YOU KNOW ...?
SHE'S HERE. SHE BROUGHT THE STONE BACK FOR YOU.
IS THAT SO...? I AM GRATE-FUL.
WAS THIS THE RIGHT THING TO DO ...?
A YOKAI SHOWING HIMSELF TO A NORMAL GIRL, TALKING TO HER IN A DREAM AND SUMMONING HER...
IF SHE TELLS ANYONE, THEY'LL THINK SHE'S CRAZY...
IT WILL NOT BE A PROBLEM. I JUST NEED THE STONE BACK.
WHAT ...?

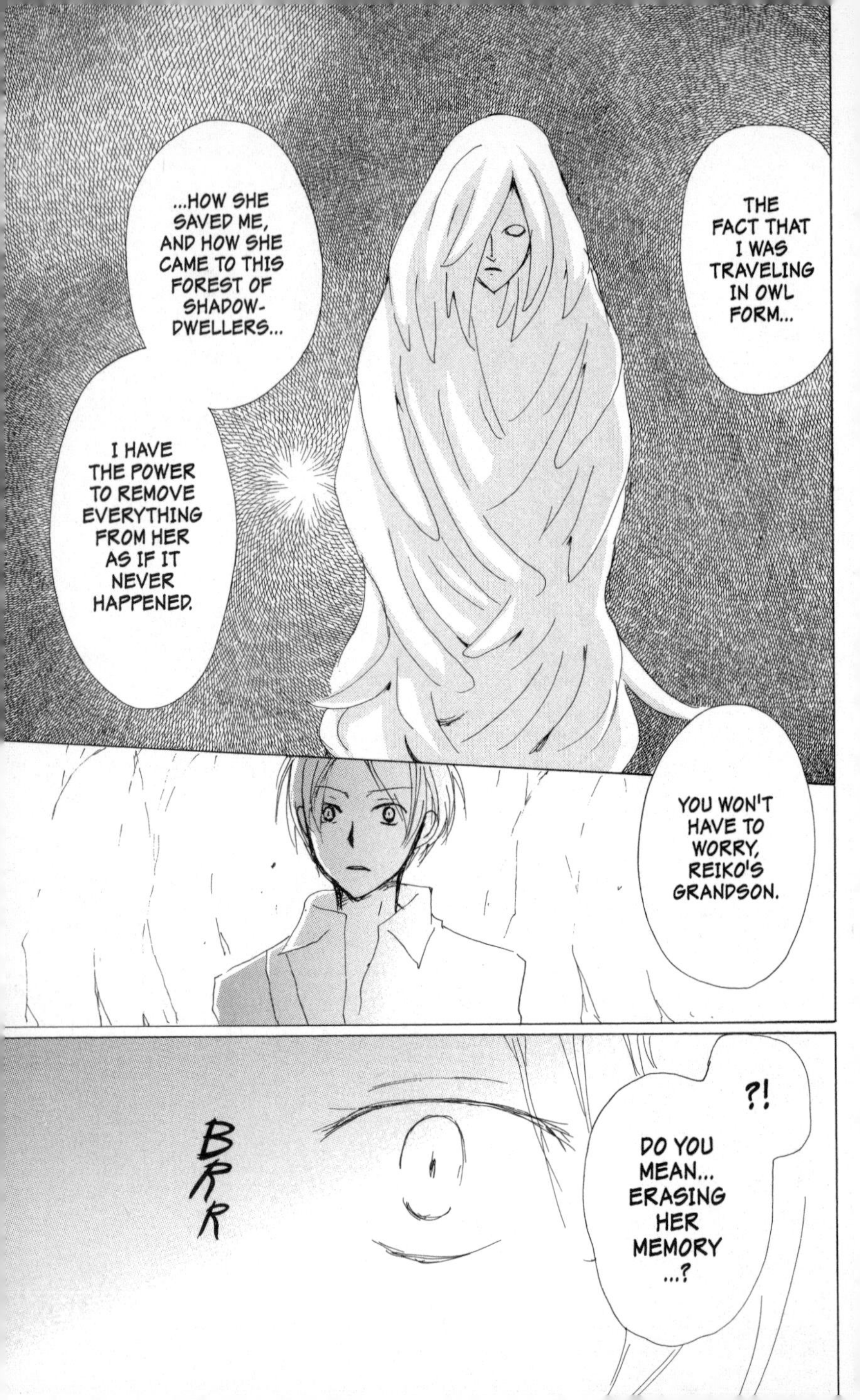
THE FACT THAT I WAS TRAVELING IN OWL FORM...
...HOW SHE SAVED ME, AND HOW SHE CAME TO THIS FOREST OF SHADOW-DWELLERS...
I HAVE THE POWER TO REMOVE EVERYTHING FROM HER AS IF IT NEVER HAPPENED.
YOU WON'T HAVE TO WORRY, REIKO'S GRANDSON.
?!
DO YOU MEAN... ERASING HER MEMORY ...?
BRR

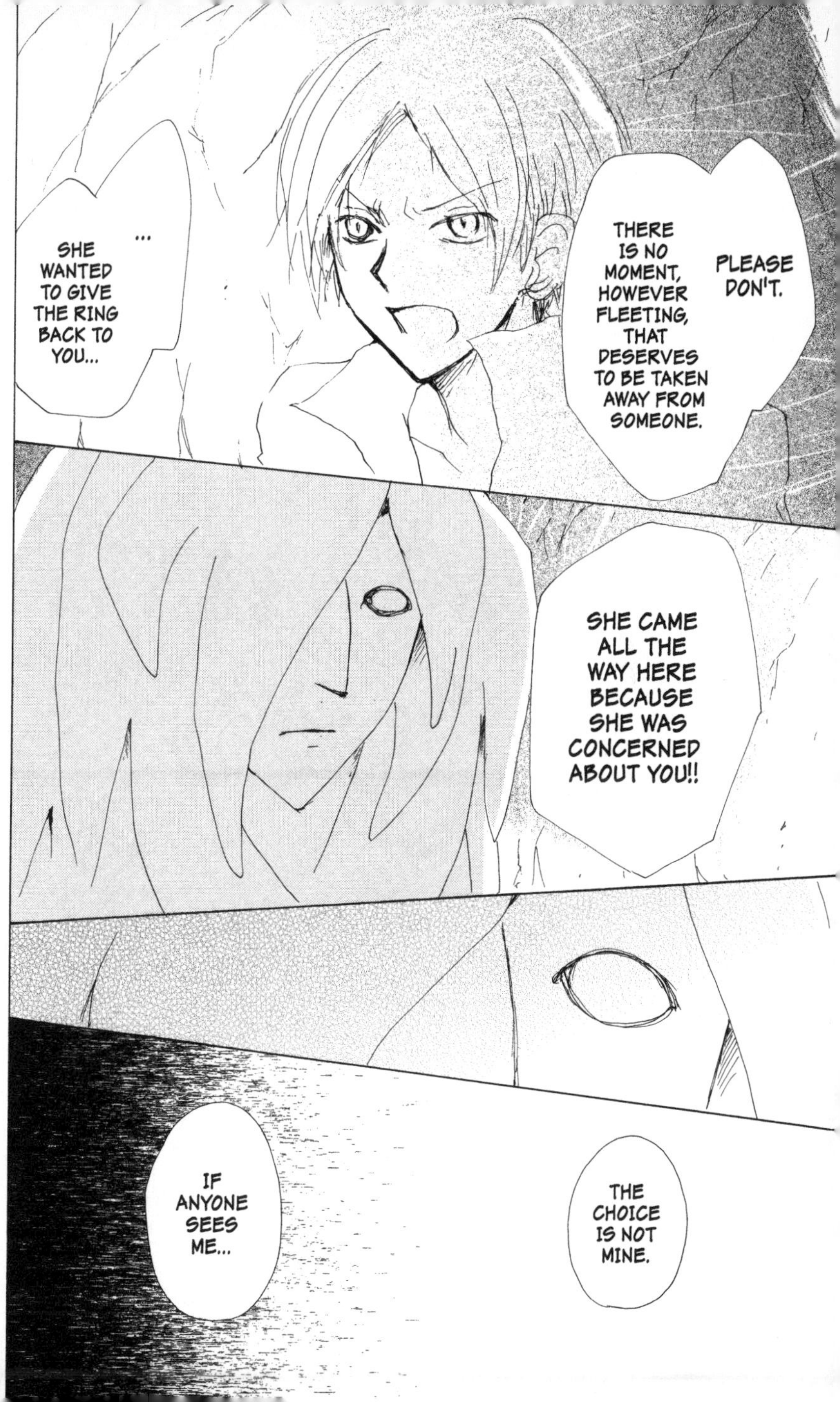
PLEASE DON'T.
THERE IS NO MOMENT, HOWEVER FLEETING, THAT DESERVES TO BE TAKEN AWAY FROM SOMEONE.
...
SHE WANTED TO GIVE THE RING BACK TO YOU...
SHE CAME ALL THE WAY HERE BECAUSE SHE WAS CONCERNED ABOUT YOU!!
THE CHOICE IS NOT MINE.
IF ANYONE SEES ME...

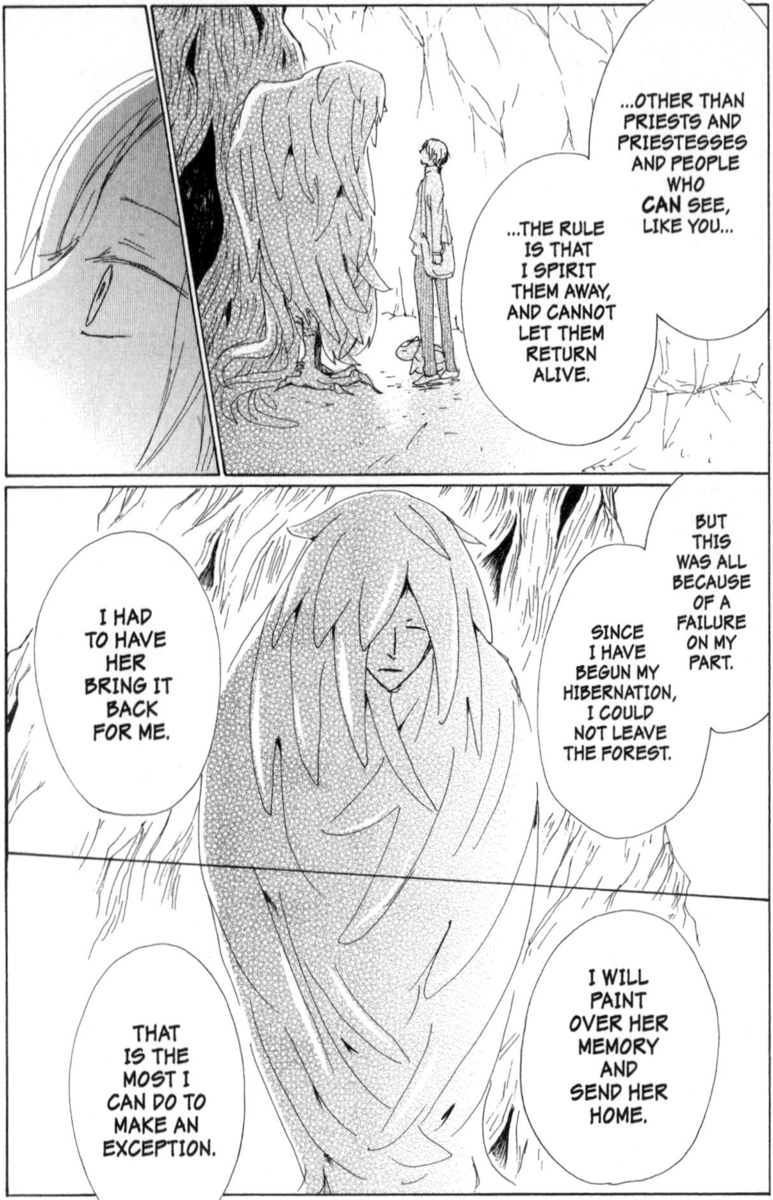
...OTHER THAN PRIESTS AND PRIESTESSES AND PEOPLE WHO CAN SEE, LIKE YOU...
...THE RULE IS THAT I SPIRIT THEM AWAY, AND CANNOT LET THEM RETURN ALIVE.
BUT THIS WAS ALL BECAUSE OF A FAILURE ON MY PART.
SINCE I HAVE BEGUN MY HIBERNATION, I COULD NOT LEAVE THE FOREST.
I HAD TO HAVE HER BRING IT BACK FOR ME.
I WILL PAINT OVER HER MEMORY AND SEND HER HOME.
THAT IS THE MOST I CAN DO TO MAKE AN EXCEPTION.

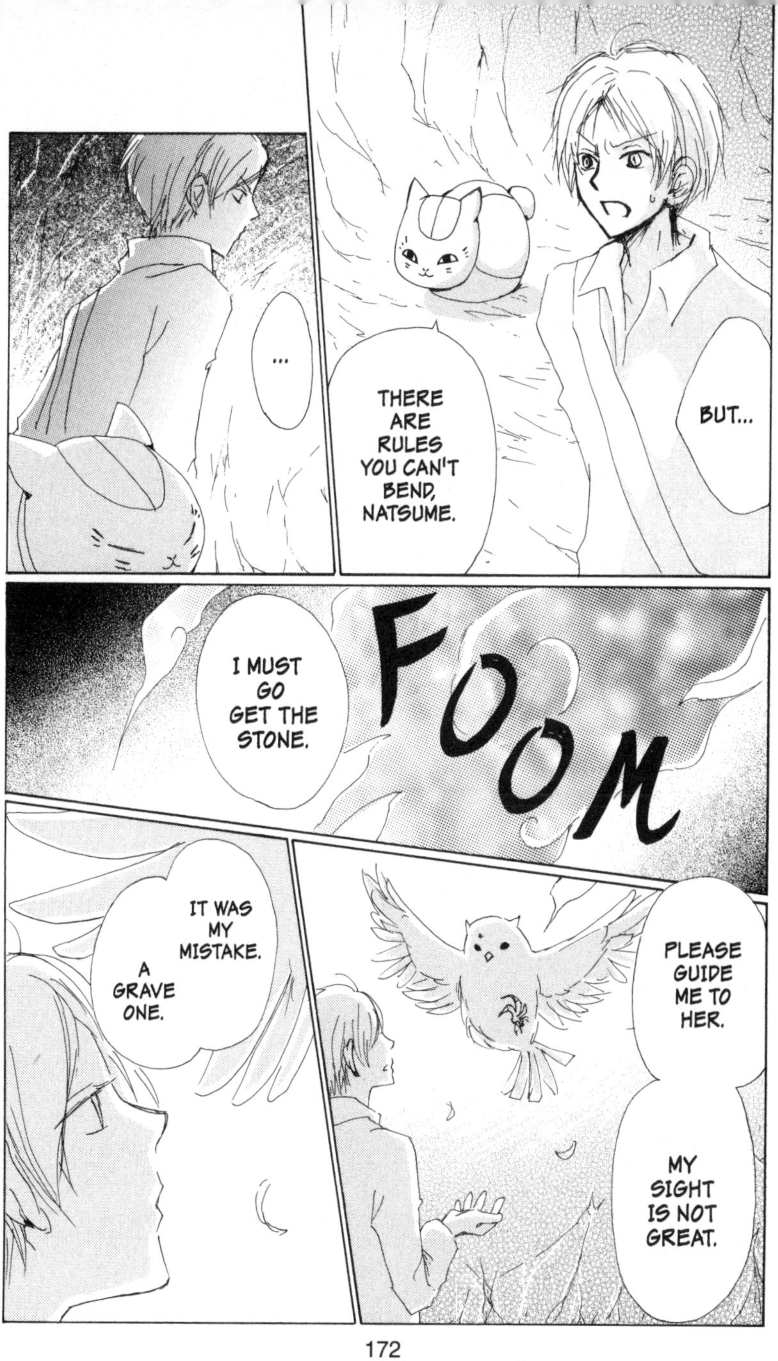
BUT...
THERE ARE RULES YOU CAN'T BEND, NATSUME.
...
FOOM
I MUST GO GET THE STONE.
PLEASE GUIDE ME TO HER.
MY SIGHT IS NOT GREAT.
IT WAS MY MISTAKE.
A GRAVE ONE.

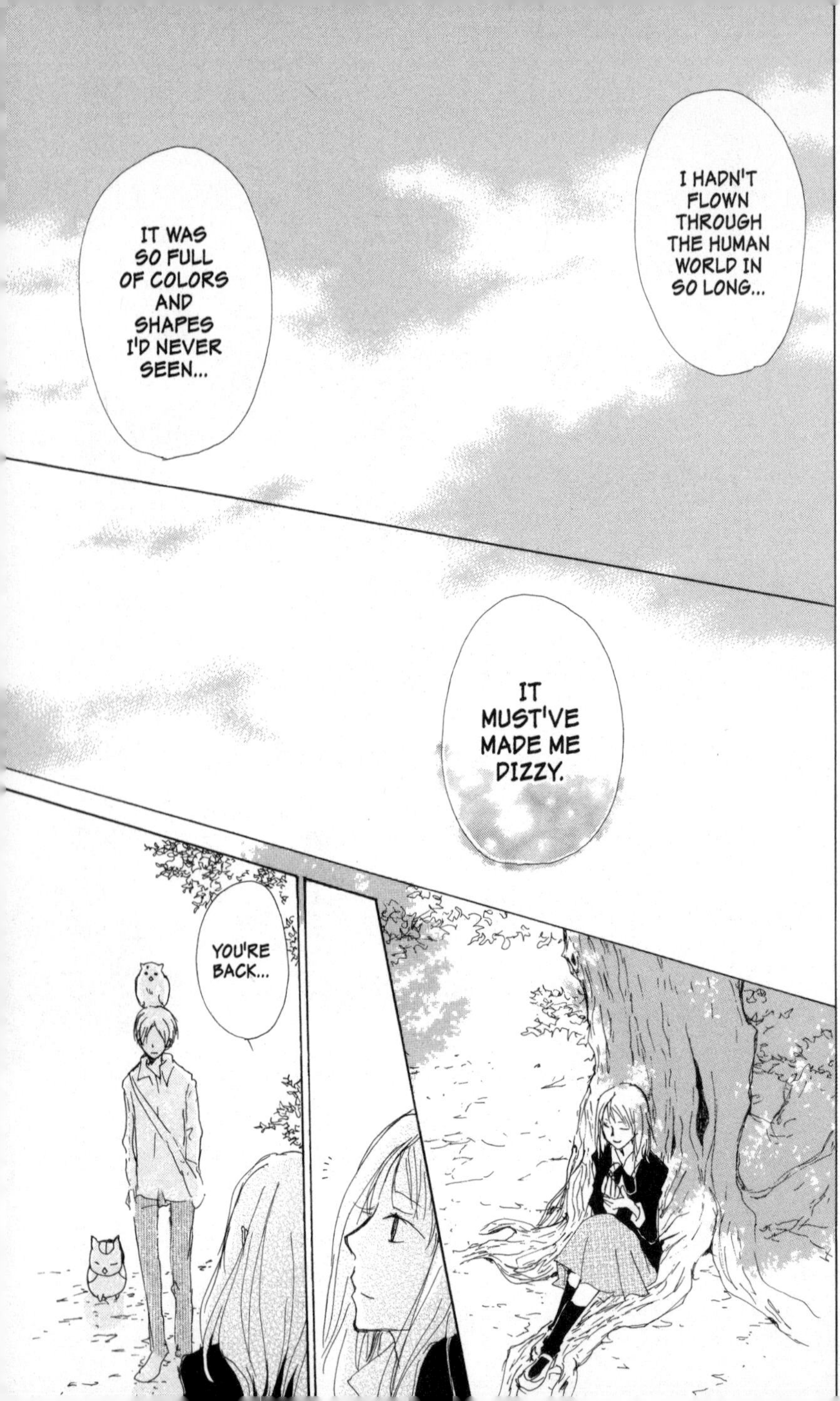
I HADN'T FLOWN THROUGH THE HUMAN WORLD IN SO LONG...
IT WAS SO FULL OF COLORS AND SHAPES I'D NEVER SEEN...
IT MUST'VE MADE ME DIZZY.
YOU'RE BACK...

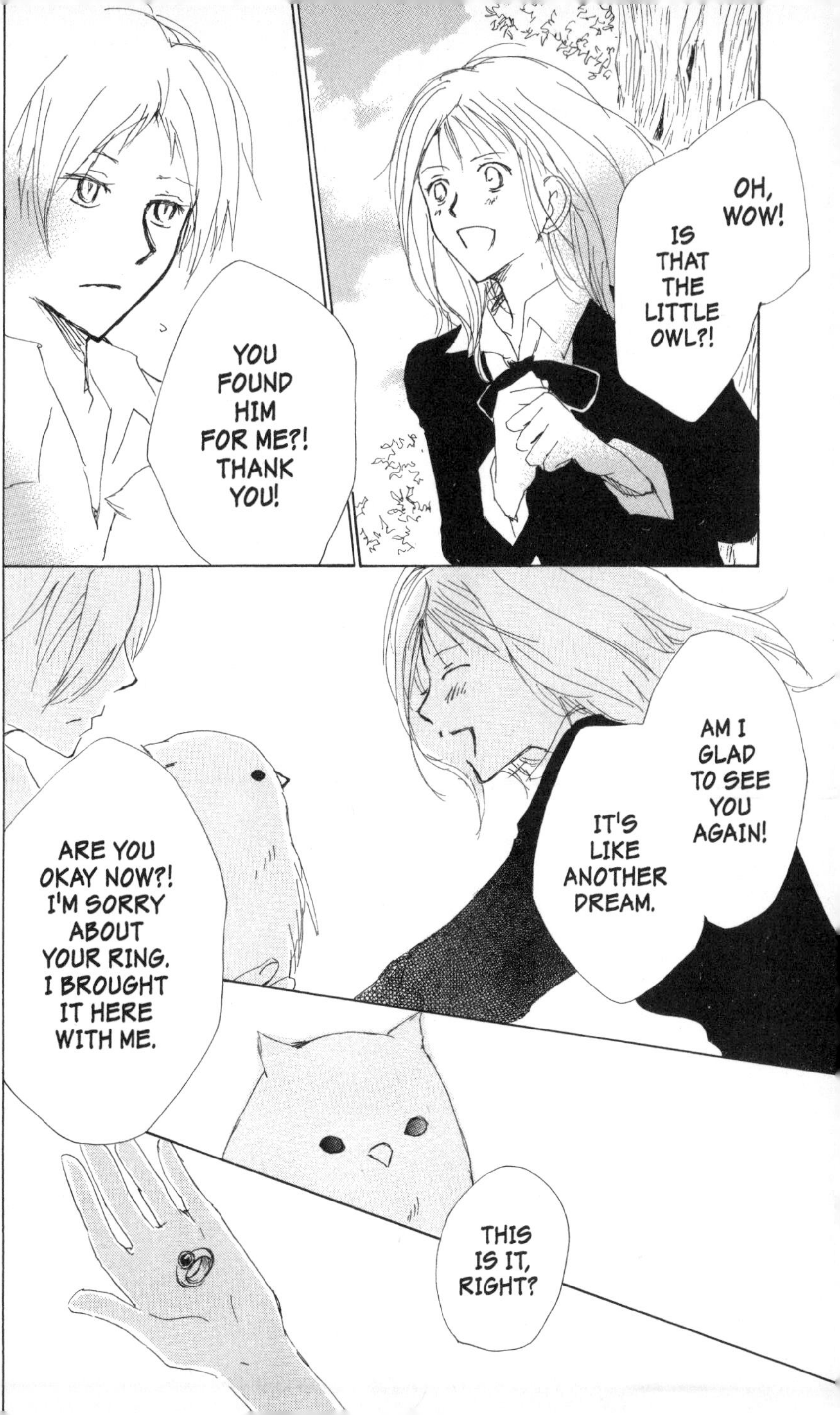
OH, WOW!
IS THAT THE LITTLE OWL?!
YOU FOUND HIM FOR ME?! THANK YOU!
AM I GLAD TO SEE YOU AGAIN!
IT'S LIKE ANOTHER DREAM.
ARE YOU OKAY NOW?! I'M SORRY ABOUT YOUR RING. I BROUGHT IT HERE WITH ME.
THIS IS IT, RIGHT?

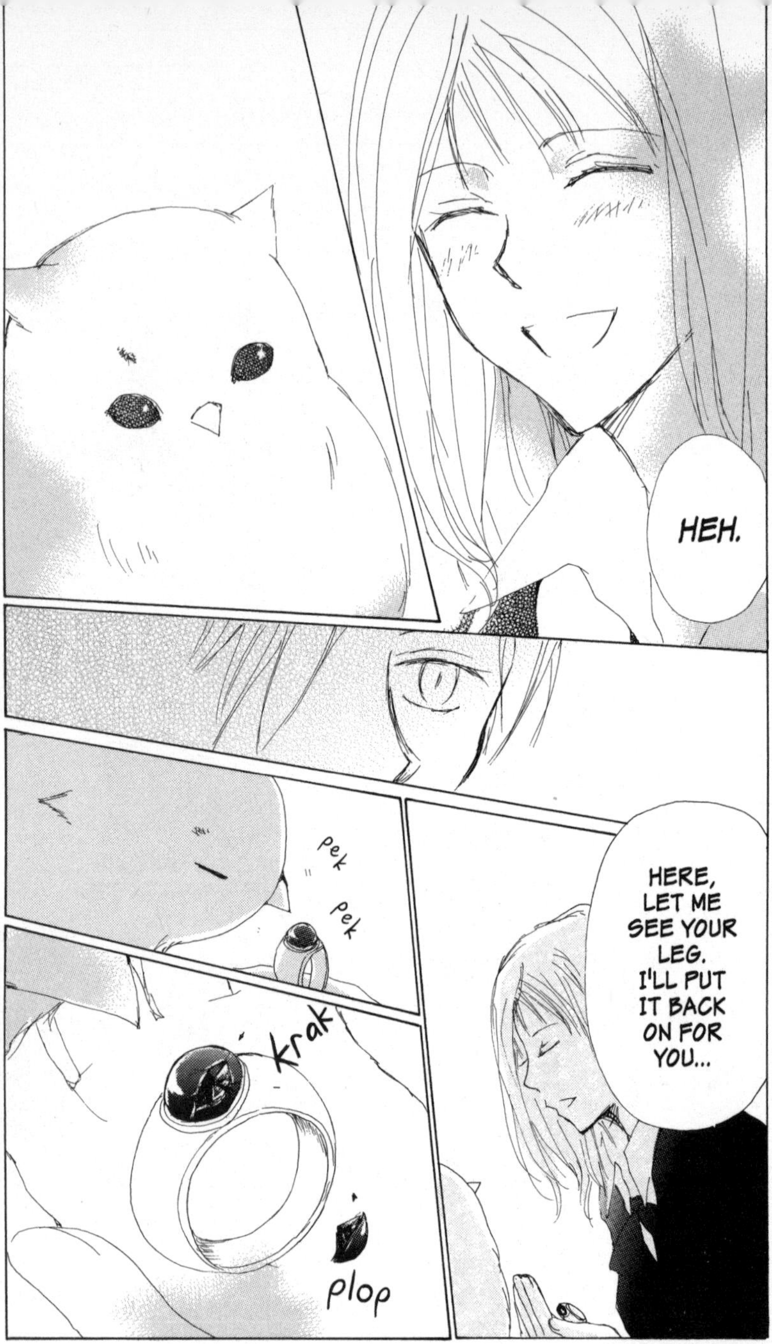
HEH.
HERE, LET ME SEE YOUR LEG. I'LL PUT IT BACK ON FOR YOU...
pek pek
krak
plop

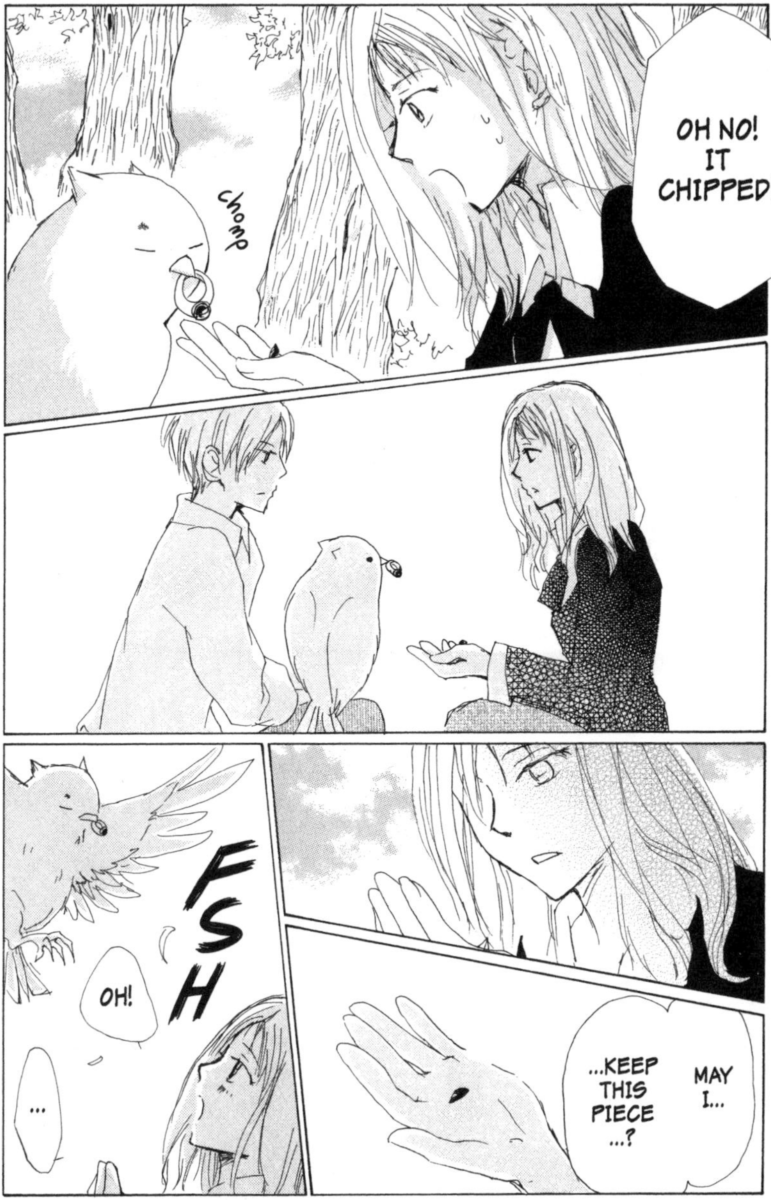
OH NO! IT CHIPPED!
chomp
MAY I...
...KEEP THIS PIECE ...?
FSH
OH!
...

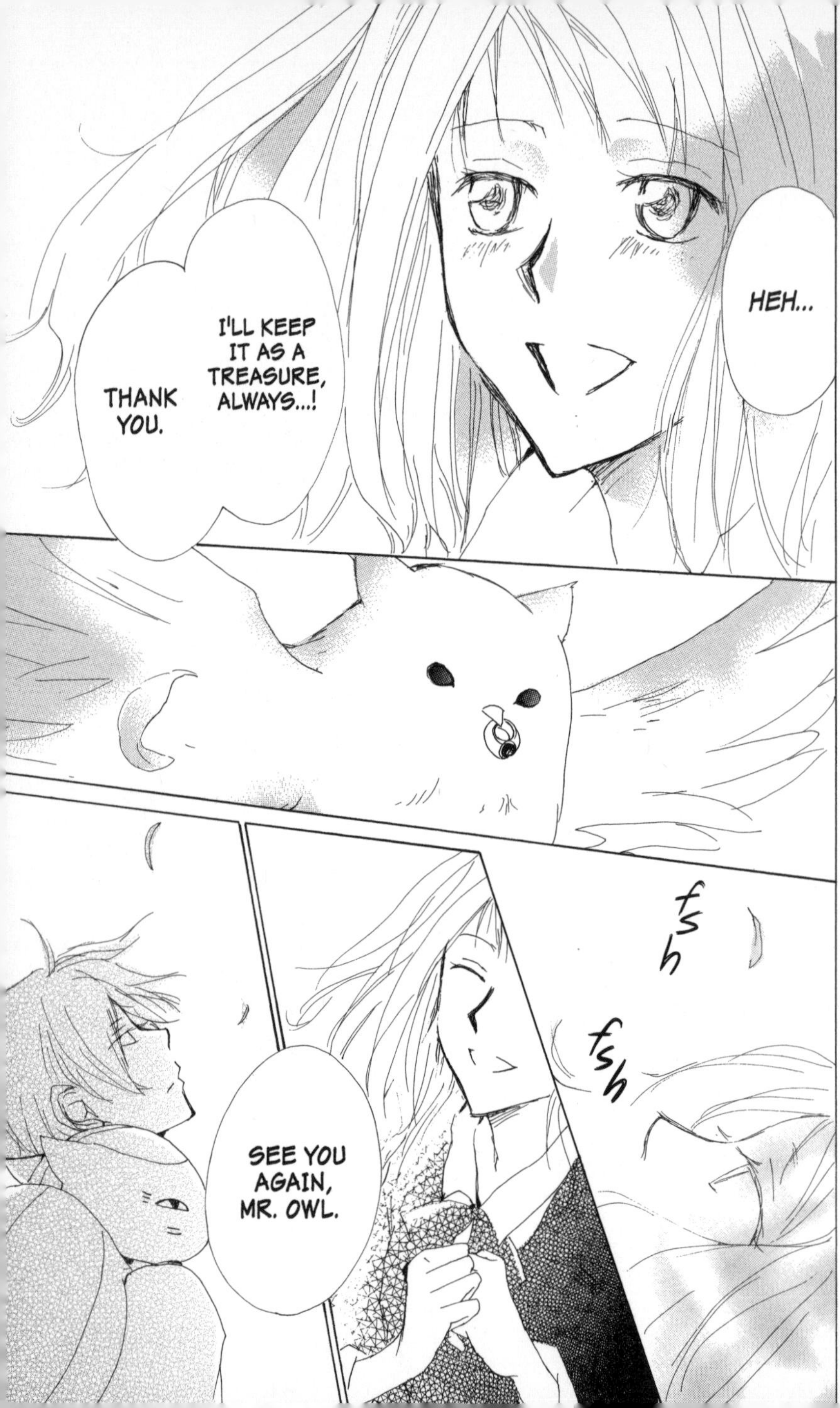
HEH...
I'LL KEEP IT AS A TREASURE, ALWAYS...!
THANK YOU.
fsh
fsh
SEE YOU AGAIN, MR. OWL.

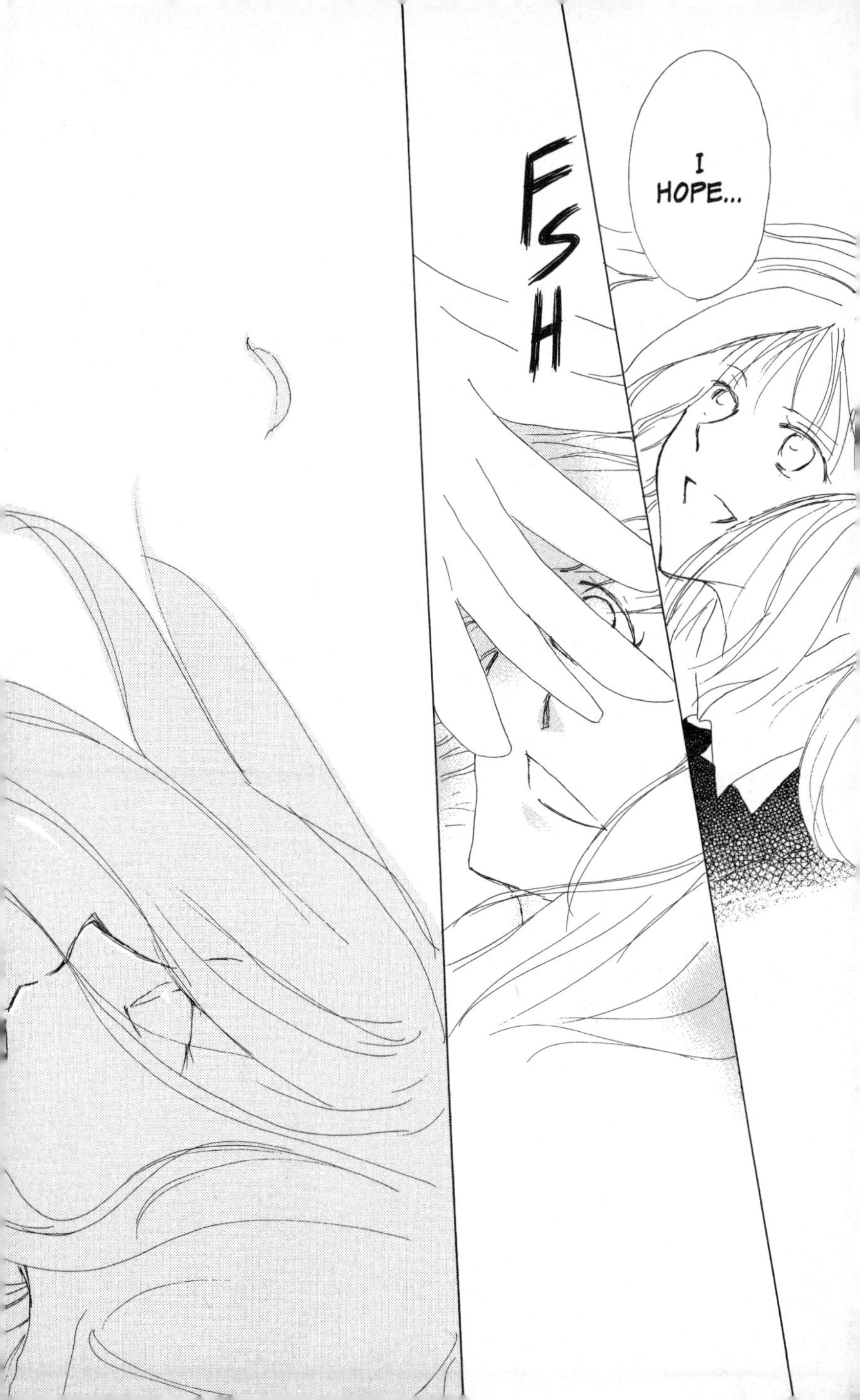
I HOPE...
FSH

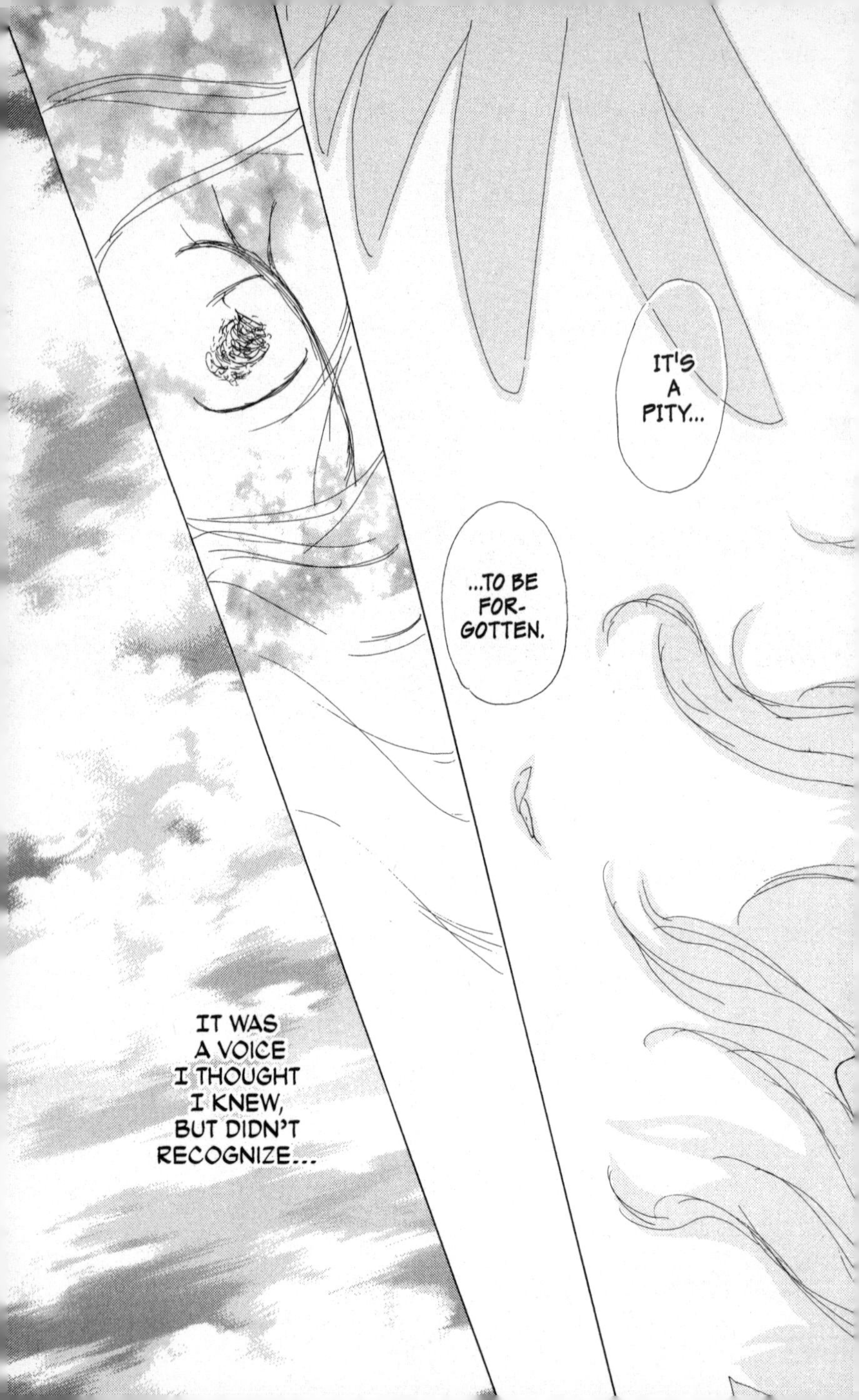
IT'S A PITY...
...TO BE FOR-GOTTEN.
IT WAS A VOICE I THOUGHT I KNEW, BUT DIDN'T RECOGNIZE...

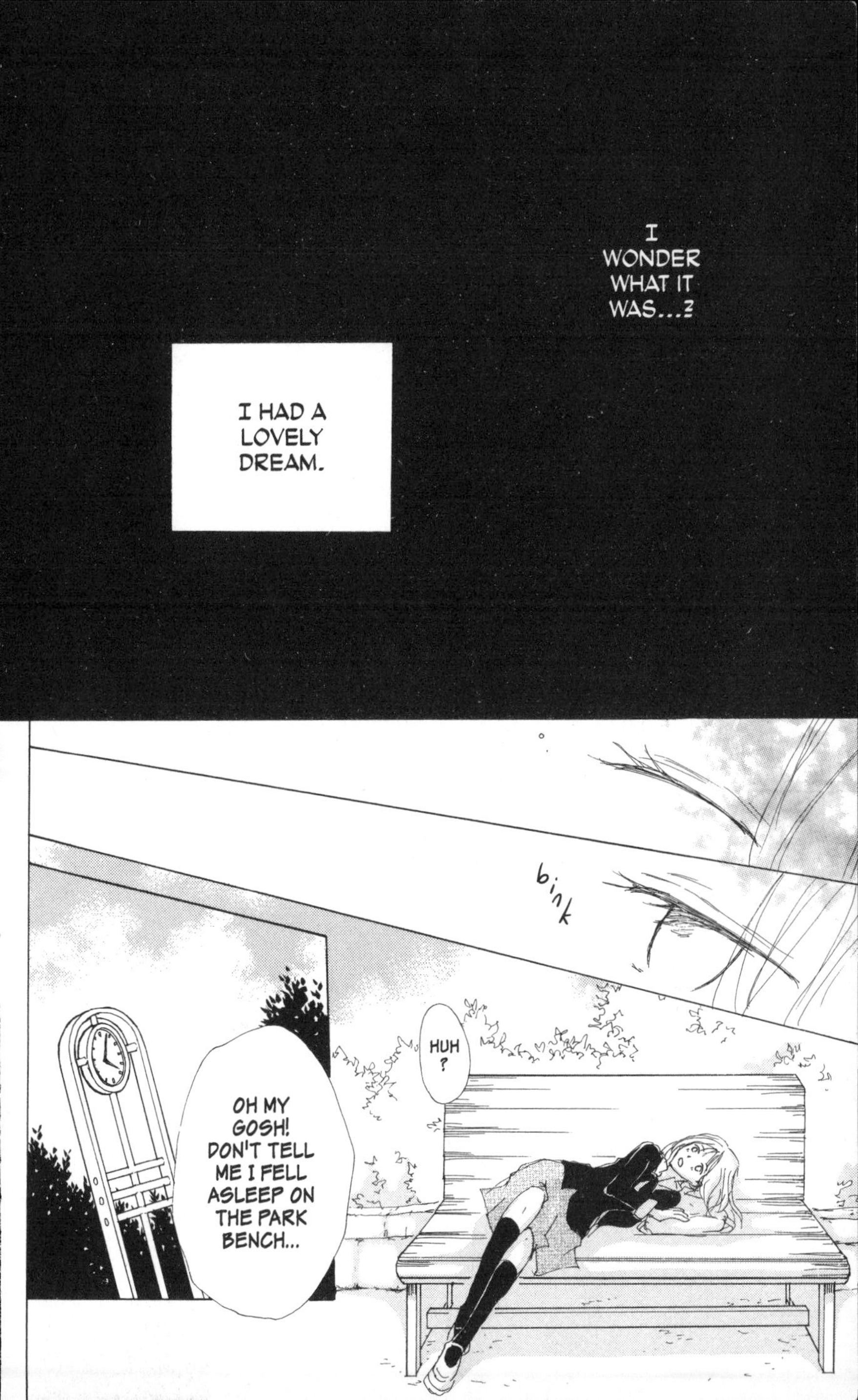
I WONDER WHAT IT WAS...?
I HAD A LOVELY DREAM.
bink
HUH?
OH MY GOSH! DON'T TELL ME I FELL ASLEEP ON THE PARK BENCH...

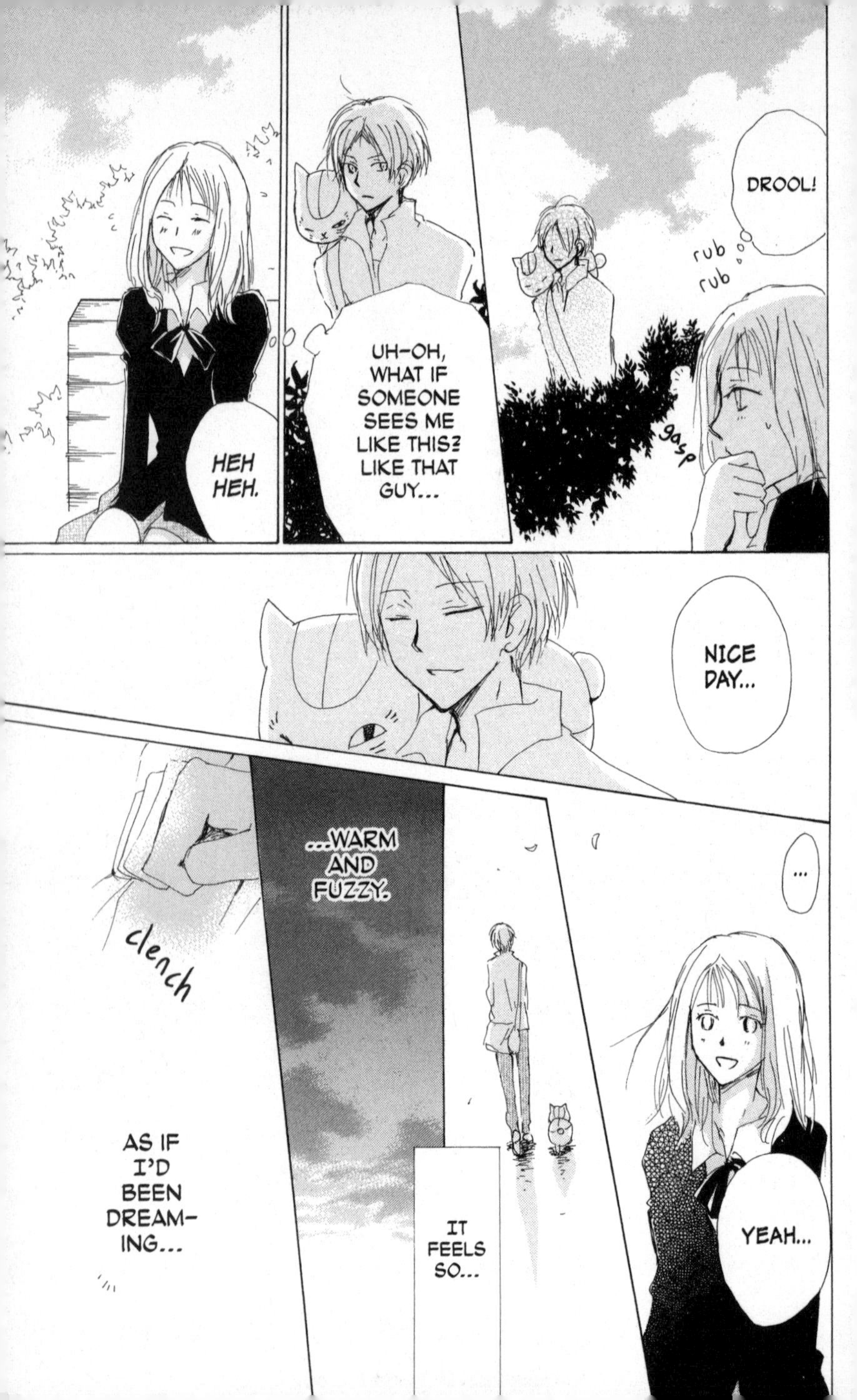
DROOL!
rub rub
gasp
UH-OH, WHAT IF SOMEONE SEES ME LIKE THIS? LIKE THAT GUY...
HEH HEH.
NICE DAY...
...
YEAH...
IT FEELS SO...
...WARM AND FUZZY.
clench
AS IF I'D BEEN DREAMING...

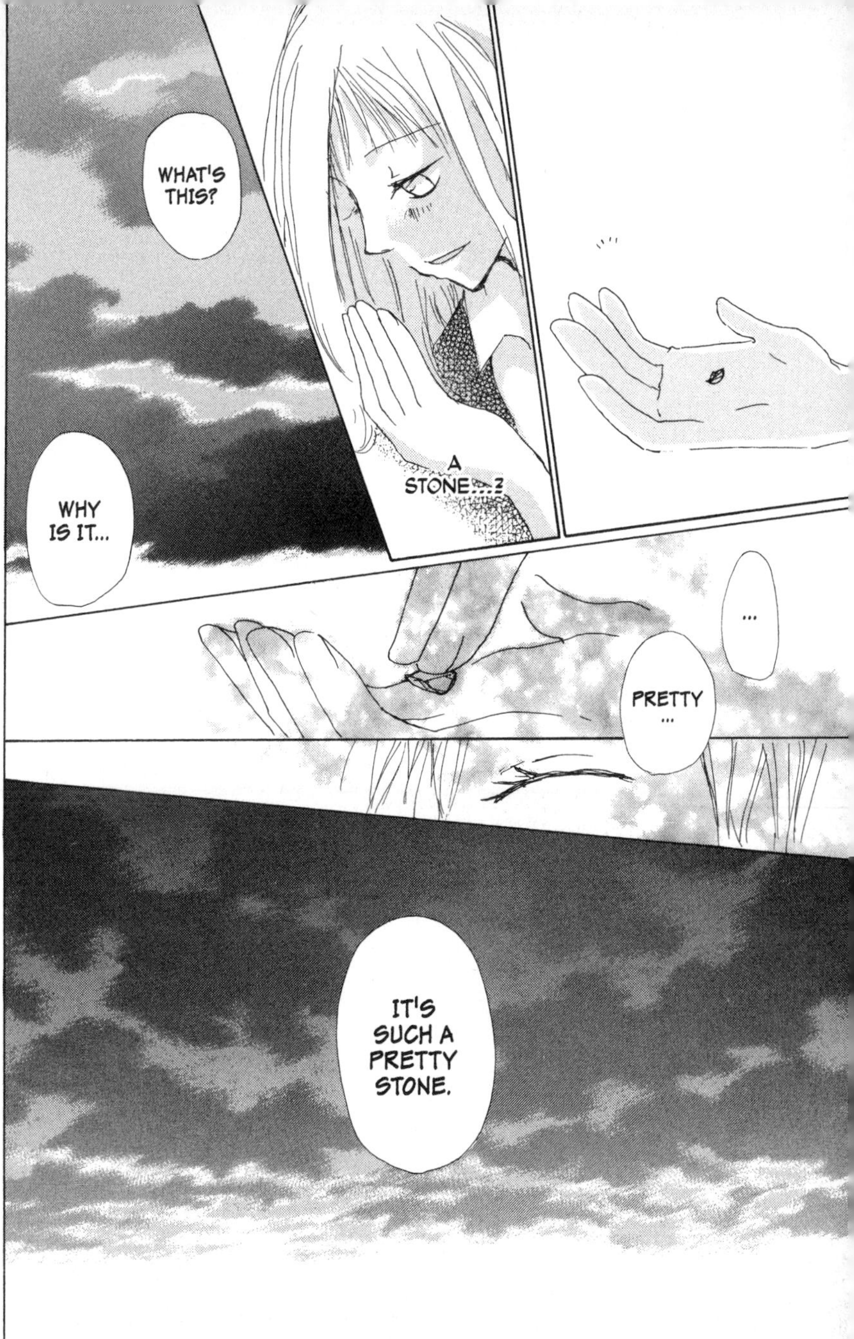
A STONE...?
WHAT'S THIS?
WHY IS IT...
...
PRETTY...
IT'S SUCH A PRETTY STONE.

NATSUME'S BOOK OF FRIENDS, VOL. 18: END

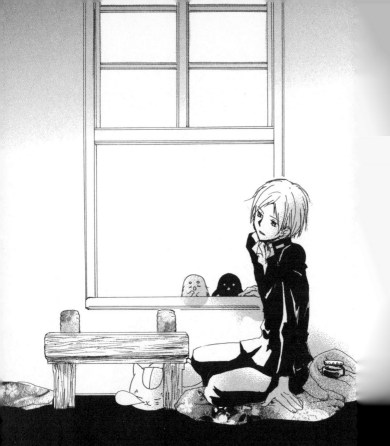

Thank you for reading.

Natsume can now maintain some distance between himself and both humans. I think he's able to be more interested in himself and exor now more able to keep a straight path without being affected by things as much as he used to. But in exchange for the stability in h patterns and actions, there might be small changes in the yokai and around him.

Please read the rest of this afterword only after reading the ent

CHAPTER 71
What I Can Do

I wanted to do a story about getting twisted around the finger of a yokai who's a bit scatterbrained. Shiro and Ake looked different in my first draft, and I couldn't get in the mood. I managed to finish it after I redrew them, so it's not quite what I initially had in mind when I wrote the plot up. That's one part I regret. But it was fun drawing a story where Natsume could be an observer and not get so worked up.

CHAPTER 72-73
Closed Room

Natsume had made up his mind to keep the Book of Friends a secret, but Natori ended up overhearing about it from another yokai—quite an undesirable situation. He decided he couldn't pretend it didn't happen. I think it had great meaning for Natsume to tell him with his own words, albeit belatedly. Meanwhile, since Natori had some clue about what it was, I think Natsume's decision to tell him meant more to Natori. I think he's the kind of guy who would act differently based on whether Natsume was willing to tell or not. I can't describe it very well, but with these two, when one of them steps forward, the other stalls out. I was happy I was able to draw Ms. Nanase again.

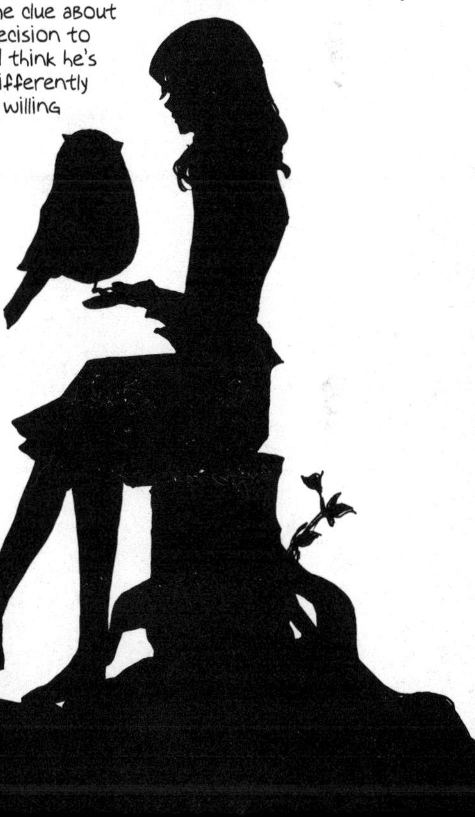

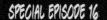

SPECIAL EPISODE 16

A Fragment of a Dream

It was fun drawing from a girl's point of view. Natsume tends to be pretty flat with his emotions, so it was exciting having a temperamental character who acts before thinking. It was refreshing being able to advance the plot with a character with no limitations on her actions after writing Natsume for so long. It was also fun drawing Nyanko Sensei being a bit friskier than normal.

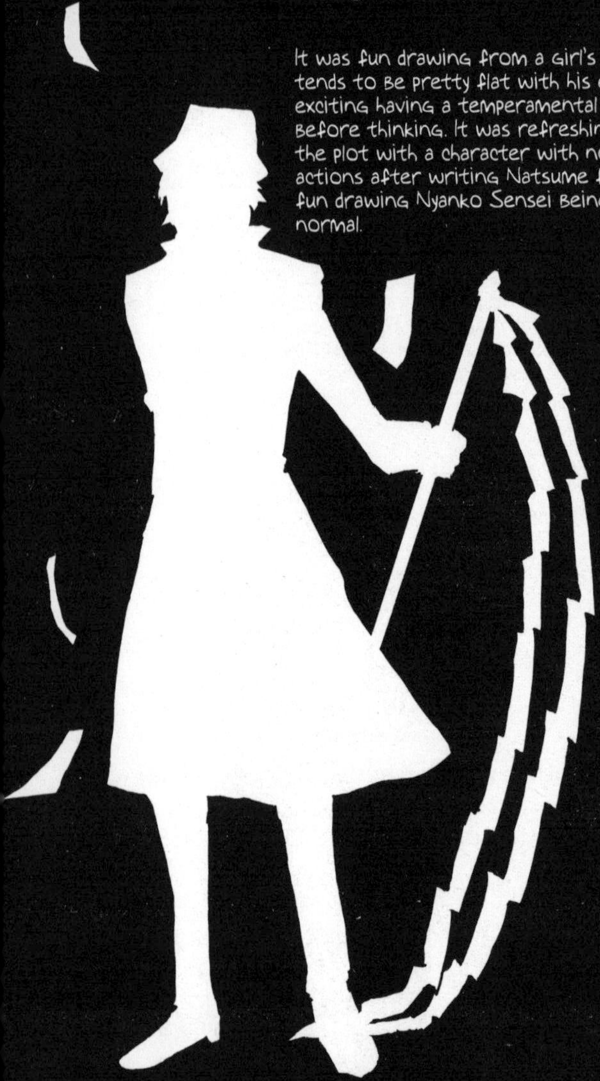

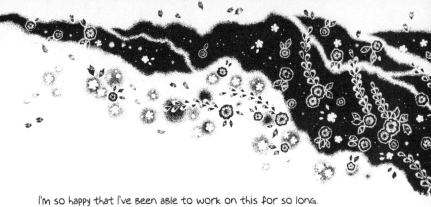

I'm so happy that I've been able to work on this for so long.
A lot of people help me out or give me support. I'm well
aware that I wouldn't have been able to do this by myself.
Because it's a long series, I have to be careful not to let
the plot or characters meander off in unrealistic directions.
The publishing rate is going to slow down for a while, but
I'll keep working hard to produce manga that people will
enjoy, at least a little bit.

Thank you so much for your support.

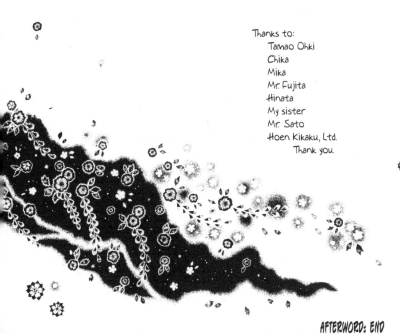

Thanks to:
  Tamao Ohki
  Chika
  Mika
  Mr. Fujita
  Hinata
  My sister
  Mr. Sato
  Hoen Kikaku, Ltd.
      Thank you.

AFTERWORD: END

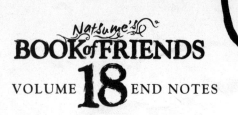

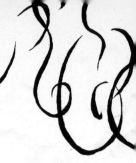

BOOK of FRIENDS
18
VOLUME 18 END NOTES

PAGE 6, PANEL 3: *DAIFUKU*
A type of glutinous rice cake (*mochi*) that is normally filled with sweet bean paste.

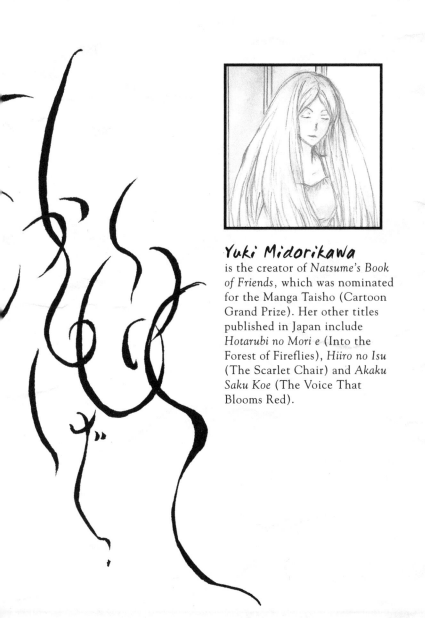

Yuki Midorikawa

is the creator of *Natsume's Book of Friends*, which was nominated for the Manga Taisho (Cartoon Grand Prize). Her other titles published in Japan include *Hotarubi no Mori e* (Into the Forest of Fireflies), *Hiiro no Isu* (The Scarlet Chair) and *Akaku Saku Koe* (The Voice That Blooms Red).

NATSUME'S BOOK OF FRIENDS
Vol. 18
Shojo Beat Edition

STORY AND ART BY *Yuki Midorikawa*

Translation & Adaptation *Lillian Olsen*
Touch-up Art & Lettering *Sabrina Heep*
Design *Fawn Lau*
Editor *Pancha Diaz*

Natsume Yujincho by Yuki Midorikawa
© Yuki Midorikawa 2014
All rights reserved.
First published in Japan in 2014 by HAKUSENSHA, Inc., Tokyo.
English language translation rights arranged with HAKUSENSHA, Inc., Tokyo.

Printed in the U.S.A.

Published by VIZ Media, LLC
P.O. Box 77010
San Francisco, CA 94107

10 9 8 7 6 5 4 3 2 1
First printing, June 2015

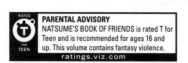

PARENTAL ADVISORY
NATSUME'S BOOK OF FRIENDS is rated T for Teen and is recommended for ages 16 and up. This volume contains fantasy violence.
ratings.viz.com

www.viz.com

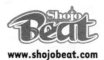

www.shojobeat.com

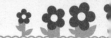
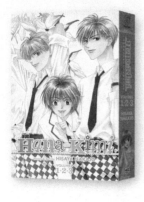
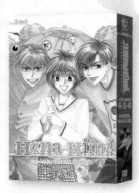
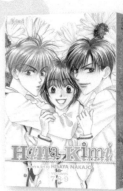

SURPRISE!

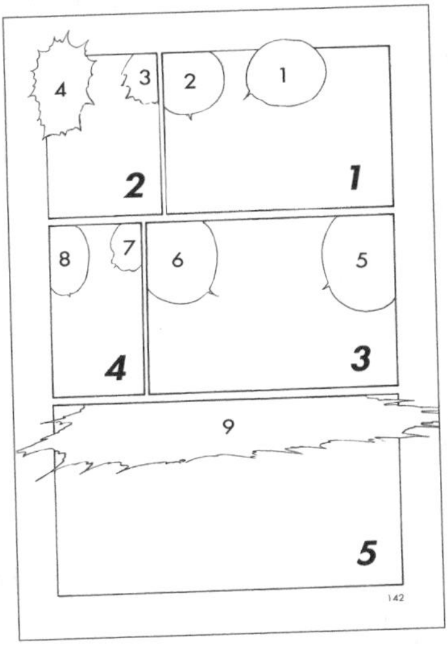
1
2
3
4
1
2
5
6
7
8
3
4
9
5
142

You may be reading the wrong way!

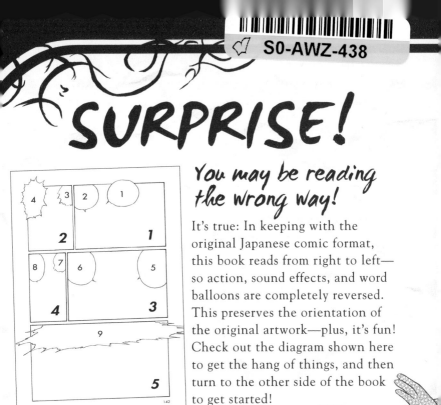

It's true: In keeping with the original Japanese comic format, this book reads from right to left—so action, sound effects, and word balloons are completely reversed. This preserves the orientation of the original artwork—plus, it's fun! Check out the diagram shown here to get the hang of things, and then turn to the other side of the book to get started!

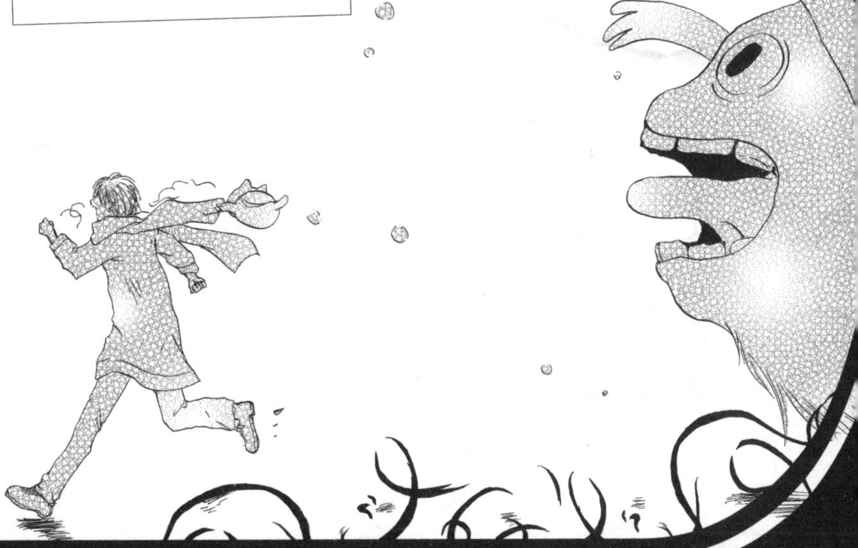